# From Bourgeois to Boojie

AFRICAN AMERICAN LIFE SERIES

*A complete listing of the books in this series can be found online at wsupress.wayne.edu*

SERIES EDITOR

Melba Joyce Boyd, *Department of Africana Studies, Wayne State University*

# From Bourgeois to Boojie

## Black Middle-Class Performances

EDITED BY
Vershawn Ashanti Young
with Bridget Harris Tsemo

 Wayne State University Press
Detroit

15  14  13  12  11     5  4  3  2  1

LIBRARY OF CONGRESS CATALOGING-IN-PUBLICATION DATA

From bourgeois to boojie : Black middle-class performances / edited by Vershawn Ashanti Young with Bridget Harris Tsemo.
p. cm. — (African American life series)
Includes bibliographical references and index.
ISBN 978-0-8143-3468-3 (pbk. : alk. paper)
1. African Americans—Race identity. 2. Middle class—United States. 3. African American arts. 4. African American in the performing arts. I. Young, Vershawn Ashanti. II. Tsemo, Bridget Harris, 1970–
E185.625.F76 2011
305.5'508996073—dc22
2010033585

*Designed by Charlie Sharp, Sharp Des!gns, Lansing, Michigan*
*Typeset by Maya Rhodes*
*Composed in Agora Serif*

*For all black people everywhere*

*It may turn out in the distant future Negroes will disappear physically from American Society. If this is our fate, let us disappear with dignity and let us leave a worthwhile memorial—in science, in art, in literature, in sculpture, in music—of our having been here.*

■ E. Franklin Frazier, "The Failure of the Negro Intellectual," 1962

# Contents

## PART I. PERFORMING RESPONSIBILITY

## PART II. PERFORMING WOMANHOOD

## PART III. PERFORMING MEDIA

# Foreword

## The Journey from Bourgeois to Boojie

Since our arrival on American soil, African Americans have always been marked by our class position. Although we were considered only three-fifths human and had no material possessions to speak of, enslaved Africans' intracultural relations were shaped by class, for white masters understood the psychosocial dynamics of divide and conquer: give one group access to the master's house and family and put the other in the fields and forbid them access to the same. Thus the distinction between house slaves and field slaves paradoxically codified a caste system that effectively divided a people along class lines, even though all slaves were subjugated subjects who possessed nothing but their will to be counted as human and to be free. What white slave owners understood was that playing a game with labor assignments would instigate tension among the slaves and keep them fighting among themselves rather than plotting against their masters. This strategy was only marginally successful in allaying slave rebellions and other forms of indirect and direct insubordination, but psychologically the strategy was effective in creating the perception that some members of the community were superior to others—indeed, that some members had literally become part of an upwardly mobile class. The irony, of course, is that those slaves who were assigned to the plantation home were actually no better off than those in the fields in terms of what they actually had materially. In fact, one might argue that because of their frequent interaction with their masters, house slaves were more susceptible to acts of physical and sexual violence. Nonetheless this division of labor created an image of what we now call the black middle class that remains today.

The divide between the "folk" and the bourgeoisie intensified in the years after emancipation as some blacks became upwardly mobile, instantiating a black middle class materially rather than only in the black imaginary. The ideological differences between working-class and middle-class blacks also intensified in the realm of racial uplift discourse—that is, the strategies thought to best move the black race forward: vocation versus education. Moreover, the black middle class became increasingly associated with whiteness and a disavowal of blackness, as the psychosocial ideologies planted in slave culture began to take root in the form of cleavages among blacks around skin color or other physical features associated with black people. Colorism was almost always undergirded by class distinctions—that somehow dark skin and kinky hair signified low class and fair skin and straight hair signified high class. Of course, these psychodramas only sustained the hegemony of whiteness and kept black folks embroiled in intracultural battles about who was more or less authentically black.

This class divide also shaped the way black leaders strategized the uplift of black people. Booker T. Washington insisted that learning a vocation was the only way to save the race, whereas W. E. B. Du Bois believed that the education of our people would be the only way to overcome subjugation. This is but one example of how class has shaped black politics. Indeed, in his famous 1926 essay, "The Negro Artist and the Racial Mountain," Langston Hughes indicts the Negro middle class as apolitical, disinterested in black culture, subsumed with aspirations of being white: "The whisper of 'I want to be white' runs silently through their minds."[1] A similar sentiment is found about forty years later in Amiri Baraka's poem "Black Bourgeoisie," in which he says the namesake of the poem

*does not hate ofays*
*hates, instead, him self*
*him black self.*[2]

In the mid-1970s this image of the bourgeois black who is more interested in competing with whites than helping his people manifests in the form of the character George Jefferson in the sitcom *The Jeffersons*. The characters George Jefferson and his wife, Louise, leave behind their working-class life in Queens to "move on up to the East Side" of Manhattan, apparently leaving behind as well any political commitment or social responsibility to their working-class roots. Although George brings with him to the Upper East Side his black vernacular speech—shortening his wife's name from Louise to Weezie and pronouncing it, for instance, with an undeniable working-class black cadence—and his suspicion of white people (he refers to his white neighbor Tom as "honky"), he nonetheless is more interested in moving his family further on up the socioeconomic ladder than he is in helping other poor blacks out of their poverty or using his wealth to speak to the plight of black folks. Further, George's character is presented as a middle-class version of earlier stereotypes of blacks, such as "Steppin' Fetchit" or "Zip Coon"—racist stereotypes that emerged after emancipation to sustain white superiority.

Less simplistic popular culture images of black middle-class figures emerged in the 1980s with *The Cosby Show*, which portrayed Bill Cosby and Phylicia Rashad as Cliff and Claire Huxtable, as an upper-class black couple—obstetrician and lawyer, respectively—who lived with their five children in a brownstone in Brooklyn Heights, New York. For the first time in television history, a black family was presented in which both parents not only were present but also were successful. And while the *The Cosby Show* was often criticized for not dealing with social issues like racism, the show did celebrate African American cultural history by featuring the work of black visual artists and black musicians, and by promoting historically black colleges and universities. And yet, not once was there ever a reference to the Huxtables' *class* roots. Indeed, no one in the Huxtable family, extended family, or circle of friends is poor or even working class, which is remarkable given that the sitcom is set in the 1980s, when President Ronald Reagan's economic policies dismantled hundreds of social welfare programs, which disproportionately affected the working poor and especially black people. But given Cosby's more recent stomp speeches in black communities around the country in which he chastises the black working poor for their lack of parenting skills and for not taking responsibility for their own lives, the absence of such people in the Huxtable family is not surprising.

Nowhere is this sentiment crystalized better than in Cosby's 2004 "Pound Cake" speech at a gala sponsored by the NAACP at Constitution Hall in Washington, D.C., to commemorate the fiftieth anniversary of the U.S. Supreme Court decision in *Brown v. Board of Education.* Cosby says,

> These are people going around stealing Coca Cola. People getting shot in the back of the head over a piece of pound cake! Then we all run out and are outraged: "The cops shouldn't have shot him." What the hell was he doing with the pound cake in his hand? I wanted a piece of pound cake just as bad as anybody else. And I looked at it and I had no money. And something called parenting said if you get caught with it you're going to embarrass your mother. Not, "You're going to get your butt kicked." No. "You're going to embarrass your mother." "You're going to embarrass your family." If you knock that girl up, you're going to have to run away because it's going to be too embarrassing for your family. In the old days, a girl getting pregnant had to go down South, and then her mother would go down to get her. But the mother had the baby. I said the mother had the baby. The girl didn't have a baby. The mother had the baby in two weeks. We are not parenting.

Cosby's evocation of the "old days" when the black community was more responsible for its members and the welfare of the community in general registers a contemporary manifestation of nineteenth-century black respectability, in which the black elite were invested in circumscribing the boundaries of blackness in order to appear respectable in the eyes of whites. The acculturation of particular signifiers of whiteness—for example, standard English, Christian morals and values, Victorian etiquette—was undergirded by aspirations to ascend to a higher socioeconomic status. And, as Cosby has himself noted, it also speaks to the embrace of the American dream that suggests that every American, regardless of race, socioeconomic status, ability, or other factors has the opportunity to be successful—materially and socially—if he or she works hard enough—a Horatio Alger story writ large.

As the embodiment of that dream, Cosby, who grew up in a working-class family in Philadelphia, seems to have forgotten how institutionalized forms of racism, with a few exceptions—he and Oprah, for example—mitigate one's opportunities to rise out of poverty. There is no one-to-one correlation between success and "working hard," especially if there is no work to be had. Ironically, one reason why black communities were so "responsible" during the time in which Cosby grew up is because of segregation. Before the civil rights movement, there were far more black-owned businesses; there were black schools, and the black church served as the social and political pillar of the community. Because of segregation black people had no choice but to patronize black businesses, which in turn sustained the community. Because black people of all classes lived among each other they had a greater sense of responsibility to the community; thus black children across the socioeconomic spectrum shared educational and social spaces and were looked after by "the community"; the black church was a site where the community gathered across generational and class lines. For good or naught, desegregation changed the landscape of the "black community" forever. While the church continued to be a space that transcended class differences, black-owned businesses dwindled, driven out of business by competition from the white businesses that blacks could now patronize; black middle-class folks began to move into previously all-white neighborhoods, leaving behind their working-class brethren, some of whom were cordoned off in public housing; and black children were bused out of their neighborhoods to schools across town in the name of integration. The dismantling of "the black community" caused by interracial desegregation in some ways instituted de facto intraracial *class* segregation, whereby poor and working-class blacks no longer lived among middle- and upper-class blacks, which simultaneously divided these groups' priorities on what was best for black people.

In his book, *Is Bill Cosby Right? Or Has the Black Middle Class Lost Its Mind?* the cultural critic Michael Eric Dyson takes Cosby to task for his attack on the black working class and on what Dyson sees as a hypocritical stance toward this group, given Cosby's class roots, his lackluster performance in high school and college, and his former political beliefs about the working poor, as detailed in his doctoral dissertation. Dyson writes:

> Given his difficult educational background, it's a good thing Cosby didn't
> have Bill Cosby around to discourage him from achieving his goals by
> citing statistics about black high school dropouts that don't square with
> the facts. It's a shame that Cosby skewered the victims of educational
> neoapartheid, the very folk that *Brown vs. Board* sought to help, instead
> of pointing to the social inequities and disparities in resources that
> continue to make American schools "separate and unequal." And for
> Cosby to overlook how the criminal justice system mercilessly feeds
> on social inequality is just as tragic.[3]

Dyson places his retort to Cosby's rhetorical assault on the working poor in a historical context that highlights both the material effects of institutionalized racism on the black working poor and the rhetorical tradition from which Cosby's comments emerge. Beyond Dyson's first titular rhetorical question regarding Cosby is the second one about the larger black middle class. The subtext of the question has more to do with a call to black consciousness than anything else. Obviously, the black middle class has not lost its mind, but perhaps it has, according to Dyson and others, lost its sense of radical politics and sense of responsibility toward those of the black community who are poor. But this view of the black middle class as monolithic or, as Valerie Smith puts it, "a space of pure compromise and capitulation, from which all autonomy disappears once it encounters hegemonic power," is too simplistic.[4] In this regard, both Cosby and Dyson are correct: the black working class and poor are partly accountable for making their way, and the black middle class needs to recognize both the ways it is implicated in the plight of the poor and the continued forms of hegemonic institutional and structural forms of racism that affect people of color regardless of their socioeconomic standing.

Mary Pattillo's book, *Black on the Block: The Politics of Race and Class in the City*, an ethnographic study of the gentrification of the North Kenwood–

Oakland neighborhood in Chicago, represents a current example of the ways in which blacks across the class divide negotiate the homecoming of the same (middle-class) blacks who fled black neighborhoods after desegregation and the economic downturn of the late 1960s–1980s. According to Pattillo, middle-class blacks served as middlemen and middlewomen, becoming brokers, as it were, who negotiated with both the black working-class residents of the community and mainly white city officials and developers to help gentrify the area. In this instance black middle- and upper-class people were very much aware of the institutionalized forms of racism partially responsible for the ravishing poverty and urban blight in the community and were compelled to reinvest in the community by moving to it for the first time or moving back after living on the North Side or the suburbs. While Pattillo asserts that the move of these middle-class blacks to this neighborhood was not all selfless (North Kenwood–Oakland is located ten minutes from downtown Chicago and less than a mile from Lake Michigan), she also suggests that their decision was based in part on a commitment to black culture and people. Thus, unlike Cosby, these middle-class blacks were, according to Pattillo, "battling on behalf of the race, including the poor of the race, for the rights and resources that citizenship and municipal residency should, but do not always, automatically entail."[5]

And we come full circle. Just as the class divide in slave culture was more psychological than material, the current cleavages among black folks around class are not simply a matter of economics or rhetoric but a bit of both. Most black middle-class people I know have at least one or more people in their family who are poor or working class, and most middle-class blacks I know grew up in poverty or in a working-class family. As someone who has ascended to middle-class status—at least in economic terms—I am always dubious about my position within "middle classness," for like so many of my (black) friends who are also middle class, my status is always a little insecure, because a portion of my money goes back home to my family, rather than into savings to pass down to future generations. In matters of style and taste I often tell my friends that I "embrace my boojie-ness." But I, like Dwight McBride, writing in another context, "claim my position as a bourgeois subject, [but] I do so registering my own somewhat fraught and contingent relationship to that category."[6]

The youngest of seven children, child of a domestic worker, public housing, and a single-parent home, I personally experienced material poverty but also enjoyed a front-row seat for some of the most intricate performances of middle class. In my childhood boojie was a state of mind rather than a state of being—from my mother's getting "gussied up" to go to a house party to my aunt Mary Lee's acting "seddity" to the pageantry of "crowns" in my church to my cousin's recitation of Countee Cullen's "Yet Do I Marvel," as if she were on stage at the Metropolitan Opera, I witnessed many a poor black person perform the bourgeois other. I have also witnessed black middle-class folks "getting down" on the dance floor, recalling the working-class dances of their childhood or throwing down on some soul food, eschewing the healthy foodways of the wealthy in favor of comfort food. Accordingly, I disavow hard-and-fast rules about who is and is not a part of a particular class, especially since the sense of play and performance around issues of class (not to discount people's real material economic circumstances) go unacknowledged.

The field of performance studies has been instrumental in theorizing how identity markers, including race, gender, sexuality, and class, are not givens but rather are bound to ideological and cultural discourses.[7] Indeed, the notion of performance has provided a way to discern the dialectic between the material body and the representation of the body. In other words, someone who appears bourgeois may not actually inhabit that socioeconomic position and someone who is materially situated within the middle class might not perform a bourgeois sensibility. Examples include folks who drive Mercedes and live in the projects and rappers who sing about the 'hood but who grew up in middle-class homes in the suburbs. Or it might include middle- or upper-class folk who dress down so as not to call attention to their wealth. In these examples we come to understand class as more than socioeconomic status but also as artifice. As I have argued about blackness, class—and in this context, black middle classness—is not the exclusive property of any one group.[8] It may be appropriated and performed by a range of folks whose economic position may or may not align with their ideological position or others' expectations of what constitutes bourgeois/nonbourgeois performance.

*From Bourgeois to Boojie: Black Middle-Class Performances* brings all the aforementioned history together in one volume. This important collection represents a cross-generational, cross-gender, cross-sexual, and cross-genre portrait of the various ways in which black people sign middle-class blackness. Indeed, the title metaphorically signals a generational shift in our perception of the black middle class, from the serious moniker that *bourgeois* connotes to the more playful, half sardonic, half self-mocking connotations of *boojie*. Vershawn Ashanti Young and Bridget Harris Tsemo mark that historical trajectory as well by their inclusion of senior cultural workers like Amiri Baraka and Houston Baker as well as younger scholars like Damion Waymer and Candice Jenkins. What each of these essays, poems, visual representations, and short stories represents is nothing less than the complex web that constitutes the black middle class: it could never be depicted satisfactorily by one genre or from one perspective. Thus performance is an apt trope to embody the complexity of what Young refers to in the introduction as "both everyday self-presentations of middle-class people and artistic representations of them." The contributors to this book take the editors' call to engage the material and the discursive seriously through their own personal engagement and political commitment to their various objects and bodies of inquiry. In so doing they ask hard questions about what it means to be black and to be "between the upper and lower classes in the Negro community," as E. Franklin Frazier put it.

The essays here remind me of the by now clichéd slogan "It takes a village to raise a child." At the heart of this African proverb is the belief in community and communion as a life force and progenitor of a culture. These artists and scholars have come together as a community—and in all their diversity—to uphold the traditions of their forebears but with new insights from where we are now and as we march toward the future. The journey from bourgeois to boojie embraces the journey from the cotton field to the master's kitchen, from the pimp's street corner to the doctor's office, from the assembly line to the corporate conference table, from the outhouse to the White House. Boojie, indeed.

*E. Patrick Johnson*

**NOTES**

1. Langston Hughes, "The Negro Artist and the Racial Mountain," in Henry Louis Gates and Nellie Y. McKay, eds., *The Norton Anthology of African American Literature* (New York: W. W. Norton, 1997), 1268.

2. Imamu Amiri Baraka [LeRoi Jones], "Black Bourgeoisie," in Dudley Randall, ed., *The Black Poets* (New York: Bantam, 1971), 223.

3. Michael Eric Dyson, *Is Bill Cosby Right? Or Has the Black Middle Class Lost Its Mind?* (New York: Basic, 2005), 61.

4. Valerie Smith, *Not Just Race, Not Just Gender: Black Feminist Readings* (New York: Routledge, 1998), 67.

5. Mary Pattillo, *Black on the Block: The Politics of Race and Class in the City* (Chicago: University of Chicago Press, 2007), 21.

6. Dwight A. McBride, *Why I Hate Abercrombie & Fitch: Essays on Race and Sexuality* (New York: New York University Press, 2005), 28.

7. See Judith Butler, *Gender Trouble: Feminism and the Subversion of Identity* (New York: Routledge, 1990), and *Bodies That Matter: On the Discursive Limits of "Sex"* (New York: Routledge, 1993); E. Patrick Johnson, *Appropriating Blackness: Performance and the Politics of Authenticity* (Durham, N.C.: Duke University Press, 2003); Andrew Parker and Eve Kosovsky Sedgwick, eds., *Performance and Performativity* (New York: Routledge, 1996); and Della Pollock, ed., *Remembering: Performance and Oral History* (New York: Palgrave/Macmillan, 2005).

8. See E. Patrick Johnson, *Appropriating Blackness: Performance and the Politics of Authenticity* (Durham, N.C.: Duke University Press, 2003).

# Acknowledgments

The cultural critic and sociologist E. Franklin Frazier published the original edition of his controversial text *Black Bourgeoisie* in 1955. Fifty years later Bridget Harris Tsemo and I organized a panel—"From Bourgeois to Boogie: Mapping the Economics of Identity and the Black Middle Class"—for the annual conference of the Modern Language Association. We wanted to reassess the influence of *Black Bourgeoisie* on humanities scholars and to explore the current relevance of Frazier's argument that "the black bourgeoisie has been uprooted from its 'racial' tradition and as a consequence has no cultural roots in either the Negro or the white world." Bridget headed the panel and asked Dwight McBride, Charles Nero, and me to address Frazier's view that the middle class uses its economic and social success as a way to foster a false sense of superiority over the black underclass and as a result experiences some insecurity, anxiety, and self-hatred in its unfulfilled quest to become "American" or "white" in the same way that, say, Jews, Italians, Polish, and other ethnic minorities arguably have. These contentious points were dealt with deftly, not only by the speakers but by the audience, which included Angelo Rich Robinson, who has since become a good friend and promoter of this project, and Candice Jenkins, who became a contributor to this collection.

The American edition of Frazier's book was published in 1957. In 2007 the Obermann Center for the Humanities at the University of Iowa, headed by Jay Semel, provided a large grant to Bridget and me to direct a major symposium. We modified the theme to "From Bourgeois to Boojie: Black Middle-Class Performances." Our conference, which took place in the community of Iowa City, featured Amiri Baraka and Michele Wallace as keynote speakers and included these artists, writers, and scholars: Bryant Keith Alexander, Nancy Cheryll Davis-Bellamy, Signithia Fordham, E. Patrick Johnson, Angela Mae Kupenda, Mary Pattillo, Greg Tate, and Lisa B. Thompson. Some of our colleagues from the American Studies and African American Studies departments were also intricately involved: Venise Berry, Michael Hill, Tisch Jones, Kim Marra, and Sydne Mahone.

My idea to do a book on the topic was inspired by both the MLA panel and the Obermann symposium. Both LeAnn Fields from the University of Michigan Press and Ken Wissoker at Duke University Press provided developmental assistance. But it was Wayne State University Press's acquisitions editor, Kathryn Wildfong, and African American Life Series editor Melba Boyd who skillfully and smartly helped turn an idea into the book before you. They were aided by the adept work of the Press's staff and by freelance copy editor Polly Kummel.

I save the best for last—family.

Everybody knows that blood is thicker than water. But, as I learned after the publication of my first book, blood gets thicker in print—as I'm now convinced it should be. I thought when I wrote the acknowledgments for my first book, *Your Average Nigga* (2007), that I should only nod to those family members who directly influenced the publication of the book, to those who had read and commented on the book in part or in whole. My oldest sister, Annie Rine Newman Tart, aka Bell, disagreed. An avid reader, Bell devoured the book cover to cover in a day or two, bought copies for her friends, and called to tell me her mostly favorable opinion and to debate others. In the course of our conversation, she asked why I had listed only half of my siblings, leaving her name out and omitting the names of all my brothers and one other sister. My rationale did not assuage the unintended injury. No matter who, what, when, where, or how, my family has always been there. When I need a meal, a loan, some encouragement, whatever, they are there, and Bell stands, proudly and happily, at the head of the line. So from her perspective (and now mine), that first book, as well as this and any others, should nod to the fam: My parents, Dorothy Jean Young and Richard Moore; my siblings and their partners, Robert L. Young and his wife, Marsha; Bell and her husband, Wayne; Anthony "Wolf" Newman and his former wife, Sherita; James "Teddy Man" Jones and his wife, Carol; Latonya Smith and her husband, Tony; Katrina Young and her former husband, Gennard; Y'shanda Latrice Rivera and her husband, Jose; and Lakia Shante Young.

I express my utmost gratitude to you all. Thank you.

—V.A.Y.

---

The patience of my beautiful children, Kayta and Mambi, and that of my husband, Aurelien, who doesn't always understand my work but is supportive anyway, inspires me. My mom and dad motivate me daily to forge ahead. My sister, Bernina, helps me maintain the peace of mind I need to move forward. Thank you, Bernina.

I especially want to thank the support staff of the Rhetoric Department at the University of Iowa: Sandy Mast, Kris Bevelacqua, and Cindi Stevens, for helping with all the things that matter.

I would also like to acknowledge those who contributed to this collection—both directly and indirectly: the anonymous panel reviewers for the 2005 Modern Language Association conference; Charles Nero and Dwight McBride, for being on the panel; Jay Semel and the UI Obermann Center; all the participants in the symposium; the contributors to this book, both those whose essays appear here and those who made submissions. There were so many good essays. We are sorry we could not include them all, but we look forward to reading them in print elsewhere.

Last but certainly not least, I am thankful to have worked on this project with my colleague and friend Vershawn Young. It was quite a ride.

—B.H.T.

# Introduction
## Performing Citizenship

---

*I am convinced that those of us who are earnestly concerned about the problems of civil rights and integration must measure progress not in terms of how much progress we have made recently but how far we have yet to go before we achieve full first class citizenship for the Negro.*

■ *Jackie Robinson, letter to Richard Nixon, 1958*


*I have witnessed a profound shift in race relations in my lifetime. . . . But as much as I insist that things have gotten better, I am mindful of this truth as well: Better isn't good enough.*

■ *Barack Obama,* The Audacity of Hope: Thoughts on Reclaiming the American Dream, *2006*

---

A recent survey conducted by the Pew Research Center reports African Americans today believe that "blacks can no longer be thought of as a single race" and that class performance—how middle class or lower class you act—distinguishes one race of African Americans from an-

1

other.[1] The results of this study may appear at first to be unique, representing twenty-first-century racial attitudes. But they are in fact connected to an old racial longing, a longing, for instance, that the writer James Weldon Johnson puts in the mouth of the middle-class black doctor in *The Autobiography of an Ex-Colored Man* (1912). In that make-believe memoir the nameless protagonist reports: "As I drove around with the doctor, he commented rather harshly on the [black lower] class which he saw. He remarked: 'You see those lazy, loafing good-for-nothing darkies, they're not worth digging graves for; yet they are the ones who create impressions of the race. . . . But they ought not to represent the race. We are the race, and the race ought to be judged by us, not by them.'"[2]

The racial perspective that Johnson incorporates into his fictional account, the wish for a special distinction to be made between middle- and lower-class blacks, is reflected in the behavioral instruction some parents gave their children in the early to mid-twentieth century. In 1926, while commenting on the family life of "the Negro middle class," the literary artist Langston Hughes writes that "the mother often says 'Don't be like niggers' when the children are bad." This admonishment resembles the directive the journalist Clarence Page's parents delivered as he grew up in the 1950s and '60s. "Their early admonitions against 'showing your color' and the like," he says, "were just another way to say, Don't behave like *those* Negroes, those loud, lazy, godless, shiftless, do-rag–wearing good-for-nothings who hang out on the corner and get themselves into trouble."[3]

Many in Page's generation were apparently raised similarly. The intellectual Henry Louis Gates Jr. speaks of an instance when he and his father "drove past a packed inner-city basketball court" and his father remarked: "If our people studied calculus like we studied basketball . . . we'd be running MIT." Although Gates doesn't specify whether his father is speaking to him as an accomplished adult or an impressionable adolescent, the moral of the object lesson is clear. Gates's father contrasts a disapproving representation of lower-class blacks with a vision of middle-class success. The cultural critic Shelby Steele also received object lessons from his father, lessons extolling middle-class virtues and financial success, Steele writes, "by means of negative images of lower class blacks."[4]

Thus the Pew report does more than confirm that some middle-class "blacks see a growing values gap between [the] poor and middle class." The findings also suggest that the historical longing of some middle-class African Americans to be racially distinguished from the lower class is no longer a yearning but is perceived as fact. Is it progressive, however, for Americans to view race this way—as an unstable marker of ethnic identity, as an alterable performance, influenced less by heritage or faulty concepts of biology or social construction and more by performances of socioeconomic status? Will multiplying racial distinctions on the basis of class alleviate or create social problems? And given that Americans so cherish their long-held myth of a classless society, and have come to treasure the notion of a colorblind one, just how did class become the basis for dividing one race into two?

While sociologists and social economists may have their own responses to these questions, my goal in this introduction, in addition to previewing this collection, is to analyze the performative quality of class and to discuss its increasingly significant effect on African American racial performances. To me, African American class performativity and the corresponding performances of race bear some relationship to African Americans' status as U.S. citizens. More specifically, if African American identity has been informed by what Jackie Robinson calls the struggle for "full first class citizenship," then changes in African Americans' experience of citizenship have something, if not everything, to do with the reason that class is now believed by some to be the factor that determines race.

The goal of the greater volume is to present and interrogate African American middle-class performances in the post–civil rights era. This focus arises from what one sociologist calls the "declining significance of race" and the increasing significance of class in the African American experience.[5] This change is the product of desegregation, which ideally should benefit all African Americans. Yet the increased influence of class on African American identity has benefited the middle class, if not politically and socially, certainly economically, more than it has helped the poor and lower classes. Yet, according to various sociological studies, the middle class must still contend with social and political struggles, including racism.[6] What really, then, are the differences between the "two races" of blacks? And why is understanding those differences relevant to the Pew report?

I will respond to these questions, using citizenship as a trope to examine how racial identification has come to be linked to socioeconomic class performance. I begin with a discussion of E. Franklin Frazier's *Black Bourgeoisie* (1957), the fiftieth anniversary of which inspired this collection.

I

E. Franklin Frazier's *Black Bourgeoisie: The Rise of a New Middle Class in the United States* (1957) is a short but complex sociological examination of the black middle class. His study is comprised of two parts, which I think of as sections on class performativity (part 1) and class performance (part 2). In the former, Frazier analyzes the ideologies that precede and produce the behaviors of the black middle class that he criticizes in the latter. In "Part 1: The World of Reality," he describes the persistent strategies deployed to subordinate blacks during times of racial and economic progress (e.g., emancipation, blacks elected to government during Reconstruction, and employment opportunities during the spread of industrialization).[7]

"Part 2: The World of Make-Believe" is best known because in it Frazier makes his most controversial assessment: "Having abandoned their social heritage and being rejected by the white world, the black bourgeoisie have an intense feeling of inferiority, constantly seek various forms of recognition and place great value upon status symbols in order to compensate for their inferiority complex" (111). This complex, he says, arises because the black middle class has "adopted the white man's values and patterns of behavior" (124) yet must "constantly [live] under the domination and contempt of the white man" (112).

As a result the black middle class manages its complex with "compensations," which are used to create a world of make-believe, or what performance studies scholars call "make belief"—"enacting the effects they want the receivers of their performances [and perhaps also themselves] to accept 'for real.'" Glamorous representations of fashionable blacks, expensive lifestyles, and appeals to southern white "ancestry, puritanical morals, and especially education" are used to "make belief" that the black middle class is not significantly impacted by racism.[8]

Frazier's assessments can be briefly summarized this way: the black bourgeoisie believe that their middle-class status compensates for the social inequality they experience, and, since they must live with racism, they focus their attention on what they can change (their class status) rather on what they cannot (their race), believing that economic equality with whites is attainable and will contribute to future social equality. Both perspectives are make belief, according to Frazier. "There are only eleven Negro banks," he writes, offering a strong example of the economic inequality between the races, "with total assets amounting to less than a single white bank in many small cities" (134). Frazier concludes his analysis by arguing that economic equality does not exist, that it will always be in limbo, unattainable, so long as there is any form of racial inequality, and further that the comparatively few blacks who have been able to attain upper-, upper-middle-class, or middle-class status exemplify neither the diminution nor transcendence of racism.

Frazier is even more controversial when he reports what is for me the central point of his text—that middle-class status for blacks in the United States tends to require a conservative rather than a radical racial perspective. He says that racial conservatism is expressed by an acquiescent, accommodationist, subordinate approach to race relations in exchange for increased economic security. Racial radicalism, Frazier says, is defined by the desire for simultaneous racial and economic equality, and racial radicals flat-out reject trade-offs that ask for acceptance or negotiation of racism in exchange for financial gain.[9]

These views are exemplified in two well-known perspectives on education offered by early twentieth-century leaders: Booker T. Washington and W. E. B. Du Bois. Washington says: "In all things that are purely social we can be as separate as the fingers, yet one as the hand in all things essential to mutual progress." "Separate as the fingers" refers to the segregation of the races, and "mutual progress" refers to economic advancement. For Washington the focus should be on gaining economic equality instead of fighting racial inequality. "If we make money the object of man-training," Du Bois responds, "we shall develop money-makers but not necessarily men." "Man-training" refers to developing the intellectual and emotional stamina needed to confront and challenge racial injustice. While opposing systemic racism might in the short run reduce economic opportunities for African Americans, cause them personal discomfort (even death), and provoke white backlash, Du Bois believed it would produce true economic and social equality in the long run.[10]

Frazier illustrates the prominent white perspective on the issue, showing how even the most liberal philanthropic organizations supported blacks' economic success but not advancement of their social status as citizens. Frazier says the agencies expected beneficiaries to "conform to their racial policy," and were "hostile to any [black] who showed independence in his thinking in regard to racial and economic problems"; he noted that "a teacher could be placed upon a 'blacklist' by merely refusing to submit to insults by southern whites" (86).

The real problem that Frazier exposes, the economic myth he busts, is that class is not and could never be compensation for inequality. For as long as blacks have lived in the United States, they have lived in a racially hostile society. At the same time there has always been a group of blacks who manage to acquire wealth, increase their class status, and live within the confines of social inequality. What Frazier's black middle class understands and, according to him, unfortunately accepts, is that middle-class success for blacks in the United States means maintaining or, at least not directly challenging, a system of racial inequality.

While this rehearsal is important and should be kept in mind, this collection does not concentrate on Frazier's middle class. The more particular focus is on the middle class that lives within and benefits from the post–civil rights era of desegregation. This group is associated with, and many of its members arise from, that segment of blacks whom Frazier omits from study in *Black Bourgeoisie*. Writing about those who comprise the unobserved group, he says: "They do not have the same social background as the black bourgeoisie in my study who represent a fusion of the peasant and the gentleman" (6).

Frazier describes this other group as "the Negro middle classes" who participated "in sit-ins and in other protest movements against racial segregation" and whose "social background is essentially that of the Negro folk" (6). There is a significant difference, then, between Frazier's bourgeoisie and the middle class highlighted in this collection: the former base their racial performance on caste, a class status they believe they inherit largely from free middle-class or "mixed-blood" ancestors who had some privilege during antebellum slavery ("house servants"; free northern blacks; mulatto mistresses). This caste can be considered a historical middle class on traditional economic and social terms: as people of some financial means, they promoted and upheld Victorian manners and values during Reconstruction and beyond.

The "new" group's racial performance is based on an acquired class status that links economic elevation to social justice. While the focus here is on this other group, exaggerating the distinctions between the two, without acknowledging their overlap, would be a mistake. As the historian John A. Bracey writes: "When the sit-in demonstrations started, it was the children of the same middle class that Frazier was attacking that led the demonstrations. . . . I was one of them."[11]

The important point to be made, however, is that post–Jim Crow America witnesses more blacks from the lower classes, from Frazier's "folk," ascending to this new middle class largely by way of opportunities afforded by civil rights legislation.[12] And although some African Americans still boast of their connection to Frazier's middle class, as Otis Graham does in his *Our Kind of People* (1999), comparatively few middle-class African Americans today place claims on that combination that produced the black bourgeoisie— social heritage, inheritances, and familial connections to white southern aristocracy. Yet even today's middle class, with its activist roots, as Frazier points out, "has been influenced by the genteel tradition." In other words, while the civil rights middle class may not have the caste of the bourgeoisie, the two share crucial commonalities in the performance of class. Thus the "new" group is sometimes pejoratively, sometimes encouragingly, called *boojie* (alternatively spelled boujie; pronounced boo'zhee).[13]

I have heard *boojie* used as a derogatory term in different ways to describe those who live outside their social or economic means in order to distance themselves from common blacks, for example, a single mother who lives in housing projects but refuses to speak to any of her neighbors; a single schoolteacher who buys a high-priced home in an exclusive neighborhood and wears mink; a custodian who vacations at the Hamptons or on Martha's Vineyard; the secretary who carries only Gucci purses and belittles those who use "no name" bags.

In addition, *boojie* is also sometimes used to refer to a racial sellout, an opportunistic person who was once lower class but who now counteri-dentifies with the people of her class origins in exchange for personal gain. In this sense *boojie* applies to those of the post–civil rights generation who equate proper middle-class performance with middle-class whites, believing, as Steele does, that the black middle class "has always defined its class identity by means of positive images gleaned from middle- and upper-class white society and by means of negative images of lower class blacks."[14]

On the other hand, as a positive term, *boojie* can be used to describe those from the middle class whom Frazier omits from his study, people from the "folk" background who elevate their class station, incorporate some mannerisms and values from middle- and upper-class white society into their black cultural patterns, and who sustain a positive perspective on and relationship with the black majority. What's clear in the varying usages of *boojie* is the essence of performance. Note how this is illustrated by two authors in this book who also offer definitions of *boojie.*

In the final chapter the performance artist–scholar Bryant Keith Alexander says, "For me a boojie performativity references those perceived repetitive actions performed by black people, plotted within grids of power relationships and social norms that are presumably relegated exclusively to white people; hence, by virtue of their enactment and in the presumed absence of black folk, these performances are critiqued as rejecting or abandoning some organic construction of black character and black people."

Alexander is here referring to *boojie* as a class epithet that is used to insult blacks with a folk background like, say, Shelby Steele, but who mimic white behaviors, insulate themselves in predominantly white environments, and niggle about the class performance of lower-class blacks. Of course, Alexander's point is that the epithet can go too far, be unjustly applied to middle-class blacks, who, like himself, may have white lovers and regularly move through white circles but who have not deserted the folk and do not want to be white.

*Boojie* can also be used as a subversive sobriquet to label blacks who mimic the (white) bourgeoisie that Karl Marx critiques as a self-interested piranha class. Marx spoke against a bourgeoisie that controlled the means of industrial production and that relied on labor from the underclass it systematically exploited. Of course, blacks have never controlled production in the United States, so there is not a direct correlation between Marx's bourgeoisie and the black bourgeoisie. But the metaphor still obtains.

In black Marxist ideology production is not primarily industrial but is intellectual, emotional, and spiritual, as illustrated in relationships between, say, teachers and students, church leaders and congregants, intellectuals and the community. Thus the black bourgeoisie, who lack control of industrial production, should recognize the elements of their own oppressed state (benefited by class, oppressed by race) and use their primarily social and material production, however minimal, to help uplift the black lower class. Then both groups can challenge the dominant (white) bourgeoisie that oppress them both.

In this collection's opening essay, the literary and cultural critic Houston A. Baker Jr. vivifies this black Marxist ideology in his discussion of *boojie*:

> The bourgeoisie is a moment of affiliation and transition; it is genuinely about resources, cooperative businesses, relevant group-oriented education for class advancement, and collective ownership. It creates and sustains public spheres that challenge old regimes of power and knowledge. It is a concerted enterprise at betterment, complete with operating manuals and clear marching orders. To be boojie, by contrast, is to ape the dominant bourgeoisie; boojie is black comprador performance for money and awards. Boojie is without commitment or black majority affiliation.

Obviously, *boojie* is a term that generates diverging interpretations. What is certain, however, is that the interpretations derive from the class performance of boojie blacks and their performative relationship to both the white and black bourgeoisie. The authors in this collection have not been asked to tease out these distinctions in terminology, although a few, like Alexander and Baker, do. Instead they attend to and discuss post–civil rights era (boojie) black middle-class performances from artistic, humanities-based perspectives.[15]

These perspectives follow the long tradition of artistic representations of the black middle class and are intended to complement studies that take a historical or sociological approach, like Frazier's.[16] In fact, contained herein are essays (intellectual and academic) as well as creative works (fiction, poetry, and plays) that not only depict the progress made by post–civil rights–era blacks, like Barack Obama, the first black president of the United States, but that also illustrate how far this group still has to go.

Frazier's *Black Bourgeoisie* provides the foundation for this undertaking, but this book, unlike James E. Teele's edited collection, *E. Franklin Frazier and Black Bourgeoisie* (2002), is not about the man or his monograph. Instead another honor is paid—that of acknowledging Frazier's influence on and significance to the ideas presented herein.

## ‖

In the voice-over for director William Greaves's 1968 documentary *Still a Brother: Inside the Black Middle Class*, the late actor Ossie Davis asks: "Does income alone determine what is understood by the term *middle class*?" The film then cuts to the sociologist St. Clair Drake, who responds: "In the American sense class implies a style of life." To explain he shares an anecdote about two black men earning the same middle-income wage while working for the same company in the same position.

On payday the first man stops at a bar to drink alcohol before heading home. When he reaches his house, his wife takes longer than expected to open the door. They fight publicly, and the neighbors observe the man beating his spouse. In contrast, the second man avoids the bar on his way home. His wife also takes some time to open the door. But their fight starts inside, and before he beats his wife, he pulls down the shades. Later they sit to plan their family finances. Drake explains the men's class difference: "They both might have the same amount of money, but the way in which they behave, the aspirations they have for themselves and their children differ. And therefore money alone, as we would see it, doesn't make one middle class."[17]

Later in the documentary Dr. Nathan Wright, an Episcopal minister who once organized the Newark Black Power Conference, expresses skepticism that any black person of any income level can accurately be described as middle class. In fact, he says, "there aren't any middle-class black people but *middle-class–oriented* black people" (emphasis added), a sentiment also expressed by other interviewees. Drake and Wright differently complicate the notion of middle-class identity. For Drake, although income is important, performance, or, as he says, "style," and the concealment of negative behavior, matter more in understanding the term *middle class*. For Wright race and racism impede the full development and acquisition of middle-class identity for blacks. These two perspectives, though dated, offer a context for why the term *middle class*, when used in association with African Americans in the twenty-first century, gestures toward performance and defies neat definition.

The term *middle class* is variously applied to blacks who stand anywhere between rich and almost poor. It's a wide-ranging descriptor, since many who are wealthy, like President Obama and First Lady Michelle Robinson Obama, are often identified among the black (upper) middle class. On the other end, those with incomes closer to lower class but who exhibit the manners and ideologies associated with the middle class, are included, even if marginally, in the group.[18]

Instead of contesting and seeking to narrow this use of *middle class* for this book, I accept it. In fact, an expansive, if somewhat economically imprecise, understanding of *middle class* is appropriate in this context, particularly in light of E. Franklin Frazier's own use of the term. In his 1949 textbook *The Negro in the United States*, he writes: "The middle class consists of professional and technical workers, clerical workers and sales people, skilled workers and craftsmen, and proprietors of small businesses, and public employees."[19]

In *Black Bourgeoisie* he includes teachers, intellectuals, pastors, and even gamblers. Placing such a range of occupations and individuals under the rubric of middle class may make some sociologists and economists cringe, even though they too differ on who and what factors constitute the middle class and the importance of things like, say, marriage, occupation, neighborhood, and income in relation to socioeconomic status. Still, Frazier has not escaped criticism for his broad classification. Even his sympathetic biographer Anthony M. Platt, for instance, calls Frazier's inclusive list "Frazier's muddled middle class."[20]

Yet Frazier was deliberate in his usage, noting in his textbook: "The term 'middle class' as used here refers to the class having an intermediate status between the upper and lower classes in the Negro community. Only a relatively small upper layer of this class is 'middle class' in the general American meaning of the term. Moreover, 'middle class' as used here is essentially a social class though occupation and income play some part in its place in the class structure of the Negro community" (301). Thus Frazier's middle class, and the term as deployed in this book, is not based on pure social-scientific data, nor does it describe a tightly identified economic or sociological category. Rather the term as used here refers mostly to its performative function.

Bracey explains that reading Frazier prompted him to enact a different performance of middle-class identity. He writes, "What I learned most from Frazier was not to be like the people in *Black Bourgeoisie*. If that's what we were doing with our lives, we should stop and think about it. And there was an impulse that came out of *Black Bourgeoisie* that made a whole generation of young people in the black middle class say that whatever we want to be, we don't want to be that."[21] The performative essence of the term *middle class* as used by me and by Frazier, I think, is based on how middle-class blacks use any power and influence that their status affords them in relation to the black underclass majority. This includes both social and economic power, power that, say, business people, teachers, clergy, politicians, and police officers wield.

My use of the term *performance* refers specifically to black middle-class people's everyday self-presentations and artistic representations of them. I connect my use of the term *performance,* as presentation and representation, to Richard Schechner's explanation of what constitutes a performance. "One cannot determine what 'is' a performance," Schechner says, "without referring to specific cultural circumstances." For Schechner, a theater artist and director, "the roles of everyday life are performances," just as plays, rituals, dances, paintings, and poetry are performances "because convention, context, usage, and tradition say so."[22] Analyzing the roles that middle-class African Americans play in everyday American life reveals that many still desire what Jackie Robinson calls "full first class citizenship." This citizenship status exceeds the legal definition of citizenship and is based on both economic and social equality. Therefore what I mean by the combined term *black middle-class performances* is the desire for "full first class citizenship" as expressed in the roles middle-class blacks play in everyday life and how that desire and its attendant roles are represented in art.

A problem I observe, however, one of the several that motivate this collection, is that economic equality is often publicly discussed at the expense of social equality. That is to say, discussions of class that separate blacks into different economic categories today are considered more important than considerations of race and racism—which, the Pew report notwithstanding, still join all blacks together. It's almost as if, as twin concerns, they cannot penetrate the same ear.[23] And even when they are presented together, audiences are bewildered. At least that's the reaction that Nicholas Kristof observes whites had to Barack Obama's national address titled "A More Perfect Union," also dubbed the "race speech."[24]

In his column for the *New York Times*, Kristof writes: "The Obama campaign has led many white Americans to listen in for the first time to some of the black conversation—and they are thunderstruck."[25] Although Obama's speech is a response to questions about his association with Jeremiah Wright, the Chicago minister whom some believe preaches antipatriotic, antiwhite sermons, Obama does not focus exclusively on race but also makes class central in his presentation. The economy, of course, was a primary topic of his campaign, and he says his constituency is the American middle class. Linking race to class is also appropriate in light of what he argues before and after the race speech—that attending to class difference will help secure a better economic future for the majority of Americans, not just the filthy rich. If the election results can be said to corroborate anything about this topic, it's that most Americans are interested in and hear his views on class.

But when Obama articulates the relationship of race to class, people seem unable to reconcile one with the other, which perhaps explains why whites can hear the class and economic issues but are left confused by the racial ones. And although blacks do not appear to be dumbfounded by topics of race, some believe that a focus on class makes race irrelevant. These reactions, whether from naive whites or hopeful blacks, fail to account for a key point about race and middle-class status that Obama emphasizes in his address: "That even for those blacks who did make it, questions of race and racism continue to define their worldview in fundamental ways."

The disparities that produce a racialized worldview, he notes, "can be directly traced to inequalities passed on from an earlier generation that suffered under the brutal legacy of slavery and Jim Crow." He believes this past is common knowledge: "We do not need to recite here the history of racial injustice in this country," he says. But given the public's "thunderstruck" response, a rehearsal of that history is important, particularly a rehearsal that shows how the social inequality that some middle-class blacks still protest always has been and already is about class.

Undeniably, race has always been connected to both the citizenship and socioeconomic status of blacks. The Supreme Court's decision in *Plessy v. Ferguson* (1896), which legalized segregation, illustrates just how connected they remain in our modern era. Justice John Harlan, offering the only dissent, wrote that segregation "interferes with the personal freedom of citizens."[26] It was evident to him that the legislation violated the Fourteenth Amendment rights of African Americans: "No state shall make or enforce any law which shall abridge the privileges or immunities of citizens."

With an illustrative, if xenophobic, example, Harlan argues that it is contradictory to allow Chinese people who could not at the time qualify for U.S. citizenship to enjoy the very rights and protections of the law denied to black American citizens. "There is a race so different from our own that we do not permit those belonging to it to become citizens of the United States," he writes. "But by the statute in question, a Chinaman can ride in the same passenger coach with white citizens of the United States, while citizens of the black race . . . are yet to be declared criminals" if they do so.[27]

Harlan's argument about black people's experience of citizenship is clear, but the relationship of Jim Crow–citizenship to class is not detailed. This is not because it was not addressed in the case. In fact, Homer Plessy's attorney, Albion Tourgee, made an argument against segregation on the basis that it denied Plessy financial opportunities. Because Plessy was more white than black—seven-eighths white and one-eighth African (in the then-quantifying terms of race biology)—Tourgee argued: "How much would it be *worth* to a young man entering upon the practice of law to be regarded as a *white* man rather than a colored one? Six-sevenths of the population are white. Nineteen-twentieths of the property of the country is owned by white people. . . . Under these conditions, is it possible to conclude that the *reputation of being white* is not property? Indeed, is it not the most valuable sort of property, being the master-key that unlocks the golden door of opportunity?" (emphasis in original).[28]

Tourgee's argument appears at first to be a "defense of the nearly white man, not the black," but as the literary historian Brook Thomas points out, "if [the argument] had been successful, it would have played havoc with all laws designed to make [racial] distinctions" (30). The Court, however, ignored this class argument and reached a decision that made race the only issue. Thus one way to express the lasting effect of segregation on the combined experience of race, class, and citizenship is to say that separate but equal laws concretized the belief that in the United States your race determines your class. This is why, regardless of their actual economic level, middle-class African Americans could be treated as lower class.

The writer Charles Chesnutt explores the relationship of class to the Court's ruling in his novel *The Marrow of Tradition,* first published in 1901. When a train conductor asks Chesnutt's middle-class black protagonist, Dr. William Miller, to move to the second-class car, Miller says: "I have paid my fare on the sleeping-car, where the separate-car law does not apply." While he is riding through the North, Miller sits in the first-class car that his position afforded. While he is traveling through the South, his class is ignored. Miller moves to the "Colored Only" section and finds deplorable conditions and a white man smoking. He responds: "I have paid first-class fare, and I object to that man's smoking in here."[29] Miller believes an appeal to his class capital should at least entitle him to ride in a smoke-free car designated for blacks. But the white man and his smoke stay. And race, or rather race prejudice, forestalls class privilege.

In *Marrow* Chesnutt portrays the class problem inherent in racial segregation, a problem that can be described this way: the fantasy that blacks and whites should be separated because their races are incompatible and the falsehood that blacks are inferior because they are not white became class-based realities under law. Put another way, the law forced blacks to perform their race as a lower-class identity in relation to whites. Under Jim Crow, whites, regardless of their actual status, received middle-class privileges, and middle-class blacks were uniformly denied them.

Desegregation may have eliminated separate but equal laws, but it has not eradicated the fantasy wherein race marks class. Thus many contemporary middle-class African Americans experience a psychological dilemma: their class status is linked to a white racial identity, and their racial identity is linked to a lower-class status. To reconcile this predicament many attempt unsuccessfully to identify with only one, the white racial world, or the other, the black class world, since to repeat the familiar expression, they are caught between two worlds. Or, like the elite black bourgeoisie, the Martha's Vineyard brand, where one anonymous resident called Michelle Obama "a ghetto-girl," they try to insulate themselves from both.[30] I firmly believe, and argue here, that this history prompts the people whom the Pew Research Center interviewed to mistakenly believe that desegregation undid the Jim Crow experience, where your race determined your class, and ushered in an era where your class status determines your race. On this basis some believe that if different groups of blacks perform class differently, "blacks can longer be thought of as a single race."[31]

To gloss the point, in "Race as Class" (2005), the sociologist Herbert J. Gans observes that even today, in the case of African Americans, "race is used both as a marker of class and . . . an enforcer of class position."[32] Yet there is a compromise. African Americans must prove their worth as beneficiaries of desegregation; either they must perform in socially acceptable ways, according to rules of decorum that are not defined by them or based on their cultural patterns, or they must remain segregated. Said differently, during Jim Crow middle-class African Americans were prevented from "acting white," from sitting where they could afford on the train; post–Jim Crow they are required to "act white," particularly in white-collar professions.

In this sense "acting white" simply means middle-class blacks must be cautious about talking too loudly and animatedly, wearing colorful clothes, letting their hair go natural, speaking black English, rolling their eyes, and a host of other benign behaviors that are deemed problematic only because they are associated with being black and thus lower class. If there really is no such thing as acting a race, as many argue, why are so many of the traits and behaviors associated with black people perceived as so wrong?

Yet even when middle-class African Americans today present and sustain the "proper" racial performance, they still cannot yet be considered nonblack or be considered "new people," as Chesnutt calls those in *House Behind the Cedars* (1900) who are middle class and more white than black. Therefore some have made their own categories: many middle-class African Americans who want to retain the category black for themselves characterize lower-class African Americans as not really black but niggers. Though they are not named as such in the findings, these are really the two class-based races discussed in the Pew report. But to view race this way is boorish, crude, and historically ignorant. This view shares a bed with America's legacy of racism, which actually created the very circumstances that middle-class blacks wish to avoid by counteridentifying with lower-class blacks.[33]

Post–Jim Crow middle-class blacks counteridentify with the lower class for the same reason that blacks sometimes passed as dark-skinned noncitizens during segregation—in order to avoid racism and experience privileges denied them as citizens. The writer Zora Neale Hurston writes of passing as an "Asiatic person of royal blood" at the prompting of her employer, the novelist Fannie Hurst, in order to enter the apparently segregated Astor Hotel in New York. And although the educator Booker T. Washington does not write of passing himself, he does indicate that passing as an Indian or Moroccan would facilitate better experiences for dark-skinned African Americans. He writes about an instance when an Indian student was greeted in a "dining saloon," where Washington was denied entry. "The man in charge politely informed me that the Indian could be served, but I could not. I never could understand how he knew just where to draw the colour line, since the Indian and I were of the same complexion." Another example calls more attention to the importance of passing through performance, in this case using language to perform and downplay black racial identity. Washington reports that in one town "so much excitement and indignation were being expressed that it seemed likely for a time that there would be a lynching. The occasion of the trouble was a dark-skinned man had stopped at a local hotel. Investigation, however, developed the fact that this individual was a citizen of Morocco, and that while travelling in this country he spoke the English language. As soon as it was learned he was not an American Negro, all the signs of indignation disappeared." And "the man . . . found it prudent after that not to speak English."[34]

The literary critic Joseph T. Skerrett Jr. argues that James Weldon Johnson writes so well about racial passing in *The Autobiography of an Ex-Colored Man* because Johnson was drawing from his own experience. Regarding Johnson, Skerrett reports: "On several occasions, recorded in *Along This Way* [Johnson's real autobiography], his ability with idiomatic Spanish allowed him to 'pass' for some other kind of brown-skinned man than an American Negro. In these situations his goal was to avoid the potential unpleasantness inherent in 'a suddenly presented situation that involved "race."' Johnson was personally familiar, then, both with the concept of impersonation and the experience of 'passing'—if not for white, then at least for some other kind of non-Negro."[35]

The point of these historical anecdotes is to show that the United States has always been hostile toward African American identity. And in order to benefit from the rights guaranteed them as citizens and to be treated fairly, some dark-skinned African Americans passed, ironically, as dark-skinned *non*citizens. The dark-skinned African Americans who passed as individuals of another dark-skinned race, of course, also had to disassociate themselves from other American blacks. Class passing or, rather, class performance in the twenty-first century has replaced the racial passing of the twentieth century. Both types of passing point to a societal problem, one that unjustly stigmatizes black identity. This stigma prompts blacks either to seek ways to avoid it by claiming another identity (passing) or try to disassociate from the stigma (creating a race within a race).

Given this overview of social history, it is really a wonder to me that so many misunderstand the quest to connect class equality to social equality. Too many mis-hear the articulation as just another appeal for racial justice. And that appeal is now eagerly dismissed by some blacks and many whites on the ground that blacks have achieved a good deal of social equality in the forty or so years since the end of the civil rights period.

Yet this very attitude illustrates the current relevance of Jackie Robinson's assessment that we "must measure progress not in terms of how much progress we have made recently but how far we have yet to go." Measuring future travel hinges on understanding the (immediate) past, understanding how American racial history produces contemporary performances of class and how the very governing structure of our society at one end creates a legal frame that leads us to privilege race over class and at the other to judge a person's class by his race.

I emphasize this point about class for a reason different from the one the cultural critic Walter Benn Michaels provides in his book *The Trouble with Diversity* (2006). According to Michaels, Americans enjoy believing "that the differences that divide us" are differences of race rather than differences of class, because recognizing racial difference "present[s] a solution: appreciating our diversity." He says "appreciating our diversity" is fine: African Americans, Asians, queers, Latinos are all good people. But accepting this diversity does little to address America's class trouble. He argues that Americans should recognize that the fundamental problems of the nation exist, not between races and genders but "between those of us who have money and those who don't."[36]

The problem with Michaels's view, of course, is that he merely reverses the problem of privileging race over class by privileging class and ignoring the problems that race, gender, and sexual identity pose to those seeking to acquire or sustain a middle-class status. Unlike Michaels, I support analyses that place racial identity and class on the same plane, that link them. I believe that race determines and most certainly modifies the experience of class. Note the following example concerning Condoleezza Rice.

The now-famous tidbit is offered by Coit Blacker, a Stanford professor who identifies himself as one of the former secretary of state's closest friends. He recalls going into a jewelry shop with Rice; Rice asks to see earrings. The clerk shows her costume jewelry. Rice asks to see something nicer, prompting the clerk to whisper some sass under her breath. "Let's get one thing straight," Coit recalls Rice as saying. "You are behind the counter because you have to work for minimum wage. I'm on this side asking to see the good jewelry because I make considerably more." Rice gets what she wants: a manager quickly brings her the gems.[37]

Rice's response is evidently an effort to get the benefits she deserves based on her upper-class status ("I make considerably more"). Her black identity, however, complicates the case. After all, it's hard to accept that a clerk in a fine jewelry store is unaccustomed to properly dealing with upper-middle-class people. Thus the attention Rice calls to her class is also about her race. "I may be black," the subtext of her words suggest, "but I am also upper middle class."

Although Rice's experience ends differently than Dr. Miller's in Chesnutt's *Marrow,* in terms of class performance the similarity matters. The difference, of course, is that in Jim Crow America Dr. Miller's class does not register. In post–civil rights America, Rice's class does. That's why she gets her jewels. Yet even with the outcome, race is a significant factor, since working-class clerks in fine jewelry stores do not customarily mistreat their clients on the basis of their upper-middle-class status. That would be not only absurd but bad for business. But clerks have been known to mistreat black people. It's not hard to believe, of course, that working-class clerks might mistreat white working-class people, might show them fake gems, not the good stuff, presuming what they can and cannot buy. That presumption would be an expression of classism, which is also wrong. But it is hard to accept that Rice was read as poor on a basis other than her race. The similarity, then, between Rice and Dr. Miller—what is, of course, the issue—is that they had to perform—verbally display and call attention to—their class in order to diminish their race.

How performing race differs for middle-class blacks than for, say, middle-class whites can be understood from what Schechner explains as the difference between performing that is "playing a role" in everyday life and someone "being herself." "To 'be myself' is to behave in a relaxed and unguarded manner. To 'perform myself' means to take on the appearance (clothes, demeanor, etc.), voice, and actions" of the role or persona. Both Rice and Chessnut's Dr. Miller exemplify the primary problem of racial performance for middle-class blacks: they must "perform themselves" (perform their class) in situations where they should be able to "be themselves." In other words, they must take on what I theorize in *Your Average Nigga* (2007) as the burden of racial performance, where middle-class black people are called upon in everyday social situations to be hyperconscious of their behaviors and speech and must guard how they are perceived, by constantly altering their social performance, in situations where they should be able to be "relaxed and unguarded."[38]

In view of the foregoing, it is clear why Jackie Robinson uses not one but two modifiers to emphasize that he wants all black people to experience citizenship just like any other person. Certainly, some might say, "But he and all blacks already have citizenship. If he asks for full citizenship, isn't he asking for something that no one has, not even white people?" If the question refers to blacks as legal citizens, the answer is yes. Robinson, Chesnutt's Dr. Miller, former secretary of state Rice, President Obama, and the middle-class blacks Obama says have "made it" are all citizens. The problem is lingering unevenness, disparity, inequality in the experience of their citizenship—particularly in the class experience, which is always inflected, and sometimes mitigated, by race. Thus Robinson's "full first class citizenship" is a rhetorical hyperperformance that shines the spotlight on the regular citizenship that the law says African Americans have but that an analysis of their performance of everyday life reveals they still do not.

This point, in turn, further amplifies my earlier description of the term *performance* as presentation and representation. Representation is the depiction of actions, ideas, laws, and behaviors in order to draw attention to them for some kind of aesthetic and/or rhetorical consumption, like appreciation, analysis, or discussion. Such representations, as some of my examples show, take place in literature, like Chesnutt's *Marrow of Tradition*; in film; in legal documents, like Justice Harlan's dissent; on stage; in correspondences, like Robinson's letter to Nixon; and so on. Presentation is both the unscripted and deliberate behavior of everyday life, like Rice's encounter with the clerk and Obama's act of delivering his "race speech."

The contributors to this book use representation and presentation as they specifically perform what Schechner calls "explaining showing doing." That is, they are engaged in "a reflexive effort to comprehend the world *of* performance," or representation, "and the world *as* performance," or the presentation of everyday life framed as performance. Although Schechner says "this comprehension is usually the work of critics and scholars," which the writers here are, I think it is also the work of any person (readers of this book, for instance) who seeks to comprehend the interrelationship of their everyday performances and artistic representations.[39] On this specific basis the writers herein explore black middle-class performances.

The order of appearance for the contributions to this book makes no distinctions between the creative works and academic essays. The writings—a play, essays, poetry, and fiction—are arranged to illustrate what the performance scholar Dwight Conquergood describes as a "radical intervention"—"by embracing both written scholarship and creative work, papers and performances. . . . Performance studies brings this rare hybridity into the academy."[40] The aim here, though, is to go a bit further than Conquergood's charge and also present this hybridity to the public, addressing educated laypeople and public discourses, not only academic ones.

If, as Conquergood asserts, academic discussions can benefit from artistic performances that occur with greater reception and frequency in public, then the public should likewise be able to benefit from academic wisdom. The goal here is to represent a true exchange of values between the public and the academy, instead of reifying artificial boundaries that keep them apart. I believe Frazier himself would value this approach. In his essay "The Failure of the Negro Intellectual" (1962), he writes: "It may turn out in the distant future Negroes will disappear physically from American society. If this is our fate, let us disappear with dignity and let us leave a worthwhile memorial—in science, in art, in literature, in sculpture, in music—of our having been here."[41] Artistic representation and academic analyses were important to Frazier, and that importance undergirds this collection.

The contributions are arranged into four sections, each of which is preceded by an artistic interpretation by Jean Berry, who is also our cover artist. Berry uses deceptively simple figures of unclothed, ambiguously gendered, faceless black bodies to depict each section's main thrust: Performing Responsibility, Performing Womanhood, Performing Media, and Performing Sexuality. *Performing* is shorthand for presentation and representation, since the two terms are interconnected, one sliding into the other in practice. Their interconnectedness is better explained by the performance scholar Erin Striff, who writes that performing can be understood as "how we represent ourselves and repeat those representations within everyday life."[42] The terms following *performing* in the section headings (i.e., *womanhood, sexual-*

*ity*, etc.) refer to topics found in Frazier's *Black Bourgeoisie* and remain important to understanding black middle-class performativity and performance. Let me therefore contextualize descriptions of the contributions with a brief summary of the contemporary discourse surrounding the topics.

### Section 1: Performing Responsibility

In *Black Bourgeoisie* Frazier is critical of black leaders for camouflaging their efforts to generally assimilate blacks under the rhetorical rubric of integration. He argues that by promoting assimilation, black leaders are supporting the annihilation of black culture, identity, and spirituality. Further, leadership is not only about occupying a political office, like the presidency. It is about one's responsibility to family, to community, to the race. One carries out this responsibility in various roles, as the one who has "made it" in an otherwise lower-class family, as a major figure in an academic field, as an administrator at a university, or as someone who runs a community institution designed to promote racial and economic success for blacks. The writings in this section feature leaders who fit in one or more of these categories, and they all interrogate the notion of responsibility.

In the first piece, "Bourgeois Fugue: Notes on the Life of the Negro Intellectual," Houston A. Baker Jr. offers a personal and cultural analysis of the role of black intellectuals in the struggle of the black masses. He critiques the self-interest of some leaders, arguing that personal self-reflection can help bring about necessary systemic and ideological change. He offers his analysis through an honest reflection about his life and class status as well as his intellectual transformation.

Venise Berry's short fiction, "Pockets of Sanity," explores the main character's anguished perspective on the expanding gulf between the middle and lower classes. The female protagonist struggles to reconcile her middle-class status with her family's lower-class ways. She is presented with questions about what her personal role and responsibilities are in relation to those she loves as family but loathes as performers of class.

In his chapter "My Momma, Obama, and Me: Black Leadership/Black Legitimacy," Dwight McBride adds layers of complication to the traditional story of how an African American leader should perform. In an insightful examination driven by personal experience, he writes about the performance of black political leadership in relationship to intellectual and academic leadership. He folds in the question of "alternative" sexual and gender identities to open the closet door on what is still, unfortunately, a controversial question: Can gays, lesbians, the transgendered, and queer blacks or blacks with white partners be good, effective black leaders?

In "Selling Dr. King's Dream: Blackness and Tourism in Atlanta," Sara F. Mason critiques the heritage tourism of Atlanta's tourist industry. She writes that as a tourist destination, Atlanta relies upon a dualistic construction of Atlanta as the place where history happened (the "Old South") and a place beyond history (the "New South") in order to promote a city of renewal, racial harmony, and progress. She argues that, in the process, Dr. Martin Luther King Jr.'s dream of political and economic parity is rearticulated in terms of consumption rather than praxis and that King's memorial is co-opted so that Atlanta can generate more economic capital, sometimes at the expense of social equality.

This section ends with the father of the black arts movement, the Poet Laureate of New Jersey, playwright, and activist Amiri Baraka. His poem "The Drug of White Supremacy" is controversial on the topics of race and class. His poem meditates on problematic middle-class ideologies that find their way into policies and behaviors that affect the black masses. He is not shy about calling out popular politicians, journalists, and activists who, although black themselves, engage performances that perhaps do more harm than good to the black majority. On this note of shared racial affiliation but displaying different class ideologies, he summarizes:

> Like my man, Mean William, used to say
> "Skin is Thin, But Class
>     Will kick yo' ass."

### Section 2: Performing Womanhood

Without a doubt, whatever strides African Americans have made in terms of class and citizenship have been largely the result of the efforts of black women and the roles they have played in social and economic struggles.

Black women have arguably done as much for the race as black men, if not more. To rephrase the historian Paula Giddings (à la Anna Julia Cooper), when or where black women enter, so enters the entire race.

Nazera Sadiq Wright's "Black Girls and Representative Citizenship" opens this section with a substantial historical interpretation of early twentieth-century conduct books written by middle-class blacks to train middle-class black girls to perform proper racial behavior. The aim of the proper behavior was to elevate the race. For Wright black girls became representative citizens of the black race. Wright's essay specifically examines the "language, iconography, and coded messages of decorum that surrounded the black girl figure as a citizenship model" in one popular instructional manual titled *Floyd's Flowers, or Duty and Beauty for Colored Children. Floyd's Flowers* is an important text to study, because as Wright points out, it was "part of a collection of prescriptive texts that instructed African Americans on how to act in a manner that would protect against Jim Crow laws and prevent violence by whites."

In "Black Bourgeois Women's Narratives in the Post-Reagan, 'Post–Civil Rights,' 'Postfeminist' Era," Claire Oberon Garcia examines how black women attempt to enter into a new post–civil rights era with hopes of social advancement. Garcia contrasts Ntozake Shange's novel and musical *Betsey Brown* with Andrea Lee's *Sarah Phillips* and argues that while both pay a kind of homage to historical constructions of class aspirations and social uplift, neither author accepts the limitations of those constructions.

Eileen Cherry-Chandler takes readers "down home" in her tale, "Rosalind." In this performance poem readers encounter the personal sexual struggle of a tough teenage girl, Rosalind, whose story is told by the girl she antagonizes. The two meet unexpectedly in a beauty salon, where the narrator reveals that Rosalind is 'hood, from the streets, where the narrator sometimes hangs out: "I was not raised for all the wild stuff that I do." The subtle and implicit notions of middle-class behaviors and ideologies as they conflict with working-class performances are uncovered in a story about sex, youth, and intraracial strife.

Following Cherry-Chandler is Lisa B. Thompson's play *Single Black Female.* Unlike Cherry-Chandler, who uses the black female grooming ritual of hair straightening to drive her coming-of-age narrative of class and gender,

Thompson reminds us that no matter the texture of the hair or the grooming technique—or the quality of the clothes, for that matter—black women
continue to be the female doppelgangers of Ralph Ellison's *Invisible Man.*
They struggle to be seen and heard among whites as well as other blacks.
As Thompson writes in her remarks that precede the script, "throughout the
[play] the duo humorously express the ambivalence, hope, and desires of
many single middle-class African American women in the post–civil rights
era."

## Section 3: Performing Media

The essays here address a variety of media and media-related issues raised
by Frazier. He exposes middle-class blacks who engage in conspicuous consumption, overspending in order to present a showy display of their means
of life, and placing representations of their means in black magazines, like
*Jet*, to convince themselves and the public of their status. He further examines the role of the black media, for example, newspapers, magazines, and
journals, in creating make belief, a world that paints a false picture of insula-
tion from white contempt.

The first two pieces in this section put two post–civil rights black musical traditions into conversation. Greg Tate's essay, "Of Afropunks and Other
Anarchic Signifiers of Contrary Negritude," is a simultaneous call to self-
reflection and a description of contemporary black musicians. Instead of
focusing on a black musical past, he positions himself in the present by
investigating "alternative music" by such groups as Living Colour. These
musicians are meant to represent a creativity that inspires us to think outside the box, that eschews efforts to "authentically" represent white or black
middle-class values.

Damion Waymer discusses the implications of the commodification of
rap and hip-hop music in "Hip-hop and Capitalist Interests." He identifies
the negative ramifications of rap music and argues that the ghetto-fabulous
features of the genre represent the very conspicuous consumption that Frazier critiques. What Waymer finds interesting is that middle-class blacks
criticize the flaunting of ghetto-fabulous styles but do not follow the advice
against conspicuous consumption themselves. He further cautions both un-

der- and middle-class blacks against falling prey to materialism, whatever its origin.

In "Middle-Class Ideology in African American Postwar Comic Strips," Angela M. Nelson takes a historical approach to the discussion of two strips that appeared in two black newspapers. According to Nelson, black comic strips both reflect and reject efforts to create a world of make-believe. "What is important to know about them," she writes, "is that comic strips are a direct reflection of the editors and staff of the newspapers in which they appeared." Knowing this, she says, "helps us to understand the extent to which middle-class ideologies helped shape images and representations of African Americans."

The next essay in this section, "*Put Some Skirts on the Cards!* Black Women's Visual Performances in the Art of Annie Lee," Deborah Elizabeth Whaley examines the art of Annie Lee, whom Whaley argues "envisages the variety of black female identities as articulated and practiced in everyday life." Whaley ruminates on how Lee's aesthetic approach is itself a visual performance of class, race, and gender identities, as well of sexual and national constructs. Overall, Whaley uses Lee's art to draw critical attention to "the transformative power of oppositional art by and for African American women."

Harilaos Stecopoulos's essay, "Melodrama of the Movement: Lorraine Hansberry's *A Raisin in the Sun*," argues that Hansberry's play is not, contrary to some popular reviews, an "endorsement of dominant [white] middle-class values." Stecopoulos insists that the play instead contends with the traditional middle-class values that privilege racial and class assimilation over enlightenment.

### Section 4: Performing Sexuality

The chapters in this last and arguably most important section take up class and sexuality. As the sociologist Patricia Hill Collins writes in *Black Sexual Politics: African Americans, Gender, and the New Racism* (2005), "Failing to address questions of gender and sexuality will compromise antiracist African American politics in the post–civil rights era." E. Franklin Frazier also attended, albeit somewhat problematically, to issues of gender in *Black Bour-*

*geoisie.* Frazier argues that because black men "are not allowed to play the 'masculine role' as defined by American culture," they "resemble women who use their 'personalities' to compensate for their inferior status in relation to [white] men."[43] He further reports that because many women may be married to men who neglect them for work, white women, and other activities, the women are sexually frustrated and engage in nonsexual behaviors to distract themselves from the "sexual orgasm" they desire. Certain ideas and images of the effeminized black middle-class male and the sexually truncated black female still abound in our public culture and media. And many issues surrounding sex and gender remain taboo in many African American communities and churches.

In this section's opening essay, "The Black Church and the Blues Body," Kelly Brown Douglas is concerned that " 'there's something going all wrong' in the black church." The essence of the problem, she argues, can be found in the church's "attitudes toward issues of sexuality." Douglas examines these issues by focusing her discussion on what she calls "the blues bodies," which are "nonbourgeois bodies." Her interesting class-based analysis of blues music, the blues body, and lesbian, gay, bisexual, and transgender issues reveals just how central sex and sexuality are to the performance of class within the black church.

Candice M. Jenkins's essay, "A Kind of End to Blackness: Reginald McKnight's *He Sleeps* and the Body Politics of Race and Class," focuses on Bertrand Milworth, the protagonist of McKnight's novel. Bertrand Milworth is associated with academe. As an anthropologist, he goes to Dakar, Senegal, to conduct fieldwork and is haunted there by his sexuality: his relationship with white women and his never-satisfied desire to have sex with black women. Jenkins argues that because Bertrand's self-reflective interrogation takes place in Africa, it "allows the novel to comment on, specifically, African American middle-class identity, and that identity's relationship to larger narratives of the black body."

Lisa B. Thompson posits in "Black Ladies and Black Magic Women" that the films she analyzes reject restrictive representations of black womanhood in order to "escape the clichéd depictions of sexually frustrated, but highly professional, black middle-class women." Her discussion of female gender and sexual performances both illustrates the agency black women have over their bodies and their struggles to maintain such control. Her analysis complicates pedestrian and stereotypical fantasies of black women as either oversexed or sexually bereft.

Bryant Keith Alexander offers a powerful and thoughtful closing to this entire project with his essay, " 'Boojie!': A Question of Authenticity." He addresses "issues of gender and sexuality, performances of professionalism, and racial authenticity." He discusses his romantic partnership with a white male, how his role as a professor and dean in the "white ivory tower" affects others' perceptions of his racial performance, and how the term *boojie* entraps as much as it empowers the possibilities for transgressive performances.

*There exists today a monumental divide between black intellectuals and the black majority.*

■ Houston A. Baker Jr., Betrayal: How Black Intellectuals Have Abandoned the Ideals of the Civil Rights Era

*Before the black creative intellectual can "heal" her people she must consider to what extent she must "heal" herself.*

■ Hortense Spillers, "The Crisis of the Negro Intellectual: A Post-Date"

Every book has a set of personal politics, even an edited collection. So I want to expose mine, indeed, where my politics and those of Bridget Tsemo intersect. In 1994 the historian Hortense Spillers poignantly critiqued black intellectuals for their failure to respectfully observe and take adequate note of the silver anniversary of Harold Cruse's *The Crisis of the Negro Intellectual* (1967). The anniversary of his still-influential analysis "passed without fanfare or remark," Spillers says. "The occasion of the lapse," she continues, resulted in no small part from black intellectuals' continued confusion about their roles in relationship to the larger black community.[44]

Although Bridget and I were undergraduates at the time of Spillers's writing, and therefore not the direct subjects of her criticism, we nonetheless feel convicted by her description of "the black, upwardly mobile, well-educated subject [who] has not only fled the neighborhood (in some cases the old neighborhood isn't even there anymore!) but, just as importantly, has been *dispersed* across the social terrain to unwonted sites of work and calling" (433).

We see ourselves in this description: two scholars from the urban landscape of Chicago (one from housing projects, the other from a working-class neighborhood but both from the now-gentrified, no-longer-ghettoes where we cannot afford to live) working to sustain our acquired middle-class status and landing our first university jobs in, of all places, Iowa. (I'm now at the University of Kentucky.) We do not want Spillers's critique to apply to us. We are inspired by James Teele's hope that his "volume [on Frazier] represents only the opening stage of a renewal of interest in E. Franklin Frazier's rich and rewarding work."[45] We did not want to be part of a group that allowed the golden anniversary of Frazier's *Black Bourgeoisie* to pass without note, for we would be not only forgetful but neglectful.

Engaging the performance rituals of our culture, which call on us to become retrospective on special days and sensitively analytical during commemorative times, Bridget and I invited others to join us in self-reflective critique on our panel for the 2005 Modern Language Association Annual Convention in recognition of the original publication of *Black Bourgeoisie*, in France, in 1955. Encouraged by the good attendance and response, we brought the subject home to the University of Iowa in 2007, when we received a $25,000 grant from the university's Obermann Center for Advanced Studies in the Humanities. We codirected a well-attended symposium on the occasion of the anniversary of the American edition of Frazier's book, published in 1957.

Still, conferences are intentionally ephemeral, occasions to generate thought that takes root elsewhere, in policy, in teaching, in interpersonal relations, in writing. This collection, then, is designed to substantially consider what it means for African American citizens to perform racialized class identities in the age of social progress. As I arranged the contributions, I recalled not only Spillers's words but also those of W. E. B. Du Bois, specifically, his comments on the responsibility of middle-class blacks to the greater black majority.

In his "Talented Tenth Memorial Address," written as an addendum forty-five years after the publication of his original "Talented Tenth" essay (1903), Du Bois calls successful blacks who emerged after Reconstruction "a group of self-indulgent, well-to-do men, whose basic interest in solving the Negro Problem was personal; personal freedom and unhampered enjoyment and use of the world, without any real care, or certainly no arousing care, as to what became of the mass of American Negroes, or of the mass of any people."[46] Middle-class blacks misunderstood his original message to be about personal gain when, he says, he meant the focus to be on their relationship to the black masses. He explains, "For these men with their college training, there would be needed thorough understanding of the mass of Negroes and their problems. . . . Willingness to work and make personal sacrifice for solving these problems was of course, the first prerequisite and *Sine Qua Non*. I did not stress this, I assumed it" (161).

Du Bois's advice unquestionably differs from the middle-class parental instruction that intellectuals like Page, Gates, and Steele received, instruction that negatively profiles, encourages identification against, and further stigmatizes the black lower classes. However, other middle-class black intellectuals of the same generation received different parental instruction, instruction that models Du Bois's advice. In *Betrayal*, Baker writes: "My mother and father were among the select number of African Americans of their generation privileged to earn not only bachelor's but also advanced graduate degrees." Yet his father instructed Baker and his brother to "'always speak to people.'" He told his boys, "Everyone deserves your respect."[47]

His father's lessons influenced Baker. He reminisces, "One day . . . I encountered a shabbily dressed black man, holes in his shoes, reeking of alcohol." This man could certainly be one of the "negative images" of lower-class blacks that Page, Gates, and Steele report their parents warned them to avoid. But what did Baker do? He spoke to the man. To which the man replied: "'Your father is one of the best people in this world. You spoke to me. You polite just like him. You got any spare change?'" Baker's larger point is this: "To be known in the public world of the black majority as a 'good man'—as my father was—can be a lifetime goal and calling" (8). Baker does not reference Du Bois's counsel that the black middle class respect, sacrifice for, and work on behalf of the black lower classes, but the influence and relationship are clear.

Baker's example, as well as the admonishment from Spillers and Du Bois, prompt me to consider the plight of the underclasses of blacks and to make the discussion linking social equality to economic equality not just about receiving middle-class privileges (Condi's getting her earrings) but also about equal opportunities for the black poor to increase their class status in the land of opportunity. Indeed, our goal should be to help all blacks achieve not just economic success but full first-class citizenship. Therefore I acknowledge my own membership in the larger black community and welcome the responsibility that recognition brings. And while I argue that race is an entirely erroneous concept, something far worse than a social construction, I do not subscribe to the results of the Pew report, to the idea that there are now two races of American blacks. To me this is simply wrongheaded.

I am all too aware that some might believe that not having one black community is a good thing, that the notion of community produces an over-concern with race and race politics that keeps blacks in retrograde mode, stuck in a pre–civil rights–era concept of blackness when we are now free to be individuals. "People." "A part of the American community." "Not just black people." But I want to posit that so long as whiteness is a privileged position in America, deliberations about its relation to blackness and class must exist.[48] Without them, as Frazier points out, not only the black middle class but all black people will risk "becoming NOBODY."[49]

I am also aware that some believe that trying to prove your blackness, the burden of racial authenticity, is killing too many. So many brothas are found dead in the streets and sistas lie out in the 'hood precisely because performing a certain kind of black authenticity has wreaked havoc on their lives. Resisting certain "white" cultural ways has led some to dismiss education and to perform brands of blackness that have detrimental consequences. But this spectacle is not simply an upshot or proof of black pathology; it is part of the relationship that blackness bears to the larger American drama, the American dream, which for many blacks is still a nightmare.

Yes, I too am dismayed when pretty girls get ugly much too quickly, when youthful vigor is wasted on prowess in the streets. But the United States has rested its very identity, its local—and now, especially, its global—persona on preventing these eventualities in nations around the world. So why are African Americans dying much faster than whites? Granted, members of the black middle class are dying a little slower than the underclass but only a little.[50] In other words, although some stave off the eventuality of black death—because they are more middle class, because they have access to better health care and the information that health care provides—the sad truth is that the maelstrom of the United States still produces effects that shorten the lives of all black men and women, and even when they live a long time their quality of life is overwhelmed by injuries to the spirit.

So while the effects of race, or rather the devastation that racism produces, are compounded in the direction of the underclasses, the devastation operates in all directions—even toward the middle classes. I see one function of this book, an important one, as understanding the role that black middle-class performances have in relation to black working- and underclass performances and how all these performances contribute to both the wonderful promise and lingering peril of black people's experience of citizenship in the United States of America.

**NOTES**

1. See "Blacks See Growing Values Gap between Poor and Middle Class: Optimism about Black Progress Declines," report, Pew Research Center for the People and the Press, November 13, 2007, Washington, D.C. As noted on the center's website: "This report on racial attitudes was conducted by the Pew Research Center, a nonpartisan 'fact tank' that provides information on the issues, attitudes and trends shaping America and the world" (http://pewresearch.org/pubs/634/black-public-opinion).

2. James Weldon Johnson, *The Autobiography of an Ex-Colored Man* (New York: Dover, 1995), 73.

3. Langston Hughes, "The Negro Artist and the Racial Mountain," *Nation*, 1926, available online at www.english.illinois.edu/maps/poets/g_l/hughes/mountain.htm; Clarence Page, *Showing My Color: Impolite Essays on Race and Identity* (New York: HarperCollins, 1996), 59.

4. Henry Louis Gates Jr., "Breaking the Silence," *New York Times*, August 1, 2004, A11; Shelby Steele, *The Content of Our Character: A New Vision of Race in America* (New York: HarperCollins, 1990), 97. In *Colored People: A Memoir* (New York: Vin-

tage, 1995), Gates presents a more nuanced perspective of his parents and his up-bringing that is more sympathetic to the black lower classes. However, the example here, taken from his opinion piece in the *New York Times,* illustrates the complex perspective that blacks held about class and the appropriate racial performance of their children, particularly their public performance around whites, which, I argue, is a direct response to black people's historically oppressed position in America.

5. See William Julius Wilson's *The Declining Significance of Race: Blacks and Changing American Institutions* (Chicago: University of Chicago Press, 1980).

6. See, for instance, Joe R. Feagin and Melvin P. Sikes's *Living with Racism: The Black Middle-Class Experience* (Boston: Beacon, 1994); Lois Benjamin's *The Black Elite: Still Facing the Color Line in the Twenty-first Century* (Lanham, Md.: Rowman and Little-field, 2005); and Karyn R. Lacy's *Blue-Chip Black: Race, Class, and Status in the New Black Middle Class* (2007) (Berkeley: University of California Press, 2007).

7. E. Franklin Frazier, *Black Bourgeoisie: The Rise of a New Middle Class in the United States* (New York: Collier, 1962).

8. Richard Schechner, *Introduction to Performance Studies* (New York: Routledge, 2002), 35; Frazier, *Black Bourgeoisie,* 126. According to Schechner, make-believe recognizes a distinction between reality and fantasy, whereas make belief uses everyday performance to "create the very social realities [performers] enact" (35).

9. See Frazier, *Black Bourgeoisie* (chaps. 3 and 4, esp. 65–76 and 84–97.

10. Ibid., 61, 62.

11. John H. Bracey, "Frazier's Black Bourgeoisie: Talented Tenth or a Parasitic Class?" in James E. Teele, ed., *E. Franklin Frazier and Black Bourgeoisie* (Columbia: University of Missouri Press, 2002), 88.

12. The sociologist Benjamin P. Bowser makes a similar observation in *The Black Middle Class: Social Mobility and Vulnerability* (Boulder, Colo.: Lynne Rienner, 2007). He writes: "There are very few African Americans today in professions, management, or any other white-collar work who have not directly benefited from affirmative action. . . . In this sense, the contemporary black middle class can be called the 'affirmative action' middle class" (101).

13. See Lawrence Otis Graham, *Our Kind of People: Inside America's Black Upper Class* (New York: Harper Perennial, 1999), 14. See Geneva Smitherman, *Black Talk: Words and Phrases from the Hood to the Amen Corner* (Boston: Houghton Mifflin, 1994), for a critical definition of the term boojie in the context of African American rhetoric.

14. Smitherman, *Black Talk*; Shelby Steele, *The Content of Our Character: A New Vision of*

*Race in America* (New York: Harper Perennial, 1992), 99.

15. Representing and analyzing the performance of "middle-class" and "aristocratic" identities among blacks is in line with a tradition that has considered the subject within arts, literature, and culture since the beginning of slavery in the Americas (e.g., Aphra Behn's *Oroonoko; or, a Royal Slave*, 1688). After Reconstruction and especially since the turn of the twentieth century, there has been a concentrated increase in artistic critiques and assessments of middle-class performance in African American culture and literature Charles Chesnutt's *House Behind the Cedars* (1900) and *The Marrow of Tradition* (1901); Anna Julia Cooper's *A Voice of the South* (1892); Frances Harper's *Iola Leroy* (1892); Pauline Hopkins's *Contending Forces* (1900) and her magazine novels (1901–3); W. E. B Du Bois's *The Quest of the Silver Fleece* (1911); Johnson's *Autobiography of an Ex-Colored Man*; and Hughes's "Negro Artist and the Racial Mountain."

    In his influential study of the period, *Black American Writing from the Nadir* (Baton Rouge: Louisiana State University Press, 1989), Dickinson Bruce Jr. writes: "It would also be difficult to understand much about black writing from 1877 to 1915 without some sense of the characteristics of its creators. . . . They may be described without oversimplification as members of the black middle class that was taking shape and growing in size in the Post-Reconstruction era. . . . Such a collective portrait helps indicate a common body of experience upon which they drew and helps illuminate their work (4–6).

    There are also recent notable and influential explorations of the subject in literary and cultural studies, such as Michele Wallace's *Invisibility Blues: From Pop to Theory* (New York: Verso, 1990); Valerie Smith's *Not Just Race, Not Just Gender: Black Feminist Readings* (New York: Routledge, 1998); and Candice Jenkins's *Private Lives, Proper Relations: Regulating Black Intimacy* (Minneapolis: University of Minnesota Press, 2007). There are, of course, so many more that to cite only three may appear a disservice. These three texts, however, specifically address representations in film, art, and literature, the focus of this collection, and thus come readily to mind as examples.

16. Some notable and influential examples of texts from the sociological and social historical perspectives are Mary Pattillo-McCoy's *Black Picket Fences: Privilege and Peril among the Black Middle Class* (Chicago: University of Chicago Press, 2000) and *Black on the Block: Politics of Race and Class in the City* (Chicago: University of Chicago Press, 2007); Karyn Lacy's *Blue-Chip Black: Race, Class, and Status in the New*

*Black Middle Class* (Berkeley: University of California Press, 2007); Martin Summers's *Manliness and Its Discontents: The Black Middle Class and the Transformation of Masculinity, 1900–1930* (Chapel Hill: University of North Carolina Press, 2003); and Bart Landry's *The New Black Middle Class* (Berkeley: University of California Press, 1988).

17. William Greaves, *Still a Brother: Inside the Black Middle Class*, a ninety-minute television documentary made in collaboration with William Branch for National Educational Television, first aired on NET on April 29, 1968.

18. For more on the varied inclusions within the middle class, see *Class Matters* by Bill Keller and a team of *New York Times* reporters (New York: Times Books, 2005), and bell hooks's *Class Matters: Where We Stand* (New York: Routledge, 2000).

19. E. Franklin Frazier, *The Negro in the United States*, rev. ed. (New York: Macmillan, 1957), 693.

20. Anthony M. Platt, "Between Scorn and Longing: Frazier's Black Bourgeoisie," in Teele, *E. Franklin Frazier* (Columbia: University of Missouri Press, 2002), 79.

21. Bracey, "Frazier's Black Bourgeoisie," 88.

22. Schechner, *Introduction to Performance Studies*, 38.

23. It is, of course, true, as illustrated earlier, that race and class have been taken up in various strata of academic work. Some notable academic contributions are Kimberlé Crenshaw's notion of "intersectionality" to discuss the intersections of race, class, and gender (see Kimberlé W. Crenshaw, "Mapping the Margins: Intersectionality, Identity Politics, and Violence against Women of Color," *Stanford Law Review* 43, no. 6 [1991]: 1241–99). Again, Valerie Smith's *Not Just Race, Not Just Gender* builds on Crenshaw's theoretical term. The focus of my discussion in this introduction is on how the matters of race and class are received in the public sphere, in public discourses outside the academy. Indeed, the everyday public, which also includes academics, shows that the conversations of race and class are still tenuous, problematic, little understood. The point cannot be overstated that more academic and public discussions and work are needed to bring the twinned conversation into regular consideration.

24. Then–presidential candidate Barack Obama's speech was delivered on March 18, 2008, in Constitution Hall, Philadelphia.

25. Nicholas Kristof, *New York Times*, March 19, 2008.

26. *Plessy v. Ferguson*, 163 U.S. 537 (1896). I am indebted to the editor Brook Thomas for his invaluable *Plessy v. Ferguson: A Brief History with Documents* (New York: St.

Martin's, 1997), which includes the Harlan dissent. The quote appears on p. 55.

27. Thomas, *Plessy,* 55.

28. Ibid., 30.

29. Charles Chesnutt, *The Marrow of Tradition* (New York: Penguin Classics, 1993), 54, 57.

30. See Touré, "Black and White on Martha's Vineyard," *New York Magazine,* June 21, 2009 http://nymag.com/guides/summer/2009/57472/

31. "Blacks See Growing Values Gap," 1.

32. Herbert Gans, "Race as Class," *Contexts* (fall 2005): 19–20.

33. As an aside, it can be understood from this history how a black person who demonstrates middle-class habits and manners is thought to be performing out of racial character, acting white. As an epithet then, "acting white" is not a unique black expression used to criticize other blacks who display middle-class characteristics. It is an appellation produced by U.S. laws and ideologies that police the performance of race and class. For more on "acting white" and its relationship to U.S. laws and ideologies, see Signithia Fordham's "Beyond Economic High: On Dual Citizenship and the Strange Career of 'Acting White,'" *Anthropology and Education* 39, no. 3 (2008): 227–46. See also Vershawn Young, *Your Average Nigga: Performing Race, Literacy and Masculinity* (Detroit: Wayne State University Press, 2007), esp. chap. 6, "To Be a Problem."

34. Zora Neale Hurston, *Dust Tracks on the Road: An Autobiography,* 2d ed., ed. Robert Hemenway (Urbana: University of Illinois Press, 1984), 310; Booker T. Washington, *Up from Slavery* (New York: Dell, 1965),79, 71.

35. Joseph T. Skerrett Jr. "Irony and Symbolic Action in James Weldon Johnson's *The Autobiography of an Ex-Coloured Man,*" *American Quarterly* 32 (1980): 88, 547.

36. Walter Benn Michaels, *The Trouble with Diversity: How We Learned to Love Identity and Ignore Inequality* (New York: Metropolitan Books, 2006), 6.

37. Condoleeza Rice's jewelry store episode is recounted on numerous sites on the Internet and is also published in Glenn Kessler, *The Confidant: Condoleeza Rice and the Creation of the Bush Legacy* (New York: St. Martin's, 2007).

38. Schechner, *Introduction to Performance Studies* (New York: Routledge, 2002), 171. For more, see Vershawn Ashanti Young's *Your Average Nigga.*

39. Schechner, *Introduction to Performance Studies,* 22.

40. Dwight Conquergood, "Performance Studies: Interventions and Radical Research," *Drama Review* 46, no. 2 (2002): 151–52.

41. E. Franklin Frazier, "The Failure of the Negro Intellectual," in Joyce A. Ladner, ed., *The Death of White Sociology* (New York: Random House, 1973), 66.

42. Erin Sniff, *Performance Studies* (New York: Palgrave Macmillan, 2003), 1.

43. Patricia Hill Collins, *Black Sexual Politics: African Americans, Gender, and the New Racism* (New York: Routledge, 2005), 9; Frazier, *Black Bourgeoisie*, 230–31.

44. Hortense Spillers, "The Crisis of the Negro Intellectual: A Post-Date" in *Black, White, and in Color: Essays on American Literature and Culture* (Chicago: University of Chicago Press, 2003), 428.

45. Teele, *E. Franklin Frazier*, 13.

46. Du Bois's essay is in Henry Louis Gates Jr. and Cornel West, *The Future of the Race* (New York: Alfred A. Knopf, 1996), 162. See also W. E. B. Du Bois, "The Talented Tenth," in Booker T. Washington, ed., *The Negro Problem: A Series of Articles by Representative American Negroes of Today* (New York: J. Pott, 1903).

47. Houston Baker Jr., *Betrayal: How Black Intellectuals Have Abandoned the Ideals of the Civil Rights Era* (New York: Columbia University Press, 2008), 1, 8.

48. See Mary Pattillo's *Black on the Block: Politics of Race and Class in the City* (Chicago: University of Chicago Press, 2007).

49. Frazier, *Black Bourgeoisie*, 26.

50. See R. Randall Vernellia's *Dying While Black* (Dayton, Ohio: Seven Principles Press, 2006).

# Performing Responsibility

**1**

# Bourgeois Fugue
## Notes on the Life of the Negro Intellectual

cannot utter the phrase "black bourgeoisie" without evoking Howard University in the 1960s. On a hot afternoon amid the hum and buzz of the largest city I had ever inhabited, I matriculated with the Howard class of 1965. Before I found my dormitory room in Charles Drew Hall, I heard the name "E. Franklin Frazier" a dozen times. Frazier was one of Howard's most eminent professors; he was author of the renowned monograph *Black Bourgeoisie*, an excoriating account of Negro class mimicry. When I enrolled at Howard, I had no idea Frazier's work was about *my* kind of Negro: ambitious colored citizen blessed with a modicum of talent and motivated by a fierce fondness for the codes and rewards of white society. In time I speculated that the fieldwork and case studies for *Black Bourgeoisie* could have been conducted exclusively and succinctly on my alma mater's campus.

When I was a freshman, however, I knew virtually nothing of *class*. From birth through high school the sign of difference for me was *race*. All colored people in Louisville were "Negroes." True, we were differently resourced and "churched." Collectively, though, we were on lockdown through the racial etiquette of old Jim Crow. If we possessed a black bourgeoisie, it certainly could not enjoy a movie at the all-white Brown Theater. So long as any of our number had a place to live and was responsibly employed, he was racially acceptable and socially trustworthy. In a sense, then, my formal education in the black bourgeois protocols analyzed by Frazier began at Howard. And I realized early on that I was what wealthy British gentlemen call "a scholarship boy." From my first day on campus I knew that many of my cohort had traveled extensively, shopped expansively, dressed stylishly, and spoken without an accent their entire lives. I was to them an intriguingly unrefined southern black bird whose call they worked to classify.

I don't mean to discount advantages of my rearing. My mother belonged to Jack and Jill of America, the African American women's organization that promotes leadership in children, and she and my father held graduate degrees and professional titles. I went to parties and church socials where every Negro boy wore a shirt and tie. Standard English and impeccable table manners were norms in my household. We prayed modestly and never split an infinitive. My brothers and I were spurred daily to dreams of bright futures in the ranks of a colored "Talented Tenth." So I was not entirely without para-class prerequisites when I entered Howard.

Still, my closest artistic kin at the beginning of my freshman year were Balzac's rural protagonist exhilarated by the glories of Paris and Stevie Wonder's black southern immigrant given "just enough for the city." I was bedazzled by my alma mater's cosmopolitan wonder. I joined a fraternity (Kappa Alpha Psi), took up the reigning campus slang with the passion of a convert, and found myself quick at such exchanges as "What's hap'nin?" "Yo' world, man . . . I'm just livin' in it!" "C'mon, you know that's lies and garbage. You the man!" Our argot was, I think, fashioned to suggest we were hip Negroes. With a small group of classmates I revived and edited the university's literary magazine. I received a Phi Beta Kappa key at the close of my senior year.

As commencement dragged on and on under a blistering Washington, D.C., sky, I knew I had a firm handle on class. I acknowledged my race *and* class obligations. My Howard mentors had jolted me out of my parochialism and summarily southern "local knowledge." I had journeyed in the realms of Shakespeare and Byron, Weber and Harrington, Aristotle and Aquinas, Goethe and Galileo, Faulkner and Eliot. I deemed myself fortunately classified among young "Negro Intellectuals of Promise." Hence, I felt no compelling need to hang on the words of our graduation speaker. I was restless. I wanted to move into the world, fulfill what I deemed my implicit covenant with society. I believed I had earned much, deserved more, and knew *everything*. After all, I was the Negro recipient of a handsome fellowship to a prestigious PhD program in English at the University of California at Los Angeles. Alas, there was more than one deficit in my conceited self-assessment.

The first wrong turn in my thinking was my willed indifference to the civil rights activities that marked Howard's campus life during my matriculation. Charlie Cobb, Michael Thelwell, Stokely Carmichael, H. "Rap" Brown, and others were among Howard's progressive black actors and voices during my undergraduate tenure. The black liberation struggle to which they were committed entered one of its most volatile and successful phases during my university years, and I was oblivious. My failure to heed the way the winds of change were blowing was only one of many reasons I felt only indulgent annoyance as President Lyndon Johnson (our commencement speaker) delivered his historic civil rights address on the May afternoon of my departure from Howard in 1965. When I was not creating bad poems of my own in the Western mode during my college years or delving into Western literary classics or honing social skills at fraternity parties, I scarcely gave a thought to whether the black majority had food, shelter, employment, or safe passage in the United States. Willy-nilly, despite myself, in college I had become an apolitical Negro aesthete.

The second oversight in my education became apparent during the summer internship that followed my graduation. I was hired by the *Washington Post* to join a group of ten young men and women from Ivy League institutions; we were to hone our journalistic skills and further our knowledge of the trade. In truth, I had no passion for journalism, but I needed a lucrative summer job. One of Howard's creative writing instructors had recommended me to the *Post* for a job as a copy boy. Seemingly, someone at the *Post* thought "outreach" to Howard was a progressive idea. By midsummer, affirmative action and a kindly city editor at the *Post* promoted me to intern reporter. I was the only black person in that energetic group of multitalented, ambitious Ivy Leaguers. Several were from well-known journalistic families. All had achieved status as writers and editors of college newspapers, like Harvard's *Crimson*. If I sadly missed the boat with respect to civil rights at Howard, I instantly realized at the *Post* that I knew *nothing* about concise and informative journalistic prose, especially how to write it. Further, I had no useful knowledge whatsoever about the cataclysmic international dramas of my time, for example, a raging, imperialistic, undeclared war in Southeast Asia. Of African colonies and their triumphant unshackling from knots of colonialism, I could deliver not a single coherent paragraph. It is critical to note that the white interns were activists. They sought and received face time with editors and owners of the *Post*. They grilled them about the paper's editorial policies vis-à-vis Vietnam and other world events. They were relentless in their memos and suggestions for reading to those in charge. I had nothing to contribute to such activism. I was sadly uninformed.

The sum of my deficits is as follows: At Howard University I truly learned a great deal about what Langston Hughes calls "the ways of white folk." I took such "ways" as a gold standard. I believed they were universal and mattered awfully in my class advancement. Not only this, but I chose roads of least complexity and resistance. My choice, as Gilbert and Sullivan's *Patience* expresses the matter, was "to shine in the high aesthetic line." Without a single challenging forethought, I conceded that *politics is the enemy of aesthetics*. Politics were boisterous, physical, and emotionally disruptive for the true artist/intellectual. Likewise, the international scene was a distraction from my Miltonic certainty that "the mind is its own place." I thus struck a pose as a hermetic, solitary, and creative mind whose best gifts would be known by peerless scholarship and breathtaking Negro Intellectual Poetry. Such aestheticism conditioned my behavior; my behavior earned kudos and a Phi Beta Kappa key.

I acknowledge that mercifully—and with the grace of the black arts, black power, and black aesthetic movements—I realized soon after graduation that I was a perfect storm of black bourgeois sensibility. Frazier, Carter G. Woodson, and Nathan Hare set me back on my heels.

Ironically, I experienced my epiphany of black arts, politics, and power at Yale University, where I began teaching in the late sixties. Victorian English literature was my doctoral specialty, and I was an exemplary student, moving from matriculation at UCLA to the granting of degree in three years.

With affirmative action in full effect and my preparation well certified, I gained an assistant professorship at Yale. My ambition was to be a great Victorianist and write the definitive biography of Oscar Wilde. But Yale was not an Ivy League oasis when I arrived. It was a hotbed of black activism, from demands for black community and cultural inclusion in all facets of university life to calls for a moratorium on all future university expansion into black neighborhoods bordering Yale's campus. The Black Panthers were present in New Haven in rhetoric and regalia. Bobby Seale and Erica Huggins were leaders in the huge May Day protest on Yale's campus in 1970.

Yale and New Haven's black activism brought me to my senses, brought me back "home." Black students and faculty welcomed me to the activist ranks. They recommended books, summoned me to all-night political conversations and strategy sessions, gave me tips on new black music, poetry, and drama. My new allies even taught me how to divest myself of tweed jackets and don handsome dashikis. I became joyfully reacquainted with the black "basic training" that enabled my parents to survive the perils of Jim Crow and send sons off to college. When I was growing up in Louisville, my family lived in a desolate and municipally underesourced slum called Little Africa. While Little Africa was materially impoverished, it was communally rich in black survival lore and strategies. My parents were store owners; they were community-involved citizens who taught us that our opportunities and fortunes meant nothing unless they were put into the service of the black majority. Their injunctions, in combination with the lore of Little Africa, became part of my being. I learned both in that preconscious way one learns to breathe. In the headiness of higher education I had suppressed the wisdom of the elders. But their gifts remained a subconscious reservoir just waiting to be tapped.

My black activist intellectual and cultural involvement revealed that I was "mis-educated," a deluded person of color—a danger to the black majority and myself. I was brim-full and proud of all knowledge, except the great unconscious vein derived from and valuable to my natal community. I was a masquerade, the quintessence of Professor Hare's "Black Anglo-Saxon." Here, I think, resides the distinction between *bourgeoisie* and *boojie*.

The bourgeoisie is a moment of affiliation and transition; it is genuinely about resources, cooperative businesses, relevant group-oriented education for class advancement, and collective ownership. It creates and sustains public spheres that challenge old regimes of power and knowledge. It is a concerted enterprise at betterment, complete with operating manuals and clear marching orders. To be boojie, in contrast, is to ape the dominant bourgeoisie; boojie is black comprador performance for money and awards. Boojie is without commitment or black majority affiliation.

Frazier, Hare, and Woodson critiqued "boojie blacks" as a fragmented order of colored pretenders to knowledge and as shirkers of service to anyone but themselves. In their polemics against such performance, these venerable scholars deemed boojie blacks narrowly individualistic poseurs whose minds were replete with white legend and lore. Their front ranks are driven by lust for the almighty dollar. Hence, their boojie mode of existence, so astutely and devastatingly critiqued by Frazier and others, is not, in the final analysis, positively *bourgeois* at all. It is merely an abbreviation. Like the cryptic shorthand *boojie,* their lives, desires, and accomplishments are truncated, airless parodies of power, radical politics, and serviceable enterprise in the interest of the black majority. I know, for I have been chief among sinners, a weak-kneed aesthete basking in white compliments. I have lived among the unclean and boast no claim to present purity.

As I conclude this brief reflection, I can say I have traveled some effective miles toward abandonment of my black cartoon enchantment with "Whiteland," its assumed right to judge everything, and its assumption that such judgments are universal, objective, accurate, and without racial bias. Even before I departed my first academic post at Yale University, I grew my hair to stand naturally above my scalp. I bought dashikis by the dozen, and dedicated my life to reading, teaching, and analyzing black literature and culture. In silent African prayer I told Shango it would be alright if he changed my name.

Today, as I watch an assortment of Black Public Intellectuals locked in Western guise and holding forth in soothing terms before white paying audiences about a "postracial America," lauding the election of Barack Obama as a millennial advancement of the interests of the black majority, I am irritatingly haunted by shadows of my old self. The uncanny is all around us. Boojie has re-created itself as the heart and soul of a self-styled "raceless" and postsoul aesthetic. (What, scripturally, does it mean for a people to lose its "soul"?)

I listen to jazz and hip-hop, read in black diaspora classics, and wait longingly for anything positive to happen. Best would be the birth of a real and caring black bourgeoisie, one Professor Frazier would approve and that Howard University would salute as a model for a bold and vigorous African and African diaspora curriculum. To such a vision we might all proclaim, "Ashe."

# Pockets of Sanity

A short line of cars moved slowly through the street, headlights beaming in the middle of the day, while dark murky clouds floated in a fog-filled sky. Many people on the Philadelphia streets glanced at the caravan and thought nothing of it. Another death in the city was no big deal.

Helena felt the nausea rise from her chest to her throat and swallowed it. When death is a choice, any day is a good day for the funeral. Helena Schor; her husband, Samuel; their son, Alan; and Helena's mother, Helen Simmons, filled the third car in the funeral procession. Sam, who was driving, looked straight ahead, and Alan's eyes swept the sidewalk for interesting sights. Helena sighed heavily. She wanted to say something, to talk about the situation, actually to complain about the situation, but Sam, Alan, and Helen remained defiantly quiet. They knew if they gave her the slightest opportunity, they would have to spend the rest of the ride hearing all about trifling black folks.

When the procession turned into Ivy Hill Cemetery on Easton Road and stopped near a prepared gravesite, Helena didn't get out of the car right away. She didn't want to be there, but her mother had insisted. Helen was always selling the philosophy of family as crucial to survival. But Helena didn't buy it; except for her mother, she could not name one thing that her family had done for her as a child, and there was nothing they could do now. The majority of her relatives were stuck in the ghetto like burned oatmeal in the bottom of the pot.

Samuel motioned to Helena until she finally crawled out and followed him to the gravesite. Seated in the section partitioned off for family, Helena watched as the Reverend Washington took his place in front of the mourners. The reverend looked up into the sky in a dramatic gesture before he spoke.

"I remember Titus as a man who loved life. A man with a laugh that was as big as the sky. I can almost hear him laughing now because he is happy. He has gone home."

It was difficult for Helena to concentrate on Reverend Washington's words, especially when she thought about Titus in heaven. That might have been the case ten or twenty years ago when he was a good guy, but not now, not when he died a worthless, pathetic, crackhead. As she scanned the room, Helena could see nothing but the stereotypical absurdity of her family. Uncle T-Cat, who sat directly behind her, was an old pimp-daddy who had obviously found another young gold-digger to attach to his arm. Cousin Flip had recently finished a five-year prison sentence in Holmesburg for robbery and credit card fraud. He stood blinging in the back with his baggy clothes and platinum paraphernalia. Aunt Irene and her husband, Rendell, sat at the end of the first row, heads bobbing like Uncle Remus and Aunt Jemima. Both were terrified of their own son at the end. Titus had robbed them on numerous occasions, cursed them out, and once even knocked his mother into a rose bush when she didn't give him what he wanted.

Titus's nineteen-year-old daughter, Skyla, looked like a typical hoochie. She sat next to her grandparents, with her five-year-old son, Jared, on the other side. Helena listened as the Reverend Washington recited the Lord's Prayer.

"Our Father, who art in Heaven, / hallowed be thy name. / Thy Kingdom come, / thy will be done / on earth as it is in Heaven."

All eyes suddenly focused on Skyla, who had leaped up and rushed over to the casket. The long wooden box tilted toward a big empty hole behind it as Skyla kicked and hollered and screamed for her daddy to come back.

Helena sucked her teeth with disgust at the ridiculous display. She noticed that Skyla was wearing the traditional ensemble of her generation's sexually obsessed angst. The collar of her shirt scooped much too low, showing everything but her nipples, and there was not enough material to cover her belly button. The micromini skirt she wore was so short that when she fell across the casket, the audience got a clear view of a lacy black g-string as it disappeared into the crack of her ass.

After Cousin Marc finally grabbed the girl and pulled her back to her seat, Helena shot Sam a look of repugnance that made him shudder. Aware that his wife would rant about the incident for weeks to come, Sam quickly turned back to the Reverend Washington.

"Isaiah 25:8 says that He will swallow up death in victory. Listen to me? The Lord God will wipe away tears from off all faces. Do you hear me!" Some in the crowd nodded, a few mumbled amen, and others shouted hallelujah.

As the Reverend Washington continued to preach, Helen noticed that her daughter had stopped listening and grabbed the thin, brown fingers beside her and squeezed, like she used to do when Helena was six years old and misbehaving in church. Helena frowned but did not pull her hand away.

After the funeral Helen insisted that they make an appearance at Irene and Rendell's house to show their respect. Helena, protesting, was ignored. As the car careened down Broad Street into the heart of Northside Philadelphia, Helena closed her eyes. Some days she thought seriously about leaving Philly, getting away from the horrible streets she grew up on. But her father's dream for her was that she teach at Philadelphia University, and she promised him on his deathbed that she would fulfill it.

"That's the goal, Helena," her father would always say whenever they passed the sprawling campus. "Remember, college will get you out of the ghetto and make you somebody." Before he died, her father convinced her that she needed to travel only those few blocks to college to make her life better. She did, and it was.

When she opened her eyes, they were passing through familiar territory. Kids playing on grassless earth, porches with boards missing, broken stairs, tar-spotted roofs with missing shingles, mounds and mounds of trash that never seemed to end, windows cracked, boarded up, and attached to lean-to walls that didn't know what a difference paint could make. It made her sad to think about the lost souls inside. But she refused to feel sorry for people who chose to live this way. She had gotten out, and so could they.

Her aunt Irene and uncle Rendell's house at 1620 Wallace Street looked worse than it had five years earlier, the last time Helena was there. The Yukon gold paint had peeled even more, the top wooden step on the porch, which was cracked on her last visit, had broken off completely, and the hole-riddled screen hung halfway out of the front door.

Inside, the house was not much better. The glazed chintz on the couch and loveseat was well worn; their arms were frayed, their seats lumpy. The walls were dingy and the carpet filthy. Helena earnestly accepted a hug from her cousin Althea, probably the only cousin she really liked, who had been busy straightening the cloth on the dining room table and reorganizing the paper plates and napkins.

"It has been way too long," Althea scolded.

Helena shrugged. "I know. I keep meaning to call or stop by, but life happens."

"That's the truth. Can you believe Titus is dead?"

"Yeah, I can, and the sad part about it—he killed himself. God, I hate stupidity."

"That's not fair, Helena. He had a lot of demons on his back."

"We all got demons. You just got to say, 'Satan, get thee behind me,' and keep on stepping."

Althea shook her head. "Everybody's not as strong as you are, Helena. None of us were as strong as you."

Helena snorted. "We all do what we have to do."

As the crowd gathered, Althea went back to her chores, and Helena searched the table for something to nibble on. She picked up a few carrot sticks and shook her head. All the traditional black foods of death had been assembled into a serious buffet: fried chicken, mac and cheese, potato salad, chitlins, honey ham, and black-eyed peas. She glared at her son, Alan, who stood on the other side of the table with his plate overflowing, and Samuel, who followed right behind him.

Helen cautiously stepped beside her daughter and spoke. "Let's go offer a few words of comfort to Irene."

Helena frowned, but she knew it was not a suggestion or request. She literally dragged herself over to Irene in the kitchen doorway.

"Irene, honey, I'm so sorry," Helen offered with a warm embrace.

"I know, baby sister, I know," Irene murmured. "I can't believe my baby is gone."

Helena hugged her aunt hurriedly. "You know, if there is anything I can do . . . ," she stammered, lying.

Irene nodded and lied, too: "Thank you, I'll let you know." Then she stepped forward and whispered, "Come on upstairs and put your purses in my bedroom, where I can lock them up. Some of Titus's friends are going to be here, and I don't want nothing to come up missing."

Helena tossed an annoyed look toward her mother. "I can't stay that long, Aunt Irene."

"I understand, baby, but no matter how long you're here, I want to make sure you still have your belongings when you leave."

Helen and Helena followed Irene up to her bedroom and placed their purses on a shelf in the closet. Irene locked the closet door first, then locked her bedroom door behind them, and slipped the key down between her breasts.

When they returned, they found the living room filled with well-wishers. Helena found an empty seat near the window where she could observe everything. If she had to stay, at least her family always offered good practice material for her profession as a psychologist. The television briefly caught Helena's attention. A local reporter was saying that blacks were overrepresented on death row in Pennsylvania. He explained that 62 percent of the inmates currently scheduled to be executed were black. Two young cousins scuffled, cursing at each other over a pack of gum and distracting her from the report. Helena tried to stop herself from seeing both young boys, already drenched in hip-hop garb, as adding to those statistics in a few years.

When Titus's friends arrived, Helena noticed right away. They stood huddled in a group in the middle of the floor. Simon was the only one she recognized. He and Titus had been buddies since grade school. Rumor had it that Simon was responsible for Titus's drug-filled fantasies, but Helena refused to accept any of the excuses the rest of her family clung to. Titus wasn't a stupid man. He didn't grow up in a broken home. He had bullshitted his way out of a track scholarship in college with a lack of focus, then pissed away the possibility of graduating because of poor grades and immaturity. Titus could have done great things with his life, but instead he chose death.

Helena carefully surveyed the group. They were all headed for their own hole in the dark earth. The signs of addiction were obvious: rumpled and soiled clothes, sweating, scratching and sniffling, eyes glazed over, focusing on any valuables in the room that might fit into their pockets.

"Hey, Cuz, haven't seen you in ages. How are you?" Marc asked, standing over Helena as he held his two-year-old son, Omar, in his arms.

"I'm doing very well, Marc. What about you?"

"Things are tight right now, but I'm making it."

"I'm glad to hear that. How's Candy?"

Marc's chest tightened. "She's the same sorry slut she was when we got married."

Helena grimaced. "Marc, don't say that in front of Omar."

"Why not? He's gonna have to learn to deal with these chickenheads soon enough. Look at him, he gonna be a playa just like his daddy."

"Cousin Helena!" Marc's sixteen-year-old, Evette, screamed and ran over to hug her in an Academy Award–winning performance.

"Hey, Vette. Look how pretty you're getting," Helena said, barely hugging the girl back.

"When you gonna take me to Sea World again with Alan? That was mad fun."

Helena nodded and held the phony smile in place. She couldn't tell the girl the truth, that she would never take her fast ass any place ever again. Two years ago at Disney World, Evette had disappeared for a couple of hours with some bellhop. Who knows what they did.

"I don't know when we're going to get back there, honey," Helena replied.

"Well, you should hook a cousin up, you know. I'm making all A's and B's in school now."

Helena lit up. When it came to children, good grades were the magic words. "That's wonderful! Do you have a favorite subject?"

"Not really. But I'm gonna try out for junior varsity cheerleading next week. I know all the cheers already. Watch this."

Evette began gyrating her hips violently and pumping her chest. She stomped and rocked to a funky beat that spilled out of her mouth.

"We are the Ti—gers, man-eating Ti—gers, we're number one, so you better run. We are the Ti—gers, man-eating Ti—gers, outshine the sun, just for fun. We are the Ti—gers, man-eating Ti—gers, our work's not done, 'til we have won."

Helena quickly covered her open mouth. Evette's movements were so raunchy that all the boys and men in the room had stopped their conversations to gape.

"You like it?" she asked, chest heaving, hips still wiggling.

Helena hesitated. "It was something," she finally answered.

"Hey, here come Logo in his dope ride!" shouted one of the boys who had tussled over the pack of gum earlier.

Turning to look out the window, Helena watched the infamous Logo emerge from his black Lexus with the $8,000 gold rims. She had never met him before, but she knew that Logo was Skyla's baby-daddy. She also knew through the family grapevine that he was a drug-dealing pimp who treated Skyla like garbage.

Skyla rushed to the front door on cue and opened it just as Logo stepped up to knock.

"Hey, baby," she purred.

"What up?" Logo retorted and stepped inside.

"Hey, Logo, man, you need to let me hold your keys for a little while. I could pick up a lot of honeys in that slick ride," said the young boy who announced Logo's arrival as Logo initiated a homeboy handshake.

"Niggah pa——leeez," Logo drawled. "The only way you would get to drive my car is if you was sucking my dick better than my baby." The crowd laughed along with Logo when he slapped Skyla on her behind to make sure everyone in the room knew she belonged to him.

"I'd suck his dick anytime he want me to and suck it good, if he put me up in that nice apartment, and buy me all them expensive clothes and shoes like he buy her," Helena overheard a female voice whispering. She glanced behind her, sad to see Evette standing next to another girl the same age.

Helena shifted her attention back to Logo. She couldn't understand the hype. He looked like any thug on the street or in any rap music video on BET.

The long platinum chain, gold teeth, baggy clothes, and two-carat diamond earrings in both ears were stereotypical. There was nothing special about him. He was ugly and ignorant, and, unfortunately, the media had made ugly and ignorant popular when it came to young black men.

"I'm very sorry for your loss." Logo tossed the words out toward Irene and Rendell.

"Thank you," Rendell mumbled back. "I appreciate the fact that you're taking good care of our grandbaby."

"True dat, true dat," Logo grinned. "She my baby mamma and I take care of what's mine." He pulled a wad of cash out of his pocket. "Let me give you a little something to help during this bad time." He counted out several hundred-dollar bills and handed them to Rendell. Helena was shocked when her uncle took the blood money.

Helena let the words fly out of her mouth as soon as her feet hit the floor: "What the hell is wrong with you people?"

Sam cringed, and Alan rolled his eyes up into his head as everyone turned toward Helena.

"Titus is dead from a drug overdose," she continued, screaming, "and this man is a goddamn drug dealer! Don't you get it? He is just as responsible for Titus's death as Titus is!"

Helena pointed at her uncle. "I can't believe you're taking money from this thug, Uncle Rendell, giving him your blessing to treat your granddaughter like a ho'. And the rest of you guys are acting like his sorry ass is royalty or something."

Helen stepped close to her daughter and tried to quiet her without success.

"No, Mamma!" Helena jerked away. "This shit is ridiculous! His drug business is the reason why this community is so fucked up! His drug business is the reason why Peewee went to prison last year. His drug business is the reason why we put Titus in the ground today! How can you people not see that?"

Sam hurried over to his wife and attempted to help his mother-in-law lead her to the front porch, but Helena was not through. "Accepting this sick bullshit does not make it normal. It is still sick!" She turned to her mother. "This is why I don't want to be bothered with my so-called family. Why would I choose to be around this kind of lunacy?"

When she was finished, Helena stormed out of the house. She snatched at the handle on the car door, but it was locked. She kicked the door to release her anger.

"Putting a dent in the car is not going to help," Sam reasoned as he clicked the remote fob.

Helena hopped in and buckled her seatbelt. Sam slipped behind the wheel, and Alan got in the back, protecting his plate, which he had quickly refilled.

"So was that really necessary?" Sam asked.

Helena rolled her eyes. "Hell, yes, it was necessary! I can't stand those people!"

"At least she waited until we got some grub this time," Alan joked. Sam chuckled too, remembering a family picnic several years earlier when Helena had gone off about numerous ghetto indignities just minutes after they arrived. They had left early, missing the peach cobbler, honey ham, and barbeque to eat tofu salads at home.

Alan stopped laughing when his mother glared at him.

"Helena, you cannot control other people's lives," Samuel lectured.

"I don't want to control them. I want them to take control of their own sorry-ass lives."

"Honey, just because they're not moving in the direction you think they should move doesn't mean their lives are sorry."

"You gonna sit here and tell me that grinning up in that damn drug dealer's face is not sorry? You didn't grow up in the middle of this shit like I did. You were living the good life over in Chestnut Hill."

Samuel took a deep breath. He hated it when Helena used his upper-class background against him. "All I'm saying is that there are a lot of different kinds of people in the world, Helena. Most of them are not like you or me."

"Yeah, whatever, can we go, please?"

"We have to wait for your mother."

Helena clenched both fists. "Well, where is she?"

"Look, settle down," Samuel continued. "Here she comes."

Helen slid into the backseat beside Alan. "Here." She tossed Helena's purse up into the front seat. "You just had to show your uppity behind in there, didn't you?"

"I told you I didn't want to come in the first place, Mom."

"Everything is not about you, Helena. Irene and Rendell are in pain. Their son is dead. And don't nobody need you chastising them about who they are and the lives they're living."

Sam started the car and began the drive home.

"I'm sorry, Mamma, but I just can't relate to those people. I am trying to make something out of my life. I can't let them drag me down to the gutter with them."

"Who's dragging you down, Helena? You have done everything you wanted to do, and nobody has denied you your right to do it, so how can you deny other people that same freedom?"

"It's not about freedom; it's about truth. Poor Bill Cosby told the truth, and everybody jumped on him. He may not have said it in the most politically correct way, but this ghetto mentality, accepting drugs and violence as a norm, is killing black folks, and if we don't open our eyes we can't stop it."

When he couldn't stand it any longer, Samuel finally spoke up. "Helena, you have always been way too hard on black people, including yourself."

Helena flinched. "What's wrong with being hard? These stupid-ass rappers have made being ghetto popular. It's popular to have babies, with no forethought about taking care of them. It's popular to believe they can get paid big money by dropping out of school and selling drugs. It's popular not to know how to do anything, can't talk right, got a funky attitude, and look ridiculous with their pants hanging off their butts!"

"Mamma, that's not what all rap music is about. You don't even listen to it," Alan complained.

"I can't listen to it. These big companies are pushing trash to your generation, and you guys are wallowing in it like pigs in slop." Helena took a deep breath. "All I'm saying is that there's something very wrong when the role model in that room was a damn drug dealer. I want something better for you, Alan. Do you understand that?"

Alan nodded. "I understand, but . . ."

"No buts . . . you have to do better. You have to be somebody."

"Sam, do you mind taking me home?" Helen interrupted her daughter's tirade.

"I thought you were coming over to the house for a while?" Sam asked.

"No. I don't think so."

Samuel frowned at his wife.

"Mamma, don't mind me. You know how I am when I get started," Helena said.

"That's okay, baby, I just feel like going home. I'm kinda tired."

Samuel made a left turn instead of a right onto the I-476, heading toward Helen's newly renovated condo in Germantown. As he drove, Samuel glanced into the rearview mirror at his mother-in-law. He liked Helen more than he liked his own mother. His mother was always running behind some man. But in the end it was Samuel who took care of her during the five years that she struggled with lung cancer. None of those guys that she thought were so important during his childhood hung around long enough to care. Even though he was the color of skim milk, and Helen was the color of hot cocoa, she had been more like a mother to him than his own.

Helena's stomach rumbled. "Why don't we stop someplace for dinner, my treat?" she asked softly.

"I just ate," Alan reminded her.

Sam sighed. "You want to stop and get something to take home?"

"No, that's okay," Helena shook her head. "I'll make a salad at the house."

When Sam pulled up in front of Helen's condo, he parked and jumped out of the car to open her door.

" 'Bye, Mom," Helena called as Sam walked Helen up the steps.

"See you, Granma," Alan yelled behind them.

"You okay?" Sam asked after Helen had unlocked her front door.

"I'm fine, honey. What about you? You and my daughter okay?"

"We're fine. You don't have to worry about us."

Helen hugged Samuel and waved at the car, then disappeared inside.

Back on the road, the trio sat in silence for a long time. Samuel had merged onto I-76 and headed toward Mount Airy when Alan finally got up the nerve to say what was on his mind.

"Mom, I don't get it. How can you hate black people so much when you're black?"

Helena took a minute to think about it. She actually understood her son's confusion, even though she would never admit it to him. Alan had a liberal white father and a conservative black mother. He went on vacations every year to places like Disney World, Belize, and Jamaica, while cousins his age were locked away in prison. He had a future to look forward to that was very different from what he saw in the 'hood movies and rap music videos.

"Like Chris Rock said," Helena finally replied, "I love black people, but I hate niggahs."

# Momma, Obama, and Me
## Black Leadership/Black Legitimacy

## I. My Mother, Obama, and Me

I was a child of the sixties, though not in the way that my mother and father, who were in high school during that monumental decade, were sixties children. Rather, I was literally born in the sixties—1967, to be exact. Before the Age of Obama, I never had occasion to think seriously about the meaning of the specific accident of chronology we casually refer to as "generation." The tumult, progress, and legacy of the sixties shaped my life and the lives of my parents in ways that both connect and separate us. One recent event, precipitated by Obama's election, brought this into sharp focus for me.

My eleven-year-old nephew attends the same school I did when I was his age and growing up in Belton, South Carolina. During the presidential

---

Section 1 of this chapter was previously printed in the *Sixties: A Journal of History, Politics and Culture* 2, no. 1 (2009): 70–72.

campaign the students participated in an elaborate curriculum about electoral politics that culminated in a mock election at his school. As this was South Carolina, John McCain was the winner of the mock election (held in advance of the actual November 4 vote). The day after the real election, one of my nephew's teachers announced at the beginning of class that she did not want to hear anything that day about Obama's victory; with this censorship she not only silenced the students' immense interest in a historic event but also missed an incredible teaching moment.

Later that evening my mother reached me in New York City, where I was traveling on university business. I had spoken with her the night before while watching the election returns with friends in Chicago. We had cried on the phone together when Ohio was called for Obama and marveled that neither of us thought we'd ever see a black man elected president of the United States. I felt closer to my mother in that moment than I had in a very long time. And I had the sense that my amazement at Obama's victory could not rival her disbelief.

My mother asked me about the mood in New York in the days after the election. I reported that people were still excited about it—that practically everyone I had talked to, from alums to colleagues to cab drivers and the hotel concierge, was celebrating. My mother replied, "Well, it's not like that everywhere. The local paper here didn't even have a story about Obama's victory. And your nephew's teacher today told his class she didn't want to hear anything about the election. And your other nephew [five years old] had one of his kindergarten classmates say to him, 'Yeah, they elected that monkey.' So it's not all good news everywhere."

I was shocked and angered by what my mother relayed to me. I went into action mode, asking questions and charting a response. After learning from my sister more details of my nephew's experience, she and I agreed that I would write the teacher to ask why she forbade discussion of the election and copy the school's principal, the superintendent of schools, and my sister and her husband. The teacher's conduct was especially troubling and perplexing to me as an educator, given the emphasis the school had placed on the mock election. Two weeks passed with no reply to my letter, and my sister and I grew frustrated. When we discussed our feelings with our parents, they feared that our pressing the issue might call unwanted attention to my nephew from the teacher and school officials. "You've made the point," they pleaded. "Don't rock the boat."

I was now vexed at my parents' position. How could no response from the school or the teacher be acceptable? Why shouldn't we press for a reply? Despite my parents' wishes, my sister called the school and arranged for a conference with the teacher. It went as awkwardly as you might imagine but did end with the teacher apologizing.

A few weeks later I watched *The Great Debaters*, a film that chronicles the story of the famed educator, poet, and activist Melvin B. Tolson and the team of debaters at Wiley College who in 1935 broke the color barrier and competed against and defeated the University of Southern California (portrayed as Harvard University in the film). The film has an extended sequence representing a lynching and its effects on Tolson and his debaters. The film immediately evoked for me the conversation I had had with my mother and father about my nephew.

My parents both attended segregated schools, rode segregated buses, came of age in the segregated South. My maternal grandmother was a domestic who worked in the homes of white families; my maternal grandfather was a sharecropper; my mother and her twelve siblings all picked cotton. To this day my mom reminds my nephews—as she did my sister and me—how lucky they are to be able to go to school. She and her siblings were not allowed to start school until late in the fall when the crops had been harvested. Even then they were acutely aware that their facilities and books were substandard, that the schools attended by white children were newer, had better equipment, and were maintained in good repair. And my mother and her brothers and sisters had learned all too well the perils of not "knowing your place" in the South they had grown up in. Yes, they had seen Martin Luther King Jr. and all the progress he had made on behalf of blacks and the working poor. Yes, they had seen school integration come to their small town after they had left high school. Yes, they had seen local factories and other businesses that had never hired blacks have their workforce integrated. This was a part of their story of the sixties. But they had also seen Dr. King murdered and Malcolm X as well. They had seen friends and neighbors shut out and ruined financially for standing up for their rights and the rights of others who looked like them. And they had seen people physically brutalized for being agents of change. This was the other part of their sixties story.

Black power lived side by side with white retribution, black struggle with white resistance, black progress with white intimidation. For me, all this was history. For my mother and father it indelibly colored their perceptions of themselves and the world, as well as how they could move in it. To this day my parents have completely different ways of being while in the company of white folk than when they are in the exclusive company of black folk. And color lines in Belton remain strong. My sister and I—and certainly my nephews—adhere far less to such divisions. And that has everything to do with the legacy of black progress achieved through the sixties' political and cultural revolutions.

I phoned my mother after seeing *The Great Debaters* and apologized for being so short with her about my nephew's teacher. I explained that I had come to a better understanding of where she and my father were coming from. They took their position, my mother explained, for the same reason my sister and I took ours: to do what was best for that little boy. It's just that what each of us thought was best was informed by radically different generational politics.

President Obama—born in 1961, making him closer to my generation than that of my parents—represents great hope for bridging the racial divide in our nation because of the times in which he came of age. He was the product of an interracial marriage, was raised by a white mother and white grandparents, was a young black man in a world where that was something to be overcome. But as is true of my sister and me, his perception of himself in the world is not diminished by the overwhelming culture of racial segregation and its attendant limits. I can only dream that, with President Obama in the White House, the generational politics shaping my nephews' perceptions of themselves in the world will allow them to soar in ways that I cannot yet fully comprehend.

## II. Legitimacy and Black Leadership Today

While there is much to celebrate about the historic election of President Obama, we have also, at the time of this writing (more than a year into his presidency), witnessed a great deal of both overt and subtle challenges to his authority, legitimacy, and even his racial authenticity. Conservatives in Congress seem bent upon being obstructionist toward any and every initiative he has brought forward (health-care reform is the most notable example). Unprecedented displays of disapproval during formal occasions of state when the president is speaking (specifically, Representative Joe Wilson during Obama's address to Congress on health care and Justice Samuel Alito during the 2010 State of the Union address) have received a great deal of media attention. Obama is criticized by members of the Latino community for failing to push immigration reform. He is upbraided by leaders in the African American community for being too nuanced on issues of race and for not having a more clearly articulated "black agenda." And the list goes on.

My point here, however, is not to dwell on these particulars but rather to point out that even if you are duly elected to the most powerful position in the world, you do not escape U.S. society's preoccupations with race. To quote a dear friend and academic colleague in another context, "Being black in America can be a terrible inconvenience." And to extrapolate from the writing of Rita Bornstein, an expert on leadership in higher education, there are no contexts in which black leaders are not always and already marked by their race. The fact of a black leader's blackness is always as present for those observing her as it is for the black leader herself.

It is not altogether unlike watching the evening news as a reporter reviews a story about a murder or a rape. Most black people watching that news story hear a little voice inside whispering, "Please, don't let the suspect be a black man." This quiet sentiment is reflecting a lingering strain in black anti-racist politics that cares deeply about our representative selves in the world. And the logic of that strain leads us at some level to believe that our actions bear the weight of our collective representation no matter what.

This burden of representation remains a part of not only the worry of watching the news but also of the challenges of black leadership today. As Franklin Raines, the first black CEO of a Fortune 500 company, once said, "Any time you're a 'first' in one of these highly visible jobs, there's always some pressure to make sure that you don't do something that would create an excuse for people not to choose a second or a third or a fourth." Put another way, if Obama fails, we all share in the shame. And President Obama carries the weight of that reality because it is endemic to black leadership. Whatever else the pressures and rewards of the presidency may be, for a black president these also entail a knowledge of and responsibility for the politics of racial representation. Managing those politics in any context as a black leader sometimes can feel like an albatross but can also create super-human expectations, which few real live leaders can reasonably meet.

In 2007, when I became dean of the College of Liberal Arts and Sciences at the University of Illinois at Chicago, I was the first African American (and certainly the first openly gay African American) to hold that office. Going into the job, I knew well that there would be some challenges I would face that would be familiar to any dean. I also knew there would be other challenges unique to my identity as an openly gay black leader and that I'd have to work hard to turn some of those challenges (dare I call them liabilities?) into opportunities. Successful black leaders are not those who ignore the challenges of black leadership but those who openly recognize these unique challenges and understand that these must be negotiated as part of the job.

That we are still achieving such notable firsts (Obama, the first African American president of the United States; Ruth Simmons, the first African American to lead an Ivy League university; Franklin Raines, first African American CEO of a Fortune 500 company; Colin Powell, first African American secretary of state; Eric Holder, first African American U.S. attorney general) in the new millennium signals how strongly embedded in our society and institutions are our stereotyped notions of blacks and their capacity for leadership. This is not to say that progress, real and measurable progress, is not being made.

Few were more thrilled than I when Grinnell College announced in February 2010 the election of Dr. Raynard Kington, an openly gay African American man as its thirteenth president. This appointment represents a big crack in the glass ceiling of higher education leadership. I wrote to Dr. Kington, as I know many others did, congratulating him on his election by the board of trustees and offering my professional support. I had no sooner written the note when my excitement about this news began to abate and my mind moved swiftly to the unique challenges that would face him and his family in this new role.

At some level the least of these challenges will be the near herculean task of managing and guiding the future of one of the premier liberal arts colleges in our nation. For most this alone would provide a lifetime's worth of demanding professional stimulation. But I also began to think of the albatross that Dr. Kington must also carry under the watchful gaze not only of his new colleagues, alumni, friends, partners, and publics of Grinnell but also of blacks; the lesbian, gay, bisexual, and transgender (LGBT) community; and black LGBTs as he works to make opportunities of these challenges. Comments on one blog catering to black gay men have already featured a robust discussion about whether (and later about why) his partner is a white man. This was in response to a post celebrating Dr. Kington's appointment as a triumph for the black LGBT community. The work will not be easy, of course, for Dr. Kington or for any other black leaders, but the rewards of success could not be greater. Every black leader who steps up to the demands of black leadership makes stepping up a bit easier for the next generation.

Because they are growing up in the age of Obama (and by extension the many other black leaders who have accepted the mantle of black leadership), my nephews will be able to imagine possibilities and reach their potential in ways that my parents' generation or even my own could scarcely dream.

# Selling Dr. King's Dream
## Blackness and Tourism in Atlanta

Since Atlanta's humble beginnings as the end point for the Western and Atlantic Railroad, it has repeatedly been reinvented by commercial and political interests: as a center of industry and transportation; as a cosmopolitan city and cultural center of the South; as an international destination and place to visit; as the birthplace of the civil rights movement; as *the* southern black mecca. Additionally, it has long been suggested that there are two Atlanta's—one black, one white; this divide has largely been built on the split between the black political power structure and white elites. These different constructions of Atlanta suggest a relationship between place and the production of history, race, and class. Governor Sonny Perdue's 2005 heritage tourism initiative—historic and cultural tourism—and the Brand Atlanta Campaign, implemented by then-mayor Shirley Franklin, also in 2005, point to the heritage industry and the state as primary sites where these constructions are made and remade.

As heritage tourism grows in popularity, especially with black tourists, Atlanta has, in part, looked to the past, particularly the civil rights movement, to create an imagined Atlanta for visitors' consumption. The growth of heritage tourism as a viable revenue generator has meant that one of

Atlanta's most valuable commodities is the past, creating a contradiction between private industry, which seeks to "market the city as it always is," and
the history-rich city of the tourist industry.[1] How, then, does the forward-
looking face of business negotiate the historically rich and profitable past
while also proclaiming the city's "nowness"? The answer, in part, lies in the
marketing and promotion of the Martin Luther King Jr. National Park Historic Site (commonly known as the King Center) by local and state tourism
initiatives. A closer look at these marketing efforts reveals the creation of
a normative black middle-class identity and offers an unusual window into
how black middle-class identity is represented in relation to history and historical knowledge, as well as how the market mediates these constructions.

## Heritage Tourism and the Construction of the South

Mass tourism is a quintessentially modern enterprise, particularly in its
connection to the growth of modern consumerism and the shift from an
industry-driven economy to a service economy. Moreover, since the democ-
ratization of travel in the 1950s tourism has been closely associated with a
middle-class lifestyle. And heritage tourism is one of the fastest-growing areas. Thus, as Robert Hewison notes, "While future prospects seem to shrink,
the past is steadily growing." The exact meaning of the term *heritage,* however, is somewhat elusive. As the chair of Britain's National Heritage Memorial Fund, once put it, "It means everything and it means nothing and yet it
has developed into a whole industry."[2] The black tourist further complicates
notions of heritage, especially in the South, where heritage, at least in a
commercial sense, has almost always been synonymous with white history
and culture, especially the "heritage, not hate" claims from defenders of the
Confederate flag.

   State and local tourism initiatives in Atlanta seek to capitalize on the
recent surge in black tourism by producing a commercialized official history
that projects the city as a site of renewal, racial harmony, and progress. Thus
the official narrative is limited; we must forget the terror of Indian genocide,
slavery, the 1906 race riots, lynching, the Atlanta child murders, and the
current plight of the homeless. Instead the message focuses on opportunity.

Therefore the tourist industry projects a carefully crafted image of Atlanta as a progressive and open city, full of opportunity for everyone. History becomes both a testament to, and a measure of, progress by linking Atlanta, notions of progress—as understood in relation to financial prosperity—and black history. These romantic constructions of the South are rooted in the "New South" ideals first articulated by the newspaper editor Henry Grady in the late 1880s.

Grady touted the "New South" to northern industrialists in an attempt to revive the region's economy, which had been devastated because the Civil War had killed the plantation economy. In an effort to counter the region's reputation for oppressive racial relations, he published many editorials in which he attempted to put a benign spin on the rise of Jim Crow, which he recognized as bad for business. He instead promoted cooperation between the races in the name of economic progress as an alternative approach in which everybody would win. The ideal of cooperation was echoed by Booker T. Washington at the Cotton States and International Exposition in 1895, when he suggested that "in all things purely social we can be as separate as the fingers, yet one as the hand in all things mutual to progress."[3] This speech, later dubbed the "Atlanta Compromise" by W. E. B. Du Bois, reflected a pattern of accommodation and compromise that has been a staple of Atlanta politics ever since. Nonetheless, Jim Crow laws and racial terrorism remained firmly in place for much of the twentieth century. Black community leaders realized that true political power would be achieved only through securing the right to vote and began to focus their efforts on countering intimidation, terrorism, poll taxes, and literacy tests. This struggle would define the movement for the first half of the twentieth century.

The first real success came in the early 1920s when community organizers were successful in rallying black voters and got the city to build Atlanta's first all-black public secondary school, Booker T. Washington High School. The next success came in the early 1940s when organizations such as the NAACP, the Urban League, and local women's clubs and fraternal organizations made a push to educate and register voters. These efforts were bolstered in 1946 when the U.S. Circuit Court of Appeals in New Orleans ruled that Georgia's white primary was unconstitutional, and the U.S. Supreme Court subsequently declined to review the decision. The powerful black voting bloc that emerged forced the city to desegregate the police department in 1947.[4] With the strength of the black vote firmly established, black leaders shifted the campaign to maintaining voter strength, desegregating the schools, public transportation, and housing. These battles would define the next twenty years. Compromise and negotiation continued to dominate how black leaders dealt with the white power structure, but in the 1960s the old guard was supplanted by student organizations such as the Student Nonviolent Coordinating Committee and the Congress of Racial Equality and religious organizations such as the Southern Christian Leadership Conference, led by Dr. Martin Luther King Jr. They rejected backroom deals in favor of direct action and nonviolent protest, paving the way for the civil rights legislation of the 1960s.

The relatively peaceful integration of Atlanta became a badge of honor for the city and its leaders. This truly was Grady's "New South," or so they believed. In 1959 Mayor William Hartsfield proclaimed that Atlanta was a city that was too busy to hate. Business leaders were quick to pick up on the line, and Atlanta desegregated. However, according to the historian Howard Zinn, this was far more a matter of fiscal prudence than social enlightenment: "The Southern white . . . has a hierarchy of values . . . and segregation, while desirable, does not mean as much to him as certain other values he has come to cherish."[5] Beneath the progressive policies and facade of openness, blacks still struggled for social and economic justice. As James Baldwin acidly remarked, Atlanta, "having fought for and sustained the separation of the races for so long, would transform the visible—as distinguished from the real—results of the black insurrection into a propaganda medal for itself. Our presence, 'down-town,' resounded throughout the globe as proof that the leader of the 'free' world was uncompromisingly devoted to freedom."[6] President Kennedy praised Atlanta for its peaceful compliance with federal law and urged the rest of the South to follow its example.

But just beneath the surface, it was business as usual. In 1959, while Hartsfield was proclaiming his city too busy to hate, the courts ordered the South to desegregate its public schools. Atlanta school officials managed to stall integration with a variety of maneuvers throughout the 1960s. Among the gambits was requiring black students to apply for admission to previously all-white school districts. During the spring of 1960 the Atlanta Public

School System received 133 requests for black student transfers into previously all white schools, only ten of which went through; thirty-eight were
appealed, to no avail.[7] Black community leaders continued to push for busing but with little success.

In the early 1970s an agreement between NAACP President Lonnie
King and Atlanta Board of Education continued to tacitly sanction extremely
limited busing in exchange for placing African Americans in key administra-
tive positions. This agreement, later dubbed "the Second Atlanta Compromise," was rendered meaningless as the 1970s progressed and white flight
to Atlanta's northern suburbs increased, making the question of integration
moot.[8] The city became known as a dangerous, internal other. Crime rates,
poverty, urban decline, white flight, and the notorious Atlanta child murders
case marked the city as a place of darkness, both literally and figuratively.
The seeds of this urban-suburban split were sown when Mayor Sam Massell,
thrown into a run-off race against Maynard Jackson in 1973, played upon
white fears and adopted the campaign slogan "Atlanta's Too Young to Die."

After Jackson won that race, Atlanta began to emerge as a southern
black mecca, replacing the northern cities of an earlier era that promised
new opportunities to the poor blacks of the rural South. However, it was not
the poor who returned but an ever-growing black middle class, drawn by
the promises of the Atlanta of the New South. Jackson was a true "Atlanta
man"—Moorehouse educated; the grandson of a member of Atlanta's black
elite, John Wesley Dobbs; and the great-grandson of slaves. Jackson's reign
cemented the "Atlanta Style" and created unprecedented opportunities for
black businesses.

In 1973, fewer than 1 percent of city contracts went to minorities. Five
years later that number had risen to 38.5 percent. Since then Atlanta has
become home to more black-owned companies per capita than anywhere
except Washington, D.C., leading the *Atlanta Journal and Constitution* to
dub Atlanta a "modern-day Harlem, a place of opportunity where educated
blacks can enjoy the fruits of a post–civil rights era economy."[9] As a result,
since the early 1990s blacks have returned to the South at a rate of nearly
100,000 per year.[10]

Slogans, such as Mayor Andrew Young's "Look at Atlanta Now!" in
1983 and the current "Everyday Is an Opening Day" of the Brand Atlanta

Campaign have offered updated versions of Hartsfield's original. These new slogans, however, move from the "New South," which imagines Atlanta in reference to on-going racial violence and post–Civil War industrialization, to the "Now South," which presents a post–civil rights South in which African Americans have "arrived." In short, the "Now South" is the fully realized "New South."

The "Now South" challenges traditional representations of the white South as the epicenter of racism and the black South as oppressed and projects an image of renewal and progress. The implicit request is to forget about history, focus on the present, and make money. The past is present but without any real substance or true memory. Atlanta does not need to project an image of being modern and forward looking; it evinces these characteristics.

Atlanta's large black middle class becomes evidence to support these claims. Thus the "Now South" represents privilege, black success, and opportunity, whereas the "New South" highlighted white progressiveness and tolerance. However, in the process, economic success is also recast as a market concern rather than a civil rights issue. Within this context heritage tourism has become one of Atlanta's largest revenue generators.

## Selling the Dream: The King Center and the Brand Atlanta Campaign

Atlanta's official city planning did not embrace tourism until the late 1960s, as part of a national trend to reshape downtown areas for tourism. Today tourism is the second-largest industry in Georgia. City officials love it because it creates jobs and generates tax revenues. Private industry likes that it attracts business and encourages development. A closer look at the heritage industry and the Brand Atlanta Campaign reveals how historical knowledge is framed by corporate and private interests. It further reveals how black middle-class identities are understood in relation to history and progress.

The Brand Atlanta Campaign is a commerce-oriented government enterprise that markets Atlanta to private (industry and developers) and public (tourists and residents) interests. The stated purpose of the campaign is to "re-brand" the city in several key ways. One is as a city of limitless growth and development opportunity. For business this means promoting Atlanta as a good place to do business. Tax breaks, antiunion practices—Georgia is a "right-to-work" state—and the partnership of business interests and city government are big selling points on this front. For tourism this means selling the unique tourist opportunities found in Atlanta. This includes highlighting Atlanta's many claims as an important center of black culture and history. The Atlanta Convention and Visitors Bureau touts the city as *the* place to experience black heritage: "From Martin Luther King, Jr. National Park Historic Site to the APEX Museum; from down-home southern restaurants to world-class sporting events; from the outreach programs of the Martin Luther King, Jr. Center for Non-Violent Social Change to the educational excellence of the nation's best African-American colleges and universities; from the Civil War to Civil Rights, Atlanta's African-American heritage is a year-round experience." The focus on black heritage is in large part a response to the recent surge in black tourism and an attendant demand for black-centered sites; it is also a response to industry predictions regarding minority travel.

In 1994 the Travel Industry Association of America released a report identifying minority travel as key to the growth and future of the domestic market of the U.S. travel industry. This prediction was, in part, based on the current and projected population numbers for minorities and the growth of the black middle class. According to the U.S. Census Bureau, the number of black heads of household earning at least $50,000 a year went from 1.3 million to three million between 1989 and 1999, resulting in an attendant increase in black tourism. According to the travel association, black travel volume increased 4 percent from 2000 to 2004, while travel by the population as a whole increased by just 2 percent. The industry also estimated that African Americans and other minority travelers would spend more than $50 billion annually. Finally, culture and heritage tourism were identified as key growth areas. As late as 2009 industry experts continued to identify heritage tourism, especially black heritage tourism, as an important and growing sector.[11]

Angela Da Silva, owner of the National Black Tourism Network, suggests that the growth in the heritage tourism market for black tourists has as much to do with consciousness as cash. "For so long our heritage was stripped from us," she says. "There's so many more different angles of the truth coming to light. We go there [to what she terms the "center of bigotry"] because this was the seat of our history. It's the same reason why Jews go to Holocaust sites—it's to get in touch." Another industry insider, Monique Wells of Discover Paris, suggested to a *USA Today* reporter that through heritage tourism "we [the black heritage tourist] are trying to validate ourselves."[12]

In response various tourist markets have begun to promote their own black history and culture through the development of black-centered heritage sites. Alabama, for example, has the "Black Heritage Trail," which features fifty-five destinations deemed of interest to black history buffs. Louisiana, Mississippi, Tennessee, and Virginia, to name a few, have similar initiatives in place or in the works. No publicly available research measures the success of these efforts. Moreover, it is not clear how the current economic crisis has affected black travel. Surprisingly, the Atlanta Convention and Visitor's Bureau does not track this particular demographic characteristic. However, a recent report from the bureau indicates that leisure travel, while down, remains a viable industry for the city and the state. Between 2006 and 2008 trips to the metropolitan Atlanta area decreased from 38 million to 35.4 million, although the amount of direct spending ($11 billion) remained the same.

The black tourism initiatives try to be celebratory, but sometimes they must take on a different tone, such as that chosen by the Emmett Till Memorial Commission, established by the Tallahatchie County Board of Supervisors to foster "racial harmony and reconciliation; to seek federal, state, and private funds and grants to initially restore the Tallahatchie County Courthouse in Sumner, Mississippi [where the accused murderers of fourteen-year-old Till were tried and acquitted by an all-white jury]; to explore the restoration of other buildings and sites of historical value; and to promote educational tours of the courthouse and other sites in Tallahatchie County, Mississippi." The commission is also creating a "driving tour with markers located at some of the most significant sites related to the murder of Emmett Till." The tour includes the grocery store where Till allegedly whistled at a white woman, the courthouse, and a new museum. This initiative led one commentator to suggest that history "seems to occupy a more modern racial landscape, one located at the intersection of reconciliation and economic development."[13]

Atlanta's reputation as a "black mecca" and its rich civil rights history have made marketing the city to the black tourist fairly easy, and Atlanta jealously guards its image as the racially enlightened First City of the South. Therefore the Brand Atlanta Campaign projects a carefully crafted image of Atlanta as a progressive and open city, full of opportunity for everyone, and history becomes both a testament to, and a measure of, progress. This is the "Now South," after all, and racism and oppression are a thing of the past, or so they would have us believe.

Atlanta's current theme is "the three O's": opportunity, optimism, and openness; it clearly links notions of black history and progress by urging consumers, tourist or otherwise, to "put [their] dreams in motion."[14] Visitors and businesses alike are encouraged to find inspiration in both history and commerce through ad campaigns that link King's legacy, as well as Jimmy Carter's, with Home Depot and Coca Cola.

Another clear appeal is to a young, "hip" black audience through the use of hip-hop references meant to "embrace Atlanta's hip-hop sound." The Brand Atlanta Campaign commissioned a theme song from the hip-hop producer Dallas Austin titled "The ATL"—a common hip-hop moniker for Atlanta. The song's lyrics are meant to complement Atlanta's theme of opportunity, optimism, and openness: "In a world that has room for opportunity, they say Atlanta is where you go to become your dreams."[15] Atlanta is projected as a place where anybody, no matter the color of his skin, can make money—a truly colorblind American utopia. This dream iconography can also be seen as a play on Dr. King's "I have a dream" speech. This is echoed in loft ads that feature young black urban professionals and advertise "new school living (at old school prices)" and implore the potential buyer to "elevate your lifestyle," a clear connection to black middle-class identities linked to consumption and the "boojie" performance of capital and class. These same themes dominate the marketing (and consumption) of the Martin Luther King Jr. Center.

Atlanta markets the King Center as a measure of Atlanta's racial progress, as understood through economic prosperity and middle-class values.

The center was established in 1968 by Coretta Scott King immediately after the murder of her husband, to protect his legacy and continue to educate people about his philosophy and methods of nonviolent social change. In 1981, after more than a decade of fund-raising and temporary quarters, the center opened to the public, with Martin Luther King's crypt as its center-piece. The twenty-three-acre national historic site also includes Dr. King's birth home, a library, archives, the Center for Non-Violent Social Change, and Ebenezer Baptist Church, where he, his father, and grandfather were all pastors. The King Center is owned by the King family and administered by the National Park Service. An independent board oversees programming and exhibit content. Sadly, the center's educational programming in nonviolence is virtually nonexistent, and overall the site is estimated to need more than $11 million in repairs. Despite this, the King Center continues to be a large draw for black tourists and has emerged as one of the crown jewels of Atlanta's tourist industry.

Although the site represents a complex history of racial terror and the fight for social and economic justice, the King Center is marketed almost exclusively as representing one of African Americans' prouder moments, the civil rights movement—as if to say, we got this one right, eventually. This is what the historian Glenn Eskew refers to as the "won cause" retelling of the movement, which privileges a story of grand cultural and social change resulting from heroic leadership and key moments.[16] This framing often ignores everyday struggle and the role of women.[17]

King's dream of political and economic parity is rearticulated in terms of consumption. An overall narrative of progress and, most important, financial opportunity and success dovetails with the state and local tourism initiatives that promote Georgia and Atlanta as a good place to do business. Visitors to King's birth home are told about the King family's middle-class lifestyle and how this shaped his early life. The stress on economic success over social and economic justice is also reflected in the center's recent decision to award its highest honor, the Salute to Greatness Award, to Robert Nardeli, CEO of Home Depot. Other Atlanta attractions, such as the Alonzo Herndon Home (home of the nation's first black millionaire), underscore this focus on the city as the site of black financial opportunity and success.

The emphasis on black middle-class success is supported by the many black tourists who in part see the King Center as an affirmation of their own black middle-class identity. The common refrain of black visitors is extremely consistent here: "I have what I have because of him," one told me. The many black Atlantans who proclaim that Atlanta is a "good place to be black" also provide support for these claims of opportunity. As one told a reporter, "I moved to Atlanta 34 years ago. I always wondered why the city was billed as the 'city too busy too hate.' Being an American with African and Native American ancestry, I know that was not the case. However, Atlanta did offer people of color an opportunity to compete, succeed, and/or fail."[18] The question remains, however, for which blacks? Is this statement equally true of the many blacks who are still struggling in poverty in Atlanta? At what point does class supplant race, and what are the consequences?

The King Center offers Atlanta's tourist industry a chance to both embrace and reject the past through the creation of a commercialized history. On the one hand, the center represents a history of violence and racial oppression. On the other, Atlanta's large black middle class, the vibrant hip-hop industry, and Atlanta's appeal to a younger black generation become examples of the city's ultimate redemption. The promotion of the King Center by private and public interests raises many questions about how competing interests use King's legacy. These questions were particularly poignant during the events surrounding the death of King's widow, Coretta Scott King, in 2006.

Coretta Scott King died on the eve of Black History Month and only two weeks after the national observance of Martin Luther King Jr. Day—a holiday that she fought to establish. While the King Center bears her husband's name, it is, without question, equally Coretta Scott King's legacy. Her death, both publicly and privately, was met with great sadness. In the days that followed, thousands of people stood in line, often in pouring rain, to pay their respects.

The King Center became a touchstone for mourners, as well as the curious and the press. On the morning of Mrs. King's death the King Center was a flurry of activity. A black woman next to me cried while trying to explain the significance of the day and the King legacy to her children. A few minutes later another woman angrily exclaimed, "What are we going to do? All of our leaders are dying. Our children are depending on us. Don't tell me about going back to Africa. We built America." This was met with a small smattering of applause, but she was largely ignored. Meanwhile reporters practiced their scripts and approached people for interviews. No one approached the woman who asked what are we to do, but the woman next to me, who brought her children to "be a part of history" and to see "how far we have come," was interviewed no fewer than three times. Her "sound bite" was consistent: "I want [my children] to know that we have what we have because of [Dr. and Mrs. King's] sacrifices."

This woman epitomizes Atlanta's projected image of blackness—she is middle class. She evokes Dr. King's legacy as an affirmation of her own class achievement. The reporters were drawn to her because she typifies progress and black-middle class achievement. The image was disrupted by the angry black woman who reminded everyone that African Americans have not arrived; there is more to do. But because such an assertion (and anger) has no place in the "Now South," she was ignored. That week the divide between progress and change, past and future, would be highlighted repeatedly.

Atlanta's official tribute to Mrs. King, her lying in state in the rotunda of the state capital—an honor denied her husband in 1968 by the segregationist governor Lester Maddox—was meant to signal the vast difference between the Georgia of 1968 and the Georgia of 2006. Coretta Scott King was the first African American, and the only woman, to lie in state in the Georgia Capitol Rotunda. Mayor Shirley Franklin's common refrain, "I wouldn't be here if not for her," and Oprah's proclamation that Coretta Scott King "live[s] inside the dream" were further markers of the changes.

The final memorial for Coretta Scott King was held at New Birth Baptist Church. The choice of New Birth, although on the surface practical because it could accommodate a larger crowd than Ebenezer, was at best ironic, at worst prescient. New Birth is Georgia's largest church, with an estimated membership of twenty-five thousand. It is known for its explosive growth and its charismatic senior pastor, Bishop Eddie Long, who has transformed the church into one of the "megachurches" popular throughout the South. Bernice King, the youngest child of Dr. and Mrs. King, is also an elder in the church. The teachings of New Birth center on the "prosperity gospel," which tells the faithful that God will reward them with riches. At the service former president Bill Clinton asked, "What will be the meaning of the King holiday every year? And, even more important, Atlanta, what's your responsibility for the King Center? What are you going to do to make sure that this thing goes on?" This political rhetoric actually got to the heart of the matter, unintentionally echoed by the choice of a church that preaches God's financial rewards, rather than promoting protest politics and social justice.

The irony, of course, is that the movement so closely associated with both Kings was, at the time of Martin Luther King Jr.'s death, decidedly socialist and concerned with economic parity and social justice, which he saw as deeply connected concerns. He further understood poverty as a civil rights issue. As a result Dr. King called for a radical redistribution of economic power. "We must rapidly begin the shift from a thing-oriented society to a person-oriented society," he said. "When machines and computers, profit motives and property rights, are considered more important than people, the giant triplets of racism, extreme materialism, and militarism are incapable of being conquered."[19] King was widely criticized for these positions, even by leaders within his own movement. Consequently, these views have been virtually erased from popular history. Furthermore King is often reduced to a starry-eyed dreamer and conformist who is used to support conservative agendas. The complexity of King's history and message are ignored. Instead King's legacy is used to celebrate capitalism. King's dream was not about free markets and consumption; it was about freedom from humiliation and degradation. Now freedom has come to mean capitalism— but Dr. King saw capitalism as a problem, not an answer.

The marketing of the King Center and Atlanta itself by corporate and public interests projects an image of renewal, progress, and racial harmony. This raises many questions about how we are to understand progress, especially in relation to the past. When history becomes a measure of progress and therefore something to be celebrated, it is not necessarily *remembered*. The presence of a black political power structure and a growing black middle class do lend these constructions of Atlanta a certain amount of credence; however, this seductive image hides a more sinister truth. Narratives of progress obfuscate the stark realities of history, poverty, racism, and homelessness. So, there are (at least) two Atlantas, but they are best understood in terms of the intersection of race and class, as class is the way that race has been imbued with meaning. More to the point, class has rendered blackness meaningful.

Capitalism is also imagined as a curative for racism. In the "Now South" racism is incompatible with capitalism; everyone is too busy making money to hate. And black Atlanta, which was previously associated with crime, poverty, and urban decline—the internal other—is recuperated as a site of privilege rather than alienation. Race is no longer an issue. This dangerous vision of color-blind success is supported through the commodification of Atlanta's official historical narrative. Equating black success with the eradication of racism ignores the structural and individual racisms that still prevail in the South and elsewhere. It also obscures the plight of poor blacks and the many other minorities that still struggle in Atlanta. The free market will not cure society's ills—it feeds off them. Martin Luther King understood this.

King also understood that history must be remembered. Now he, like his slave ancestors, has become a commodity. As Carl Wendell Hine wrote of Dr. King, "Now that he is safely dead let us praise him, build monuments to his name. Dead men make such convenient heroes: They cannot rise to challenge the images we would fashion from their lives. And besides, it is easier to build monuments than to make the world a better place."[20] The Atlanta brand promises success, progress, and renewal but at what cost? When we forget history, or alter it to suit our own interests, it "loses its value as an incentive and example; it paints noble men and noble nations, but it does not tell the truth."[21]

## NOTES

1. "Hospitality Roundtable," *Atlanta Business Chronicle,* November 11, 2005, www.atlanta.bizjournals.com/atlanta/stories/2005/11/14/focus12.html.
2. Robert Hewison, *The Heritage Industry* (London: Methuen, 1987), 24.
3. Franklin E. Frazier, *Black Bourgeoisie: The Book That Brought the Shock of Self-Revelation to Middle-Class Blacks in America* (New York: Free Press, 1997), 67.
4. Edward A. Hatfield, "William Holmes Borders (1905–1993)," *New Georgia Encyclopedia,* December 14, 2007, www.georgiaencyclopedia.org/nge/Article.jsp?id=h-1600.

5. Howard Zinn, *The Southern Mystique* (Cambridge, Mass.: South End Press, 2002), 23–24.

6. James Baldwin, *The Evidence of Things Not Seen* (New York: Henry Holt, 1995), 24.

7. Clarissa Myrick-Harris and Norman Harris, "Atlanta in the Civil Rights Movement, 1940–1970," Atlanta Regional Council for Higher Education Publication, 2004, pp. 12–13, also available on line at www.atlantahighered.org/civilrights/atlantasstory. asp.

8. Ibid., 13.

9. Bruce A. Dixon, "Black Mecca: Death of an Illusion," *Black Commentator* 154 (October 13, 2005), www.blackcommentator.com/154/154_cover_dixon_black_mecca_pf.htm.

10. Tara McPherson, *Reconstructing Dixie: Race, Class, Gender, and Nostalgia in the Imagined South* (Durham, N.C.: Duke University Press, 2003), 15.

11. Michael Bennett, "The Importance of Heritage Tourism," *Black Meetings and Tourism*, December 2008–9, 91–92.

12. Dionne Walker, "Southern Heritage Tourism Luring a Growing Market of Black Americans," USAToday.com, July 25, 2005, www.usatoday.com/travel/destinations/2005-07-25-black-tourism_x.

13. Emmett Till Memorial Commission, 2007, www.winterinstitute.org/etmc/index. htm; Drew Jubera, "Decades Later, An Apology for Emmett Till Slaying," *Atlanta Journal-Constitution*, October 5, 2007, www.ajc.com/news/content/news/stories/2007/10/01/apology_1002.html.

14. "Hospitality Roundtable"; Rachel Tobin Ramos, "Georgia Campaign Fixes on Success," *Atlanta Business Chronicle*, June 13, 2006, http://Atlanta.bizjournals.com/atlanta/stories/2005/09/19/story5.html.

15. Shirley Franklin, interview by Michelle Norris, *All Things Considered*, National Public Radio, November 14, 2005.

16. Glenn Eskew, *The Won Cause: Memorializing the Movement through the Birmingham Civil Rights Institute* (Atlanta: Georgia State University, 1998).

17. See Charles Payne, "'Men Led, But Women Organized': Movement Participation of Women in the Mississippi Delta," in G. West and R. L. Blumberg, eds., *Women and Social Protest* (Oxford: Oxford University Press, 1990).

18. Leon Stafford, "'Opening Day' Dropped as Atlanta Changes Pitch," *Atlanta Journal-Constitution*, October 18, 2007), www.ajc.com/money/business/stories/2007/10/18. html.

19. Martin Luther King Jr. "Beyond Vietnam: A Time to Break Silence," address to Clergy and Laymen Concerned about Vietnam, Riverside Church, New York, April 4, 1967, www.ratical.org/ratville/JFK/MLKapr67.html.

20. Scott W. Hoffman, "Holy Martin: The Overlooked Canonization of Dr. Martin Luther King, Jr.," *Religion and American Culture* 10, no. 2 (2000): 141.

21. W. E. B. Du Bois, *Black Reconstruction in America, 1860–1880* (New York: Free Press, 1992), 711.

# The Drug of White Supremacy

*The rise of petty bourgeois and bourgeois negroes*
*exposes them to deep infection of White supremacy*
*(e.g., Armstrong Williams was Strom Thurman's office manager)*
*The "Integration" of schools*
> *of workplaces*
*has produced more crazy negroes than ever before*

*The drug of integrated success has injected many negroes with sickness*
> *"racism is really classism"*
*America is still alienated from Black people*
> *And they don't even want to know why*
*"Black history is a lot of bitching"*
> *—Blk Student Univ of Md.*
*"I am not in favor of Black History Month"*
> *—Morgan Freeman*
*The use of such negroes is a trick*
> *to trick the world that the U.S. is a democracy!!*

*Who is these Negroes to deny it*
*who is 16th most richest*
*in the clumsy known world*
*(511 billion a year, a buck for each tear)*


*Can't count all your children*
*who wd scrape and crawl,*
*lie and self crucify*
*to claim that black aint what they is, and*
*demand to be what they want and cant get away from*
*but still can't see the we that actually be yo self*
*brother man*
*the kid*
*the sweet loving sister*
*all yall worship*
*the fall, the disappearing boat, the racist quote, the negro in them green boots*
*who is dancing on your neck*
*what the heck they say*
*They got a way, to make you love it*
*"here is a letter from one of your sons and one of your fathers, one of the beaten,*
*misshaped by Heathens, one of the hungry"*


*In the crowd of the mass of lonely*
*who say they are not who they claim they cant be*
*who demand to be blind*
*who crave from behind*
*who kick they own ass*
*and be ignorant of class*
*tho they in the back where Stevie*
*called they name, but when they claim to be sane, they disagree with the we*
*who could verify that same*


*Why*
*is that the question*
*I asked Who*

*and all but the knowers*
*booked lied or fled*
*preachers shook they head*
    *was better that I bled*
*Called me*
    *crazy*
*you too, and him who they*
*killed and booed in Jersey for dying*
*they who eat your blood, murder your*
*children, explain you into silence asylums and eternal reformatories of ugly*
    *white disaster*

*Nobody asked you, minority*
*we archived your inferiority, your singing lacks sonority, you broke*
*and has wiggling titties that wont buy our goods*
    *you know what you need*
*to know if you could*
*you lie, you hurt, bleeding in the hood and kneel before*
*liars, molesters, punks, skunks, drunks, dishonest god builders and anything*
*wrong or glittering pitting your life against the jewelry of scum and*
    *distortions of where you from*
*got seeds who*
*get paid to act like bums*

*Who is you*
*Why is you*
*How you doing*
*and Who*
*is*
*Stanley Crouch, Skip Gates, Condoleezza Rice, Clarence Thomas,*
*Armstrong Williams, Roy Innis, Mobutu, Butulezi, Colon Bowel, Tshombe,*
*Playtoy Ben Yesman, Ward Connerly*
    *the herd of new old negro creeps,*
*count them in the bed to go to sleep, the negro in Haiti, who name is*
*actually Torture, Seaga, Floyd Flake*

*The negro nine who sent Rap up for*
*life, here I will name them if you see them*
*Spit in their face, wrap them in confederate flags so the world understands*
*their disgrace*
          *traitor whores*
*slavery's still bleeding sores, they are*
*Richard Wood, who wd never acquit, Lynn LeCraw wants to convict, will*
*kill, Fred Horton who voted for death, Jill Hood, Bush bumper sticker*
*across her mouth, this is the south, something called Nazarene sd Rap killed*
*at some bar, Terry Walker, a snake and a mason thrilled cracker*
*substitute, sd Rap resisted arrest, Edna Moore*

*Cops tell the truth, James*
*Heard a killer sez he cd forget he is biased, Ernestine Reese sd Muslims*
*don't go to Heaven, William Covington wont kill wont acquit, Panthers*
*are militants, Neil Brown, Republican, want to kill, Sam Jolley believes*
*cops but wants the facts, Jennifer Price Her Masters thesis "kids that carry*
*guns," Calvin Wise, former cop ex person, angry at SNNC, wants to convict*
*Clifton Thomas, sd "no heaven for Muslims."*

*Now is them Negroes or Niggers or Black Folks or what*
*and is they your*
*sisters your brothers*
*and if they ain't why do they claim and you agree*
*yall is the same*
          *Some dumb shit*
*Like my man, Mean William, used to say*
          *"Skin is Thin, But Class*
                    *Will kick yo' ass."*

# 2

# Performing Womanhood

# Black Girls and Representative Citizenship

onduct books written by black activists at the beginning of the twentieth century advocated a race that was cultured, malleable, law abiding, and religious. These texts were produced as black populations were migrating from southern states to northern and western cities during the Great Migration. Because this movement changed the geography of race relations through a collision of classes, manners, dialects, and lifestyles that resulted in unease among the black elite, conduct books offered specific behavioral protocols to manage and reconstruct racial representation.

The conduct books were written to protect African Americans against violence caused by poor race relations. During the post-Reconstruction era, a period lasting from 1877 to World War I, which the historian Rayford Logan labels the nadir, or the lowest point, in American race relations, African Americans were concerned about the constraints placed on their political rights.[1] Restrictions on voter registration and voting methods, such as poll taxes, literacy and residency requirements, and ballot box changes, disfranchised most blacks and many poor whites. Violence in the form of rape and lynching of African Americans intensified race relations. The mass publication of white supremacist literature, such as Thomas Dixon's illustrated novel, *The Leopard's Spots: A Romance of the White Man's Burdens, 1865–1900* (1902), and its sequel, *The Clansman: An Historical Romance of the Ku Klux Klan* (1905), contributed to harmful racist ideologies by presenting untruths of rampant black criminality.

In response to the violence of the period, black activists encouraged a view that proper conduct, harmonious courtship, and marital relationships could gain blacks access to the social and political events from which they were largely excluded.[2] To promote these Victorian ideals, black activists published instructional manuals that taught readers how to adopt genteel characteristics representative of the cultured, well-mannered "New Negro." As Henry Louis Gates Jr. observes, "the image of the New Negro . . . served various generations of black intellectuals as a sign of plenitude, of regeneration, of a truly reconstructed presence." He argues that this "New Negro" was generated between 1895 and 1925 to counter the image in the popular imagination of the black person as devoid of all characteristics that separate the lower forms of human life from the supposedly higher forms. To promote this representative subject, black intellectuals wrote prescriptive instructional manuals with exemplary characters who modeled moral integrity and behavioral codes that whites would recognize as embodiments of bourgeois manners.[3]

The behavior of black girls was an important topic in conduct rhetoric at the turn of the century. The rhetoric assumed a patriarchal agenda in which black girl figures acquired education and learned to care for others. Rather than use their education to prepare for uplift work in the public sphere, black girls were to defer to male leadership and return to the domestic sphere. They were to follow rules of "duty" and "beauty" that prepared them for their future roles as wife and mother.

One popular instructional manual, *Floyd's Flowers, or Duty and Beauty for Colored Children,* offers a good example of the language, iconography, and coded messages of decorum that surrounded the black girl figure as a citizenship model. Written by the educator and activist Silas X. Floyd and illustrated by the artist and educator John Henry Adams, this conduct book was first published in 1905 and republished in 1925 as *Charming Stories for Young and Old.*[4] *Floyd's Flowers,* a breakthrough for its time, was widely read at the beginning of the twentieth century. Its compilation of one hundred short stories provided black parents with advice on how to raise their children as morally correct citizens and productive members of society. Using girls and boys as protagonists, Floyd prepared readers to face prejudice at an early age and taught protocols on racial etiquette and lessons on moral refinement.

Although Adams's illustrations now seem pedestrian, with simple drawing and shading, their messages resonated deeply with racial aware- ness, economic inequality, and a collective sense of well-being. In later edi- tions photographs replaced sketches. The human subjects in these photo- graphs refuted caricatured images and thus completed the cultural work that Floyd's text could not achieve on its own. Thus, as Katharine Capshaw Smith writes, the image of the black child became emblematic of racial ten- sions of the period. In turn, then, the black girl in *Floyd's Flowers* became a representative feminine figure fully aware of the racial climate at the nadir.

Analyzing this little-known literature adds to the conversation of ca- nonical texts of this period that we read for messages about racial perfor- mance. We no longer have to lean as heavily on novels like Wallace Thur- man's *The Blacker the Berry* (1929), Jessie Fauset's *Plum Bun; or, a Novel with- out a Moral* (1929), Nella Larsen's *Quicksand* (1928) and *Passing* (1929), and Claude McKay's *Banana Bottom* (1938) because we can and should look at the various other works that connect behavior, instruction, and, as I posit here, the black girl.

## Conduct Book Discourse

The ideology and rhetoric of conduct has a long history, beginning in late fifteenth-century Europe and gaining prominence between 1540 and 1640. Until then, birth had been the principal determinant of rank for all social groups, an indicator of social status that was considered an intrinsic God- given attribute. However, that perception slowly changed to the more mod- ern notion that individuals create their own identity through their own ac- tions. Upper-class groups feared they would have to share their rank and privileges and thereby be displaced. Hence they created distinctions set forth in conduct theory—what Frank Whigham labels "a rhetoric of bodily demeanor"—a sophisticated rhetoric that effected an epistemology of personal social identity introducing a new understanding of one's place and role in society.[5] Courtesy literature sought to regulate the surge of social mobility that occurred between ruling and subject classes in late fifteenth-century England.

Eventually, conduct discourse moved away from determining social classes and entered the domestic realm, regulating women into prescribed, gendered roles.[6] Embedded in conduct books for ladies was the notion that girls lacked guidance and that advice will provide the warnings, information, or encouragement needed to become self-governing women. In her work on conduct rhetoric in women's writing, Nancy Armstrong argues that, in the eighteenth century, conduct literature began to target women and their sexuality rather than men and political life. The primary function of this eighteenth-century literature was to essentialize what it meant to be a woman and remove her from political events that society had designed for men. Conduct literature for women, Armstrong argues, took the place of devotional manuals for wives and daughters of the aristocracy and of courtesy books for would-be court ladies.[7]

*Floyd's Flowers* was part of a group of texts by black intellectuals who adapted the rhetoric of conduct books to address black readers. The adapted texts included W. E. B. Du Bois's *Morals and Manners* (1904) and Booker T. Washington's *Working with Your Hands* (1904). In *Morals and Manners* Du Bois addressed the "Negro Problem" when he claimed, "There is without a doubt a deep-seated feeling in the minds of many that the Negro problem is primarily a matter of morals and manners and that the real basis of color prejudice in America is the fact that the Negroes as a race are thotless [sic] in manners and altogether quite hopeless in sexual morals, in regard for property rights and reverence for truth."[8] Consequently, Katharine Capshaw Smith claims that "an anxiety about crude public behavior courses through most conduct material, as elites betrayed their fears that blacks would be judged as a whole through the behavior of the lower classes among them. For the black aristocracy, race solidarity resulted from political necessity as well as moral obligation."[9]

As Kevin Gaines argues in *Uplifting the Race*, racial progress based on conduct and outer appearance signified the black elite's awareness that its destiny was inseparable from that of the masses.[10] As African Americans left the South during the Great Migration, black intellectuals encouraged the masses to learn certain rules of decorum in order to acquire a sense of personal worth and dignity in an antiblack, racist society. Floyd thus suggested that girls who publicly exhibited lower-class behavior negatively affected how the dominant culture perceived the black race—with serious consequences.

Booker T. Washington joined Du Bois and Floyd in arguing that, with proper cultivation, African Americans would improve their condition and prevent threats of violence. In his essay "Industrial Education for the Negro" (1903), Washington states that African Americans must "learn the secrets of civilization—to learn that there are a few simple, cardinal principles upon which a race must start its upward course." Adoption of these "secrets of civilization" will cultivate productive citizens.[11]

These texts elevated the black elite's role as instructors to the black reading public and were designed to contribute to the moral good of black people and the nation at large.[12] Floyd adapted lessons from these texts to teach his readers how to manage the body through a conservative agenda that promoted propriety, morality, and decorum. Many black conduct books addressed effective parenting to give children a life of happiness and encourage their capacities and possibilities; among these were *The Brownies Book*, edited by W. E. B. Du Bois and Jessie Fauset between 1920 and 1921. It consisted of stories and advice and sought to promote racial pride and unity among black children.

In another book, *Golden Thoughts on Chastity and Procreation, including Heredity and Prenatal Influences* (1903), the coauthors, Professor and Mrs. J[ohn] W. Gibson, discuss how young girls should avoid discussions, speak politely, and apologize readily; they must shield themselves at their own expense and not tell personal jokes. Similar to the Gibsons' text is *Don't! A Book for Girls* (1891), in which Robert Charles O'Hara Benjamin instructs against "idleness, flirting, dancing, vindictiveness, backbiting, gossip, and slangy speech."[13] Dr. Mary Wood-Allen, national superintendent of the Purity Department of the Women's Christian Temperance Union, wrote *What a Young Girl Ought to Know* (1897), a sympathetic manual that discusses sex, nutrition, sleep, breathing, health, exercise, menstruation, and creative power.[14]

Floyd draws from these conduct books and repackages their messages into a book on racial etiquette. The frontispiece of Floyd's manual reinforced his upper-class status and his credibility as a teacher of such etiquette. It paired authenticating photographs of Floyd and Adams with stenciled images of their European equivalents: Floyd is placed next to a white male scholar surrounded by books; Adams is juxtaposed with a painter who holds his brush to a canvas and wears an elaborate hat and sophisticated clothing. Through its European references the frontispiece expresses a genealogy of authority in which black men validate their roles as instructors and advisers to the black reading public.

## Floyd's "Dutiful" Girls

An example of how Floyd represented the role of black girls in racial progress is depicted in one of the stories, "Thanksgiving at Piney Grove." Grace Wilkins is the daughter of Solomon and Amanda Wilkins and grew up on a farm in the Piney Grove settlement of the black belt of Georgia. A sketch features Grace with unruly hair and a plain face with little expression before she attends one of the normal and industrial institutes for the training of black boys and girls of the South. After her first year Grace returns at age fourteen to spend the summer with her parents, who immediately notice a new hygiene routine that Floyd describes in detail. Floyd writes that "Grace dressed differently and talked differently; and her mother said, speaking one day in confidence to her husband shortly after Grace's return, 'Dat gal's sho got a new walk on her!'"[15]

At school Grace learned the fundamental skills for caring for her body and her overall appearance. Floyd describes Grace's new hygiene routine: "Grace brought back a toothbrush with her from school. That was something which she had never had before. She used that toothbrush every morning and night. That was something that she had never done before. She was now careful to keep her hair combed every day. That was something that she had been accustomed to do on Sundays only or on special occasions. She washed her face two or three times a day now" (40).

Grace's new practices "made a deep and abiding impression upon Solomon and his wife" (40). The intentional simplicity of the narrative's rhetoric, combined with her parents' southern dialect, accentuates Grace's physical transformation from an unruly girl into a "Grace-ful" woman. Her tooth-brush, combed hair, and washed face become markers of cultivation. In his autobiography, *Up from Slavery* (1901), Booker T. Washington reinforced the use of the toothbrush to his students at Tuskegee Institute. Washington writes, "In all my teaching I have watched carefully the influence of the tooth-brush, and I am convinced that there are few single agencies of civilization that are more far-reaching." Washington reinforced the "gospel of the toothbrush" as an essential component of education for African Americans.[16]

Furthermore, Grace's transformation critiques the role that race and ancestry have on the physical and psychological development of the black race.[17] Grace's parents repeatedly suggest that her newly acquired rituals in hair maintenance, dress, and hygiene are habits she "had never had before"; thus Grace's behavior is not inherited from her parents but rather learned from lessons taught in school. Floyd teaches readers that despite their lineage or ancestry, elevation in class and the acquisition of new behaviors are neither innate nor inherited; rather, they can be learned.[18]

Through Grace's story Floyd shows readers his interpretation of the "Old Negro" in the form of Grace's parents and the "New Negro" in Grace's cultured, educated image. This contrast conveys a gap in class and in generation that he hopes his lessons will close. Floyd suggests that Grace's lessons will also reform her parents. Smith argues that the black child, including girls, gained a role in transforming the image of the race. She writes that many black intellectuals were "deeply invested in the enterprise of building black national identity through literary constructions of childhood, suggesting that the child who reads the texts has a duty to reform backwards parents." Grace's parents were reformed, "join[ed] in heartily in the movement," and assisted Grace in building her own school.[19]

In conveying a multiplicity of characters and voices through the dialect of Grace's parents, her instructors, and her own transformation into a "New Negro" figure, Floyd teaches readers that change from an old to a new way of life will enhance African Americans' access to citizenship and equal rights. Floyd's text also reveals the kind of education that might lessen the gap between the cultured elite and the masses.

After Grace opens the Piney Grove Academy, a school for black children, she holds a Thanksgiving Day ceremony in which she teaches lessons on Frederick Douglass, Booker T. Washington, and Paul Laurence Dunbar. At the end of the ceremony the town's pastor announces the intention of his son to marry Grace, whom he views as "one of the best women in the world" (46). Floyd positions Grace as the politically aware, intellectual center of her community *and* as a woman in line with the values of the cult of domesticity. Thus Grace not only achieves leadership status as head of a school but gains marriage as an additional reward. Grace's preparation for leadership, then, consists of social and cultural awareness as well as gendered expectations.

The image of Grace at graduation embodies what Floyd perceived as the culmination of successful, self-governing womanhood: Adams's illustration reveals Grace in a full skirt, crisp blouse, and overall well-groomed appearance. Expressing their views on the impact of illustrations on a reader, the Gibsons, authors of *Golden Thoughts*, note that "it is important to study the illustrations as well as the content, because, combined, they tell their own story; they tell the coming of a new aristocracy, a people powerful in strength, morals, culture, wealth and refinement." The artist John Henry Adams defines this "new aristocracy" in his sketches of black femininity. In "Rough Sketches: A Study of the Features of the New Negro Woman," Adams explains that the model black female is "an admirer of Fine Art, a performer on the violin and the piano, a sweet singer, a writer mostly given to essays, a lover of good books, and a home making girl." Adams's sketch is intended to capture Grace's transformation from an uncultured girl to an ideal woman who is educated, a "lover of good books, and a home making girl."[20]

The collaborative work of Floyd's text and Adams's images directly confronted negative racial representations. The literary scholars Cherene Sherrard-Johnson, Anne Carroll, and Caroline Goeser, among others, argue that the collaboration of text and image functioned to change public opinion. As Sherrard-Johnson notes in her work on images of the New Negro woman, collaborative texts are "visual and literary cross-fertilization" and operate as a counterrepresentational strategy to combat negative images of the black woman in the early decades of the twentieth century.[21] By using his own stereotypical images, such as Grace's image before she is educated, with her lopsided grin and messy hair, Floyd hoped to teach readers how to recognize the damage these images did to the perception of African Americans.

Floyd channels Grace's independence and achievement into the gendered role of wife. Her story begins with change and ends with marriage. This growth suggests that marriage, rather than her achievements, is Grace's ultimate reward for her education and cultivation. Although Grace portrays all the attributes of a woman qualified to educate and mobilize her race as head of her own school, she will teach texts written by men, maintain a gendered role as wife, and fulfill marital obligations.

Floyd also reinforced black girls' domestic roles and their contribution to the collective well-being of the black race in the other stories. In "Mary and Her Dolls," for instance, the representation of a young black girl, Mary, and her love for her black dolls channels her budding progressive awareness of social and economic inequality into a lesson on her future. The story opens with a description of how dolls and other toys are a privileged but salutary part of children's upbringing.

> Was there ever a time when little boys and girls, especially little girls, did not love dolls and did not have something of that nature to play with? It is not only amusing, it is inspiring to see the little children making merry with their dolls and their toy animals and their little express wagons and their wooden guns and their toy steam engines and their whistles and their balloons . . . and a hundred and one other things.[22]

While Floyd mentions a number of playthings for children, dolls are the focal point of the story. Mary's father, Dr. Smithson, asks her to give one of her five dolls to a less fortunate girl. Since he is clearly a member of the black middle class, Mary's refinement and awareness can be attributed to her father's influence. Rather than part with her precious dolls, however, Mary decides to use her own money, with which she had intended to purchase "a little iron bank," to buy a doll for the less fortunate girl (76).

Mary's independent spirit in maintaining her own money represents a modern outlook that conveys a mature, if not maternal, way of thinking: "She was glad that her papa had understood how she loved her dolls and glad to find that none of her beloved children was missing" (77). The sketch of Mary and her dolls reinforces how an independent spirit is channeled in favor of a domestic, dutiful role learned early in life. Like Grace's mother, whose role is peripheral, Mary's mother is never given any attention. Instead Mary, with her maternal guise, assumes the role and posture of her mother. In Adams's illustration Mary seems to replace her mother. She appears older than her suggested age and maintains the posture of a mother with a long, clean, neat, matronly, nonseductive dress, prim short hair, and furrowed eyebrows that accentuate a look of deep concern. Floyd's stories both work in conjunction with and sometimes altogether replace the tutelage gained from the biological mother. Thus *Floyd's Flowers* offers advice and instruction on nurturing to children and parents.

Textual images of black girls playing with dolls appear throughout *Floyd's Flowers* and suggest that the acquisition of black dolls fostered racial pride and increased black consciousness. In her work on racial destiny in African American culture, Michelle Mitchell provides extensive documentation of how the National Baptist Convention recognized the need to make "colored dolls" more accessible to black consumers to promote the idea that dolls helped shape black children's self-esteem. In 1908 the convention launched several such initiatives. Baptist women organized the Negro Dolls Clubs in 1914 and hosted "doll bazaars" during Christmas, while black Baptists opened the National Negro Doll Company. Mitchell's recounting of the history of black dolls explores how "race dolls were powerful toys," as black reformers "considered the placement of certain kinds of material culture within domestic spaces to be a symbol of collective progress." Although Floyd discusses "the power in dolls," he specifically emphasizes the dolls' connection to "domestic life, skills, and the acquisition of maternal feeling."[23]

Thus Mary's appearance and her dutifulness were designed to inspire young readers. Her dress and demeanor are as simple, uncomplicated, plain, unpretentious, and straightforward as she is. Her appearance, along with her determination to keep and care for dolls as she would her own children, rather than give one away, reinforces ideals of domesticity. Mary's gradual awareness of social class and her obligation to maintain the gendered role of caring for her dolls in preparation for motherhood conveys Floyd's image of a woman prepared to maintain her family's safety and cohesiveness.[24]

## "True Little Ladies": Floyd's Beautiful Girls

In conjunction with duty and commitment to the domestic sphere, the figure of the black girl defined female beauty. Beauty ideals involved both behavioral characteristics (manner, mood) and exterior appearance (dress). They encompassed all aspects of respectability and informed girls how to adhere to social codes of behavior through their outward appearance and interaction with others. The figure of the girl functioned as an expression of beauty, with the goal of regulating how African Americans represented themselves in public places.

In "Directions for Little Ladies," Floyd offers specific behavioral instructions that dictate how a girl should act at home, in public spaces, and in everyday life. "A true little lady" will always say, " 'I thank you' whenever someone assists her"; she is "never loud and boisterous on the streets, in public places, or at home"; she is clean and well-dressed because "every true little lady hates dirt"; "she will not tattle or seek to gossip; she loves Sunday school and church; she loves her mother and will help her mother in any way; finally, a true little lady will be a Christian." These guidelines appear to leave little space for girls to develop their imaginations or to participate in precocious or playful activity.[25]

In stories that focus on the amoral behavior of black girls, such as in "The Loud Girl" and "The Don't Care Girl," Floyd warns of behavioral characteristics that diminish "beautiful traits," such as yelling and maintaining a poor appearance. Floyd claims that the "loud girl" and the "don't care girl" are "two things of which we have seen enough of in this world" and that children who exhibit such behavior are "things; they are hardly worth the dignity of being called human beings." The "loud girl" contests the qualities that Floyd defines as beautiful. She is "always an object of pity and she is a sorry object for her own contemplation." The "don't care girl" is "the worst girl in all this world" because she "doesn't care what people think or say about her conduct; the girl goes to every 'hop,' to every party," and she "stays out late at night with the boys." Floyd's stories send a cautionary message that girls who exhibit good behavior will not become victims of sexual abuse by white men, a pervasive threat during slavery that persisted throughout the late nineteenth and early twentieth centuries. Floyd further suggests that by behaving like ladies, black girls can eliminate the tarnished reputation of black women, who have been stereotyped as impure, immodest, and overly sexual.[26]

In "The Loud Girl" an illustration depicts two girls (one older and taller than the other), both of whom exhibit immodest behavior. Their gestures— one clenches her hands into fists, while the other raises her hands in the air as if ready to clap—suggest aggression. Their broad stance, gaping mouths, boyish hats, and rumpled clothes depart from the feminine ideal of the period. The stakes only increase when girls engage in rowdy behavior and wear unfeminine dress in public places. As the story of "The Loud Girl" demonstrates, three girls ride in a streetcar and make a ruckus while eating chocolates, talking, laughing loudly, and throwing candies at one another; passengers who enter the streetcar stumble over the girls' outstretched legs. The behavior and dress of the three girls suggest a highly charged, unruly performance that contributes to the girls' diminished moral character and questions their class.

> They all wore boys' hats. One wore a vivid red jacket with brass buttons, and another had on a brass belt. A third one had on a most conspicuous plaid skirt. This third one had a box of bonbons, and when the three were seated she opened the box and offered it to her companions, saying as she did so, in a voice loud enough and shrill enough to be heard in every part of the car: "it's my treat; have some, chums!" (47–48)

Floyd critiques the girls' inability or unwillingness to observe how their behavior in public affects others' perceptions of them. The story teaches readers how behavior, dress, voice, and manners affect perceptions of class for African Americans. The occurrence of this behavior on a streetcar, a public space in an urban setting, suggests that the girls will attract the kind of attention that will only lead to assumptions about their sexual mores.

Floyd's streetcar scene echoes a similar scene in Pauline Hopkins's novel *Contending Forces: A Romance Illustrative of Negro Life North and South* (1901), in which black girls cause a ruckus on a streetcar. In a chapter in which black people from the community gather in a parlor to discuss "questions of the day and their effects upon the colored people," Mrs. Davis relates a story in which she chastises a group of black girls who act unruly on a streetcar:

> Some o' them was a-standin' up in thet car, an' every once in a while I noticed thet a passenger'd squirm as ef suthin' had hit him. Finally I got so mad I jes' couldn't see along with sech antics from them critters a-disgracin' theirselves and the whole o' the res' o' the colored population, an' I jes' elbowed myself into thet crowd o' young jades—what's thet (as Will murmured something under his breath), was they gals? Yas, they was; young *jades*, every one o' them! Now what do yer think they was a-doin? . . . *They was a-trampin' onto the feet of every white man an' woman in thet car to show the white folks how free they was!* I jes' took my ambriller an' knocked it into two or three o' them thet I knowed, an' tol'em' I'd tell ther mothers.[27]

Although Mrs. Davis is a respectable member of the black community, Hopkins gives her dialect speech to signal agreement with someone from this class who has a sense of manners and congeniality. Mrs. Davis's concern is not only that the black girls act so badly that their behavior affects "the whole o' the res' o' the colored population" but that they demonstrate bravado and "show white folks how free they was." Her choice of the word *free* is sarcastic and suggests that the girls are unwilling to subscribe to rules of propriety and choose to act as free as they wish. The severe self-imposed restrictions black people were under to avoid violence necessitated strict etiquette lest the community be judged and condemned by the behavior of one or a few.

As his stories confirm, Floyd's writings attempted to protect girls from the dangers rampant in the Jim Crow era. However, certain female race activists during this postbellum period nevertheless had to act loud in order to advance racial progress. The activist Ida B. Wells wrote inflammatory articles and spoke publicly and openly about violence toward African Americans. Her actions demonstrated an unwillingness to stay silent despite being constantly in danger. Yet, while she spoke clearly and directly against injustice, she did not behave in a manner that would have distracted from the delivery of her message. The ironic tension in "The Loud Girl" is that the attributes that Floyd assigns to the "loud girl" reveal the kind of girl who could channel her passion and become a woman who is self-assured and confident. She will refute the "good opinion" of others, speak boldly, and "shoot her head way up in the air" when she addresses others. In other words, the characteristics that describe the "loud girl"—loud, bold, defiant—actually depict someone who is strong willed, independent, and outspoken—qualities that could be admired rather than shunned by society. Nevertheless, the politics of respectability, as Evelyn Higginbotham suggests, attached shame to such qualities because of the fear not only of derogatory racial stereotypes but also of rape by white men.[28] Black intellectuals like Floyd criticized any type of outward behavior that could be construed as sexual. These codes of behavior were defined by a patriarchal agenda meant to steer the girl and woman to a domestic sphere and keep them there.

Floyd's treatment of boy figures in *Floyd's Flowers* demonstrates that they too cannot act in an unruly way. While unruly girls are told they are "the worst girl in all this world" (49), Floyd encourages unruly boys to behave because they were "made for better things" (53). In "The Rowdy Boy," "A Plucky Boy," "Directions for Little Gentlemen," and "The Bad Boy—How to Help Him," Floyd describes behavior unacceptable for young black men. For example, Floyd asserts that one can clearly identify a "rowdy boy" anywhere in society because "there are certain marks or appearances which he carries about with him and which are never absent," such as smoking, poor dress, lateness, and criminal behavior (51). The story of "The Rowdy Boy" ends with a final word of advice: "Don't be rowdy, boys; don't be rough; don't be rude. You were made for better things" (53). Acting unruly will prevent boys from achieving "better things," which implies that, unlike girls, who remain in the home, boys leave their homes and make an impact on the world.

Floyd portrays the model black girl not as active but as "modest and quiet," as the caption under her sketch states (49). She is not expected to speak much or make a verbal impact. She is good natured, delicate, and gentle. Her body is calm and self-contained rather than out of control, with flailing arms and legs. Her stature is tall and upright, as captured by her full image filling the entire page, rather than the three-quarters of a page provided for loud girls (46). In her hand she holds a closed fan, which suggests modesty and propriety and mimics her body, which appears closed, drawn in, and turned away from any confrontational stance. Her neatly coiffed hair and long full skirt are properly maintained—she does not need to wear a cap, nor are her clothes wrinkled or disheveled. Overall, she exhibits true womanhood, guided by a quiet demeanor, crisp outward appearance, and the absence of vices. The picture thus demonstrates that Floyd's proper model of black girlhood focuses less on the improvement of her intellect than on the development of moral character and outward appearance.

Because the good-natured girl appears to be lighter in skin tone, while the shade of skin on the "loud girl" is noticeably darker, the illustrations in Floyd's text seem to suggest that character is contingent on skin tone. Furthermore the sketch depicts the model black girl's hair as long and shoulder-length, rather than short, coarse, and curly like that of the "loud girl." Stereotypical racial characteristics make character claims: darker-skinned girls are loud, while lighter-skinned girls are "modest and quiet." This differentiation between the darker-skinned girl as unruly and the lighter-skinned girl as demure and attractive suggests that Floyd aligned his text with the white supremacist discourse that equated dignity with white or lighter-hued skin. His text encouraged an idea of uplift that centered class distinction on color and superficial exterior characteristics such as dress and hair, regardless of one's merit or intellect. This mind-set points to an intraracial division along class *and* color lines that creates further divisions among African Americans, a lessened sense of community, and heightened perceptions of class difference.

Conduct rhetoric stipulated that for the black race to advance, the black woman and girl had to maintain the image of the race by remaining at the center of the domestic economy to teach discipline, caution, and morality. Floyd's stories about Grace's transformation and Mary's nurturance taught readers how appearance, domesticity, and education might control the race's image and could protect against attacks on the collective character and individual bodies of black people. However, as Floyd reveals, there were "loud girls" and "don't-care girls" who were unconcerned with protocol and navigated their own way in the city, on streetcars, and in workplaces, unwilling to be restricted by outdated protocol.

Floyd's text aimed to negotiate the public image of African Americans by reinforcing a return to domestic ideals. His text became a parenting guide whose instructive rhetoric and images replaced the black mother with black male figures in the form of Floyd and Adams, the pastor in Grace's story, and Dr. Smithson, Mary's father, who become authoritative, protective figures who guide the girl into a domesticated role. These black men were the visible members of the middle class, while the black mother, speaking in the dialect of the "Old Negro" in Grace's story and absent altogether from Mary's story, assumes a marginal role in raising her children. Thus Floyd's text teaches readers that the middle-class black male figure will assume the role of uplift for the black race, while black women and girls support him through maintaining the domestic sphere. What results are girl figures who might have enjoyed imagination and play in their youth, as Mary does with her dolls, but whose youth and imaginations are channeled to deferential domestic roles.

While the rules of conduct instruction, like that in *Floyd's Flowers,* did repress the full range of women's behaviors, they did not stop many independent-thinking women from making an activist impact on racial uplift. For example, the political writings in "The Colored Girl" (1905) by Fannie Barrier Williams, the work of Ida B. Wells, and representations of black girls in Zora Neale Hurston's novels, specifically, her own autobiography, *Dust Tracks on a Road* (1942), ran counter to many of the bourgeois values of that time. Thus the black girl as a model of the New Negro is a rich and complicated representative model of African Americans' diverse attempts at acquiring full citizenship at the turn of the twentieth century.

## NOTES

1. Rayford Logan, *The Negro in American Life and Thought: The Nadir, 1877–1901* (New York: Dial, 1954).
2. Claudia Tate explores black women writers' adherence to Victorian ideals such as marriage as a political means. She examines how domestic novels emphasized

bourgeois decorum as an important emancipatory cultural discourse and argues that these novels must be read against the cultural history of the period, an era that was symbolically embedded in Victorian ethos. These novels portrayed courtships and wedded bliss that allowed African Americans to enter the social and political events from which they were largely excluded (Claudia Tate, *Domestic Allegories of Political Desire* [New York: Oxford University Press, 1992], 5).

3. Henry Louis Gates, "The Trope of the New Negro and the Reconstruction of the Image of the Black," *Representations* 24 (Fall 1988): 130–31.

4. Silas X. Floyd. *Floyd's Flowers; Or Duty and Beauty for Colored Children*, illus. John Henry Adams (Atlanta: Hertel, Jenkins, 1905); Silas X. Floyd, *Charming Stories for Young and Old* (Washington, D.C.: Austin Jenkins, 1925). Other editions of *Floyd's Flowers* include *Short Stories for Colored People Both Old and Young* (Washington, D.C.: Austin Jenkins, 1920) and *The New Floyd's Flowers: Short Stories for Colored People Old and Young* (Washington, D.C.: Austin Jenkins, 1922).

   Known as a prominent author and educator, Floyd graduated from Atlanta University in 1891 and served for five years as a public school principal in Georgia. By 1902 Floyd had received honorary degrees from Morris Brown College and Atlanta University. His work can be found in several periodicals of the early twentieth century, including *Sunday School Times*, the *New York Independent*, and *Lippincott's Magazine*.

5. Frank Whigham, *Ambition and Privilege: The Social Tropes of Elizabethan Courtesy Theory* (Berkeley: University of California Press, 1984), x–5.

6. Catharine Beecher's advice book, *A Treatise on Domestic Economy for Use of Young Ladies at Home and at School* (1841), prepared girls for marriage and household management. The magazine *New England Offering* (1848–50) offered discussion of sexuality, reproduction, and health for girls.

7. Nancy Armstrong, introduction to Nancy Armstrong and Leonard Tennenhouse, eds., *Ideology of Conduct: Essays on Conduct and the History of Sexuality* (New York: Routledge, 1987), 4.

8. W. E. B. Du Bois, *Morals and Manners among Negro Americans*, ed. W. E. Burghardt Du Bois and Augustus Granville Dill (Atlanta: Atlanta University Press, 1914), 5. At a conference addressing the moral improvement of the black race, Du Bois countered the stereotype, crediting the work of the National Association of Colored Women for uplifting the race. He claimed being "pleased to call the attention of the country to the fact that much of the real work of social uplift and moral awakening

is being carried on by Negro women in their clubs and institutions" (7).

9. Katharine Capshaw Smith, "Childhood, the Body, and Race Performance: Early Twentieth-Century Etiquette Books for Black Children," *African American Review* 40, no. 4 (2006): 798.

10. Kevin Gaines, *Uplifting the Race: Black Leadership, Politics, and Culture in the Twentieth Century* (Chapel Hill: University of North Carolina Press, 1996).

11. Booker T. Washington, "Industrial Education for the Negro," *The Negro Problem* (1903; repr., New York, 2003), 99, 18. Washington argues that "it has been necessary for the Negro to learn the difference between being worked and working—to learn that being worked meant degradation, while working means civilization; that all forms of labor are honorable, and all forms of idleness disgraceful" (9).

12. See other instructional manuals such as *The New England Offering* (1847–50), which discusses sexuality, reproduction, and health for girls. Lydia Maria Child's *The Juvenile Miscellany: For the Instruction and Amusement of Youth (1826–1836)* is said to be the first American children's magazine that included information geared for children, including discussions of proper behavior, essays on virtue, and biographical sketches of notable figures.

13. Professor and Mrs. J. W. Gibson, *Golden Thoughts on Chastity and Procreation, including Heredity and Prenatal Influences* (Naperville, Ill.: J. L. Nichols, 1903); Michelle Mitchell, *Righteous Propagation: African Americans and the Politics of Racial Destiny after Reconstruction* (Chapel Hill: University of North Carolina Press, 2004), 121.

14. Mary Wood-Allen, *What a Young Woman Ought to Know* (Philadelphia: Vir, 1905).

15. Floyd, "Thanksgiving at Piney Grove," in *Floyd's Flowers,* 39.

16. Booker T. Washington, *Up from Slavery: An Autobiography* (New York: Doubleday, 1901), 110.

17. See Richard Yarborough, introduction to *Contending Forces: A Romance Illustrative of Negro Life North and South,* by Pauline Hopkins (New York: Oxford University Press, 1988), xxxv.

18. See Katharine Capshaw Smith, who claims that "the child's body becomes the site on which the character of the new black identity can be staged" and that "through education and uplift, the supposedly fixed nature of public identity can change and be witnessed in the new, cultured body of the black child" ("Childhood, the Body, and Race Performance," 799, 806). See also Saidiya Hartman, who argues that "the emphasis on hygiene expresses larger concerns about national well-being since hygiene legitimated, if not invited, the policing of dwellings but also the setting

of guidelines for marriage and other forms of social association, particularly those considered dangerous or destabilizing of social order" (Hartmann, *Scenes of Subjection: Terror, Slavery, and Self-Making in Nineteenth-Century America* [New York: Oxford University Press, 1997], 158).

19. Katharine Capshaw Smith, *Children's Literature of the Harlem Renaissance* (Bloomington: Indiana University Press, 2004), x; Floyd, "Thanksgiving at Piney Grove," 41.

20. Gibson and Gibson, *Golden Thoughts*, 74; John Henry Adams, "Rough Sketches: A Study of the Features of the New Negro Woman," *Voice of the Negro* (June 1907): 238–41. The quote I used is from a caption to a picture accompanying the article.

21. Cherene Sherrard-Johnson, *Portraits of the New Negro Woman: Visual and Literary Culture in the Harlem Renaissance* (New Brunswick, N.J.: Rutgers University Press, 2007), 3. See also Anne Elizabeth Carroll, *Word, Image and the New Negro: Representation and Identity in the Harlem Renaissance* (Bloomington: Indiana University Press, 2005), and Caroline Goeser, *Picturing the New Negro: Harlem Renaissance Print Culture and Modern Identity* (Lawrence: University Press of Kansas, 2007).

22. Floyd, "Mary and Her Dolls," in *Floyd's Flowers*, 76–77.

23. Michelle Mitchell, *Righteous Propagation: African Americans and the Politics of Racial Destiny after Reconstruction* (Chapel Hill: University of North Carolina Press, 2004), 178, 195.

24. For more information on dolls in American culture, see Miriam Formanek-Brunell's *Dolls and the Commercialization of American Culture* (New Haven: Yale University Press, 1993).

25. Floyd, *Floyd's Flowers*, 264–65. In her work on etiquette books for black children, Katharine Capshaw Smith claims that "amending the child's body would come through modifying the child's thought" ("Childhood, the Body, and Race Performance," 802).

26. Floyd, *Floyd's Flowers*, 49–51.

27. Pauline Hopkins, *Contending Forces: A Romance Illustrative of Negro Life North and South* (New York: Oxford University Press, 1988), 110–11.

28. See Ida B. Wells, *Crusade for Justice: Autobiography of Ida B. Wells,* ed. Alfreda M. Duster (Chicago: University of Chicago Press, 1978), and Evelyn Higginbotham, *Righteous Discontent: The Black Woman's Club Movement in the Black Baptist Church, 1880–1920* (Cambridge, Mass.: Harvard University Press, 1993).

# Black Bourgeois Women's Narratives in the Post-Reagan, "Post–Civil Rights," "Postfeminist" Era

lack bourgeois memoirs and novels published late in the twentieth century engage a cluster of related questions: What significance, if any, does class have in American constructions of race, and how does gender inflect the experience of race and class? Where does the black bourgeois woman fit into the historical and psychic narratives of American identity? How does her liberation project relate to the liberation of black people as a whole? Black middle-class women's narratives and memoirs of the late 1980s and 1990s tend to fall into two camps in their responses to these questions: those that analyze the impact of gender constructions on black middle-class experience to affirm that class distinctions are ultimately insignificant in the U.S. civil rights struggle, and those that use the black middle-class woman's social position as a means of deconstructing the categories of race, class, and gender and of rejecting the fundamental tenets of identity politics.

In this chapter I examine two black women's autobiographical novels from the late twentieth century that serve as examples of these two ideological stances, Ntozake Shange's *Betsey Brown* and Andrea Lee's *Sarah Phillips*, and discuss the conflicting implications of their visions of race and gender relations in the United States in the new century.[1] The eponymous heroine of Shange's novel feels that she must embrace a working-class identity to perform the work that her middle-class parents have raised her to commit herself to; she attempts to synthesize the aspirations and values of the traditional black bourgeoisie with a political agenda that recognizes the insignificance of class distinctions among an oppressed people. The protagonist of Lee's novel, on the other hand, finds herself in a free fall that may be either liberating or catastrophic, as she realizes that the historical constructions of identity evoked by the title of the earliest flashback in the novel, "New African," are not tenable in a postmodern world.

An understanding of these black middle-class performances and an articulation of what is at stake in them takes on a particular urgency at the dawn of the twenty-first century, when the United States is witnessing a backlash against civil rights legislation and affirmative action policies, Bill Cosby is on a self-appointed mission to save the struggling classes from themselves, and a 2007 Pew Research poll purportedly demonstrates that a substantial number of African Americans no longer consider that the middle class shares a racial identity with the struggling class of African Americans. Meanwhile, limited access to an effective education—still the primary marker of class within the black community—continues to shut out increasing numbers of black people from class mobility. In an age when the first black presidential candidate was dogged by accusations of elitism—and suggested that it might not be appropriate to include in affirmative action programs affluent black children like his own—while the *New York Times* declares that the United States is in an era of "post-black" politics, these two texts provide radically different ways of imagining the role of the black middle-class woman in negotiating a society that many people are also eager to label postfeminist.[2]

## "On Being Young—A Woman—and Colored"

Sixty years after Marita Bonner's essay chronicling the effects of the limiting constructions of femininity and blackness on an educated young black woman won *Crisis Magazine*'s essay contest in 1925, Lee's *Sarah Phillips*

(1984) and Shange's *Betsey Brown* (1985), autobiographical novels that focus on the challenges of growing up black, female, and middle class, were published within months of each other. On the face of it, the novels share many similarities in their portrayals of sheltered, bookish black girls coming of age in the midst of the civil rights struggles of the sixties and the waning influence of the traditional black bourgeoisie. Both narrators acutely delineate the mixed messages about race and sexuality that they receive from their families, and both protagonists resist the protection their families attempt to offer them by taking social and sexual risks. However, Lee's novel (her first, and really a collection of linked stories structured around a racial "ah-ha" moment in each) inspired a fascinated horror among many African American readers and generated surprisingly few critical responses that attempted to grapple with the text's ambiguity and ambivalence toward conventional literary racial identities.[3] *Betsey Brown*, on the other hand, offered a more comfortable read. In *Betsey Brown* the tensions generated by class and color distinctions are ultimately synthesized into a black identity rooted in working-class female culture that serves both as a source of creativity and as political defense. In *Sarah Phillips* the power of Sarah's familial past is both overwhelming and impossible to come to terms with; there is no hint of a neat and satisfying remedy—emotional or political—to Sarah's characteristic feelings of loss, ambivalence, and unease. A reconciliation of the paradoxes of her position as a black middle-class woman in a white supremacist society would entail not only the destruction of present structures of oppression but also a complete erasure of her past.

Both texts provide fascinating views of the black bourgeoisie's racial, gender, and class anxieties in an era shaped by the civil rights and feminist movements. During this period literary theory put *race* in quotation marks and notions of "racial authenticity" were deconstructed along with other ideas of primordial and essential truths. The backlash against the very affirmative action policies that had contributed to the growth of the new black middle class encouraged a refashioning of the idea of racial solidarity. Shange's and Lee's novels, like many memoirs and autobiographical novels of this era, problematize issues of racial authenticity, representation, and sexuality in ways that pose political and cultural challenges with which we are still grappling in the twenty-first century. The protagonists of both novels leave childhood just as their nation is witnessing a radical revision of the places of both blacks and women in U.S. society. Both novels take as their central concern the estrangement of the black middle class from the larger black working-class community. Shange's novel defines growing up as rejecting the mores and values of the black bourgeoisie and identifying with and integrating oneself into the black working class; Lee also emphasizes the necessary rejection of the traditions and performances of black bourgeois behavior but presents her protagonist as adrift and mourning the loss of ties to the bourgeois world.

The perils and possibilities of racial integration play major roles in both eponymous novels. Both heroines grow up in neighborhoods seemingly far removed from the violent landscape of the civil rights struggle in the southern states, yet their self-perceptions are formed by those distant and mediated—through the media and adult conversations—civil rights battles. The recipients of inconsistent and ineffective protection afforded by their class, Sarah and Betsey must confront racism in subtler ways than the black children they see in news photographs, and they come to the realization that their families' education and material comforts are no armor against the world's assumption that they are inferior beings. As they explore their nascent sexuality, each discovers that while she cannot follow the script for conventional bourgeois womanhood, performing the role of sexy exotic is equally unsatisfying. Their childish perceptions, sharpened by their emergence into adolescence, reveal that class, gender, and racial identities are matters of performance and choice rather than fixed essentialized identities.

Betsey's story takes place in St. Louis in 1959 against the backdrop of recently mandated school desegregation, but the city's "poverty, meanness and shootings Betsey was only vaguely aware of" (14). Sarah lives in a tiny suburban enclave peopled by black "doctors, ministers, and teachers who had grown up in Philadelphia row houses—the lawns and tree-lined streets represented the fulfillment of a fantasy long deferred, and acted as a barrier against the predictable cruelty of the world" (39). Both girls are called upon by their activist parents to integrate their respective local schools. The issue of integration forces the girls into roles that highlight the performative nature of class and race.

*My skin is yellow*
*My hair is long*
*Between two worlds*
*I do belong*

■ Nina Simone, "Four Women"

## Sarah Phillips: An Expatriate in Her Own Country

*Sarah Phillips,* which is structured as a series of vignettes, each centered on a racial "incident," presents Sarah as an adventurer who tries on and plays out different identities. Indeed, each vignette of the novel records her refusal to perform the conventional roles dictated by her class, race, and gender. From her literal fight against receiving baptism at her father's hand to her role-playing in a group of European men's sexual fantasies, each of her rejections of a proper black middle-class girl's identity is accompanied by feelings of ambivalence and loss.

Sarah's father, a popular minister at a Baptist church in inner-city Philadelphia, is also a civil rights leader on the national stage, yet he does not insist that his children be involved in any meaningful way with church life or the civil rights struggle (he tells Sarah, who wants to accompany him to the March on Washington, that it is too dangerous for little girls). The majority of his congregation, like his own family, lives in the suburbs and returns to the inner-city only for weekly church services. Sarah, a self-described "suburban child," thinks of the church as "a dreadful old relative in the city, one who forced us into tedious visits and who linked us to a past that came to seem embarrassingly primitive as we grew older" (19). Indeed, Sarah also feels "privately embarrassed to have a parent who freely admitted to going to jail in Alabama" (21) and states that she "cared little about history, and found it hard to picture the slaves as being any ancestors of [hers]" (26) when her father explains that the baptismal song was created by southern slaves. It is interesting that the representative of the church and its historical significance in black life is not Sarah's father, the Reverend Phillips, but an old family domestic employee named Bessie Gray. Bessie, not Reverend Phillips, attempts to drag Sarah to the altar to take her father's hand and to be baptized, and it is to Bessie that Sarah expresses her refusal to play the expected role of the minister's daughter. The narrator describes Bessie as a stereotypical lower-class black woman: her religious faith; her loyalty to her "white children"; her dark skin, which she covers with "a thick orange face powder"; her strength of will (which, in the end, is no match for Sarah's) all mark her as the embodiment of a mode of black womanhood that Sarah despises and rejects. Sarah prefers to fashion an identity from "the remote dimension" of books rather than the historical community symbolized by the church congregation.

Part of Sarah's alienation from conventional constructions of her race and class stems from her early awareness of the fragility of her class status and the limits of the protections her relative privilege affords her. The fantasy of Franklin Place, the suburban black enclave, is disrupted and damaged beyond repair when Sarah is seven and she and a friend encounter a group of Gypsies. Upon observing Franklin Place, with its rambling houses, expansive lawns, and swim club ("constructed by neighborhood parents for their children, who couldn't swim elsewhere" [39]), a Gypsy woman tells Sarah and her friend that "'it's a real crime for colored to live like this'" (43). When Sarah relates her encounter to her family at the dinner table, she is confused by her father's response: "'Well, everybody's got . . . to . . . feel . . . better . . . than somebody,' said Daddy. . . . He had the compressed look about his cheeks that he got whenever he was about to tell a joke, one of the complicated civil rights jokes. . . . 'Most of the world despises Gypsies, but a Gypsy can always look down on a Negro. Heck, that fellow was right to spit! You can dress it up with trees and big houses and people who don't stink too bad, but a nigger neighborhood is still a nigger neighborhood'" (44).

The incident and her father's response deeply disturb Sarah, but in a typical move she displaces her thoughts and feelings about the class and race issues it raises and develops a vague fear of being stolen. For several nights in a row the seven-year-old wakes up "with a jolt, thinking, 'Gypsies!'" but the older narrating Sarah reflects: "It was not that I had really feared being stolen: it was more, in fact, that they seemed to have stolen something from me. Nothing looked different, yet everything was, and for the first time Franklin Place seemed genuinely connected to a world that was neither insulated nor serene" (46).

*Unreality* and *isolation* are key words in E. Franklin Frazier's characterization of the black middle class in the first half of the twentieth century. In his schema the small black middle class is estranged from both the white and black worlds. While the nonblack world hovers like a threatening penumbra at the edges of Sarah's sheltered bourgeois world, Sarah and her family's relationship with working-class blacks is even more problematic and ambiguous. Sarah envies the rowdy, stylish, sexualized city youth who integrate her genteel Quaker summer camp and idealizes the vision of the civil rights movement "which made blood relatives of people like my father and the cab driver" (50), yet she is confused by her father's sometimes joking, sometimes serious, distinction between himself and "Negroes":

> Daddy taught Matthew [her brother] and me to stick out our chins and say "Negro" with near-military briskness when we spoke of ourselves in the classroom of our Quaker school, and occasionally he brought home for us stacks of books filled with the strenuous exploits of heroic slaves. . . . Yet sometimes, when Daddy was sitting quietly with my mother in the evenings, he would talk unflatteringly about Negroes, referring to them as *we* or *us.* "Yes, that neighborhood has gone downhill, now that *we* have moved in," he would say. "There's nobody like *us* for spoiling a community." And once, when Mama was urging him to make some changes in the garden of our house, he looked at her and said in a withering voice, "You seem determined to make the house vulgar. Do you want it to *look* like it belongs to a colored man?" (48)

Sarah's childish inability to distinguish between her father's taking on the voice of white racist perspectives and his own internalized racism or to understand his sometimes ironic, sometimes inspiring, use of the racial *we* reveals the confused allegiances of the old black middle class. With a child's relentless clarity of vision, the narrator describes the double-voiced performances that the black middle class, even today, feels are necessary to both move ahead and survive. In what is perhaps the pivotal chapter of the novel, the Reverend Phillips's ironic self-mocking tone is echoed in the title, "Servant Problems," which also evokes and critiques Frazier's scathing characterization of the bourgeois woman's trivial life. The title is a class-based cliché, like "Good help is hard to find," a theme that Shange uses ironically in *Betsey Brown.* Like Betsey, Sarah discovers that class distinctions between "Negroes" do not exist in the white world; in the white world Sarah is interchangeable with a black maid, both on stage and in real life.

Sarah has left her liberal, Quaker grammar school ("where race and class were treated with energetic nonchalance" [53]), to integrate an exclusive girls' school, where Sarah finds herself politely but firmly excluded from the school's social life.[4] The narrator situates Sarah's experience in the landscape of the racial upheavals across the nation: "I came to Prescott in the mid-sixties. . . . *Life* had recently published pages of pictures showing flames blossoming from storefronts in Newark and Washington, but in the countryside around Saddler's Creek no one was burning anything but leaves" (53).

She remembers another photograph she had seen several years earlier, of a southern black girl, accompanied by a policeman, entering a school through a jeering crowd. At least Prescott students did not jeer or throw things, but they expressed hostility to Sarah's presence all the same with "a set of almost imperceptible closures and polite rejections" (30). Her only friend is a misfit white girl whose own racism seems to take on a more benign guise when she asks "admiringly, 'Don't you think it's romantic to be a Negro?'" (55). However, Sarah's relationship to the white world of Prescott is clear; her relationship to the almost hidden black world of the school's maids, cooks, and janitors is not (should she or should she not wave to the cook across the lawn?). Sarah accidentally stumbles upon a maid's room one day and discovers that "contiguous to the bright, prosperous outer life of the school was another existence, a dark mirror image, which, like the other world in a Grimm's tale, was only a few steps off the path of daily routine. . . . I tried to forget what we'd seen. Thinking about the black people working at the school made me uncomfortable; I didn't know what to feel about them" (57).

Sarah also does not know how to relate to them until several weeks later, when, after auditioning brilliantly for a school play, she finds that she has been awarded the role of Rheba: "Who was Rheba? Somehow neither Gretchen nor I could recall her. I leafed through the play and read aloud, *From the kitchen comes a colored maid named Rheba—a very black girl somewhere in her thirties. She carries a white tablecloth and presently starts to spread it over the table*" (58). Sarah has been assigned a peripheral inappropriate part in the play on the basis of the white teacher's constructions of her racial identity, just as Prescott's community has assigned her a peripheral role in the life of the school. Although Sarah's status is that of a middle-class student paying the same tuition and wearing the same uniform as her white counterparts, Prescott puts her in the same category as the thirty-, forty-, and fifty-year-old "girls" in the hidden rooms of the campus buildings. As a result of this incident Sarah no longer averts her eyes when she passes the cook and other black staff; although she still does not wave to the cook, she "looked seriously at him, as if he had something to teach" her (59).

She refuses the theatrical part but learns to perform a role as a way of coping with the new knowledge she has: she develops a new way of laughing that "burn[s] her insides like vinegar." This new way of laughing brings her "closer to growing up" than the development of her breasts and makes her "life at Prescott . . . easier" (58). Unlike Betsey, however, Sarah does not come to identify with the black working class as a result of her realization that the white world does not make class distinctions among blacks. Rather, her new knowledge initiates her determination to escape from "the past," "the unbearably familiar" (93), which Sarah defines specifically as the black bourgeois world of her parents. After a family dinner attended, to their parents' disapprobation, by her brother's white girlfriend, Sarah carelessly carries the Phillips's heirloom crystal glasses—a symbol of the family's history and pride—and wishes that she "had the courage . . . to [throw] them against the wall" (66). In her own mission épater le bourgeois, Sarah embarks upon a career as a sexual libertine, using her body to perform white male fantasies.

The opening of the novel finds Sarah at twenty-one playing the role of exotic sexual plaything to three Frenchmen. Propelled to Paris by "a loathing of everything that made up my past," Sarah inhabits a world that "suited her desire for amnesia" (4). This world is one created by her putative lovers and based on their fantastical constructions of her race and sexuality. Clearly evocative of the slave auction block, one of their favorite games was one in which Sarah "stood naked on a wooden box and turned slowly to have my body appraised and criticized. The three boys were funny and horny and only occasionally tiresome; they told me I was beautiful and showed me off to their friends at the cafés and discos and at the two Drugstores" (6–7).

When clothed, Sarah favors masochistic cigarette jeans so tight "they left a mesh of welts on my belly and thighs" (7) and miniskirts so short that one of the men, Henri, tells her that she "looks like a prostitute" (10). However, one of Henri's fantasies gives Sarah the jolt that propels her back to the United States and a coming to terms with her own—and her family's—past. Like Helga Crane, the protagonist of Nella Larsen's 1926 novel, *Quicksand,* who recognizes herself in the performance of black minstrels in a European city, Sarah feels a sense of recognition in a racist, stereotyped narrative of her genealogy: " 'Did you ever wonder, Roger, old boy . . . why our beautiful Sarah is such a mixture of races, why she has pale skin but hair that is as kinky as that of a Haitian? Well, I'll tell you. Her mother was an Irishwoman, and her father was a monkey. . . . Actually, it's a longer story. It's a very American tale. This Irlandaise was part redskin, and not only that but part Jew as well. . . . And one day this Irlandaise was walking through the jungle near New Orleans, when she was raped by a jazz musician as big and black as King Kong, with sexual equipment to match" (11).

Sarah is not, she insists, disturbed by the puerile racism of the tale but by how it "illuminated . . . with blinding clarity the hopeless presumption of trying to discard my portion of America" (12). Sarah's "portion of America" is that of the black bourgeoisie, whose relationship to American history and aspiration is conflicted, ambivalent, and inconsistent. *Sarah Phillips* does not offer its readers a comfortable and coherent reconciliation of class and racial identity, only the hope that a thoughtful tracing of the ambiguities of this class and its psychic effects on its members will, as Sarah says, "turn out to be enough" (117) to illuminate the inherent absurdities and dangers of constructions of race, gender, and class.

*Whose little girl am I?*

■ Nina Simone, "Four Women"

## Betsey Brown: Native Daughter

I have already noted some of the many similarities between Shange's *Betsey Brown* and Lee's *Sarah Phillips*. Both novels track the formation of racial, gender, and class performances and identities of two bourgeois girls growing up on the eve of the civil rights movement of the 1960s. Both protagonists are observant, bookish, sensitive girls highly conscious of their individuality. Both novels relate a series of discrete incidents that prompt the girls to reflect on their own social positions as females in middle-class educated families. Both girls challenge the definitions by which their families and their societies seek to limit them. The narrator of *Betsey Brown*, however, uses the eponymous character to affirm the integrity of a black female identity that transcends class lines.

The Browns, like the Phillipses, seek to create a domestic sphere and a neighborhood that serves as a bastion against the racial cruelties of the larger world: "Jane and Greer knew about these things. They'd been chastened since birth by the scorn and violence the race had known. They'd been brought up on lynchings and riots, name-calling and 'No Colored Allowed.' The neighborhood had saved them, they thought. With the Negro-owned businesses, the hairdressers and the laundry, the schoolteachers and the shadows of the great trees, the neighborhood had sheltered them from what they knew was on the outside: the white people" (91–92). While Sarah saw her haven of a neighborhood as "slightly unreal," a "fantasy [that] . . . acted as a barrier against the predictable cruelty of the world" (39), one that harbored its own fragility and dangers, the Browns see their spacious house and self-contained neighborhood not only as a defensive shelter but also a site from which to launch an offense: "Weren't many places where the likes of them could live in St. Louis and know the nooks and covies of fifteen- and twenty-room houses. Weren't many places where the likes could be themselves and raise their children to own the world, which was the plan never spoken" (31).

The role of the black bourgeoisie in this text conforms closely to that which dominated bourgeois writing before publication of Frazier's *Black Bourgeoisie*: the professional classes are not exceptions to the general conditions of black American life but representative of the possibilities and potential of black people as a group. While Sarah's family lives in a black suburb far from the inner-city community her father's church serves, Betsey's family lives within the city. At the opening of the novel Betsey is "only vaguely aware of" the "poverty, meanness, and shootings" that rankle the city (14), but the poor crime-ridden portion of the black neighborhood is only a few blocks from the mansions of the judges, doctors, prizefighters, and lawyers.

Sarah has always attended integrated schools; Betsey goes to an all-black school that draws its students from all classes until the law allows her to attend integrated schools. While Sarah grows up with the impression that Franklin Place is disconnected geographically and psychically from larger communities of black people, Betsey sees her connection to "the black masses" through her parents' daily lives. Her family holds its bourgeois position because her parents are professionals who serve a segregated community: Dr. Brown depends upon his work at the public health clinic to support his private practice; Jane, Betsey's mother, is a psychiatric social worker who in the morning dresses "as if she were going shopping at Saks" but earns her living "at the segregated public hospital with the mad niggahs" (26). Betsey's insular world does not float, as Sarah's does, in some miniature space of its own between the affluent white and the larger, poorer black worlds: "The nice thing bout segregation was the colored could be all together, where the air and the blossoms were their own, as clear as it was impossible for white folks to put a veil over the sun" (43).

Betsey's narrative is, like Sarah's, structured around racial and sexual moments of insight. In an incident analogous to Sarah's encounters with the Gypsies, Betsey sees her family's status through lower-status white people's eyes when two white police officers escort her brothers home after they have allegedly been caught trespassing. The officers are impressed by the Browns' elegant home, and Betsey overhears them saying that the Browns "'aren't them common types of colored.'" The police officers make it clear that in deference to the Browns' class status and their unfamiliarity with St. Louis mores, the officers will allow this incident to end with only a warning; however, if there is a "next time," the Brown boys will be treated like any other black criminals: "'Well, on accounta you special, in a sense, we are gointa let the boys by this time, but only once'" (45). Betsey sees that in the police officers' eyes, the distinction between playful, well-brought-up boys and juvenile delinquents is erased by race. Her family may be "special kind of nigras" but they are still "nigras." She understands that the young uneducated police believe themselves superior to her well-dressed, well-spoken mother just because they are white.

The meaninglessness of class distinctions in the black community is also brought home to Betsey in her relationships with other black people. "Servant problems" also function in this novel as a discourse of class and race; the Browns have trouble keeping much-needed household help. The Browns hire a newly arrived southern woman, Bernice, despite their distrust of her as a "body with no upbringing." The children regard Bernice with contempt because she's ugly and "doesn't know how to talk." Betsey rejects the older woman's attempts to forge an alliance with her, and by not taking responsibility for the chaos she herself has caused, Betsey makes her parents fire Bernice. Proud of this display of power, Betsey brags about this adventure to her friend Veejay, the daughter of a maid, who explodes with anger:

> "Y'all act just like white people, always trying to make things hard on the colored. Lying on them and making a mess of things. Thinking it's so funny. I don't even know if I want to be your friend. That could have been my mama lost her job on accounta you. . . ." Veejay turned to go anywhere away from Betsey. She'd known that Betsey was from over there where the rich colored lived, but she liked her anyway. Till now, that is. Now Betsey was the same as anybody who made fun of her mother doing daywork and looking after white children while her own waited anxiously at the door for her to come home. (67)

Her conscience stung, Betsey makes a vow to herself "to do her best not to hurt or embarrass another Negro as long as she lived" (70).

In *Sarah Phillips* Sarah learns that the notion that race can transcend class divisions is illusory: a cab driver whose conversation convinces the eight-year-old Sarah of the magical unifying force of the civil rights movement ends up cheating her father when he hands him the wrong change for the ride. In Betsey's world, as several incidents demonstrate, as long as there is white racism, class distinctions that work to divide black people from each other are irrelevant in the face of structural and social racism.

Gender, like race, transcends class in *Betsey Brown*. The black bourgeois woman has been haunted by the idea of the lady. Partly in response to the image of the wanton black woman, portrayals of black middle-class women in American literature often go to the opposite extreme. Sarah, despite her self-declared persona as a bohemian adventurer, adopts the stereotypical role of a sexual exotic. Betsey's mother, Jane, although a sexually vibrant woman, is too trapped by her heritage of bourgeois prudery to be a useful role model or even a source of information about sexuality for her daughter. Betsey must turn to other women for images of sexual possibilities: two black women and a white girl from the lower classes.

Although Susan Linda comes from a racist family whom the Browns describe as "white trash," she is included in Betsey's circle of preadolescent black girlfriends because Susan Linda shares their questions, fears, and fantasies about sex. This relationship shows the power of gender to cross class and racial borders. Regina, a teenager from an indigent family who is hired to help Mrs. Brown around the house, provides Betsey with her first glimpse of heterosexual romantic performance as she witnesses Regina's passionate encounters with Roscoe, a young man who has promised to give Regina the fantasy of marriage, home, and family. However, after Regina gets pregnant, is abandoned by her lover, and fired, Betsey discovers Regina working as a prostitute at an establishment that is a beauty parlor by day and bordello by night. This encounter leads Betsey to another of her epiphanies; she realizes that all black people are connected in ways significant enough to undermine the illusion of class distinctions:

> There were different kinds of Negroes. She bet money some of these Negroes wouldn't give a stone's throw if something happened to Roscoe, they didn't care what would happen to Regina's baby. "Niggahs" they'd say. . . . Yet they couldn't go anywhere else to have their hair done but a bordello. . . . There was a difference between being a little girl and being a woman. She knew now. She'd never see Regina again, but they'd never be separate, either. Women who can see over the other side are never far from each other. (138–39)

In this novel the operative class distinction in the black community is not between those who "act white" and those who do not, but those who, because of their educational and economic achievements, refuse to acknowledge that the plight of the black lower classes is a less varnished version of their own reality in American society. Betsey observes that the only difference is that the toiling and criminal classes do not have the means to buy a little bit of protection from white racism. Even so, the wives of judges and doctors in this last generation of the old bourgeoisie will have to have their hair done in bordellos and live a few blocks from their maids, the gamblers, and the prostitutes.

The third woman to provide Betsey with a model of black woman-hood is Carrie, another of the Browns' domestic helpers. Carrie serves as an alternative maternal figure to Jane. Whereas Jane is a classic bourgeois "high yellow" (fair skinned, light haired, and fine featured), Carrie is dark, wild haired, and large. While Jane's response to her daughters' questions is, "'Just keep those panties up, you hear?'" (197), Carrie's lesson is direct, moral, and practical:

> "Now I want you to know that you don't need to sit like a statue if some boy takes a whistle at ya. You just smile and go on. There's no trouble worse than fear. You ain't 'sposed to be afraid of men and young boys, but what young beau wants to hear you saying, 'My mama said you only after one thing and my knees are locked, so there.' . . . A kiss or two can undo all that mama talking. Go ahead and enjoy bein a girl, but be careful . . . just hold off from those no-good niggers with the devil in they eyes. Now that's my advice." (196)

Although Carrie is an uneducated, domestically employed, low-status woman, the narrator portrays her as a powerful and appropriate role model for the educated, ambitious, bourgeois Betsey. Carrie is sexual but possesses agency and perspective on her own sexuality; she has a firm moral sense but is pragmatic while giving just due to emotion.

In fact, the end of the novel finds Betsey performing Carrie's role in the house, once Carrie has been jailed and, of course, fired from the Brown household. Betsey is the only family member who mourns Carrie's absence. Betsey compensates for her loss by appropriating Carrie's identity: "Betsey never mentioned her feelings to her mama cause then Jane would just re-mind her that she always picked the most niggerish people in the world to make her friends. . . . So Betsey didn't say anything. Betsey just took Carrie's place in the house. Did everything like she would have done except she did use the regular bathrooms" (207). The novel closes with a romantic view of the successful integration of a bourgeois girl's intelligence and sensibility with a black folk woman's identity. Class distinctions melt away in the heat of racial and gender bonding.

*What do they call me?*

■ Nina Simone, "Four Women"

## Conclusion: Back to the Future?

Shange's and Lee's novels were widely reviewed. Critical and popular reaction to Lee was racially polarized. White reviewers either read her novel, as a *Washington Post* reviewer did, as "a short course on the life of the black middle class" or focused on how little Sarah's life seemed affected by her race, as a *Boston Review* critic said.[5] Patricia Vigderman marveled that so many details of Sarah's childhood were similar to her own "white and middle class" experiences and wrote that Lee's novel "is a very gracefully written book about black identity that makes what Sarah and I share seem more important than what we don't."[6] Black readers and critics misread the novel in another way. They tended to conflate the narrator with the author and criticized what they saw as Sarah's (and Lee's) disavowal of her blackness, although the novel is framed by Sarah's realization that she cannot escape her black bourgeois past. Mary Helen Washington, writing in the *Women's Review of Books*, saw in *Sarah Phillips* a dangerous literary harbinger and warned that "in these conservative times there are fewer and fewer novels which deal with racism or poverty, and a novel by a black writer which exalts class privilege and ignores racism is bound to find wide acceptance."[7]

Shange's *Betsey Brown*, on the other hand, became a best-seller and then a less-successful musical and revival. Reviewers noted "the vibrant and gutsy world" of the novel, and where Sarah's attempts to "reinvent herself" outside her family's history were seen as a failure, readers noted Betsey's ability "to redefine herself in her own context, outside the expectations of the white or 'colored' world and beyond the prescriptions of traditional, female roles of the docile daughter and dutiful wife."[8] Nancy Willard praised the novel in the *New York Times* as "a healing book" that, despite its engagement with topical issues of racial strife, is celebratory: "Does this book have some kind of ax to grind? Thank heaven, no, although Miss Shange's characters confront plenty of problems."[9]

Perhaps ironically, Shange's novel epitomizes a kind of "rearguard" sensibility that is quite problematic. First, the narrative is predicated upon ideas of racial and sexual authenticity that are never questioned or unpacked. The text relies on clichéd characterizations of poor black folk culture (highly sexualized, criminal, and familially unstable), and the text roots "real" black identity in that culture. Second, it employs stereotypes that have been used since the nineteenth century, most crucially that of the dark, sexually expressive, religious black folk woman who serves as a font of wisdom for her upper-class charges. On the other hand, black bourgeois women are fair skinned, sexually repressed, and conflicted. Reviews of the musical adaptation note that Betsey's father, depicted as a vibrant apostle of racial pride in the novel, becomes a pontificating one-dimensional tyrant on stage. *Betsey Brown* relies on familiar clichés and facile optimism as its response to the black bourgeois dilemma.

The narrator's ambivalence and the narrative's ambiguity make *Sarah Phillips* a more difficult read, despite its luminous prose. This book bravely, if not flawlessly, engages the paradoxes of black bourgeois identity and performance in a world of mixed messages about the nature, meaning, and function of blackness and class in fin-de-siècle America. At the close of Lee's novel, Sarah is in free fall, in a state of transition and openness very different from Betsey's commitment to a clear black identity and liberation project: "Exhausted as I was, I had a brief new impression: that the world was a place full of kids in transit. . . . I was one of them, and although I didn't know what direction I was heading in, and only had a faint idea yet of what I was leaving behind, the sense of being in motion was a thrill that made up for a lot. I sat and squeezed my eyes tighter and hoped that it would turn out to be enough for me" (Lee 117). Is this thrill freedom? And if it is, is it enough for a satisfying adult life? The text does not presume to give us an answer. As both novels are *kunstleromans* as well as bildungsromans, they also present two differing views of the role of the black bourgeois writer. Shange's protagonist is a part of her community, and her educational privileges and social opportunities allow her to speak for those who do not have the tools and the access to large and public forums to tell their own stories. The reader knows that Betsey, "a woman who can see over the other side," is going to become an artist who gives voices to the women of the beauty parlors, bordellos, prisons, and kitchens. Sarah, on the other hand, is aware of the problems and paradoxes of representation—not only of "her people" but of a unified coherent self. The reader of *Sarah Phillips* is left with the suspicion that Sarah's figuring out her relationship to her past and her family's history is going to be a rough, painful, and lifelong work.

The little burst of black bourgeois women's writing at the end of the twentieth century had a variety of causes. Certainly the legacy of second-wave feminism and publishers' interest in the new frontier of feminist writing created an arena for black bourgeois women to tell their own stories in fiction and memoir. I also believe that these texts were part of a response to questions about the gains and losses of the civil rights movement of the 1960s; they are part of larger conversations in print and other media about the value of the ideal of integration. The flight of the black middle class from traditionally segregated neighborhoods and what seemed to be a widening gap between the lives and aspirations of the black middle class, the working class, and the so-called underclass inspired new reflections on the relationship between race and class in African American communities and on the notion of racial identity and allegiance.

## NOTES

1. Ntozake Shange, *Betsey Brown* (New York: St. Martin's, 1985); Andrea Lee, *Sarah Phillips* (New York: Random House, 1984).
2. On "post-black" politics see, for example, Charles M. Blow, "Black in the Age of Obama," *New York Times*, December 4, 2009.
3. Laurence Hogue, "The Limits of Modernity: Andrea Lee's *Sarah Phillips*." *MELUS* 19, no. 4 (1994): 75.
4. Years later Andrea Lee wrote about her return visit to the real-life school that provided the model for Prescott in the novel, as she enrolled her own daughter there.
5. Jonathan Penner, "Mixing Memory and Desire," review of *Betsey Brown*, *Washington Post*, November 4, 1984.

6. Patricia Vigderman, review of *Sarah Phillips, Boston Review,* February 1985, 23.

7. Mary Helen Washington, "Young, Gifted and Black," review of *Sarah Phillips, Women's Review of Books* 2, no. 6 (1985): 4.

8. Andrea Stretton, "Joy and Courage Win over Despair," review of *Betsey Brown, Saturday Review,* October 4, 1986; Claudia Tate, "Growing Up 'Colored,'" review of *Betsey Brown, Washington Post,* June 17, 1985, D9.

9. Nancy Willard, "Life Abounding in St. Louis," review of *Betsey Brown, New York Times,* May 12.

# Rosalind

## Prologue

*Time? Tell them it is early winter in the 1970s.*

*Setting? A small black storefront hair salon.*
*Narrator? She sits.*
*Wears a plain top,*
*wide-leg jeans.*
*Platform sneakers. Her hair: undone.*

*Tell them: to hear thunder*
*then gentle rain.*

The original prose rendition of "Rosalind" appears in the July 2010 issue of *Triquarterly Online*, an online journal of writing, art, and cultural inquiry sponsored by Northwestern University, www.triquarterly.org.

# 1: Shadow

*Window panes crystalize and frost. Lights wink and glow bright.*
*Darkness blurs the world outside the place owned by*
*my grown cousin Claude.*

*He gestures for me to hop in his chair,*
*he ties an apron around my neck.*
*He asks after my great aunt who raised me.*
*"How's my auntie?"*
*I say, "Ma Dear is fine."*
*I feel him search my hair for new growth.*

*He turns me to the mirror where I see*
*rain become snow beyond the street entrance.*

*Then a human shadow blocks the door.*
*It wiggles the knob. Hesitates. Presses against the door glass.*
*But the door doesn't budge. The pressing persists, then*
*finally the door gives way.*

*Who is this overgrown girl?*
*Her sopping head and broad wet shoulders*
*push through.*
*She has commonly round hips.*
*She has the big bare brown legs*
*with knee scars deep and dark.*

*Then*
*I realize that the face under the scarf*
*is one I do not want to see,*
*nor do I want her to see me.*

## 2: She Is Rosalind

*Two days before she threatened to cut my friend LaNell.*
*Why I got in it? I don't know. Ain't that stupid?*
*We knocked her down to the muddy ground*
*before all her little friends, and there were these men*
*standing and watching while warming their hands over a flaming barrel.*
*And there were other grown folks looking out of the windows*
*who say nothing,*
*don't move a damn muscle.*

*So we took Rosalind's knife, ran, and I hid it away.*
*And it has been this way for the past two days.*
*Waiting for Rosalind to find me*
*and flat-out kick my ass.*

*I whisper to Claude,*
*"That girl that just came in. Do you do her hair?"*
*"Oh no. No way. Not me," he answers.*
*"That is one of Mimi's clients."*
*Mimi rents the other booth*
*in Claude's salon.*

## 3: Make-over Paradise

*Rosalind*
*sits in the same chair where I waited.*
*Leafs through the same magazine.*
*She angles her head like me.*
*She fingers each glamored page like me.*
*And it scares me and angers me.*
*Like me she is entranced,*
*Her mind gone to the makeover paradise*
*that promises contentment.*

*What lengths we go through to be acceptable in another's sight—*
*What bullshit we bear to please the world*
*—but I suspect Rosalind puts up with much more than I do.*

*She unpicks the knotted scarf around her neck.*
*Each fingernail spotted with ruby nail polish*

*twists the fabric into a hard, tight ball.*
*This day she wears a dull white T-shirt*
*with a neckline plunge weighted*
*by her mature breasts.*

*Rosalind raises her deep-set eyes.*
*One arm obscures her waist*
*while the other pulls the magazine pages*
*closer to her face.*

## 4: Payment Due

*I was crazy to pick a fight with this girl.*
*She had done nothing to me. (For awhile at least.)*
*Because when I was new, she says I got payment due*
*to her,*
*and I say I ain't got nothing. I do not pay nor do I play,*
*even though I was scared shitless.*

*This is what I told LaNell:*
*We must act on her threats. We cannot wait.*

## 5: Secrets

*At any moment I will be discovered.*

*I was not raised for all the wild stuff that I do.*
*Claude, Ma Dear, and all her friends—*
*and all the friends she chooses for me—*
*would die.*
*I privilege them with only half of myself.*
*The secrets of my wholeness*
*are completely my own.*

*They may already know—*

*So every moment I go unnoticed*
*by them and Rosalind is a reprieve.*

*I don't know how long*
*my luck will last.*

# 6: Magic Fire

*Mimi bursts through the door and flutters like a wet bird.*
*I love the way she whirls around the salon and can snatch*
*three-dollar tips with the speed of a rattlesnake.*
*She tells us, "All that rain is turning to snow."*

*Now in the mirror I resemble Ma Dear.*
*White chemical suds make my hair stand in a great pyramid*
*while the temperature on my scalp rises.*

*Then Claude rinses away the magic fire,*
*and my new straight, silky strands lie easy on my brow and neck.*
*My head feels moist and cool.*

*I look like the Indian girl Ma Dear always wanted.*
*Being old school, she believes a woman's hair is her glory, provided it is lustrous,*
*long, and*

*straight. Easy to comb.*
*And thank God black women have found a way.*

# 7: Eyes

*I discover when I glance at the mirror*
*not to look into it—but just to look at it.*

*Rosalind stares at me.*

*Her eyes leap into my line of vision, and I drink my breath.*
*Claude asks me some dumb questions about school.*
*I hear. I answer*

*but my eyes never leave Rosalind's.*

*Mimi ties an apron around Rosalind's neck.*
*She says to her, "I won't have any shit out of you*
*today." As she slathers the girl's head white.*

# 8: Bitch

*Rosalind's eyes break their hold on mine.*

*I can beat her to the door and get home before Mimi is finished with her.*
*I can crawl out the back window while Claude has a smoke, Mimi takes a phone*
*call, and Rosalind waits alone.*

*But my escape is boarded up with thick plywood and*
*brand new burglar bars. Nothing open but a wedge of light*
*and draft from a corner windowpane.*
*I sit on the toilet seat with foot propped against the backroom door.*

*I close the hook just as Rosalind pushes and spills through the door crack,*
*blows spit and fire on my face: "BITCH! Where's*
*the knife? Where's my muthfuckin knife?"*

*Her head looks like it floats on its own.*
*Her eyes are orange with thin, patchy eyebrows.*
*Sulfur from her dribbling white relaxer reeks;*
*I want out of the nasty little trap I'm in.*
*I hold my breath and push back with all my might,*
*but I am no match against a force that snaps the*
*hook off the door.*

# 9: Mimi

*"Rosalind! What the hell is the matter with you?!?"*
*I hear Mimi's approach and the front entrance door*
*slam. Rosalind says to her, "Uh, I thought she was in trouble!"*
*I don't contradict her and stay hidden behind the door.*

*Mimi pushes Rosalind back to peek at me through the cracked door.*
*She must think I am really using the toilet. And when she asks,*
*I tell her that I am all right, though I feel she doubts me.*
*She hustles Rosalind to the shampoo station.*
*I listen to Mimi through the door with the broken latch.*

*"Why is it every time you come here there's some mess?*
*I'm through with y'all. Tell your mama don't send you over here*
*no more."*

*"My MAMA did not send me over here," says Rosalind.*

## 10: Protection

*I must get out before she does.*
*I leave the backroom, and Claude waits by his chair with a*
*blow dryer. Unfortunately, Mimi sets Rosalind's hair with amazing speed.*
*While Claude waits for his curlers to heat,*
*Mimi tells Rosalind to keep the curlers,*
*collects her fee, and gives her a plastic cap*
*to protect her hair outside.*

*As Rosalind leaves, Claude bends my hair into*
*Sunday school shape, and I worry.*

*Rosalind is outside in the dark waiting for me.*

*Then Claude says, "I think you should sit tight*
*and let me drive you home." Then a client comes in*
*and another and another until I can't take the wait any more.*
*"I'm going outside for some fresh air," I say.*

*He hands me a plastic cap and warns me not to work up a sweat*
*and endanger my hairstyle before Ma Dear's inspection. I pull it on my head, and*
*I am out of the door looking at freshly powdered snow on the sidewalk.*
*I inhale the soft cold air.*
*I want to buy barbeque potato chips and orange pop down the block.*

## 11: Trophy

*I want to remember*
*the afternoon with LaNell after the fight. How we shook*
*with relief before I said, "She's coming after us again."*
*I flicked open the blade of the cherished weapon*
*the way I had seen it done. It clicked and unraveled*

*with a snap. They called it a butterfly. LaNell asked me,*
*"What are you going to do with it?"*
*"I am keeping this, honey. This my trophy. Where*
*I'll keep it? That's my secret."*
*"How can you be so sure?" she said.*
*"Because I can," I said.*

## 12: No Ho

*As I slip on the snow,*
*the other people on the street laugh at me.*
*Among them, Rosalind stands nearby*
*enjoying a slight smile that empties*
*from her face as she moves closer.*

*Impulses say "run!" But I must hold still on the slick pavement.*
*She approaches with her hands in her jacket pockets.*
*I can move my cold fingers into mine, too.*
*We face each other, and we each wear cheap shower caps.*

*"You know I should kick your ass right now, but you*
*tell me where my knife is," she says.*
*"I ain't got it on me," I say.*
*"I ain't got time for this. What the hell are you doing,*
*trying to be so bad? You a fake. Why don't you be who you are?"*
*"What?"*
*"This is not your thing. You a square. You a house girl."*
*Which is true. Then I speak.*
*"So why do y'all have to fuck with people like me*
*and LaNell? We don't want to have nothing to do*
*with you!"*

*"Could be you get on my nerves, too. Being Miss Proper.*
*That's what gets me mad. I can't feel cool with y'all hanging around.*

It don't make no sense to me. You got any money?
See the knife ain't mine—it belong to this dude, and if I don't come up with the
knife, then I got to take care of it, you know what I sayin'?"
I say yes but she says, "Naw. I don't think
you know what I mean. You don't have no men
messin' with you, do you?"
I say nothing because
I am still virgin and living in my dreams.

"Just what I thought," She says. "This man
my mama got is all over me. He pays for my hair
sometime. I could ask him, but I'm tired of his shit.
He wants me to sing for him all the time.

I bet you know somebody that's got some money?
The guy that owns that shop is related to you, right?"
I don't answer but I say, I say, "I can get your knife back.
But you can't bother me
and LaNell no more."
"Then fuck you and LaNell," she says. I tell her the knife
is at my house, and as we start down the street Rosalind
whispers, "I ain't nobody's ho."

# 13: Butterfly

Why should Rosalind have to degrade
herself because of me? I have no use for
her butterfly other than to remind me
of my courage. Ma Dear calls it vanity.

So trembling from cold and relief
we reach the steps to my house,
I am not sure if Ma Dear wants me to invite
Rosalind inside because she claims to

*know all about the girl's family, and she*
*does not like them. So I ask Rosalind to wait outside.*

*Only the small lamp in the living room is on.*
*I see Ma Dear sitting in her chair by the phone.*
*I stomp the snow from my feet.*
*She calls my name.*
*I leave my shoes and enter the room.*

*When I face her,*
*I see the butterfly knife lying across*
*her lap opened. Its menacing blade is white*
*in the lamp's light.*

*Ma Dear's lips are tight. Her eyes are shadows.*
*She says, "Claude called me. He was worried."*

*I slip the shower cap from my head,*
*and lumps of frizzy matted hair*
*tumble out.*

*She points to the knife. "I'm not even*
*going to ask you what this is. I'm just*
*too tired. But you can believe on Jesus*
*that I will in the morning. Now go to bed."*

*How do I get word to Rosalind outside*
*waiting in the snow? As I face the entrance*
*to my room, Ma Dear says one more thing:*
*"If I catch you in that window, I'm gonna*
*beat your behind twice."*

*So I close my door. Put on my nightgown.*
*Sit on the edge of the bed. On my clock, I watch the hours*
*turn. The world outside grows colder, dribbles*

*and freezes on my window with the drab lace curtain*
*that overlooks the street. I fear touching it.*
*I don't want to see how Rosalind's footsteps*
*are obscured by new flowing snow.*

# Scenes from *Single Black Female*

n June 2006 my play *Single Black Female* opened off-Broadway at the Peter Jay Sharp Theatre, produced by the New Professional Theatre and directed by Colman Domingo.[1] The irreverent show, originally billed as a new comedy about sex, love, and shopping, depicts the frustrations faced by middle-class black women as they encounter bad dates, abrasive gynecologists, and insensitive relatives. Rendering the lives of SBF 1 and SBF 2 as they help each other survive the narrow odds of finding partnership in a unfriendly landscape gave me the opportunity to create characters who complain that "we did what we were suppose to do! We earned ourselves law degrees, PhD's, IRAs, and 401Ks. We bring all this to the table and Tiger Woods marries a nanny? We could have avoided all those student loans if that's all men want."[2] Throughout the show the duo humorously express the ambivalence, hope, and desires of many single middle-class African American women in the post–civil rights era.

Written in response to the material I unearthed while researching representations of middle-class African American women when I was a doctoral student at Stanford University, *Single Black Female* became my dissertation's alter ego. After spending the day in the library, I would spend my evening giving voice to those silenced and invisible in the media. The two-woman show about unmarried African American urban professionals was my reaction to what I considered the abundance of unsophisticated and unimaginative depictions of blacks in contemporary popular culture. I hungered for adequate representations of middle-class black women navigating the quandaries of race, gender, and sexuality that preoccupied me and the other women I knew and respected. Most renderings fail to adequately reflect the lives of black women. Where were the witty, quirky, and clever African American characters? For that matter, where were the representations of black women suffering existential angst? Where were the stories of middle-class women who neither focus on nor completely ignore racial issues? The women I know are smarter, more sophisticated, and lead more complicated lives than what popular culture conveys. Also, while most middle-class women understand their unique place within African American culture, many in the current generation no longer want to accept old expectations about proper behavior. *Single Black Female* is my attempt to represent the difficulties and joys of navigating the madness of dating in the new millennium.

## Characters

**SBF 1:** A thirty-eight-year-old African American woman. A literature professor with dreadlocks and a bookish androgynous style accented with "Afrocentric" accessories. She wears Dansko clogs and eccentric eyeglasses.

**SBF 2:** A thirty-five-year-old African American woman. An attorney. SBF 1's best friend, confidant, and alter ego. Sports a flowing perm and wears sexy business suits.

## Setting

The present. A comfortable yet stylish brownstone in Harlem, New York. The main room is furnished with wooden chairs, a walk-in closet, sofa, television, stereo, and a dining room table. The stage also has various props (books, clothing, hats, shoes, etc.) to help the actors create each vignette/character. The titles of each scene are projected overhead on the window shade. Musical selections by female musicians and singers, a video monitor, voice-over audio, and slides provide an electronic component that supports a postmodern, fast-paced, surreal environment.

# Prologue

**SBF 1.** We are often asked what SBF stands for. Those three letters represent many things.

**SBF 2.** Sistas, black and free.

**SBF 1.** Sincere blissful friend.

**SBF 2.** Soulful bad freaks.

**SBF 1.** Staying black forever.

**SBF 2.** Saucy, bold, and fierce.

**SBF 1.** Sad blue funk.

**SBF 2.** Sweet bangin' fuck.

**SBF 1 & SBF 2.** *(in unison)* We be

Us be

Single

Black

Female

**SBF 1.** Diva.

**SBF 2.** Bitch.

**SBF 1.** Goddess.

**SBF 2.** And nobody wants to hear us. *(beat)* You undoubtedly heard of the black male crisis—well, there is also a very serious crisis for the black woman.

**SBF 1.** *(PowerPoint lecture)* The National Center for Health Statistics informs us that "the marriage rate for white women is 76 percent higher than the rate for black women."

**SBF 2.** Teach!

**SBF 1.** According to the U.S. Census, 41.9 percent of black women in America have NEVER been married.

**SBF 2.** Damn!

**SBF 1.** And 57 percent of black children reside in single-parent homes.

**SBF 2.** Now what if a sista has a college degree or two—

**SBF 1.** Or three? She's more likely to be hit by a meteor than find a husband!

**SBF 2.** What happens to the black family if we don't find love? What will happen to the African American legacy?

**SBF 1.** Tonight, let us introduce you to the world of the single black female.

**SBF 2.** Wait! This ain't *Sex in the Inner City*! Let's be more specific: Welcome to the lives of single middle-class black women.

**SBF 1.** Remember Ellison's *Invisible Man*? Well, we are the invisible women. Black professional intellectual leftists with conservative fiscal ideologies—

**SBF 2.** Except for a sale at Barney's!

**SBF 1.** We're the New Negro African American Black Colored Girls who only *consider* therapy. And even though nobody wants to hear us—we are tired of being ignored! We will no longer be QUIET!

**SBF 2.** You're anything but quiet. Sullen, or remote when angry—but never . . . quiet!

**SBF 1.** You're right about that.

**SBF 2.** Still, nobody wants to see us, let alone really think about us.

**SBF 1.** But it's about time we get some accurate press.

**SBF 2.** We must thank Supreme Court Justice Clarence Thomas for putting us on the map.

**SBF 1.** Right, before his dreadful Senate confirmation hearing, nobody thought we existed.

**SBF 2.** We STILL believe you, Anita!

**SBF 1.** And now we have sweet little Condi Rice to thank for making us popular the world over.

**SBF 2.** Isn't she single, too? Maybe if the child could get her hair right!!!

**SBF 1.** Don't talk about Condi now! That might prove a little too dangerous.

**SBF 2.** True.

**SBF 1.** People, before Ms. Oprah Winfrey became a media icon, the image of black womanhood was a bit stale and not very complex.

**SBF 2.** Yes, who can forget the long reign of Aunt Jemima, Sapphire, and Jezebel?

**SBF 1.** Now, we concede there were a few bright moments, especially during the late twentieth century. The seventies gave us *Julia*—thank God for Lady Diahann Carroll. The eighties gave us attorney Claire Huxtable, a Cosby creation. But the nineties gave us—

**SBF 2.** The supreme ghetto ringmaster, Jerry Springer!

**SBF 1 & SBF 2.** *(Ad-lib typical talk-show guest fight scene, complete with hysterical dialogue.)*

**SBF 2.** We still haven't recovered from those sistas. And we cannot neglect those hoochies shaking their rumps on BET. *(SBF 2 does booty shake.)*

**SBF 1.** Why would anyone go on those shows? Dance in those videos? I can't understand it.

**SBF 2.** Now, we do get some occasional exposure to remind us that black middle-class women are part of the American dream.

**SBF 1.** But, even in the twenty-first century the networks still won't cast a black woman in the role of the Bachelorette! And, no, "I Love NY" does not count!

**SBF 2.** That's because they want us to think a man wouldn't want us even if we come with a million bucks! All we can get is *Flavor of Love*! Flavor Flav! That's some bullshit! No, we're not in style.

**SBF 1.** And we are not all the same, but we're looking for the same thing. To put it simply? Love. Unfortunately, our generation is more single than double. This is her story and mine . . . and hers and hers and hers. *(Pause)* And maybe his, too. Our story.

**SBF 2.** Well, at least what we are willing to share tonight.

**SBF 1 & SBF 2.** *(In unison)* Come on in.

# Scene 1: Identity

**SBF 1.** There are obvious signs if you get beyond the door.

**SBF 2.** Once invited inside her cozy home, it's easy to detect.

**SBF 1.** You spot the kitchen and dining ware.

**SBF 2.** On her shelves sit numerous Pottery Barn ceramic bowls and serving platters.

**SBF 1.** Don't forget the stemware—

**SBF 2.** The finest liqueurs and drinking glasses for every occasion!

**SBF 1.** Margarita glasses hand-blown from Mexico and filled with Herradura tequila.

**SBF 2.** And dipped with coarse sea salt.

**SBF 1.** Champagne flutes.

**SBF 2.** Only the French do bubbly, right?

**SBF 1.** Thanks to hip-hop, Cristal has gone so ghetto!

**SBF 2.** You are wrong for that. Highball glasses for a few shots of Glenfiddich single malt after a long day in court.

**SBF 1.** Four martini glasses with pitcher.

**SBF 2.** Dry, very dry.

**SBF 1.** Wait! Don't forget those four jelly jars for the ethnic touch!
(*Both laugh.*)

**SBF 2.** Damn! We sound like alcoholics.

**SBF 1.** An SBF typically owns an impressive collection of cookbooks.

**SBF 2.** As well as a healthy stack of takeout menus for those nights she doesn't cook.

**SBF 1.** Like six out of seven nights? Please. Who has the time? I order Chinese or Thai takeout for those evenings in front of the HDTV. And for those down-home nights? (*Southern blues music starts to play.*)

**SBF 2.** Amy Ruth's, baby! Soul Fixins'! AMEN!!!

**SBF 1.** For dessert? Red velvet cake!

**SBF 2.** Sock it to me!

**SBF 1.** SBFs also keep current subscriptions to *Essence*, the *Nation, Metropolitan Home,* and *Vibe*—

**SBF 2.** You read *Vibe*?

**SBF 1.** Oh, yes, I must keep up with my students. Now, for outerwear.

**SBF 2.** Clothing depends on whether she's an artsy boho—

**SBF 1.** Or a classy hoho?

**SBF 2.** Hey! Hey now! Watch it.

**SBF 1.** She's always well draped and politically—

**SBF 2.** And culturally—

**SBF 1.** Sophisticated. In the summer you'll find her at the Studio Museum of Harlem sporting flawless white linen.

**SBF 2.** She's got to have her kente cloth bumpin' in February for Negro History Month.

**SBF 1.** Must be head to toe in deep dark chocolate for that night on the town. You know *Vogue* says that chocolate is the new black. Doesn't anybody realize that black folks have been chocolate for years?

**SBF 2.** Talk, girl. By the time an SBF reaches about thirty years old, she's found her style—now she's just trying to find somebody to like her style.

**SBF 1.** Where to meet us?

**SBF 2.** *(SBF 1 & SBF 2 start to fan themselves with local funeral home fans and mime greeting other parishioners.)* At Abyssinian Baptist Church.

**SBF 1.** Or at Brooklyn Tabernacle's 11 a.m. service. Amen!
*(Sound of gospel music. SBF 1 & 2 start to dance around like they caught the Holy Ghost.)*

**SBF 2.** Praise Jesus! Glory! Glory!

**SBF 1.** Wait! Who has all day to spend in church? It's the twenty-first century! This is not the South, you know. We are in NEW YORK CITY!

**SBF 2.** You can also find us at the bank—

**SBF 1.** Telling the manager to go to hell.

**SBF 2.** Or at the video store. You can usually find several single black women deep in the line at Blockbuster on Friday and Saturday nights.

**SBF 1.** Lines? Please, I got Netflix! Yes, you can also find us at the stylist all day, any day.

**SBF 2.** No more beauty shop for me! A facial every two weeks, manicure and pedicure once a week, and a full body spa at least once a month. It's the role of the black middle class to integrate.

**SBF 1.** The spas?

**SBF 2.** Yes, the revolution, one massage at a time. Each of us has a role. I'm doing my part. I love the look in the eyes of those old Upper East Side white society matrons when they see my naked black ass sauntering toward the sauna.

**SBF 1.** Somehow I don't believe that's what Martin, Malcolm, or Huey and Bobby had in mind.

**SBF 2.** *(Quietly)* Don't judge, I'm just doing what I think is right. You know what Audre Lorde taught us: the personal is political! After all, we are all women who come from fine stock. Our mothers and grandmothers were strong black matriarchs.

**SBF 1.** Whom we've learned to forgive for not being stronger. Not to mention forgiving Daddy.

**SBF 2.** Hooray for therapy!

**SBF 1.** We are three paychecks away from being on welfare and two art openings away from being culturally insignificant.

**SBF 2.** We all have a constant preoccupation with our *bee*hinds and *hair*lines.

**SBF 1.** We are mirrors for each other. *(beat)* A typical SBF carries—

**SBF 2.** In her Marc Jacobs purse—

**SBF 1.** Or her Coach briefcase, a healthy supply of that Mango body butter.

**SBF 2.** Don't wanna sport ashy elbows.

**SBF 1.** She needs stylish business cards and a trusty iPhone.

**SBF 2.** Don't forget the one thing she cannot leave home without—American Express! Platinum. In case of depression, crack open wallet and spend, spend, spend!

**SBF 1.** In her closet an SBF can never have too many—

**SBF 2.** Seven jeans or St. John suits.

**SBF 1.** During her lifetime an SBF can never have too many—

**SBF 2.** Dates—

**SBF 1.** Stocks—

**SBF 2.** Season tickets for the symphony—

**SBF 1.** And flowers.

**SBF 2.** Don't forget the condoms. These days it's BYO!

**SBF 1.** But an SBF better be careful if she has—

**SBF 2.** Too much weight. Too many wrinkles. Too much debt.

**SBF 1.** Or too much unresolved anger? Relax. Breathe, breathe, breathe.

**SBF 2.** Thank you, girl. After all, being single is a middle-class black thang! You need to understand.

**SBF 1.** Why? Do you think looking for an appropriate partner is only a black middle-class woman's obsession? Why worry about what a person does for a living so long as they give you good lovin'?

**SBF 2.** Class makes us different. I can't really explain. You try.

**SBF 1.** Explain difference? Difference as defined by Derrida or Henry Louis Gates Jr.?

**SBF 2.** Here we go! I don't want to deal with Gates, what do you think this is, the *New Yorker*? Are we on *Charlie Rose*? Turn the channel! This is our subconscious, damn it!

**SBF 1.** Okay, you pick the theorist.

**SBF 2.** Let me tell you like my mother would. There is something wrong, folks, when both Mike Tyson and Evander Holyfield are able to marry black women who have MD's! These women are medical doctors, for God's sake!

As for me? I can't do the "he's a plumber, why can't you love him?" thing. I tried it several times. Don't call me stuck up, but, sorry, my panties get moist when I weave my basket through the aisles of Whole Foods, picking up organic cranberries and shiitake mushroom soup.

**SBF 1.** In the morning she brews a South American blend of coffee from Dean and DeLucca. Her last man? Bro went to heaven at the local 7-Eleven.

**SBF 2.** He grabbed a fast cup of joe from McDonald's with his Egg McMuffin. I wind down in the evening with a glass of pinot blanc and—

**SBF 1.** Didn't he think pinot blanc is a light-skinned Filipino?

**SBF 2.** The last one I dated woke up every morning to Three 6 Mafia's "You Know It's Hard out Here for a Pimp."

**SBF 1.** Girl here likes the hopeful nuances of Rachmaninoff's Prelude No. 21 in B Minor. As for cuisine? I recall that boyfriend wrapped his lips around a fried chicken wang and could not let go!

**SBF 2.** I like turkey breast sliced thin on rye with a whisper of Dijon mustard.

**SBF 1.** She has to have her *Wall Street Journal* every morning. He reads the back of the cereal box!

**SBF 2.** And his idea of "must see TV"?

**SBF 1.** *Cops*!

**SBF 2.** My favorite show of all time? *The Sopranos.*

**SBF 1.** That was not TV, that was HBO!

**SBF 2.** My dream dinner is scallops and fettuccine in a white wine sauce with garlic and butter. His dream? Black-eyed peas, corn bread, and greens.

**SBF 1.** Hold up! Wait! Wasn't that you at the family reunion chowing down on some pig's feet doused in hot sauce? We ain't got that much class or that much education. What about our people? Our community? Maybe that's why we're alone.

SBF 1 & SBF 2 turn and look at a slide show of various black "family" photographs. The photos reflect diverse families: big and small, urban and suburban, gay, middle class, and working class. Intermingled should be pictures of single women ending with a rapid succession of single women's photos until they are the last image. Lights fade down.

## NOTES

1. See Anita Gates, "Brainy Women, Still Looking for Love," *New York Times,* June 20, 2006, E4. Reviews of other productions of *Single Black Female* appeared in *Variety,* the *Los Angeles Times, LA Weekly,* and the *San Francisco Examiner.*

2. Lisa Thompson, *Single Black Female* (1998), unpublished manuscript, 73.

3

# Performing Media

# Of Afropunks and Other Anarchic Signifiers of Contrary Negritude

L
ike other emblems and aspirants of civilization, the black bourgeoisie has produced a unique set of discontents, malcontents, miscreants, and class traitors. In the 1940s and 1950s some escaped from their class obligations by becoming beboppers and beatniks; in the 1960s a rebellious new generation eschewed Cadillac dealerships and croquet to become Freedom Riders, Black Panthers, revolutionary poets, and free jazz musicians like Cleveland's teen-golfing-champion-turned-dada-saxophone-colossus, Albert Ayler.

The 1970s saw some of my Chocolate City Gold and Platinum Coast homies rise up en masse as fans and even members of Parliament Funkadelic; Mandrill; Earth, Wind and Fire; Rufus; and the Ohio Players. Hip-hop has of course spawned a host of suburban and urban street poets—like Ice Cube, the product of a two-parent home with a college degree in architectural drafting, who once answered my question of whether he was ever in a gang by saying, "Oh, hell, no, Dad wasn't having it."

The 1980s and 1990s would also see the advent of the black punk rocker, a species recently anthropologized in James Spooner's epochal documentary *Afro-Punk*. This group was shown to have its own peculiar set of behaviors around the thickets of racism, racial identity, Afrocentricity, class alienation, class privilege, class betrayal and interracial dating, black rage, black pleasure, and black feminism.

What can now be said about the Afropunks—an "only in America" diasporic tribe—is that they were the kids who found that their pent-up urges for rebellion, authenticity, or negrocity could not be satisfied with hip-hop, R&B, or participation in Jack and Jill. They were part of the first black MTV generation, which meant they were the kids who knew their Spandau Ballet from their Clash, their Depeche Mode from their Flock of Seagulls, their Slits from their Smiths, their X-Ray Spex from their Bow Wow Wow.

The groundbreaking black punk-inflected bands of the 1980s, such as Bad Brains, Fishbone, and Living Colour, were actually populated with musical virtuosos and black music historians who could have played any single genre they chose—jazz, reggae, soul, calypso, country, gospel, hip-hop—but instead chose a genre that allowed them to mosh them all up as the creative moment inspired—and they often did so, with extremely pronounced senses of irony, wit, style, outrage, and outrageousness.

So for the District of Columbia's own Bad Brains, that meant not just bending reggae, punk, funk, fusion jazz, and metal into a seamless lightning-fast hybrid but becoming Haile Selassie–worshipping Rastafarians instead of the pharmacology majors and Olympic swim team members their parents had envisioned. For LA's own Fishbone, whose assimilation blues ensued from being bused out of South Central to the San Fernando Valley, the decision to go punk and ska meant becoming a black PoMo Circus bent on exploding and caricaturing everything from blaxploitation movies, nuclear holocaust flicks, and Pentecostal church services to Jamaica's the Skatalites and the Sex Pistols.

For Brooklyn's own Living Colour, this meant creating a musical space where Van Halen, John Coltrane, and the Mighty Sparrow were all fair game for a race-mixing and sometimes race-baiting musical orgy, as heard in such songs as "Elvis Is Dead" and "Funny Vibe." In the latter Living Colour sings,

*No, I'm not gonna rob you*
*No, I'm not gonna beat you (Beat you)*

*No I'm not gonna rape you . . .*
*And I try not to hate you, so why you want to give me that funny vibe?*

We know now that these bands were ramping up the common everyday black schizophrenic and rhizomatic experience and using their code-switching facility to conjure up a highly skilled musical and visual spectacular in the process of offering yet another stylish testament to New World African modernity.

All three bands, Bad Brains, Fishbone, and Living Colour, established a new tradition of excellence and bravura in African American music that continues to inspire those who come after and also seek to render unto Jah, Jezebel, and Jehosophat a twenty-first-century black music, one capable of drawing on the entire legacy of Euro-Asiatic Afro-diasporic instrumental and vocal performance forms as they damn well please. Their heirs apparently include Tamar-Kali, Whole Wheat Bread, FunkFace, Imani Uzuri, Cipher, Suffrajett, and Game Rebellion.

All discovered mechanisms in their chosen, proactive, and self-invented genres for reconciling the differences between their black identities and those black identities we routinely see depicted across a broad negroidal representational spectrum—a spectrum that might casually be said to include BET, the NAACP Image Awards, Source Awards, Vibe Awards, *Essence, Jet, Ebony, Soul Train,* Tyler Perry films, Spike Lee Joints, Grammies, Oscars, Emmys, MTV, Europe, the *Tavis Smiley Show,* the Nation of Islam, the Lincoln Center Jazz Orchestra, HBO's *Pimps Up Hoes Down* series, *Girlfriends,* and *The Wire,* not to mention various NWA, Snoop, Puffy, Jay Z, Lil' Kim, Lil Jon, Ludacris, Nelly, Lil Wayne, Lil Mama, Beyoncé, and Rihanna videos.

In other words, like their predecessors Sun Ra, Albert Ayler, Miles Davis, Nina Simone, Arthur Lee, Sly Stone, Jimi Hendrix, George Clinton, Lee Screatch Perry, Grace Jones, and, increasingly, Lauryn Hill, they are all proud to be nigras from outer space. They not only know it, but they like it like that. They see you, but they wouldn't want or even know how to be you, though some of them have kids in college and paid-up mortgages; love Dave Chappelle, Luther, and Oldskool hip-hop; are quick to quote Malcolm in a heartbeat; said "fuck Reagan and Thatcher" in the 1980s; and more recently said "fuck Bush" and now "hail Obama" or "damn Obama" on a regular basis.

Like most folk of extreme artistic temperament born under the sign of black modernity, they are natural-born ikonoklasts, free-thinking intellects, and diehard individualists who wouldn't know how to fit in a box, any kinda box, not even one built to their own specifications. Their hard-core stance and "My Way" integrity seems beyond anything but momentary recuperation by the not-dying-fast-enuff rock music industry—an industry that apparently finds them a more fearsome threat to American hegemony and apartheid than anybody's gangsta rap.

What they left us to ponder as a collective legacy is not just the Ellisonian fluidity of black identity but that such identity by necessity needs to be aggressively, promiscuously, procreatively, metamorphically, rebelliously fluid and that if you want to claim some of that for yourself in the face of gentrification and other forms of genocidal race annihilation, you may need to get aggressively, promiscuously Afropunk—rockingly procreative, metamorphic, and buck wild in your own damn self.

# Hip-hop and Capitalist Interests

---

*HIP-HOP*

*It is art*

*It is culture.*

*It is music*

*It is entertainment.*

*It is HIP*

**H**egemonic, **I**nfluential, **P**owerful.

*It is extravagant spending*

*It is mimicking the possessions of performers*

*It is class conflict*

*It is conspicuous consumption*

*It is HOP*

**H**erald **O**bsessiv**e** **P**urchasing

---

The Miami rapper Trick Daddy raps quite simply and bluntly in his 1998 hit titled "Nann Nigga": "You don't know nann nigga / that dress fresher than me / and you don't know nann nigga that wear mo' Polo shit than me"![1] Trick Daddy's promotion of Polo in his lyrics is not meant so much to challenge listeners to identify a better, fresher dressed niggah as to persuade them to join him in sporting specific name brand apparel. When the song came out, my friends and I followed Trick without question. We were already donning Tommy Hilfiger—Tommy shirts, Tommy cologne, Tommy jeans, Tommy briefs—and if there had been Tommy toothpaste, we would have had that, too. Once, while hipping along to the hop of the song, one of my homeboys said, "See, I told you, Polo is the shit! Tommy ain't got nothing on Ralph Lauren." Of course, before the song this homeboy was the Polo oddball among our Tommy crew. But the song changed that. So what did the rest of us do? What else? We stepped up our Polo game. We weren't stupid enough to ditch our Tommy clothes. We knew another song was bound to come out the following month, extolling how fly we'd be in a Tommy jacket. We now had Polo and Tommy—a diverse wardrobe.

Ten years later, while shopping at Walmart with my wife and brother-in-law, I jokingly recalled the powerful one-liner of Trick Daddy and revised his lyrics for a little ditty of my own. I tapped my wife and sang: "You don't know nann niggah who dress cheaper than me, and you don't know nann niggah who wear mo' Walmart shit than me!" We fell out laughing.

It's obvious that times have changed for me. While hip-hop remains a part of my life, the lyrics no longer hold the same sway over me. They do not influence my spending and behavior as they once did. And this is not because hip-hop artists have stopped encouraging excessive consumption of the attire they advertise in their music. And it is also not because consumers—poor and middle class alike—are no longer influenced to purchase beyond their means. It is because my viewpoint on life has changed. Material possessions do not make the person. They become dated, break, stop working, and most likely will lose their value. Therefore it is paramount that I choose to store my treasures in things that won't decay. Instead of buying some nice shoes, I would rather invest in the enlightenment of people. So, I ask, why does hip-hop have the power, like Eric B. and Rakim, "to move the crowd"? Why, in 2002, when Nelly rapped about needing two pair of Nike Air Force One's did all sorts of folks flock to buy these sneakers, and not just one pair but two? Why is it that when I tune in to BET's highly popular show *106 and Park*, I witness star-struck youth dressed in the garb that the latest lyrics suggest?

It is obvious that following the dictates of these lyrics affects poor black folks more adversely, since they have to sacrifice more necessities in order to keep up with the Joneses of the hip-hop world. While they may realize that they cannot afford one pair of high-priced sneakers—let alone two—simply telling them to stop is ineffective; it is not as persuasive as the lyrics. Indeed, telling me to stop did not persuade me, and I am an otherwise reasonable and intelligent man. I ask, then, what is really behind the lure of the lyrics? Why are such lyrics aimed at poor people when even producers and performers are aware of the adverse affects?

Hip-hop, which originated as, and is still prominently considered, African American art, has emerged as a dominant force in popular culture. Its beginnings can be traced to working-class blacks and Puerto Ricans in New York, and now hip-hop has morphed into a multimillion-dollar industry with vast influence. Hip-hop reached its phenomenal success during a period when Americans of all backgrounds and walks of life were on a huge spending binge. During the subprime lending boom of the 1990s and early 2000s people tuned in to watch shows such as *Flip This House* and *MTV Cribs*. Americans dreamed of buying relatively inexpensive investment properties, fixing them up, and selling them for large profits. Many Americans had plans to get rich. They thought that resources would not dry up. They spent often and frivolously. This sort of lifestyle served as the basis for much of the content of rap lyrics—and the lyrics continue to be influenced—often manipulated—by wealthy corporate interests.

The consumer represents one side of the story. Production and corporate interests represent another. Perhaps this is the important side to consider. Indeed, corporations present artists with lucrative financial opportunities. OutKast, P Diddy, T.I., and Jay Z have all been linked in their music and their advertising with corporations that have become aware of the financial benefits of targeting the hip-hop public. For example, the brand management scholars Federico de Gregorio and Yongjun Sung assert that Maven Strategies, the first agency devoted exclusively to negotiating branded insertions within songs (with a particular emphasis on the hip-hop genre), arranged to have mentions of Seagram's gin inserted in five hip-hop songs that subsequently were released. Petey Pablo, in his 2004 song "Freek-a-Leek," gave an in-song promotion for Seagram's gin, rapping, "Now I got to give

a shout-out to Seagram's gin, 'cause I'm drinking it, and they paying for it."
Gregorio and Sung found that most artists were still not engaging in such
direct quid pro quos, but whether hip-hop artists are rapping about products they personally enjoy or are rapping about a product because they are
being paid to do so, the effect is the same: encouraging poor people to buy
items that they do not necessarily need or perhaps cannot afford. The corporations recently have been actively pursuing this public by using myriad
measures to infiltrate this market. For example, in 2003 the rap group Out-
Kast reached an agreement with Polaroid to bring Polaroid cameras (which
retail for about $80) on stage with them during their performances. The
hip-hop mogul Sean "P Diddy" Combs has converted his music career into a
marketing empire: his Blue Flame company helps companies build brands
that are targeted to trend-conscious consumers. The Atlanta-based rapper
T.I. had a sponsorship deal with General Motors until he pleaded guilty to
felony weapons charges. The list goes on and on. This trend appears likely to
continue long into the foreseeable future. Although corporate sponsorship
has long been a staple of musicians' tours, what makes the hip-hop situation
unique is that this genre—more than any other, according to Gregorio and
Sung, has been deemed the most appropriate for brand placement.[2] Hence,
fans have come to accept and even expect that hip-hop lyrics will contain
product placements and brand promotions—which means that hip-hop fans
are paying to listen to commercials designed to convince them to buy expensive goods. The same outrageous arrangements do not exist to the same
degree for other musical genres such as country, pop, rock, and classical.

Clearly, corporations and hip-hop artists are benefiting—at least financially—from these relationships. However, in many ways the black poor in
general, and specifically the poorer publics who engage in conspicuous consumption, are actually pawns of corporate greed and of the mostly white
power structure of the music and entertainment industry. Can they truly
afford the things that they are indirectly being encouraged to buy? I would
argue that those hip-hop artists are rooks in this vicious game of consumption: the artists benefit financially from their participation in the exploitation of their poorer fans. In the eponymous 2002 film Spiderman, the title
character says, "With great power comes great responsibility!" Although
Spiderman is not a hip-hop artist or a hip-hop critic, his words certainly are

applicable to this situation. W. E. B. Du Bois spoke of the Talented Tenth, whose role in society was to educate and enlighten the masses. Few rappers take on this role in their music or onstage personas.

While rap artists claim to be pro-black in terms of racial identification, they sometimes act in ways that are antiblack in the class struggle. That is to say, they are caught between a racial rock and a socioeconomic hard place because their corporate sponsors exploit the poorest segments of the black community. This dilemma is most evident when we assess the impact of these hip-hop lyrics on the masses of blacks who can never even hope to develop true wealth because they are encouraged to spend beyond their means, while the rappers who claim to identify with these fans get richer still because they share in the corporate exploitation of lower-class blacks. But I argue that if white-owned corporations did not support the celebrity artists who glorify conspicuous consumption, there might be a larger space for the more socially conscious rappers, such as Mos Def, Common, Talib Kweli, Dead Prez, and the Roots, whose messages create awareness of social issues, challenge societal ills, and champion knowledge and betterment of the self. The solution is not to force corporations to develop specific rules to follow for marketing their products to the black masses; rather, the challenge is for these corporations to engage in responsible advocacy and marketing practices. Corporations and their hip-hop mouthpieces should at least engage in some level of reflection about which products they are going to promote to vulnerable populations. This outcome, however, is not likely given the current situation in which most black rap artists find themselves: rap about conspicuous consumption or join the poorly paid underground of rappers selling mix tapes online. Moreover, if these corporations continue to engage in exploitative behaviors, black journalists, academics, social justice scholars, and politicians who write for and/or who have access to the mainstream press should use their ability and their influence to inform white liberals about what some deem unethical corporate behavior. Together, these voices might be able to pressure the large corporate interests to behave more responsibly.

Although the hip-hop masses in general and the underclass specifically are engaged in the kind of conspicuous consumption that caused Frazier to criticize the black middle class in 1957, what is complicated about the contemporary case is that, while the underclass, the masses, are trying to demonstrate and perform an affluent way of life, the likes of Bill Cosby and others criticize them for it. These critics say that blacks spend too much money on designer clothing and fancy cars instead of investing in their futures. I am not defending Cosby's criticism because it does not offer solutions. It tears down without providing a means of building up. Sure, Cosby points out the perceived problem of conspicuous consumption, but he does not address the psychological benefits that people gain from having the "finer things" in life.

A more beneficial approach would be to understand why these individuals are participating in this world of make-believe . . . or, better yet, address why they want to keep up with the Joneses, the Smiths, the T.I.'s, and the Lil Waynes. Frazier speaks to these very concerns in his groundbreaking text, saying that entertainers "who very often have a lower-class background in the social hierarchy of the Negro community, exercise a far greater influence upon the morals and manners in the Negro community than actors and entertainers in the white community." He further asserted that "their prestige is owing partly to the glamor of their personalities, but more especially to their financial success, which is due to their support by the white world."[3]

## Hip-Hop and the American Dream Myth: The World of Make-Believe

Rapping about material products and accumulation did not originate with corporate interests in the hip-hop consumer market, as many may believe (although the two, today, are strongly intertwined); however, an age-old psychological factor at least in part accounts for the content of rappers' lyrics. Although the black bourgeoisie was not immortalizing their material possessions in song, Frazier found that affluent blacks had shifted away from piety and the Puritan work ethic and moved toward standards of living that were marked by extravagant social activities and expensive, fashionable dress. The reason for this, Frazier stated, is that in order to compensate for feelings of inferiority, "the black bourgeoisie has created in its isolation what might be described as a world of make-believe in which it attempts to escape the disdain of whites and fulfill its wish for status in American life"

(27). This group, with a determination like none other, lived and embodied this world of make-believe by constantly showcasing their achievement of the American dream—even if some, as Frazier asserts, were living far beyond their financial means.

The American dream is rooted in a vision of success. The social analyst Alex Thio has asserted that "the American ideology of success . . . encourages the populace (1) to raise their level of aspirations and (2) to believe in the established society as one with abundant opportunities."[4] And although few Americans actually embody the American dream, all forms of media—including hip-hop music and videos—perpetuate the myth that achieving the American dream and material wealth is within everyone's grasp.

The echoes of the American dream in today's hip-hop lyrics are readily apparent. Wealth, as Alan D. DeSantis defines it, means that "one can procure money, property, and the good life that accompanies such acquisitions . . . [and] secure products and services that aid a lifestyle marked by relaxation and self-indulgence."[5] Both components of his definition appear regularly in hip-hop lyrics.

In an analysis of the hip-hop artist Jay Z's 1996 song "Feeling It," the hip-hop scholar and critic Jeffrey Ogbar notes: "[Jay Z] raps about a typical 'Big Willie' life, complete with driving in a Lexus . . . revels in his fantasy mobster world of materialism and crime . . . brags about his 14-karat gold pen, pearls, diamonds, and caviar . . . raps that materialism is king [and] if people are not talking about 'large money' then what's the point?"[6] Expressions of such hopes, concerns, and aspirations are manifested throughout hip-hop lyrics.

As evidenced by their material possessions, these hip-hop artists have achieved the American dream. As the scholar Dana Cloud once said about Oprah Winfrey, the stage persona of the rap artist "resonates with and reinforces the ideology of the American Dream, implying the accessibility of this dream to black Americans despite the structural, economic, and political obstacles to achievement and survival posed in a racist society."[7]

Cloud claims that the persona we know as "Oprah" is "constructed in the biographical narratives that frame her rise to stardom in the late 1980s as a black person who, refusing identification with the politics of black liberation, 'proves' that the American Dream is possible for all black Americans" (116–17). In Oprah's narrative her hard work, sacrifice, and dedication allowed her to pull herself up by the bootstraps. In a similar vein the southern rapper T.I., in his 2003 song "Doin' My Job," talks about his hard work, sacrifice, and dedication to the profession of drug dealing. T.I. rapped that he was "always stuck in the grind summertime to wintertime"—selling drugs and hustling.[8] Arguably, he too pulled himself up by the bootstraps, and his hard work ultimately led to his newfound wealth, which he raps about in subsequent songs.

Whether rap artists have actually achieved the American dream or are pretending in their lyrics that they have, their words can serve as an escape from the socioeconomic conditions and constraints of urban life in which many rappers and fans are mired.

## From Shit to Sugar: And You Can Do It, Too

According to Frazier, "new recruits" to the black bourgeoisie came from the "successful underworld Negroes, who . . . gained their money from gambling, prostitution, bootlegging, and the numbers," and "the 'sporting' and criminal elements began to acquire a dominant position among Negroes" (109–10). Other members of the black bourgeoisie exercised "considerable influence on the values of Negroes" but "did not occupy a dignified position in the Negro community" because the masses regarded the black bourgeoisie as simply "lucky in getting money" (194), whereas these "new recruits" from the underworld became lionized as they engaged in conspicuous consumption, despite not having been born with the proverbial silver spoon. A plausible explanation for this differentiated respect from the masses is that the underworld members of the black bourgeoisie provided a blueprint to financial success—even if it was through illegal means. They were not "lucky in getting money"; rather, they seized an opportunity to rise in social status. Although most rappers' income is not from numbers or prostitution, the game and access to the table remain the same: these artists are paid by large corporate interests, yet many artists claim to have reached their elevated social status because of their drug dealing and street-hustling ways. Money provided in the underworld is still deemed a viable means to earn a higher social status.

This plays itself out in many rap lyrics. For a rapping emcee, establishing street credibility appears to be paramount. Some of the most popular rappers ever, the late 2Pac, Eminem, 50 Cent, Snoop Dog, and the late Notorious B.I.G., had a rags-to-riches tale, and each experienced great success after establishing his street credibility in his lyrics. Notorious B.I.G. detailed his rise in "Juicy," his mainstream debut. In one verse he stated:

*I made the change from a common thief*
*To up close and personal with Robin Leach*[9]

He truly believed that he was living the lifestyle of the rich and famous.

As I mentioned earlier, these rappers have the power to move the masses. Their celebrity, coupled with their rise from poverty, makes them iconic in the eyes of the black lower class, that is, the black masses. Rappers today have become the great black hope to many people.

# (H.I.P.) Hegemonic. Influential. Powerful.

The embrace by the black masses of actors and entertainers, as well as those who moved up to the bourgeoisie from the underworld, appears to be as tight as it was in Frazier's day. But where the actors and entertainers realize the American dream through legitimate jobs, the drug dealers and other underworld figures attain a life of luxury through illegal activities. Rappers are iconic because they have one foot in each camp. Yet rappers, through their lyrics, elevate the achievement of material wealth, status, and leisure through illegal means and in so doing are challenging conventional conceptions of the American dream. But are celebrations of criminality and consumption responsible?

Critics have argued that hip-hop lyrics are detrimental to society because they promote violence and overindulgence in consumer products. Although he was not speaking about hip-hop, the media critic and sociologist Herbert Schiller argued that corporate advocacy and the corporate voice (which arguably drives the hip-hop market) are harmful because corporations have the power to set the public agenda. Moreover, he claimed that the corporate ownership of public space is squeezing out citizens who want to engage in the public debate of socially important issues. According to Schiller, American consumers, including African Americans, have become mindless sheep led by the all-powerful shepherd, corporate influence.[10]

## It's Bigger Than Hip-Hop . . . Hip-Hop . . . Hip-Hop

As I said, I was a child who bought into and accepted hip-hop lyrics; conspicuous consumption did not feel optional for me—it was necessity. Engaging in conspicuous consumption afforded me a certain level of psychological comfort and enabled me to participate with my peers without fear of ridicule. To get the respect from others—to be treated well and be accepted—I had to front, model, and clearly perform my class status. This is the primary reason why so many vulnerable members of the public participate in these performances of conspicuous consumption. I recognize that I was a victim of savvy corporate campaigns that were marketing the latest footwear to urban, black, and hip-hop communities. At one time Nike did not have the complete stranglehold on the athletic footwear market that it does today. If you weren't wearing Nike Air Jordans or the Air Max, the only suitable shoe was the rival Reebok Pump, which was famously endorsed by Shaquille O'Neal. My mom finally bought me a pair of the hideously expensive Reebok Pumps, after I begged her endlessly. I couldn't tell her the real reason I wanted them so badly: I could not take the ridicule at school any more. I was teased incessantly for wearing the "no name" boots that my mom purchased for me at Sears. They were really nice boots, but they did not have a logo on the bottom or the side. I went home each day nearly in tears. What is sad is that nearly twenty years later, my friends remember how badly I was picked on, and they still joke about how I tried to pass those boots off as Colorado brand footwear. Some still think it's funny. To me, it was a painful time in my childhood.

Is escaping ridicule that important? To some, of course, it is. Back then it was of paramount importance to me. I never questioned why it was so important for me to have clothes and shoes with culturally and socially accepted logos on them. All these years later, do any young members of the hip-hop public openly question why their peers think it's so important to follow the trends set by rappers?

Analysts of contemporary hip-hop lyrics argue that they focus on consumption because it is what sells. This is a reasonable argument, but it fails to address the underlying reasons for their popularity. Foremost among these underlying reasons is, to my mind, the American dream. People want to listen to these lyrics because they give them something to hope for—dream about. That's what they did for me. People may not identify with rappers' particular struggles, but they can identify with struggle nonetheless. They may dream about "making it" just like their favorite rapper has. Is this unreasonable? There's something to be said for having an escape from the daily grind, and perhaps these lyrics provide it.

# It Was All a Dream . . .

While I have been discussing Frazier's critique of conspicuous consumption among the black bourgeoisie, the famous words of the late-great hip-hop artist Notorious B.I.G. have been bouncing around my brain: "It was all a dream."

Frazier asserted that some middle-class Negroes sought escape from their frustrations by developing, for example, a serious interest in Negro music. He implied that such an outlet was primarily a means of coping for lower-class blacks. It therefore follows that they would regard the success of a black musician as the achievement of "one of their own" and that they would embrace him. On the other hand, many middle-class Negroes, who were satisfied to live in the world of make-believe, had to find a solution to the real economic and social problems that they faced and sought escape in illusions of wealth. Part of the problem, Frazier perceived, was that "they have had little experience with the real meaning of wealth and . . . they lack a tradition of saving and accumulation. Wealth to them means spending money without any reference to its source."[11]

In his essay about television, black Americans, and the American ideology of success, Herman Gray, a cultural studies scholar and popular culture critic, noted that "one message of these representations of success and failure is that middle . . . [and upper-class] class blacks (and whites) succeed because they take advantage of available opportunities while poor blacks and other marginal members of our society fail because they do not."[12]

A study released in November 2009 by the Selig Center at the University of Georgia estimated that black buying power will be worth about $1.1 trillion by 2014. At first glance this appears to be, but is really not, a huge number. In fact, Frazier questioned the buying power of blacks as early as 1951. Frazier found that "the myth that Negroes were spending 15 billion dollars in 1951 was widely circulated by whites as well as Negroes since it served to exaggerate the economic well-being of Negroes in the United States and to whet the appetites of the black bourgeoisies, both Negro businessmen and Negroes employed by American corporations, in their efforts to reap benefits from the increased earnings of Negroes"—though he never reported what blacks' spending power actually was at the time.[13]

What black buying power is and what it means is beyond the purview of this essay; however, let's assume that the myth persists today, perpetuated in part by African American leaders who constantly remind us of the power of the black dollar. Moreover, many of African Americans' performances are prompted by and are complicit with the notion of this myth. The Selig Center reports that current spending power for blacks is estimated to be nearly $910 billion. A recent e-mail I received from the NAACP reminds me that African Americans contribute more than $700 billion per year to the U.S. economy, and a sizable portion of those dollars is spent in stores such as Target. The purpose of this e-mail was to convince African American consumers to threaten to boycott Target to force the company to clarify its position on economic opportunity for African Americans. Throwing around such large dollar figures could lull African Americans into the belief that they have real economic power and that their dollars actually can make a difference. Attributing a false economic power to African Americans can be seen as yet another ploy initiated by the black bourgeoisie (in this case the NAACP) to offer themselves and the black masses psychological comfort for their economic shortcomings. One rapper who apparently swallowed the economic vitality myth whole is Jay Z, who not long ago proposed a boycott of the high-end champagne company Cristal. The reaction of Frederic Rouzaud, managing director of Louis Roderer Cristal, was that his firm would do whatever was necessary to retain the black community's business but to state outright that he did not want his brand to be associated with hip-hop and gangsta rap. Jay Z vowed to no longer support Cristal, even though he probably recognizes the minimal economic impact of his boycott. I'm guessing that he feels that the boycott makes a statement to his largely African American fans and has little or no understanding that his boycott can be used to demonstrate the inherit flaw in the myth of the power of the black dollar.

But what if the economic vitality of African Americans is not a myth? I suspect that if a certain popular athletic shoe company had snubbed the black consumer dollar the way Cristal did, a boycott of its shoes might be far more effective. So the myth might have a kernel of truth to it, but calling for boycotts on the basis of a myth is an exercise in futility. The trick is to leverage the economic clout that blacks do have by carefully selecting the products and circumstances that warrant a boycott. Cristal wasn't it.

Perhaps the question we should be asking is why blacks at all socioeconomic levels are engaging in such conspicuous consumption. Frazier might answer that blacks' "larger incomes have enabled them to propagate false notions about their place in American life and to create a world of make-believe" (129), although when he wrote *Black Bourgeoisie,* "Negroes were not only at the bottom of the economic ladder but . . . all the pretended economic gains which Negroes were supposed to have made had not changed fundamentally their relative economic position in American life" (11).

One explanation for this mass consumer bingeing may be that although a large percentage of blacks may be struggling financially, they feel some sense of achievement if they have a gold watch and nice shoes. Frazier observed that the black bourgeoisie, "having become less isolated and thus more exposed to the contempt and hostility of the white world, but at the same time cherishing the values of the white world, the new black bourgeoisie with more money at their disposal, have sought compensations in the things that money can buy" (126). Lower-class blacks are following the example set for them by newly affluent blacks—among them, the rappers—and by the middle-class blacks whom Frazier was criticizing. In short, the pervasiveness of the myth of the American dream is one reason for the prevalence and pervasiveness of paeans to consumption in hip-hop lyrics, as well as why these lyrics tend to be so influential among consumers of all races.

A final example will illustrate this point. In her song "Bossy," Kelis sings, "I am the one that told Young Stunna [Lil Wayne] that he should switch to BAPEs." Then, in his "Hustler Musik" video, you can see Wayne wearing a BAPEs sweater. What are BAPEs, you might ask? In 2009 one of *Billboard*'s top songs was Soulja Boy's "Crank Dat"; it was on *Billboard*'s top 100 list for more than fifteen weeks. In this song Soulja Boy has a line that says, "Haterz get mad cuz / I got me some Bathing Apes"— a reference to BAPEs. As I looked at reviews of the song, I found a lot of people wondering the same thing: What are/is BAPEs?

It's a clothing line created by a Japanese designer who worked with the rapper Pharrell "Skateboard P" Williams to open the first American Bathing Apes store in New York. I'm guessing that young blacks (and others who follow hip-hop culture and trends) will flock to these stores to purchase the latest new thing in apparel, continuing the vicious cycle of conspicuous consumption.

Often, rappers are paid to rap about products—they receive a nice fat check from a corporation after they rap about its product in a highly popular song—or they just rap about products to show what they are consuming now that they have made it to a higher economic status. Although these rappers are black in terms of racial identification, their lifestyles do not mirror the class struggle that many blacks face. These rappers are the corporate mouthpieces used to exploit the poorest segments of the black community. Rap lyrics indirectly encourage poor blacks to spend beyond their means, while the rappers themselves, who claim to identify with these black masses, get richer because they share in the corporate exploitation of their lower-class fans. Rappers should use their elevated status for entertainment, to provide feel-good music, but they also need to recognize that this music can be used as a platform to raise awareness about and challenge societal problems. Sadly, it does not appear that corporate interests are likely to support this style of rap music because it is not highly profitable.

Corporations would much rather support a rapper whose aim is to get rich by any means. I'd like to mention a line from one of 50 Cent's songs from his first album, "Get Rich or Die Tryin'": "It feels good to spend fifty grand and think nothing of it." Many, including me, will agree that it would feel good to be able to spend large amounts of money without any reservations or second thoughts, but, for many people, especially blacks, this simply is not reality. Yet class performances might indicate otherwise. In reality, shouldn't we all be so lucky as to share in 50 Cent's dream? His current reality is make-believe to many. And it is a shame that so many young blacks are going deeply into debt because they are caught up in status and trying to live a dream that is someone else's reality.

Hip-hop is a culture. It is a movement. It is a social phenomenon. However, it is powerful and cannot be discounted or looked at simply as a form of entertainment. The messages delivered are hegemonic, influential, and powerful, and members of the underclass, who are engaged in the same kind of conspicuous consumption for which Frazier criticized the black middle class in 1957, are mere pawns of corporate greed and of the mostly white power structure of the music and entertainment industry.

Media, including music and hip-hop, can be considered agents of socialization—shaping and influencing people's identities and identity formations. Media are often our only gateway to other worlds. This means that many people are taking images of conspicuous consumption in hip-hop culture as their view of reality. We need to find the courage to change the script and create songs similar to the one that I sang jokingly in Walmart. Or perhaps we can go one step further and expose the Wizard behind the curtain—that is, corporations which are reaping the profits from the lyrics sung by rappers who promote their products.

## NOTES

1. Adam Duggins and Maurice Young, "Nann Nigga," First and Gold Publishing, 1998, lyrics as posted at www.lyricsmode.com/lyrics/t/trick_daddy/nann_nigga.html.

2. Federico de Gregorio and Youngjun Sung, "Giving a Shout out to Seagram's Gin: Extent of Attitudes Towards Brands in Popular Songs," *Journal of Brand Management* 17 (2009): 218–19.

3. E. Franklin Frazier, *Black Bourgeoisie: The Rise of a New Middle Class in the United States* (New York: Macmillan, 1962), 109.

4. Alex Thio, "Toward a Fuller View of American Success Ideology," *Pacific Sociological Review* 15 (1972): 381.

5. Alan D. DeSantis, "Selling the American Dream Myth to Black Southerners: The *Chicago Defender* and the Great Migration of 1915–1919." *Western Journal of Communication* 62 (1998): 480.

6. Jeffrey Ogbar, "Slouching toward Bork: The Culture Wars and Self-Criticism in Hip-Hop Music," *Journal of Black Studies* 30 (1999): 168.

7. Dana L. Cloud, "Hegemony or Concordance? The Rhetoric of Tokenism in Oprah Winfrey's Rags-to-Riches Biography," *Critical Studies in Mass Communication* 13 (1996): 116.

8. Michael Love Smith, Clifford Harris, and Kanye West, "Doin' My Job," 2003, Ye World Music, Domani and Ya Majesty's Music, Stone Diamond Music Corp., Wb Music Corp.; Emi April Music Inc., lyrics as posted at www.lyricsmode.com/lyrics/t/ti/doin_my_job.html.

9. Christopher Wallace, Jean Olivier, Sean Combs, and James Mtume, "Juicy," 1994, Emi April Music, Big Poppa Music, and Justin Combs Publishing.

10. Herbert I. Schiller, *Culture, Inc.: The Corporate Takeover of Public Expression* (New York: Oxford University Press, 1989).

11. Frazier, *Black Bourgeoisie,* 188–89.

12. Herman Gray, "Television, Black Americans, and the American Dream," *Critical Studies in Mass Communication* 6 (1989): 376.

13. Jeffrey M. Humphreys, "The Multicultural Economy 2009," *Georgia Business and Economic Conditions* 69, no. 3 (2009): 1–16, www.terry.uga.edu/selig/docs/GBEC0903q.pdf; Frazier, *Black Bourgeoisie,* 145.

# Middle-Class Ideology in African American Postwar Comic Strips

ostwar black comic strips present ideologies that reflect both what E. Franklin Frazier calls a middle-class "world of make-believe" (false perceptions of class status and influence) and critiques of this perception. Not all comic strips of the era are limited to addressing this debate, however, nor are all even concerned with representing these views. What is important to know about them is that comic strips are a direct reflection of the editors and staff of the newspapers in which they appeared. Considering this factor helps us to understand the extent to which middle-class ideologies helped to shape images and representations of African Americans following World War II.

From 1946 to 1959 black newspapers expanded their purpose from campaigning for freedom to providing black news as well as editorial guidance, sports news, church information, entertainment news, advertisements, and cartoons and comic strips.[1] Black comic strips are open-ended dramatic narratives about a recurring set of core characters of African descent told in a series of drawings, often including dialogue in balloons and a narrative text, and published serially in newspapers.[2] They are primarily authored by people of African descent but have occasionally been authored by people of

European descent. Black comic strips amuse or engender pleasure in inter-racial (black and white) audiences and emerge from self-conscious inten-tions, whether artistic, economic, or political, to illuminate African Ameri-can characters and/or black experiences, real or created. The three types of traditional black comic strips are comedy (gag), family, and action.[3]

Two postwar black newspapers from Toledo, Ohio, the *Toledo Sepia City Press* and *Bronze Raven*, emerge as sites for the cultural phenomenon of comic strips. Of the seven black newspapers published in Toledo from 1943 to 2008—*Sepia City Press, Bronze Raven, Toledo Script, Toledo Observer, Toledo Journal, Sojourner's Truth,* and *Midwest Urban,* only *Sepia City Press* and the *Bronze Raven* included comic art.[4] Significantly, the *Sepia City Press* and *Bronze Raven* were published between 1945 and 1955, a time of revolution-ary cultural change in the United States that profoundly affected African American life and culture in political, economic, and social arenas. Black newspaper reporting was a primary vehicle for reflecting this change and for voicing the thoughts of African Americans in reaction to this change. The period after World War II marked the first time that representations of blacks in popular culture and mass media changed for the better, even though old representations—blacks as domestics and servants or as child-like—still appeared. It was also a time of explosive creativity for African Americans themselves.

Although black newspapers have served an important social and po-litical role in African American life and culture, Frazier criticized the black press for being the "chief medium of communication" that created and per-petuated the "world of make-believe" for the black bourgeoisie. Frazier ar-gues that magazines like John H. Johnson's *Ebony* essentially represented the interests and outlook of the black bourgeoisie and that such periodi-cals exaggerate blacks' economic well-being and cultural achievements. The magazine also emphasizes "black societies" (black social organizations and clubs comprised mainly of middle-class blacks in northern urban areas) in order to help its bourgeois readers to escape their "inferiority and inconse-quence in American society."[5]

A review of the issues that Toledo's independent black newspaper *Bronze Raven* explored from 1951 to 1956 provides a brief illustration of Fra-zier's concerns and alarm. The *Bronze Raven,* established by Frances Belcher and her husband, Richard Belcher, was published weekly from September 1948 to January 10, 1976, and was the longest-running African American newspaper in northwestern Ohio until 1975. For twenty-eight years the *Bronze Raven* served in several capacities as a conveyor of local, state, and national news for adults and youth, covering events like sports, commencement services, church services, marriages, burials, concerts, and occupational promotions and the efforts of the National Association for the Advancement of Colored People (NAACP). It was a good example of Frazier's observation, for the *Bronze Raven* counted among its beats the "Toledo Social Set." It included black elite organizations such as the Women's Auxiliary of the Belmont Savings Club; the Blue Ribbon Savings Club; the Y's Men, an organization of the Indiana Avenue Branch of the YMCA; and local chapters of national black sororities and fraternities. Society news also targeted various events, including bridal showers and holiday dinners, as well as debutante balls, family vacations, and other leisure activities. Furthermore, the *Raven* (as the paper called itself) emphasized the display of material consumption by featuring stories on families that purchased automobiles, television sets, and appliances. Advertising was primarily from small businesses, both black and white, in Toledo: auto dealers, appliance stores, furriers, bowling alleys, jewelers, dry cleaners, barber and beauty shops, gasoline service stations, hotels and inns, and numerous restaurants and nightclubs.

After World War II the black comic strip series *Barry Jordan* (July 17, 1954–July 16, 1955) in the *Bronze Raven,* and *Little Magnolia* (which appeared sporadically in the first half of 1949) and *Swing Papa* (April 3, 1948–August 1948) in the *Toledo Sepia City Press,* explicitly exalted African American urban life as a major cultural narrative.[6] Through the use of middle-class culture, the strips also implicitly represented the norms of the patriarchal nuclear family, consumerism, consumption and affluence, individualism, "black society," and heterosexual romantic love and marriage.

Of more importance, blackness in *Swing Papa, Little Magnolia,* and *Barry Jordan* is mediated, figured, and represented by the trope of middle-classness. The significance of middle-class ideology in the black postwar comic strip is that it exalts, celebrates, and centers black urban life rather than black rural or religious life. The strips also speak to the urban black middle class, expressing a vision of urban black life in America that is equal to whites' socially, culturally, educationally, economically, and (implicitly) politically. Black middle-classness therefore becomes synonymous with racial integration, peace, harmony, and equality, a recipe that complements the rhetoric of equal civil rights evinced in the activities of the NAACP and similar organizations, and suppresses social contradictions of inequality, racism, discrimination that exist in society.

The mediation of blackness through middle-class ideology in *Swing Papa*, *Little Magnolia*, and *Barry Jordan* is expressed through three typical conventions in comic art: character, setting, and ritual. *Character* refers to the imaginary people represented in fictional comic strips. *Setting* refers to the social spaces the characters share and in which they live. Rituals are participatory activities in which comic strip readers take part by reading weekly and by "drawing pleasure from the repetitive formulas, genres and myths of popular culture."[7]

*Swing Papa* and *Little Magnolia* were featured in the *Toledo Sepia City Press*, a black independent newspaper that published weekly from April 3, 1948, to May 13, 1950. *Swing Papa* was syndicated with the Story Script Syndicate and appeared in consecutive issues of the newspaper from April 3, 1948, to August 7, 1948.[8] The creators of *Swing Papa* were Harold "Dave" Quinn, a World War II veteran from Toledo and the artist for the strip, and O'Wendell Shaw, a former Toledo editor of the *Ohio State News*, editor of the *Sepia City Press*, and writer for the strip.[9]

Information about Shaw is sparse. We have no evidence that he was a native of Toledo and no information about how long he lived there and edited the paper. However, Shaw does appear to have had experience with writing in other venues before and after his stint at the *Sepia City Press*. For example, Shaw is the author of *Greater Need Below*, a novel published in 1936 by the Bi-Monthly Negro Book Club and reprinted in 1972. In his foreword he says that *Greater Need Below* is based on "some phases of life in a typical southern Negro-manned, state-supported college." The "greater need below," as explained to the novel's heroine, Ellen Vance, by the dean of women at her college, is the need for black teachers to go "below the Mason-Dixon Line" to teach because the "white people down there will not teach the thousands of colored boys and girls" there. In Donald Franklin Joyce's research on black-owned book publishers in the United States, he finds that the

Bi-Monthly Negro Book Club published one book (by Shaw) and speculates that the publisher intended to publish books about the African American experience for an adult African American audience. After the *Sepia City Press* and *Greater Need Below,* Shaw published a short monograph in 1962 on how to write for weekly newspapers.[10]

Quinn, the artist for *Swing Papa,* was a native of Toledo and a commercial artist who designed logos for area companies and institutions. Born in 1926, Quinn was the fourth of ten children. He spent his childhood in East Toledo and graduated from Scott High School in 1944. Quinn earned an athletic scholarship to play football at Wilberforce University near Dayton. He attended the African American college briefly until he was drafted into the U.S. Army Air Corps. After the war he returned to Toledo and attended the former Laingor Commercial Art Studio and School, graduating in the late 1940s. In the 1960s Quinn created the bulldog logo for the historically black Scott High. He worked at the Ace Sign Company for twenty years and was vice president and co-owner of Creative Arts and Signs, which specialized in signs, art, and truck lettering. He was also the owner of his own business, Dave Quinn and Associates, during the 1970s. Quinn retired in the 1980s and died in Toledo on July 29, 2001.[11]

*Swing Papa* ran in the Feature Section of the *Sepia City Press,* which included sports, theater, comics, gags, and stories of community interest. The strip consisted of three to eight panels that were comparable in size to comic strips found in the *Blade,* the mainstream newspaper of Toledo, then and now. The hero of *Swing Papa* is Bret Harvey, an African American musician who is also an amateur detective. The series is an adventure continuity comic strip, set in the city, an example of the formula I call "black urban romance and adventure."[12] Its primary purpose is to engage its readership through entertainment but also by gaining readers' identification with the characters' middle-class affluence, unlimited consumerism, individualism, social and economic mobility, violence, and heterosexual love relationship, all centered in a separate-but-equal black world. Rituals of order, consumption, and consummation (conformity and assurance, and romanticism and lifestyle) are found in *Swing Papa.* Elements of the black repertoire used in this strip include music, oratory, the nightclub, middle-class ideology, and the hero.[13]

Bret Harvey is "maestro of the devastating 'Swingsters Sweet' orchestra," and his primary instrument is the tenor saxophone. Shaw describes the strip as providing a "true-to-life story of the glamour, tinsel and [romance] of the Negro entertainment world, featuring music, adventures, travel, beautiful women and suave men." Indeed, *Swing Papa* has a fast pace from the first installment, when Bret Harvey "succumbs to the seductive wiles" of Marta Grayfield, a "glamorous 'hanger-on' from the realm of society and wealth." *Swing Papa* makes conscious references to Toledo in general and to places and businesses within the city, including Park Hurst, an affluent black neighborhood; the Trianon Ballroom; Deluxe Cab; Bellman's and Waiter's Club; Thomas Hotel; Latin Club; Lion's Department Store; Indiana Avenue; City Park Avenue; and Rosy Cab. Although *Swing Papa* started out in an unidentified city, by the fifth installment much of the action occurs in Toledo.

Bret's suave manner, physical appearance, and interactions with Marta remind the reader that the strip is both urban and hip. Marta's hair is meticulously done, and Bret's is processed, which was a symbol of status among men in the black music community. They both wear fashionable clothes, and urban markers, including nightclubs, taxicabs, and city street corners, are abundant. The strip features romance, music, adventures, and travel. In one strip Bret and Marta arrive in Toledo and are met by Chick Lewis of the *Sepia City Press* and Sepia City Mayor Bob Howe.[14] Before Bret performs that evening, the mayor of Sepia City presents him with a key to the city of Toledo. More physical action and adventures continue in the May 15, 1948, installment when the last panel introduces two robbers who are confirming with each other that Bret is the bandleader then in the city. The reader is cued to their negative role by their noses, which are far larger than those of other characters, the hats they are wearing, and one robber's beard and sideburns, both signifiers of hypermasculinity. The men bump into Bret and steal his wallet. For a time Bret and Marta chase the robbers in a taxicab. Later Bret jumps onto the robbers' vehicle and has a fistfight with the driver from outside the car. The car crashes, and Bret falls to the ground. Coincidentally, the police witness the entire car chase and are present to subdue and arrest the criminals.

*Swing Papa* envisions a black Toledo where black male musicians are the cultural heroes of the urban landscape and where the entertainment world is vibrant and alive but racially segregated. Through *Swing Papa* Quinn and Shaw illustrate an expression of black life and culture that is adventurous, glamorous, and fantastic. They tell a story of life in Toledo that is exciting but not based on the city's social conditions. *Swing Papa* is not calling attention to important social and cultural issues in black Toledo such as voting, the nonexistence of black principals in the Toledo public school system, or black membership drives for the Young Men's Christian Association, Frederick Douglass Community Association, and NAACP. *Swing Papa* also does not highlight the important issues in black America, such as civil rights and banning segregation in all public transportation, that were featured in the news sections of black papers.[15] *Swing Papa* presents a "world of make-believe," but it is firmly grounded in 1950s black Toledo culture.

While many old and new mainstream cartoonists were moving away from gag strips by the 1940s, black cartoonists still used the form as a viable and effective format for their artistic vision. *Little Magnolia* is one such example. *Little Magnolia* was written and drawn by Al Hart and appeared in discontinuous installments from January 15, 1949, to May 7, 1949, in the *Sepia City Press*.[16]

Magnolia was a traditional gag strip with four panels that include a punch line in the final panel, and it ran in the Feature Section. *Little Magnolia* is a self-contained black comic strip that revolves around a precocious preteen named Magnolia and her parents, friends, and other adults. Rituals of integration dominate the installments of *Little Magnolia,* showing the protagonist and parent or friend in the first panel introducing the "situation," moving to an illustration of the "situation" in the next two panels, and then resolution in the final panel. This strip uses little of the black repertoire, but Magnolia's living environment and home explicitly convey middle-class status. Her home, which appears to be an apartment, has a spacious living room and kitchen, comfortable furniture, and art objects. The apron on Magnolia's mother strongly suggests that she is a homemaker. Magnolia's father appears to be a professional because he is shown with a vest, shirt, and tie when at home and completely attired with suit jacket when at work.

*Little Magnolia* is a cultural narrative about black middle-classness, which includes heterosexual marriage, the nuclear family, and conspicuous consumption. As such, it, like *Swing Papa,* supports Frazier's claim of a "world of make-believe."

*Barry Jordan,* published in the *Bronze Raven* from 1954 to 1955, was created by Jimmy Dixon, a Toledo native who the newspaper editors deemed had "great possibilities in the field of art." Dixon created another comic strip series, *Li'l Moe and Joe,* about two preadolescent boy heroes. A brief biographical sketch by the *Bronze Raven* editors provides additional information about Dixon: "Jimmy Dixon entered the U.S. Armed Forces in 1945 and worked for two years on the European edition of the *Stars and Stripes* newspaper as a staff artist. Dixon was discharged from the Army in 1948 and

worked in various art studios in Toledo. He entered art school in New Jersey and later went to New York, where he worked on *The Spirit* comic strip, for two years. He also did free lance comic book work for various comic book companies in New York. He is living with his parents, Mr. and Mrs. Hubbard Moore at 33 Tenth Street."[17]

Dixon's participation in writer-artist Will Eisner's *The Spirit,* a Sunday newspaper comic book insert, is well documented because the strip's history is so well documented (among its scriptwriters was Jules Feiffer). It premiered on June 2, 1940, and continued until October 5, 1952. The Spirit was a masked superhero who wore a blue suit and red tie. Dixon, who worked on the strip in 1951 and 1952, was among several assistants employed by Eisner to draw or ink backgrounds, ink parts of main characters, or ghost-draw the strip entirely.[18]

There was no special "comic strip section" within the newspaper for *Barry Jordan* until November 13, 1954, when the *Bronze Raven* added "The National Foto News."[19] The *Barry Jordan* series appeared on the bottom half of a page in the "Foto News." *Barry Jordan* took up the upper half of that space, and *Li'l Moe and Joe* appeared just below it. Dixon's panels ranged from as few as six and to as many as eleven panels and were almost twice the size of nationally syndicated weekly strips in mainstream newspapers at that time.

Barry Jordan is a musician who is also an amateur detective. The series is an adventure continuity comic strip, set in the city. Jordan is an "ace tenor sax-man," and his trio included two other African American men, Bucky and Slim. The novelty of Jordan's persona is that he is, first, a competent and successful musician and, second, an equally competent and successful amateur

detective battling the "evil" lurking in and around hotels and clubs in the Midwest. The components of the black repertoire used in this strip include music, the hero, oratory, the nightclub, and middle-class ideology.

Physically, Jordan is attractive to women, specifically, the blues singer Dee Dee Torch and the Kenny twins, Karen and Kay. However, for the duration of the series, he is single with no references to a spouse, significant other, children, parents, or siblings. In fact, Jordan's closest friends appear to be Bucky and Slim. Barry Jordan is modern and urban and had appealing physical characteristics. He is shaded brown, has well-groomed hair (natural, not processed), clear muscular features, full but not oversized nose and lips, and a firm square jaw. He also wears fashionable tailored suits. The setting of *Barry Jordan* also stresses the city landscape: nightclubs, taxi cabs, and city street corners. Barry Jordan is not shown in his place of residence. At times he is in the nightclub where he is working, and most often he is "in the street" or at the scene of the crime he is engaged in solving.

As the strip illustrates, Jordan was a significant departure from the caricatures of African Americans drawn by whites in earlier comic art. White cartoonists from the late 1890s to the late 1920s exaggerated the physical characteristics of blacks to grotesque and distorted proportions. This typography of the African American, the "Sambo," was characterized by an "eight-ball" head with white, round, bulging eyes; thick, white, clown-shaped lips; objectified hairstyles (for example, the unkempt hair of the Buckwheat character in *The Little Rascals*, if headgear was not drawn); totally black skin; and nondescript clothing or a uniform of some sort to denote the character's occupation as a servant or domestic.[20]

Thematically, *Barry Jordan* is a morality play involving good guys and bad guys. The theme illustrates its relationship with both the classical detective story and the hard-boiled detective story. In the two fully developed plots, the crimes are organized and carried out by both men and women. Furthermore most crimes that Jordan encounters are not violent and ugly in the sense of bloody murder, brutal torture, and gun brandishing. Rather, Jordan is faced with crimes of the intellect. From July 17, 1954, to July 16, 1955, Jordan faces three major crime situations. The first occurs at the interracial Island Casino Club in Toledo, where Jordan solves a case that involved an "infidelity racket." Married men who frequent the Island Casino Club are being extorted for money after having private meetings with the club manager's "wife," who in fact is the club hostess, Kay Kyles. She would take a man to her dressing room for a drink. As he drinks, he becomes more comfortable and intimate with Kay, who then presses a buzzer to call for the club manager, Mr. Blakie. Pretending to be her husband, he enters the dressing room, accuses the man of inappropriate behavior with his wife, and begins to beat him up. To save his skin, the man offers to give money to Mr. Blakie. The second plot is called "The Fire Bug," involving an arson ring targeting nightclubs. The final plot line, which is never resolved because the strip ended on July 16, involved the disappearance of "beautiful women" from the "Float." (It appears to be a large raftlike object with a ladder and diving board.)

Rituals of order operate in the *Barry Jordan* series. As a whole it made a covert political statement because it represented the wish fulfillment of an African American man fully integrated into the American social order: Jordan's world is racially integrated, he relates with whites and blacks with equal ease, he has an acceptable occupation and a successful career as a musician, and, finally, Jordan possesses an intellectual, mental, moral, ethical, and artistic capacity superior to the other characters.[21] However, the series does not make overt political statements about racial injustice, discrimination, or segregationist practices, as did characters in Morrie Turner's *Wee Pals* and Brumsic Brandon Jr.'s *Luther,* both of which ran in the late 1960s, and as do characters in the popular *Boondocks* by Aaron McGruder.[22] Rather, Barry Jordan's presence in postwar comic art *is* the political message that Dixon conveyed. That is, Dixon protested earlier portrayals of African American males by creating one who was not feckless, jet black, lazy, dumb, and dishonest.

The conventions that mediate blackness in black comic strips help to create a picture of either total assimilation into or total segregation from mainstream American society. While these strips are grounded in middle-class ideologies, how the characters interact with the larger society differs greatly. *Swing Papa* and *Little Magnolia* are examples of pluralist (separate-but-equal) discourses. Black comic strips from 1920 to the present show black characters that are just like white characters except for minor differences of habit and racial perspective and show that blacks face the same experiences, situations, and conflicts as whites, except that blacks live in separate communities. In these strips black individuals or families are isolated and living in separate but equal worlds.[23] Jimmy Dixon's *Barry Jordan* is an example of assimilationist (invisibility) discourses. These comic strips, created between 1930 and 1969, treat the social and political issues of black presence in particular and racism in general as individual problems. These strips are assimilationist to the extent that the worlds they construct are distinguished by the complete elimination or, at best, marginalization of social and cultural difference in the interest of shared and universal similarity. *Barry Jordan* was devoid of significant African American traditions, social struggle, racial conflicts, and cultural difference.[24]

In conclusion, through the publication of *Barry Jordan, Little Magnolia,* and *Swing Papa,* black readers of the *Bronze Raven* and *Toledo Sepia City Press* witnessed the mediation of blackness through middle-class ideology. These images provided a prescriptive way of life for urban blacks in postwar America, served as a formative period of black representations, and set a precedent for contemporary African American images.

## NOTES

1. Charles A. Simmons, *The African American Press: A History of News Coverage during National Crises, with Special Reference to Four Newspapers, 1827–1965* (Jefferson, N.C.: McFarland, 1998), 1; Roland E. Wolseley, *The Black Press, U.S.A.,* 2nd ed. (Ames: Iowa State University Press, 1990), 5–6, 17–19); M. Thomas Inge, ed., introduction to *Dark Laughter: The Satiric Art of Oliver W. Harrington.* Jackson: University Press of Mississippi, 1993), vii.

2. M. Thomas Inge, ed., *Comics as Culture* (Jackson: University Press of Mississippi, 1990), 631.

3. See, for example, Thomas Cripps, *Black Film as Genre* (Bloomington: Indiana University Press, 1978), 3; Mark A. Reid, *Redefining Black Film* (Berkeley: University of California Press, 1993), 5.

4. The seven newspapers are the *Toledo Script* (September 1943–February 1949[?]), *Toledo Sepia City Press* (April 2, 1948–May 13, 1950), *Bronze Raven* (September 18, 1948–January 10, 1976), *Toledo Observer* (July 24, 1971, apparently the only issue), *Toledo Journal* (1975–present), *Sojourner's Truth* (April 24, 2002–present), and *Midwest Urban* (January 15, 2008–December 14, 2009). For additional information, see Stephen Gutgesell, *Guide to Ohio Newspapers, 1793–1973: Union Bibliography of Ohio Newspapers Available in Ohio Libraries* (Columbus: Ohio Historical Society, 1974), 343, 347. In addition, microfilm reproductions of the *Bronze Raven* begin with the January 6, 1951, issue, not the issue of September 18, 1948.

5. E. Franklin Frazier, *Black Bourgeoisie* (Glencoe, Ill.: Free Press, 1957), 174.

6. *Little Magnolia* ran in the *Toledo Sepia City Press* January 1949–February 2, 1949, February 26, 1949, March 19, 1949, and April 2, 1949–May 1949.

7. Douglas Kellner, "Television, Mythology and Ritual," *Praxis* 6 (1982): 143.

8. No installment appeared in the July 31 issue, and the editors provided no explanation concerning its absence.

   Minor auxiliaries of the black press (and mainstream press) less formally tied to publishing include news services, feature syndicates, and the dissemination of broadcasting and public relations. Feature syndicates are firms that sell comic strips, panel cartoons, personal columns, and other content for release everywhere on the same date. In the mainstream press major syndicates include King Features Syndicate and United Features Syndicate.

It does not appear that black newspapers had features syndicates created by blacks available to them until 1984, when Syndicated Writers and Artists was founded. However, the *Toledo Sepia City Press* lists a copyright year for *Swing Papa* as 1948 and cites the "Story Script Syndicate" as the syndicate responsible for this strip. In the May 22, 1948, edition of the *Press*, the editor describes the Story Script Syndicate as "an interracial group of writers and artists who have joined hands in a nation wide effort to open new and broader avenues of outlet for the productions of Negro writers and artists." Few references are made to this syndicate before the paper closed in 1950. See Wolseley, *Black Press*, 349, 354; and "Toledo Magazine Attracts Patrons throughout Nation," *Toledo Sepia City Press*, May 22, 1948, 4.

9. See *Toledo Sepia City Press*, April 2, 1948, 4. The *Sepia City Press* listed the newspaper for which Shaw had worked as the *Ohio State News*. The Ohio Historical Society (OHS) Online Collection Catalog lists an African American newspaper within the same time period as Shaw's editorship as the *Columbus Ohio State News*. The OHS's microfilm holdings for this paper date from March 11, 1944, to September 27, 1952. The OHS holding is most likely the correct title for the newspaper because Shaw appears to have strong connections to Columbus, Ohio, through the Bi-Monthly Negro Book Club.

10. O'Wendell Shaw, *Greater Need Below* (1936; repr., New York: AMS Press, 1972), 7, 10; Donald Franklin Joyce, *Gatekeepers of Black Culture: Black-Owned Book Publishing in the United States, 1817–1981* (Westport, Conn.: Greenwood, 1983), 57–58. Shaw's monograph was *Writing for the Weeklies: How to Earn Sparetime Money as a Weekly Newspaper Correspondent* (Columbus, Ohio: Russwurm, 1962).

11. "Artist Created Bulldog Logo Used by Scott High School," *(Toledo) Blade*, August 1, 2001, B4, http://0-infoweb.newsbank.com.catalog.toledolibrary.org/iw-search/we/.

12. See also John Cawelti, *Adventure, Mystery, and Romance: Formula Stories as Art and Popular Culture* (Chicago: University of Chicago Press, 1976), 39–42.

13. I define "black cultural repertoire" as the specific devices, techniques, figures, objects, expressive art forms, or products of people of African descent that form part of their culture (whether as context, texture, or text) and are often derived from the folk tradition (see Stephen F. Soitos, *The Blues Detective: A Study of African American Detective Fiction* [Amherst: University of Massachusetts Press, 1996], 37). These form a foundation of a black aesthetic and are used to create black pop-cultural products. The twelve key components of the black repertoire from which black popular culture draws are the city, food/cuisine, rhythm, percussiveness, call-response,

musicality, oratory, the hero, worship service and party, religion and spirituality, church and nightclub, and middle-class ideology.

14. See the strip of May 1, 1948, in the *Toledo Sepia City Press.* Bob Howe's obituary in the *Toledo Blade* of April 9, 1970, noted, "Sepia City was an unofficial government started by Negro communities throughout the country to advance the race educationally, economically, socially and morally." See also "Primaries begin for Mayor of Sepia City," *Bronze Raven*, March 5, 1955, 1.

15. R. W. "Bob" Howe, "Viewed from Sepia City," *Toledo Sepia City Press*, April 10, 1948, 4, and June 5, 1948, 4; "Editorial: Toledo's New Principals," *Bronze Raven*, June 18, 1955, 2; "Congress's Record Shows Failure on Civil Rights," *Bronze Raven*, July 3, 1954, 1; "House Approves Bill to Ban Jim Crow Travel," *Bronze Raven*, July 31, 1954, 1.

16. Information about the cartoonist Al Hart in books, articles, encyclopedias, and reference books about comic art is nonexistent. His work does appear in the *Pittsburgh Courier*, the leading African American newspaper that ran black comic art in the 1940s and 1950s. The almost four-month run of *Little Magnolia* in the *Sepia City Press* provides little assistance, and Tim Jackson's online resource, "Pioneering Cartoonists of Color," has no record of Al Hart. At present, the only reference to his work that scholars have found is in black Toledo's *Sepia City Press.*

17. "Toledo Artist Begins Comic Strip in Raven," *Bronze Raven*, July 17, 1954, 1.

18. Michael Barrier and Martin Williams, eds., *A Smithsonian Book of Comic-Book Comics* (New York: Smithsonian Institution Press and Harry N. Abrams, 1981), 269–71; Grand Comics Database Project, "Will Eisner's The Spirit Archives #22," www.comics.org/details.lasso?id=356571; "Will Eisner's The Spirit Archives #23," www.comics.org/details.lasso?id=393110; Grand Comics Database Project, "Will Eisner's The Spirit Archives #24," www.comics.org/details.lasso?id=538252.

19. "The National Foto News" was a separate special insert subtitled "America's Most Outstanding Negro Pictorial Weekly." "The National Foto News" featured photographs with news briefs about national and statewide African American celebrities.

20. Ian Gordon, *Comic Strips and Consumer Culture, 1890–1945* (Washington, D.C.: Smithsonian Institution Press, 1998), 60–61, 72; Steven Loring Jones, "From 'Under Cork' to Overcoming: Black Images in the Comics," in Charles Hardy and Gail F. Stern, eds., *Ethnic Images in the Comics* (Philadelphia: Balch Institute for Ethnic Studies, 1986), 21; Martin Sheridan, *Comics and Their Creators* (Westport, Conn.: Hyperion, 1971), 41, 205.

21. James W. Chesebro, "Communication, Values, and Popular Television Series—A Four-Year Assessment," in Horace Newcomb, ed., *Television: The Critical View*, 4th ed. (New York: Oxford University Press, 1987), 33–34.

22. Jones, "From 'Under Cork' to Overcoming," 27; Ben McGrath, "The Radical: Why Do Editors Keep Throwing 'The Boondocks' off the Funnies Page?" *New Yorker*, April 12, 2004, www.newyorker.com/fact/content/?040419fa_fact2McGrath.

23. Herman Gray, *Watching Race: Television and the Struggle for "Blackness"* (Minneapolis: University of Minnesota Press, 1995), 87.

24. Ibid., 85.

# Put Some Skirts on the Cards!

## Black Women's Visual Performances in the Art of Annie Lee

*We owe it to ourselves to analyze the visual, [while realizing] the necessity for analyzing the past, doing something to shape the present, and anticipating the future.*

■ Michelle Wallace, "Why Are There No Great Black Artists?"

O
n November 14, 2008, the largest African American museum of its kind, the Charles H. Wright Museum of African American History, hosted an exhibition and signing by one of the most well known artists of the late twentieth century, Annie Lee (figure 13.1). The event included an unveiling of her commemorative painting of President Barack Obama that would become one of the paintings in her woman-centered *Obama Series*. Lee's art is particularly noted for its performative aesthetic, where the subjects of her work appear as characters engaged in a process of movement, and for her use of partial silhouette, where the character's facial features are absent. The latter aspect of Lee's art accounts for its popularity among spectators, consumers, and collectors, because the absent facial features allow for an embodiment of the character. This aesthetic aspect of

Lee's art situates her work as dialogic, visual performances. "I try to give a message without expression," Lee acknowledged during an interview by the *Michigan Chronicle* about her Wright Museum showing. She continued, "It's a challenge for me to make the movement of the figure give the message that I'm trying to get across."[1] Lee's ability to use the visual form to relay the performance and affirmation of cultural identities through an aesthetic combination of movement and masquerade makes her work a prime site for an interrogation of the relationship of black identity performances, class, and visual cultural studies.

Annie Lee's formal training includes study at the American Academy of Art, and she holds a master's degree in interdisciplinary arts education. She is a gallery owner, art distributor, and acclaimed artist who markets her art through her own businesses, Just Original Images, Ltd., and Sass 'n Class. The focus in Lee's work is African American men and women, yet the majority of her work makes women the primary subject and shows them in a position of agency. Lee's images of women have five consistent themes: performances of race and nation; working-class consciousness; leisure activities, such as hairstyling and card playing; endorsements of middle-class sensibilities that value the ideological presuppositions of the conjugal family; and heterosexual couplehood. Lee's thematic focus, though seemingly conservative at first glance, propagates a version of black Americana that presents at once the pleasures of everyday life without denying the perils. (*Americana* refers to art that depicts distinctly American scenes.) In so doing, her art provides images of cultural resonance, new ways of seeing the black subject, and a varied cultural politics of identity.

In order to explore Lee's productive suture of African American women's performances and visual representation, I analyze the paintings and figurines of Annie Lee as an example of mid-twentieth-century to early twenty-first-century iterations of nation, class, gender, race, and sexuality. I argue that Lee's art constitutes relatable visual performances, thereby creating what the feminist art critic Salah M. Hassan describes as a process of auto-inscription. The theory of autoinscription refers to the process in which consumers may insert their subjectivity into the piece and encode and decode the artwork according to their identities and worldview.[2] To convey what autoinscriptive art means for the productive convergence of the performa-

tive and the visual, I will analyze how Lee envisages the variety of black female identities as articulated and practiced in everyday life. Key questions I
take up include the following: How does Lee's aesthetic approach constitute
performances of class, race, gender, national, and sexual constructs? What
meanings does the process of mass consumption hold for African American
women as spectators and collectors of Annie Lee's art? Finally, what are the
empirical imperatives that provide evidence for viewing the cultural work of
Lee's art as constituting the transformative power of oppositional art by and
for African American women?

## Got'cha Back . . . Boo! Performing Gender and Nation in Annie Lee's Obama Series

In the painting *New Tenants (Obama)*, Annie Lee illustrates the relationship
of African American culture, class ascension, and national identity.[3] The
painting shows President Barack Obama, Michelle Obama, and daughters

Annie Lee, second from left, signs one of her Sass 'n Class figurines for a collector. *Courtesy of Charles H. Wright Museum of African American History's Archive and Research Center*
(November 14, 2008).

Sasha and Malia as they walk toward the White House. Next to the White House is a basketball court that stands in erect opposition to the massive white compound painted with strategic strokes of stark white, yellow, and gray. The family members hold hands as they approach a path lined with green bushes on both sides. Etched in the middle of each bush is a word or phrase that refers to policies of the outgoing Bush administration. Words or phrases such as "high gas prices," "war on terror," "recession," "foreclosure," "Iraq," and "Iran" are mediated with pat rhetorical answers such as "change," "hope," and "yes we can." To the left of President Obama, daughter Malia holds an American flag. To the right of First Lady Michelle Obama, daughter Sasha holds a white scruffy dog under her right forearm. The president, in the middle, tucks a basketball under his left armpit. The president and First Lady are holding hands, and from their joined hands dangle a ring of large, golden keys. The Obama daughters are dressed casually, in bold colorful play clothes, and they have hairstyles that are a combination of plaits and coiled curls. In aesthetic contrast, the First Lady appears in pearls, a conservative red sheath dress, and a "Jackie O"–inspired, relaxed flip hairdo. The president wears a navy suit and has a rhythmic lean as he walks forward; he presents an example of the masculine cool cultivated by African American bebop musicians of the 1950s. In its colorful details of African American expressive culture and the vexed question of African American patriotism, *New Tenants (Obama)* invokes a gendered and intergenerational narrative of performing race, class, and nation.

*New Tenants (Obama)* is half Americana and half cultural criticism. It displays the contradiction of American nostalgia and the real domestic and international challenges facing the nation-state. The bushes with etched wording, the clothing and artifacts of the four subjects pictured, and their movement toward a basketball court and the White House convey that people of African descent in the United States perform national citizenship while simultaneously living and expressing cultural identity. As the epigraph to this chapter asks of visual artists, Lee in *New Tenants (Obama)* considers the African American past, shows how African American cultural forms shape the present, and anticipates the future of African American cultural representation. The Obamas' visual representation in *New Tenants* also shows that despite their move toward the White House, they remain entangled, as the etchings on the green bushes convey, within the imperial "costs" of nation making and empire. The painting also depicts the sense that the Obamas may feel pressure to perform the self- and societal imposition of black middle-class identity. *New Tenants (Obama)* is one in a series of paintings by Annie Lee that depicts this intersection of racial representation, class identity, and nation with a focus on black womanhood.

Annie Lee's *Oval Office* is similar to the iconographic statement of *New Tenants (Obama)*. In this piece, she visualizes the First Family by infusing references of nation and patriotism with significations of African American culture. The environment of the office is a simile for the real building. Yet, Lee paints signs associated with blackness and American patriotism to reconfigure the image of the Oval Office as a portrait of African American family life. The president in this image sits at a desk, while Michelle Obama looks over his shoulder to seemingly offer advice; Sasha and Malia are on the floor in front of the desk and appear busy with homework and play. To the right of the desk is a basketball, which invokes African American expressive sports culture. A significant decision on Lee's part is to assert African American women's central role in the president's administration, signified by her use of the First Lady as an assumed co-decision maker through form and posture. While the facial features of the subjects are characteristically absent, the spectator knows whom the image means to depict. However, an autoinscriptive aesthetic is still at work here, not through the aesthetic choice of anonymity, which the subject of the painting makes impossible, but rather through its ability to change the narrative of the White House to one in which African American culture and life are central.

In the painting *Got'cha Back . . . Boo!* Lee follows the theme of presidential decision making as cooperative with African American womanhood, by using vernacular language structures, as evidenced by the title, and by painting the First Lady at work at a desk. To the right of the First Lady Lee has positioned an American flag in the foreground; on the wall directly behind her is a yellow and green map of the United States. A clock gives the time as three o'clock. The map's colors stand in stark contradiction to the American flag, and the wall clock provides a satirical wink to the now-infamous "It's 3 a.m." ads used by Senator Hillary Rodham Clinton during the 2008 presidential race.[4] *Got'cha Back . . . Boo!* declares that there will be a woman in the Oval Office to take the call at 3 a.m.—an African American woman who will perhaps help formulate a decision.

Lee inflects whimsical humor through the painting's title and African American womanhood through its representation of Michelle Obama as decision maker, but *Got'cha Back . . . Boo!* underscores a middle-class sensibility of material commodification and respectability that has a history of distancing itself from the African American masses. Further, the image conveys that the First Lady is busy at work addressing concerns of national interest, yet she also exhibits a hyperfemininity: her posture accentuates the curve of her hips, she wears a sleek lavender dress, white pearls, and a perfect coiffure and sports a French manicure. Such depictions are a common representation of womanhood that uses hyperfemininity to mediate the threat of domination or emasculation in the workplace. However, given the historical representation of African American women as nongendered objects or hypersexual seductresses, this depiction of the First Lady is an uncommon depiction of African American womanhood in visual culture and in the public sphere. Thus the mixture of Lee's symbolic choices in *Got'cha Back . . . Boo!* for example, the focus on femininity, Afrocentric map, clock time, and the vernacular utterance of the painting's title, presents a historically situated illustration that complicates any hasty reading of bourgeois upper-class elitism.

The *Obama Series* shows a concentrated effort to intervene in and expand frameworks of African American representation and constructions of class in art while also drawing from key historical moments in civil rights history to predict changes in social relations. *Change* is a painting that revisualizes Norman Rockwell's painting *The Problem We All Live With*—a now metonymic visualization of the struggle of integration in the 1960s. Rockwell's painting depicts the real life of Ruby Bridges, a young girl who was one of many to desegregate the New Orleans public school system. In contrast, Annie Lee's *Change* is a post–civil rights image. Bridges walks hand-in-hand with an African American male student, two white male students, and one white female student. The children carry signs that read "change" and "yes we can." At the middle of this visual narrative is Lee's reincarnation of

Bridges, whose sign reads "YES i can." Above the schoolchildren Lee paints in a shadow-like aesthetic four figures in caps and gowns that signify graduates as a specter of historical consciousness and judicial decision making.

*Change* may appear to invoke a troublesome neoliberal and post–civil rights rhetoric of assumed progress in social relations, because of the apparent successes of the civil rights movement of the 1960s. However, Lee's visual and narrative decision for Bridges to carry a sign that says "YES i can" repositions Bridges not as a young girl requiring protection to carry out a judicial decision but rather as an agent of change. In this way, the painting does not use the broader context of an Obama administration to suggest an erasure of racism in America. To the contrary, *Change* centers the African American female subject as indispensible in the cross-racial and intergender crusade for social justice. The painting *Change* is congruent with Lee's apparent vision in the *Obama Series,* a vision that shows African American women performing the prospects and perils of the nation within middle-class discourses of propriety. Yet the artist's broader range of class consciousness directs attention to the multivalent and multiclass experiences of African American women.

## Blue Monday: Performing Class Consciousness and Body Politics

Lee refigures ideologies of everyday life for working-class women in the late twentieth century from the vantage point of a myriad of African American female experiences in her first piece to gain widespread recognition, *Blue Monday,* which is the most mass-produced and popular painting done by the artist to date. Perhaps more than any other image of Lee's, *Blue Monday* stands out as a significant visual statement of a working-class consciousness. While working as a clerk in the engineering department of a railroad, Lee began to visualize an image that would explain how she felt each morning as she faced her workday. Lee says that while contemplating her approach to the piece, she had wondered if anyone else felt as tired and broken down before the start of a workday as she did.[5] *Blue Monday* was thus born out of Lee's own experience as a working-class woman and her yearning to make that experience meaningful for the African American female subject.

The painting positions a woman with hair in plaits, wearing a white slip and black cotton slippers while sitting at the edge of a bed with her shoulders raised high. Lee's paint strokes blend to create a continuity of blues, browns, and shades of white and gray, and the face of Lee's subject appears indistinct through a blending of warm browns, oranges, and yellows. *Blue Monday* is more than self-description about work exhaustion and accompanying depression. *Blue Monday* no doubt hails African American women spectators, because the image reflects a common sentiment of their working lives. An online brochure published by Avisica, a gallery specializing in African American art, attests to how Lee's *Blue Monday* resonates with African American women: "We can't tell you how many times we have seen women grab at Annie Lee's famous 'Blue Monday' print, proclaiming, 'that's me!'"[6]

Lee's series of satirical "sizism" pieces—*Does This Come in Three X?* and *You Hungry?*—does not directly illustrate meditations on class for the masses of African American women. Rather, the two images address imaging of the body. Lee's *Does This Come in Three X?* pays attention to realistic contours of the body and visualizes the exasperation full-figured women experience as they peruse racks in department stores that do not cater to women who fall outside standard clothing sizes. Lee's subject in *Does This Come in Three X?* holds up a small garment in front of her full shape, thus visually indicating the disjuncture between the standard-size clothing found in department stores and the real-size woman. Comparatively, *You Hungry?* extends Lee's focus on African American women's reconceptualization of their relationship to their bodies; she paints two middle-aged women with round protruding stomachs and widely formed legs standing side by side in leotards as they look down at their feet. Her placement of the two bodies in proximity exudes comfort rather than anxiety. Their clothing and posturing suggest they are engaged in the performance of dance or aerobic exercise, but they are not working toward an emancipated body form. Both *Three X* and *You Hungry?* encourage food consumption and healthy living, instead of deprivation and acquiescing to unrealistic, hegemonic constructions of beauty. The placement of her subjects in familiar settings and within known circumstances—whether the morning before a grueling workday or the suggestion of the limitation of standardized sizing—creates the humor and wit of art commonly associated with Americana.

# Burn Ya Baby? Performing Black Hairstyling Practices as Black Americana

The goal of Americana art is to represent universal themes of everyday life. Lee's insistence on visualizing female subjects of African descent in familiar settings emanates from a desire to paint with a specific demographic in mind while at the same time introducing a multiplicity of images that refigure the universal as the particular. In her insistence on painting the everyday subject, Lee creates a particular form of Americana relevant to African American experiences. Lee's numerous paintings of African American hairstyling and beauty salons are highly representative of black Americana, as hair grooming is central to African American women's everyday lives. Lee's art reveals that she is committed to displaying the variety of skin tones, hairstyles, and hair textures that mark African American life and their relationship without being preachy about the politics of hairstyling in the black community. An example of this is Lee's *Burn Ya Baby?*, a painting of a beautician consoling a hot comb–scorched customer. The sharply painted hairstyling tools, photos on the salon wall, and softly brush-stroked full-figured bodies provide contrast to the absent facial features of the two women.

*Burn Ya Baby?* documents the humorous (even if painful) moment that many women of her generation can relate to: the early morning pressing-comb sessions when your mother accidentally burns your ear and you jump. She knows she burned you but acts surprised when you squeal in your seat. *Burn Ya Baby?* acknowledges the centrality of hair grooming to African American experience. Like Lee's images of the real-size body, her depiction of the salon locates the difference between how women experience hair grooming as a part of everyday life and reconciliation, rather than as a form of performative ethnic assimilation. This artistic position is key to the formation of African American female subjectivity, as hairstyling within African American communities, argues the cultural critic Kobena Mercer in his essay "Black Hair/Style Politics," is a multivalent cultural practice. Mercer writes that the problem with critics of black hairstyling is that "they rarely actually listen to what people think and feel about it."[7] *Burn Ya Baby?* is part of a large series of Lee's paintings that replicate African American women's actual hairstyling experiences in honest and unapologetic ways.

Lee's *Hot Comb*, a painting of a woman straightening her afro; *All That Glitters*, which depicts the all-day drama of a hair appointment in a black beauty salon; and *Extensions*, which shows several women in the midst of a hair-weaving session all illustrate the world of black hair care. The detail of the women's setting and obfuscation of their identities through the technique of the silhouette situates black hairstyling as a cultural practice that represents what bell hooks calls women's culture of intimacy. hooks writes that hairstyling for a black woman is that "exclusive moment when Black women meet at home or in the beauty parlor to talk with one another, and to listen to the talk."[8] These gender-specific, or woman-centered, images resonate with the African American female spectator at the very core of her feminine identity. Although not overtly sexual, these images present a creation and manipulation of a sexualized connotation, as hair grooming is one site where sexual identity is located on the body. The hegemonic function of hairstyling and its influence on male sexual desire is not a question in Lee's work. Rather, with humor and realism she simply documents the moment and expression of hairstyling as an everyday cultural practice that women negotiate and enjoy in their gendered and racially specific spaces.

## Put Some Skirts on the Cards! Performances of Leisure

Lee's series of African American women playing bid whist and dominos represents a woman's sphere of leisure that is usually associated with male culture. In *Put Some Skirts on the Cards!* Lee makes an explicit statement, which is clear from the title. The title represents the moment in the game bid whist, a card game similar to bridge that is popular among African Americans, where players show their hand. This image and her series of paintings about card playing also point out that African American women use card playing as a space to convene and express pleasure. Each painting in this series situates African American women together, sometimes with male partners, conversing, playing, and finding amusement with each other. The game is only one site of their enjoyment. Card playing takes on other dimensions here, as the women create time to engage with each other and relish the release of conversation about their lives. It is significant that Lee's paintings of card playing mostly depict women playing cards in the kitchen, thereby transforming what is typically thought of as a domestic site into a site of collective everyday pleasure for, rather than from, women.

Six No Uptown and Misdeal, two other prominent pieces in her card-playing series, bear a similar comedic aesthetic toward this practice. In Misdeal Lee's performative technique is particularly striking: the characters laugh, some lean back in their seats, while others lean over the table, thus showing their excitement at card playing. Lee's animated characters bring the spectator into the action. Similar to the people depicted in Lee's other paintings, each card player in this series represents the diversity of colors, hairstyles, and realistic body shapes of women of African descent. For the most part these women are in women-centered spaces, with other women, or in spaces formerly occupied by other women. The subjects in most of Lee's paintings, many of which have been mass-produced as prints, posters, and figurines, shop, play, and gossip with each other on the streets, in their homes, at the beauty salon, and in church. Annie Lee's chosen environment for her paintings underscores the importance of spaces that allow African American women to enact cultural forms and practices that hold meaning for the enjoyment of their everyday lives.

## Love Song: Performing Conservative (?) Sexual Expression

Many of Lee's images intervene in the dearth of sexual representation and romantic love between middle-class African American women and men. Lee's art provides a representation of African American female sexuality that shows women as autonomous sexual and sensual beings in a variety of contexts. The typical visual representation of African American men and women is that they are asexual, hypersexual, or sexual adversaries; there is a scarcity of images that depict romantic and tender moments. Written and visual texts that explore intimate and sexual images of African American women and of African American women with African American men are scarce. To intervene in this omission, several popular and academic books aimed at a mass audience take up the subject of black love and sexuality in its numerous forms. Paula Woods and Felix Hiddell's *I Hear a Symphony,* about long-term heterosexual couplehood and love, bell hooks's trilogy on love, *All about Love, Communion,* and *Salvation,* and Tricia Rose's ground-breaking oral history, *Longing to Tell,* a collection of stories of black women's sexual lives, mark a topical and methodological shift in sexuality literature.[9] These texts use or reflect African American people's actual voices in discussing everyday incarnations of love and pleasure and the impact of sexuality on African American women and men and on their emotions. Similarly, Lee's thematic approach to love and sexuality highlights the everyday sexual lives of African American people. Her paintings on romantic love portray egalitarian and/or heterosexual relationships and sexualities that animate moments of intimate interaction.

Lee's paintings of sexual intimacy appear in the popular lithographs *Jumpin' the Broom, Sunday Evening Radio, Love Song,* and *Primpin'.* The first shows an African American male-female couple formalizing their nuptials as they leap high over a wooden broom. The male figure wears a brown and orange suit and hat and the female figure a full white dress, brown boots, and large veiled headpiece. Orange and shades of yellow engulf the image of the couple and add dimension to the bodies' midair movement. This culturally specific practice designed to replace Eurocentric wedding ceremonies brings a black aesthetic to Lee's version of Americana. Further, *Jumpin' the Broom* reveals how African Americans invent practices out of necessity and survival.

In *Sunday Evening Radio* a nuclear African American family sits in front of the hearth listening to the radio, and in the painting *Love Song,* Lee shows an African American male-female couple cuddling in a large chair as they listen to a record playing on a Victrola. In contrast, Lee's *Primpin'* depicts two women who are styling their hair and admiring their reflections in a mirror while standing intimately close to each other. *Sunday Evening Radio* and *Love Song* place African American subjects in a traditional, although largely ignored, visual format of family and male-female love. While *Primpin'* may imply a sexual relationship or friendship, part of the success of the image comes from the ambiguity and tension created by the placement of the women's bodies in a tight space. All four images produce a representation of African American love or intimacy largely absent from visual culture, but, more important, *Jumpin' the Broom, Sunday Evening Radio, Love Song,* and *Primpin'* extend the possibilities of visual representation rather than confining it to a stagnate representation.

Lee's work fills a void for a segment of the African American viewing public, but the popularity of her work arises from the reality that spectators view her images as palatable and not threatening. Despite the sexual ambiguity and progressive implications of *Primpin'*, her work does fall within the genre of black Americana art and safe sexual boundaries. Indeed, Lee's silhouettes are far from the scatological horrors of slavery, sexualities, and race done by Kara Walker and the abstruse work of other contemporary artists that have gained large-scale recognition.[10] Thus while her images may seem less than overtly radical or sexually transgressive, the historical construction of race, gender, and class, as her paintings, particularly of the Obamas, illustrate, changes the cultural meanings of those visual representations.

## Sass 'n Class: Performing Race and Gender through Art Collecting

The responses to Annie Lee's work by women who collect it attest to the cultural work her art performs for consumers. An Annie Lee Collector Club now exists, and Lee's work is a mainstay of Jo's Collectors Club, a club of African American women who collect affordable lithographs and ceramic figurines. JoAnn Griffin, the initiator of the club and an art gallery owner, told a reporter for the *Detroit News,* "Lee is an artist [who] can relate to the masses and to the Black experience and I think that's easily confirmed by the way collectors respond by purchasing her work."[11] As bell hooks observes in her book on race and visual politics, *Art on My Mind,* the largest impediments to art collecting by the masses of African Americans are that they do not have the disposable income or the display space needed to collect.[12] Lee's affordable autoinscriptive art represents the significance of her paintings insofar as consumption is concerned. Given the reasonable prices of her prints and posters, women are able to collect Lee's art in significant quantities, and the figurines she introduced in 1996 that replicate scenes in her paintings allow women to collect her art in several forms. African American women who collect the lithographs (few purchase the original paintings, which usually cost $4,000 to $12,000) and matching figurines create a collective installation of Lee's images for a fraction of what it would cost to collect multiple pieces of elite or folk art. The number of African American families that may occupy the White House is a foreseeable few; however, a consumer may buy a depiction of the Obamas in the White House for $40.

Sass 'n Class is Lee's commercial venture that reproduces her paintings as figurines and miniprints and on commemorative plates, greeting cards, cookie jars, throws, and coffee cups. The company uses sales figures for the lithographs to determine which images might sell well in the form of figurines or other types of material culture. Sass 'n Class has also begun to re-create historically African American neighborhoods of the mid-twentieth century in figurine form, thereby visually preserving an aspect of African American history that, as an article in the *Michigan Chronicle* notes, "pays tribute to old neighborhoods and building scenes that feature full-of-life people deeply rooted in . . . spirit and memory."[13] Instead of fragmenting the market for Lee's paintings and lithographs, Sass 'n Class's marketing strategy expands Lee's market. While her images have sold in more than two thousand art galleries in the United States, black beauty salons, independent retailers, and churches—places frequented by everyday African American women—also sell the pieces. This may increase sales in all areas of each form of the reproduced images (silhouette, figurine, plaques, etc.), instead of placing these forms in competition with each other. A lithograph of Lee's is approximately $25 to $50 unframed, a figurine runs about $40 to $60, and one can purchase Lee's coffee cups, calendars, and tote bags for less than $20. Reproductions sold in beauty salons by independent distributors sell for just under $20. For less than $100, then, a consumer is able to collect several forms of Lee's work.

African American women collect Lee's work because it is affordable, and it reflects their experiences and emotions. Lee's work offers African American women the opportunity to engage in art collection in a way that is congruent with the parameters of their lives. This, in turn, forges a new and less restrictive creation of an alternative visual public concerned with the needs and everyday life visions of African American women. Women exchange the images replicated in Annie Lee's greeting cards as a practice in shared identities and emotions, they purchase a coffee cup to bring a sense of that varied identity into their working or home lives, and the placement and display of a miniature plate or print will accommodate a spectrum of physical spaces.

There remains a dearth of scholarly attention to art made with an African American female spectatorship in mind. Additionally, African American artists who have come to the attention of the art world and art critics are often male artists who produce elite or folk art. I have thus shown what Lee's art does and has the capability to do for understanding how the African American female subject performs race, gender, class, and sexuality in a multiplicity of visual sites. Lee's work forges a performative aesthetic that imagines a visual public typically left outside the discourse on public art and the politics of visual representation. Although other African American artists visualize the everyday lives of African American women in their art and visual productions, Lee's work serves a mass market for the demographic depicted in her art. That is to say, while the acclaimed artists Faith Ringgold, Betye Saar, Emma Amos, and Elizabeth Catlett also place black women as revolutionary social subjects in their art, and their work appears prominently in museum collections and in art criticism, everyday black women can afford to buy and collect Lee's art.[14]

Cultural criticism of black performance and visual culture becomes sharper by acknowledging the limits placed upon African Americans in the field of performance and visual representation, and by acknowledging the construction and consumption of counterimages. The cultural work and possibilities of Lee's art exist within her creation of an African American woman–centered visual public. The paintings' bricolage, that is, Lee's unconventional mixture of silhouette and performative detail, create an auto-inscribed aesthetic that collectors respond to with their purchasing power. Lee's technique encourages African American female spectators to look back at their deformed representation and beyond their absence in visual culture and venture into a space of viewing and collecting pleasure. A focus on the performative aspects of visual culture, the various modalities of difference, and mass consumption, I argue, allows for an intervention in the limited approach to African American art and visual culture, where high and folk art take primacy, thereby eliding popular and mass-circulated art.

The art historian Sharon Patton points out that black Americana art, or "American scene painting" that depicts the working and middle classes, gained popularity among African American artists in the 1930s; the two most popular who worked in this genre were Palmer Hayden and Archibald J. Motley. When art critics dismissed Hayden's work for its focus on everyday life, because they felt it was too insignificant and common for fine or high art, he declared that he was "painting an era" and that his works "made a symbolic reference to comedy, tragedy, and the pleasures of black life."[15] Similarly, Lee's painting process and what that process means to her and her viewing public are instructive concerning the importance of mass-circulated art. With each piece, Lee conveys an autoinscriptive message and she is painting with an African American female spectator in mind. Given that African American women are buying her art, and they buy a lot of it, the impact of her work is tremendous. I return, then, to Annie Lee's painting of four women intensely playing bid whist while an African American man and his female partner look on with interest in *Put Some Skirts on the Cards!* Lee's intuitive painting about the moments African American women find in their lives to enjoy each other and create space for what they enjoy is representative of my argument(s). Given that visual criticism often leaves the art produced by and for African American women negated, appropriated, or on the margins of discourse on contemporary art, I have meant to "put some skirts" on the intellectual and male-dominated card game of visual culture, criticism, and politics.

### NOTES

1. "Power of Pictures: Annie Lee Graces Detroit, Wright Museum," *Michigan Chronicle,* December 16, 2008.
2. Salah Hassan, introduction to *Gendered Visions: The Art of Contemporary Africana Woman Artists* (Trenton, N.J.: African World Press, 1997).

3. Many of Annie Lee's works, including most of those discussed in this essay, are posted at various sites on the Internet.

4. See Chris Cillizza, "Clinton's '3 a.m. Phone Call' Ad," *Washington Post Online*, February 29, 2008, http://voices.washingtonpost.com/thefix/eye-on-2008/hrcs-new-ad.html.

5. "Annie Francis Lee Biography," *HistoryMakers*, April 5, 2007, www.thehistorymakers.com.

6. "Art Talk: Why Buy Black Art," Avisca.com, January 5, 2000, www.avisca.com/art_talk.htm#WHY%20BY%20ART.

7. Kobena Mercer, *Welcome to the Jungle: New Positions in Black Cultural Studies* (New York: Routledge, 1994), 104.

8. bell hooks, "Straightening Our Hair," in Juliette Harris and Pamela Johnson, eds., *Tenderheaded: A Comb-Bending Collection of Hair Stories* (New York: Pocket Books, 2001), 11.

9. See Paula Woods and Felix Liddell, eds., *I Hear a Symphony: African Americans Celebrate Love* (New York: Doubleday, 1995); bell hooks, *All about Love: New Visions* (New York: HarperCollins, 2000); bell hooks, *Salvation: Black People and Love* (New York: William Morrow, 2001); bell hooks, *Communion: The Female Search for Love* (New York: HarperCollins, 2002); Tricia Rose, *Longing to Tell: Black Women's Stories of Sexuality and Intimacy* (New York: Farrar, Straus and Giroux, 2003).

10. For an analysis of Walker's work, see Gwendolyn Shaw Du Bois, *Seeing the Unspeakable: The Art of Kara Walker* (Durham, N.C.: Duke University Press, 2004), and Hans Ulrich Obrist, Nancy Spector, Susanne Neuburger, and Vitus H. Weh, *Kara Walker: Safety Curtain* (Cologne: Verlag der Buchhandlung Walther Konig, 2002).

11. Rhoda Bates-Rudd, "Brunch Recognizes Chicago Artisan, Fetes Annie Lee, Known for Her Paintings, Ceramics," *Detroit News*, May 17, 2000.

12. See the essay "Art Matters" in hooks's *Art on My Mind* (New York: New Press, 1995).

13. Patrick Keating, "Creating Heartfelt Art, Usually with a Message," *Michigan Chronicle*, May 24, 2005.

14. On Ringgold, Saar, Amos, and Catlett see Sharon Patton, "Living Fearlessly with and within Difference(s): Emma Amos, Carol Anne Carter, and Martha Jacobson-Jarvis," ed., David Driskell *African American Visual Aesthetics* (Washington: Smithsonian Institute Press, 1995); Beverly Guy-Sheftall, "Warrior Women: Art as Resis-

tance," in *Bearing Witness: Contemporary Works by African American Woman Artists* (New York: Rizzoli International, 1996); Leslie Hammond, *Gumbo Ya Ya: Anthology of Contemporary African American Women Artists* (New York: Mid March Arts Press, 1995); and Jontyle Theresa Robinson, ed., *Bearing Witness: Contemporary Works by African American Woman Artists* (New York: Rizzoli International, 1996).

15. Patton, "Living Fearlessly," 138.

# Melodrama of the Movement
## Lorraine Hansberry's *A Raisin in the Sun*

When the hip-hop performer and cultural impresario Sean "Puffy" Combs lent his celebrity to the role of Walter Lee Younger in the recent ABC version of *A Raisin in the Sun,* he only confirmed what many fans had long known: Lorraine Hansberry's kitchen-sink drama has legs. From the original Broadway production of 1959–60 to the first film version (1961) to the Tony Award–winning musical *Raisin* (1973) to the first television production (1989) to the 2004 Broadway revival (also starring Combs), Hansberry's civil rights–era play remains an important, indeed classic, text for U.S. cultural consumers and African American cultural consumers in particular. Yet for all its appeal, *Raisin* has also raised the hackles of many intellectuals. During the 1960s such figures as Harold Cruse and Amiri Baraka found *Raisin* to be little more than a sop to white liberals eager to imagine that postwar embourgeoisement would eventually come to include all Americans, regardless of color.[1] For these critics *Raisin* was not so much a moving commentary on the empty promises and broken realities of the postwar African American dream as it was a maudlin affirmation of white bourgeois domesticity.

That critique did offer a cogent account of the *white* reading of the play. As the awards, magazine coverage, and general mainstream acclaim accorded the 1959 Broadway production of *Raisin* suggest, Hansberry's appropriation of white ethnic melodrama seems to have provided many white theatergoers with a way to find in the civil rights struggle a reflection of their own journey into suburbia. For most whites, I think it's fair to say, *Raisin* constituted black confirmation of the American dream. Yet what Cruse and Baraka's indictment of *Raisin* did not do is explain why African Americans of the late 1950s and early 1960s identified with the trials of the Younger family. As James Baldwin wrote of the play in 1965, "Black people recognized that house and all the people in it and supplied the play with an interpretive element which could not be present in the minds of white people: a kind of claustrophobic terror, created not only by their knowledge of the house but by their knowledge of the streets."[2] That is, Cruse and Baraka did not consider the possibility that Hansberry's melodrama is not so much an endorsement of dominant middle-class values as a sensitive engagement with the multiple contradictions that attended most black dreams of life among the bourgeoisie.

In what follows, I read *Raisin* as a text that revises traditional melodramatic dynamics in order to explore the intersections of race, class, and gender at a historical moment when an increasing number of African Americans imagined that they might enter the nation's middle class. Sensitive to the political uses of affective culture on the one hand, and conscious of the racist and patriarchal biases of that culture on the other, Hansberry revitalized a hackneyed genre in order to celebrate the black female tradition of resistance and its central place in the burgeoning civil rights movement. Black women in *Raisin* celebrate the domestic in a sentimental manner, but this endorsement of home serves in large part to ensure that a black working-class family will remember and support the long-standing history of struggle against white racism and capital. If the angry young man of the play, Walter Lee Younger, attempts to emulate white capitalists regardless of the cost, his wife, Ruth; sister, Benethea; and mother, Lena, all tease from consumer culture lessons of "racio-familial history" important to the struggle. In other words, *Raisin* is less a symptom than a diagnosis of the black ambivalence about normative (white) notions of embourgeoisement. Little wonder, then, that in 1989 Amiri Baraka would revise his earlier assessment of the play and claim that "*Raisin* speaks of and to and for the masses of the black community as no other play ever has."[3]

Before I turn to Hansberry, however, some overview of the social context of melodrama at the end of the 1950s is in order. During the mid- to late 1950s the preoccupation with cold war ideology and the ostensible superiority of the U.S. capitalist way of life that informed so much of the decade began to change. Senator Joseph McCarthy's fall from grace at the middle of the decade and Nikita Khruschev's denunciation of Joseph Stalin at the Twentieth Party Congress set the stage for a slight but significant thaw in the cold war. This thaw was important enough to allow Soviet Premier Nikita Khruschev to visit the United States and then–vice president Richard Nixon to visit Moscow. For average Americans the reduction of cold war tensions not only eased anxieties about the superpower standoff, it also enabled them to feel more comfortable about voicing their dissatisfaction with the false promises of the so-called Affluent Society. If the postwar boom seemed to offer all Americans the comforts of bourgeois bliss, a significant economic downshift in 1958 and full-blown recession in 1958 revealed the absurdity of such a claim.[4] The slight increase in the perceived freedom of expression and the dip in economic prosperity provided an opportunity for people to begin thinking for themselves and voicing their dissent more openly. The late 1950s would witness the public rediscovery of socialism by New York intellectuals such as Irving Howe and Philip Rahv, the easing of the blacklist, the scandal of the rigged quiz shows, and, after the federal intervention in the Little Rock desegregation case, a new interest in the ongoing black struggle for civil rights. The cold war had hardly disappeared—the Cuban missile crisis was right around the corner—but the opportunity for social and cultural change seemed to have increased.

Public intellectuals such as Arthur Schlesinger Jr. recognized that the shift in social mood had its cultural correlatives. In his *Esquire* magazine essay "The New Mood in American Politics" (1960), Schlesinger lists the cultural signs of a new social awareness on the part of the populace—the Beats, Lenny Bruce, Billy Graham—and argues that the popularity of those cultural phenomena suggested that the sixties would resemble the radical thirties more than the complacent fifties.[5] Schlesinger proved prophetic. Bob

Dylan would borrow from Woody Guthrie's folksinging; Angela Davis would learn Marxism from the historian Herbert Aptheker; and the playwright Luis Valdez would appropriate techniques from the Living Newspaper theater.

Lorraine Hansberry also attempted to redefine the texts of the "red decade" for a new time of change, but unlike the vast majority of her contemporaries she turned to a more surprising cultural resource: the ethnic melodramas affiliated with the Popular Front.[6] Rarely read, let alone performed, today, such ethnic melodramas as Clifford Odets's *Awake and Sing*, Theodore Ward's *Big White Fog*, John van Druten's *I Remember Mama*, and Philip Yordan's *Anna Lucasta* focused on gender and generational conflicts in order to draw parallels between domestic tensions and national problems. The realism of these plays, while always palpable, stands in tension with an overriding delight in affect, sensation, and the problem of moral life; like the classic nineteenth-century melodramatic fictions analyzed by Peter Brooks, these ethnic theatricals "express [Manichean] forces and imperatives . . . bring them to striking revelation [and] impose their evidence."[7] Yet at the same time Hansberry's turning to the kitchen-sink plays of a leftist variety renders them more ethnic and more anticapitalist than most of their generic kin. Often drawn from the writer's own experience, such works as *Awake and Sing* and *I Remember Mama* tend to focus on self-consciously "other," proletarian, and (often) matriarchal households struggling to maintain their values amid the temptations of a crass consumerist society. Their Manichean imperatives, to borrow from Brooks, drew from and contributed to the rich Popular Front culture of the 1930s and 1940s.

The ideological charge of these "red" melodramas did not survive the passing of the Popular Front and the rise of the Affluent Society and its new medium, television. As George Lipsitz has argued, the ethnic and proletarian sentiments central to Odets, Ward, Yordan, and other Popular Front playwrights underwent a transformation in such television shows as *The Life of Riley, Life with Luigi, The Goldbergs*, and *Amos 'n Andy*—all urban family dramas that tended to promote consumerism and devalue memories of working-class privation.[8] Rather than use a thirties legacy to promote white or black working-class solidarity, the "kitchen sink" quality of this Odetsian legacy ensured that television's appropriation of red ethnic melodrama would assist corporations eager to push new appliances, furnishings, and other domestic commodities on the new members of an expanding middle class.

Though Hansberry rarely acknowledged her connections to the ethnic melodramas of the Popular Front, let alone their 1950s televisual progeny—she preferred to cite Sean O'Casey's *Juno and the Paycock*—she was familiar with the red cultural legacy through her close relationship with Paul Robeson's *Freedom* magazine cohort, and *Raisin* unquestionably reflects a 1930s influence. The poverty, cramped domestic setting, strong maternal presence, invocation of long-standing traditions, presence of an old world, general sense of a need for social change all link Hansberry's work to 1930s ethnic melodrama. The critics certainly thought so; many of the most influential contemporary reviewers compared *Raisin* to Clifford Odets's *Awake and Sing*. Promoters of *Raisin* such as Kenneth Tynan and Gerald Weales, and Harold Clurman, the first director of *Awake and Sing*, linked the two plays in an approving manner. In Tynan's words, "I was not present at the opening twenty-four years ago of Mr. Odets *Awake and Sing*, but it must have been a similar kind of occasion, generating the same kind of sympathy and communicating the same kind of warmth."[9]

While most critics acknowledged *Raisin*'s debt to 1930s culture, some reviewers found that connection less than commendable. Tom Driver of the *New Republic* decried the influence of ethnic melodrama on Hansberry, arguing that "the emotions Raisin engenders are not relevant to the social and political realities." Amiri Baraka, Nelson Algren, and Harold Cruse offered even sharper attacks on the Odetsian qualities of Hansberry's drama. Cruse in particular would find Hansberry's turn to the 1930s indicative of her flawed approach to the black struggle. "If all things social in Negro-white relations had been equal over the past twenty-five years," writes Cruse, "all the material in *A Raisin in the Sun* would have long ago been done on the radio." Insofar as *Raisin* suggests "an Odets play with Negro replacements," it represents for Cruse a drama about a working-class black family well on its way to middle-class comfort.[10] For Cruse as well as Baraka and Algren, Hansberry's reliance on the 1930s ethnic melodrama form suggested that she viewed contemporary African Americans as situated in much the same socioeconomic position as Jewish Americans twenty-five years before—waiting for the bourgeois material comforts the postwar era would soon

bring them. In their financial windfall and impending move to a new suburban home, the African Americans of *Raisin* seemed poised to travel the
same road to assimilated embourgeoisement that many white ethnics had
successfully traversed.

Hansberry proved self-conscious about her decision to choose a seemingly antiquated and sentimental form for her first foray into the world of
theater. As she put it somewhat defensively to the *New Yorker* in 1959, "I'm
aware of the existence of Anouilh, Beckett, Durrenmatt, and Brecht, but I
believe with O'Casey that real drama has to do with audience involvement
and achieving the emotional transformation of people on stage. I believe
that ideas can be transmitted emotionally."[11] Yet if Hansberry believed in the
social and political value of melodrama, this hardly meant that she accepted
at face value a genre that had by the late 1950s moved from the Old Left the-
aters to corporate-sponsored television shows. Hansberry recognized that
using a civil rights–era setting and invoking themes of racial identity and
racial conflict would not prove sufficient for her political needs: creating a
melodrama for the civil rights era also required her to reimagine the patriarchal family dynamics upon which such domestic melodramas typically
relied. Rejecting the notion that all ethnic melodrama necessarily reflects
and supports white patriarchy, Hansberry reinvents the genre as a form that
foregrounds the female relationships of a black working-class family. *Raisin*
emphasizes interfemale emotional and political bonds (as well as tensions),
not only to demonstrate how black women sustain the black family but also
to make the more surprising claim that black female connection stands at
the heart of the civil rights movement itself. Thanks to black women, Hansberry argues, the black working-class home constitutes a site of politicized
memory that often functions as a crucible for social change. Rather than
serving as an emblem of the status quo, the domestic sphere in Hansberry's
view is a staging ground where black women, and eventually black men,
gather together to commemorate injustice and sally forth to wage battle for
a better world. For this melodramatist the family is a radical feminist means,
not a conservative patriarchal end.[12]

The play begins with the Younger family in an uneasy state of flux. When
Big Walter, the paterfamilias, dies, a contest ensues between Mama and her

son, Walter Lee, about who will take his place. This contest emerges most clearly through the question of what the family will purchase with Big Walter's insurance money. Will it be a liquor store, as Walter Lee demands, or will it be a house and assistance for Benethea to attend medical school, as Mama desires? In focusing on the question of insurance money and its role in bringing to light tensions in a working-class household, Hansberry recalls *Awake and Sing* and *Anna Lucasta*. Yet while Hansberry, like Clifford Odets and Philip Yordan, uses the shock of a sudden financial windfall to dramatize issues of consumerism and generational conflict, she also uses this crisis to reimagine the family dynamics of the Old Left ethnic melodrama. Through her representation of the debates about the insurance money, Hansberry demonstrates that, while neither Mama nor Walter Lee has a mandate to take charge of the family, the predominance of women in the Younger household leaves little doubt that Walter Lee's bid for familial power will not so much elevate him to the position of powerful father as situate him in the role of embattled male. In seeking to claim authority for the insurance money, Walter Lee precipitates a major conflict with all the women of his family—a conflict that will structure much of the action of the play.

Given this battle, it should come as no surprise that Walter Lee views black women as a frustrating obstacle to his aspirations. As he puts it, "That is just what is wrong with the colored woman in this world. . . . Don't understand about building their men up and making 'em feel like they somebody. Like they can do something."[13] Walter Lee desperately wants to "do something" because he finds it intolerable that his family must endure the ugly realities of tenement life: the cramped living space, shared bathroom in the hall, "armies of roaches," rats, lack of sunlight, the "entire experience of living in a beat-up hole" (20). Unfortunately, he has little chance of securing a well-paid job and moving his family to a better house. The increasing automation of Chicago industry during the 1950s eliminated many jobs in steel mills, slaughterhouses, and other factories, and employment options for working-class men were few and far between. Songs in praise of the Promised Land gave way to the Eisenhower blues as the number of white-collar jobs exceeded the number of blue-collar jobs for the first time in U.S. history. Instead of making things or turning the earth, as his father believed a man should, Walter works as a servant, driving his employer, Mr. Arnold, all over Chicago, opening and closing car doors, waiting outside restaurants in the Loop. And when he skips work, Walter Lee spends his time loitering at sites of industry—steel mills and dairies—paying silent homage to the productive jobs he might have had. Little wonder, then, that Walter Lee dreams of owning a liquor store and buying luxury goods for his family; if he can't join labor, he might as well join capital.

Hansberry understood that many African Americans dreamed of filling the "big, looming, blank space" of their future with money and commodities. The allure of the postwar Affluent Society encouraged such fantasies even as white capital militated against their fulfillment. Yet she was not content to imagine a civil rights movement born of the inevitable contradictions that obtain between the egalitarian promises of consumerism on the one hand and the ugly realities of segregation and poverty on the other. To the contrary, the author of *Raisin* believed that the movement should originate more from the wellspring of black working-class memory than it should from a frustrated desire for a luxury lifestyle. Thus for Mama Younger, the allure of middle-class dreams facilitated by the $10,000 insurance policy can never obscure the white capitalist exploitation that contributed directly to her husband's death. "Ten thousand dollars, they give you. Ten thousand dollars," Mama states at one point, underscoring the glaring discrepancy between her husband's existence and the paltry payoff of an insurance policy (55). Rather than let the $10,000 become a floating signifier, a sort of postwar gold doubloon that allows each member of the family to indulge his or her own fantasies of consumption, Mama attempts to ensure that the money will always remind the family that Big Walter perished at the hands of a nation that produces black poverty and black death.[14]

The sensitivity of Mama, Ruth, and, to a lesser extent, Benethea to the depredations of both racism and capitalism reflect Hansberry's belief that black women had a particularly acute understanding of oppression. While hardly immune to the siren call of consumerism—consider Benethea's many expensive hobbies—black women seem particularly sensitive to the many losses incurred by black families under an exploitative white regime. In an interview with Studs Terkel in 1959, Hansberry explained: "Obviously the most oppressed of any group will be its women. . . . Obviously, since women, period, are oppressed in society, and if you've got an oppressed group they're *twice* oppressed. So I should imagine that they react accordingly: As oppression makes people more militant . . . then *twice* militant, because they're *twice oppressed*. So that there's an assumption of leadership historically."[15] Hansberry's comment on the black female "assumption of leadership" reminds us that black women were at the forefront of the struggle during the 1950s and early 1960s. In the words of the activist Ella Baker, "the movement of the fifties and sixties was carried largely by women."[16] Indeed, during the 1950s the three most visible civil rights protests by blacks were started and sustained by black women: the mother of the murdered Emmett Till took her campaign for justice from city to city, demanding that her son's killers be punished; Rosa Parks began the 1955 Montgomery bus boycott and the heavily female Montgomery Improvement Association that supported it; and in 1957 Daisy Bates began the desegregation of Central High in Little Rock. In offering the nation a melodrama about the black family in struggle that focused largely on Mama and her rejection of Walter Lee's infatuation with capital, Hansberry affirmed the black community's understanding of black mothers and black women as militants. To deploy a cultural form that centered on the black mother and her domestic sphere was not so much to celebrate a white bourgeois ethos, as *Raisin's* critics claimed, but rather to affirm the prominent place of black working-class women and their culture in the movement.

No aspect of *Raisin* better highlights the gap between white bourgeois culture and black working-class domesticity than the way in which Mama and Ruth imagine objects of the home. While Walter Lee views commodities as mystical phenomena that can change the future, Mama, Ruth, and to a lesser extent Benethea understand that commodities betray long and often painful histories of toil and sweat. Thus the curtains Ruth buys have hand-stitched hems, the bureau Mama wants to purchase requires new handles and a little varnish, the Clybourne Park house gets the description "made good and solid" (120). And how could it be otherwise? After all, the stage directions inform us that virtually every aspect of the Youngers' tenement home is a sign of work: "Everything had been polished, washed, sat on, used, scrubbed too often." Mama and Ruth cannot discuss common domestic objects without teasing from them a story of toil, and that impulse, in turn, suggests the articulation of insurgent political feeling, the expression of the desire to, as Mama puts it, "push on out and do something bigger" (80). Drawing on her childhood memories of moving into a house in a so-called white Chicago neighborhood—a family move met by white mob violence and protracted legal battles—Hansberry has the Younger women demonstrate how a quotidian engagement with domesticity can lead a black family to confront white racism head on. The ethnic melodrama becomes in Hansberry's hands a way for black women to commemorate the past in defiance of a white consumer society intent on producing amnesia and denying black rights.

This isn't to deny the absence of any direct political action by the Younger women. One can point, for example, to Benethea's half-serious desire to burn their tenement building down (41); yet this moment is unusual, even for the outspoken college student. Adrienne Rich has argued that Hansberry has difficulty rendering representations of black female anger and resistance—that the dramatist felt constrained when it came to offering the audience images of black women in protest.[17] Indeed, for Rich, Hansberry compounds this problem by presenting her audiences with frequent representations of strong black male characters and their confrontations with white racists. Yet Rich's insistence on a black female heroine who stands up to the white status quo in a traditionally heroic fashion ignores a crucial fact: in *Raisin* Hansberry represents black female anger not by resorting to an individualist ethos but rather by stressing the ways by which black women bond through everyday life in the face of a consumerist ethos that would seek to render all questions of justice matters of profit. While it is Walter Lee who makes the major speech in denunciation of white racism and white capital at the end of *Raisin*, Hansberry emphasizes throughout the play that it is the Younger women who find in the quotidian—domestic rituals and domestic objects—new inspiration for resistance.

Instead of looking for heroic spectacles of black feminist anger in Hansberry's melodrama, as Rich would have us do, I would argue that signs of black female resistance appear in Hansberry's representation of the Younger women's communal life—in those sentimental but unspectacular moments of communication that occur when the three women articulate their own dreams, share memories, and generally engage with the often hollow promise of middle-class life in a white capitalist nation.[18] Hansberry was herself very much the angry black female figure Rich seeks, famous, among other things, for schooling Robert Kennedy on racial oppression at a well-known civil rights meeting in 1963.[19] Yet Hansberry was also a bisexual feminist profoundly invested in interfemale bonds ranging from the platonic to the sexual.[20] This isn't to say that when Mama and Ruth share their hopes they are expressing their secret longing for one another; such a claim would be absurd. It is rather to suggest that Hansberry represents the Younger women's relationships in a manner that resembles a less intense, familial version of the powerful black female friendship Deborah McDowell describes so vividly in her reading of Nella Larsen's work.[21] At the very least, readers should recognize that Hansberry's personal investment in interfemale connections provided her with an important perspective with which to radicalize still further the ethnic melodramas inherited from the 1930s.

Hansberry's seemingly banal dedication, "To Mama, in gratitude for the dream," well suggests the importance of black female bonding to this melodrama. By invoking her mother's legacy here, Hansberry begins reconstructing domestic space, the space of melodrama, as a site of black female engagement with the promise and perils of middle-class dreams. In some respects Mama's and Ruth's existence in the domestic sphere is drudgelike and stifling—hence Ruth's fantasy that Mama spend the insurance money on a trip for herself—but, as Hansberry is also quick to point out, their time together in the home provides both women with an opportunity to generate empowering relations. Ruth's and Mama's connections emerge especially clearly through a common investment in a dream of a better home, yet they also emerge because Ruth and Mama, and, to a lesser extent, Benethea, cannot avoid collaborating on an attempt to help Walter Lee abandon his obsession with "things" and rediscover the importance of working-class family. By joining together to discuss, argue about, and even confront Walter Lee, the Younger women do more than simply devote their lives to a man or simply react to male agency. They use the crisis of black manhood that he represents as an occasion to better articulate their common dreams of social change and validate the central importance of black female solidarity in achieving them. For all his talk of liquor stores, pearls, and the good life, Walter Lee is not simply a problem or a cause of worry and irritation for these women; he also represents an opportunity, however inadvertently, for them to find common ground and thus to establish feelings of community in defiance of consumerist individualism. Terry Castle has argued in her revision of the Girardian/Sedgwickian erotic triangle that when two women bond over the figure of a male, they can at times appropriate agency and power for themselves while relegating to the male the position of mediator.[22] For Castle the triangle seen as so central to conceptions of patriarchal power in the West should be understood as potentially refigurable in a manner supportive of female agency. An analogous dynamic is at work here in the three women's response to Walter Lee. While hardly a passive presence, Walter Lee does become the sort of mediating figure that helps bring them together.

Hansberry's dramatization of this revisionist power triangle exceeds Castle's description of the dynamic, however, for in this melodrama the Younger women bond through Walter Lee, not simply to gain more power in the household or in their personal lives but rather to further articulate their common dream of a better domestic life that will allow them to redefine middle-class existence in a black mode. In doing so, they become political actors who decide to move into a house in a so-called white neighborhood.[23] Hansberry cleverly shows that Mama and Ruth only begin sharing their dreams—setting the stage for the family's move into a white neighborhood—because they have been talking about Walter Lee. Early in the play, for example, Mama convinces Ruth that Walter Lee's liquor store plans are misguided and then shares with her daughter-in-law the idea that perhaps they can use some of the money to place a down payment on a house. Ruth's enthusiastic response to this idea asks us to recognize how seemingly banal everyday interactions can lay the groundwork for what is, in a white capitalist nation, a radical collaboration on the part of African American working-class women. By discussing her husband with her mother-in-law, Ruth begins to build a connection with another black woman. From this moment forward the play demonstrates repeatedly how responding together to Walter Lee's crisis produces an ever stronger connection between Mama and Ruth and thus renders their collaborative dream all the more powerful (79).

This black female collaboration reaches a dramatic climax when Hansberry has Mama reveal that she has purchased a small house at the very moment that Ruth tells her husband that she is pregnant. The two women's joy about the house stands in stark contrast to Walter Lee's lack of interest in the pregnancy and his rage about the cost of a humble abode that does not measure up to his dreams of future luxury. In this extraordinarily emotional moment, the two women's collaborative investment in domesticity comes to at least momentary fruition—"So you went and did it!" (77), Ruth says to Mama. Yet this moment of black female triumph, of black female willingness to brave the white racists of Clybourne Park, is rendered even more powerful and even more exclusively female by Walter Lee's disgusted rejection of the house and his refusal to claim the baby Ruth subsequently plans to abort. The two women's collaborative excitement about moving into a house, their willingness to brave white racism, is at once challenged and bolstered by Walter Lee's disapproval. "Is there a whole lot of sunlight?" Ruth asks Mama, and Mama replies that indeed there is. In vacillating between representing the two women's emotional bond and representing their anxious confrontation with Walter Lee, the play does more than oppose the two events; it suggests that for Ruth and Mama bonding over dreams and bonding over crises end up producing the same all-important black female connections (79–80).

To stress Mama's relationship with Ruth is not to deny the heartfelt, at times romantic, relationship between Ruth and Walter Lee, as well as the familial relationship of Walter Lee and Mama. For all her reluctance to imagine melodrama as a means of affirming traditional patriarchal and paternal values, Hansberry does not jettison a faith in the extended nuclear family and traditional family ties. Yet as the scene I have just examined suggests, Hansberry's most radical use of the family dynamics typical of traditional melodrama emerges through her subtle insistence that female same-sex connections render the black working-class family the place where the struggle continues despite the temptations of contemporary consumerism. And she makes this point clearer still by deploying Benethea, the most overtly political Younger woman, as a figure who constitutes the extreme of the continuum upon which the audience may locate Ruth and Mama's political negotiations and articulations. Benethea helps reveal that the Younger women's bonding can be explicitly and recognizably political. Benethea demonstrates her ability to accomplish this explicit politicization of black female connection when, for example, she bonds with Mama over her new

African friend, Asagai, and, in doing so, teaches Mama about the colonialism Africans were beginning to throw off in the late 1950s and 1960s (99). In this scene and others like it, Hansberry uses Benethea to draw more sharply for the audience the ways in which black female connections play a constitutive role in the emergence of a black militant consciousness. Although the audience might expect that Benethea, given her more extensive education and more overtly political behavior, represents the opposite of Ruth and Mama, Benethea's protests and demands display how the Younger women constitute radicals in the making.

Benethea helps teach both Mama and Ruth about politics in a way that links black resistance to black memory and black history; she offers Mama a lesson in colonial history (99); she defines the word *assimilationism* for Ruth (72). Yet for all her book learning, Benethea tends to think of the black past in exclusively racialist terms; she tends, by and large, to focus only on Africa and the African heritage—instead of considering the more specific class-bound history of black people in the United States. Benethea's Afrocentrism, while prophetic of black middle-class culture in the mid-1960s, is, for Hansberry, too far removed from the everyday labor of ordinary black Americans to serve as a call to arms at this historic moment; such Afrocentrism does not approach change from the bottom up and thus violates what is a central tenet of Hansberry's understanding of black female militancy: the primacy of black working-class women's memory to the movement.[24] Hansberry emphasizes what she understands as the close connection between a black female tradition of resistance and black working-class memory by having Mama offer both Ruth and Benethea, and at times the entire family, stories of her black working-class experience. This isn't to say that Hansberry, niece of Leo Hansberry, one of the foremost African American historians of Africa, discounts the importance of Africa to black Americans; it is, rather, to suggest that she understands black working-class memory as more important, particularly during the postwar era, when corporate America wanted all Americans to abandon any sense of working-class identity and embrace consumerism. For the black female tradition to continue to inspire the black community with a desire to organize and fight racism, that tradition must remain capable of helping the community remember the injustices and losses of the past. Remembering not only the African heritage but also the

African American working-class heritage is important to the struggle for equal rights in the affluent society.

Mama's lesson about the important role of black working-class memory in the black female tradition of resistance and thus in the movement it-self emerges most visibly in her spectacular grief for her husband. Yet this lesson also arises in other, seemingly more banal, conversations with her daughter-in-law. Consider their discussion of Mama's small plant. Tiny, be-draggled, ever deprived of sunlight, the plant seems so painfully sentimen-tal that many commentators have considered it all too typical of Hansber-ry's supposedly unreflective acceptance of white discourses of domesticity. One hostile critic titled his review of *Raisin* "A Plant Grows in Chicago," thus linking the play to Betty Smith's "lefty" ethnic novel, *A Tree Grows in Brooklyn* (1943). Yet closer examination of the women's discussion suggests what this sign of home may signify in less predictable terms as well. When Ruth asks Mama, "You . . . sure . . . loves that little old thing, don't you?" Mama first explains that the shabby yet resilient bit of greenery suggests the toughness of her children who have also survived a lack of sunlight. But then Mama offers a more biographically and historically specific explana-tion for her interest in the plant: "Well, I always wanted me a garden like I used to see sometimes at the back of the houses down home. This plant is close as I ever got to having one." Instead of standing for Mama's unexam-ined acceptance of the postwar middle-class dream, the plant represents her attempt to acknowledge and transcend the poverty and disfranchisement endured by most sharecropping Africans Americans in the South. This does not conclude Momma's riff on the plant, for after establishing the connec-tion between the object and white southern oppression, she extends her im-plicit critique of Dixie to Chicago and the northern ghetto as well: "Lord, ain't nothing as dreary as the view from this window on a dreary day, is there?" (38). The garden denied Momma down south becomes the space and sunlight denied Momma in the city; the abject conditions of the black farm laborer slip into the abject conditions of the black urban domestic, where Jim Crow codes flourish far better than plants. Instead of allowing consumer fantasy to license family amnesia, as Walter Lee would have it, Mama uses this small and sentimental object to teach Ruth about the unfulfilled expectations of so many black Americans who undertook the Great Migration from southern poverty to northern privation. Ruth's collapse at the end of Mama's speech because of her secret pregnancy only emphasizes the burdens African Americans must continue to endure in northern cities.

Of course, Hansberry demonstrates most powerfully how domestic discourse can speak in black oppositional accents during those scenes devoted not to Mama's plant but to the house and garden the elderly matriarch hopes to purchase. Late in the play Hansberry segues from a moment in which Ruth, Benethea, and Walter Lee inform Mama that they have been warned not to move into their new house to a moment in which all the Youngers thank Mama for placing a down payment on a house for them. What is immediately surprising about this scene is that instead of affirming Mama's unique qualities, her children decide to rename her. The card that accompanies the gift of gardening tools does not say, "To Mama," or "To Lena," or even to "Mrs. Younger," but instead offers the following dedication: "To Our Own Mrs. Miniver" (110). As contemporary audience members would no doubt have known, the name Mrs. Miniver refers to the titular heroine of William Wyler's highly acclaimed and extraordinarily popular World War II–era film. The Academy Award winner for best picture in 1942, *Mrs. Miniver* chronicles the experiences of a plucky and beautiful middle-class white British mother (played by Greer Garson) during the darkest days of the war. During the film Mrs. Miniver goes shopping, flirts with her husband, gives her name to a prize-winning rose, tends to her suburban home, consoles her children during frequent air raids, and even captures a downed German pilot while defending her house. She represents the zenith of white middle-class motherhood—a woman at once beautiful, respectable, and protective of her family. By naming Lena "our Mrs. Miniver," the card suggests that she has become a respectable, supportive mother—a nonmatriarchal figure with a functional family—yet this transformation unfortunately seems to require Mama to undergo a change not only of class but also of race. While Mrs. Miniver represents motherhood, domesticity, and even the Popular Front—World War II is dubbed the People's War in the film—the narrative links all these wonderful qualities to white bourgeois identity. In their eagerness to suggest that Mama's courageous acquisition of a new house places her in the tradition of the brave, talented Mrs. Miniver, the Youngers have unfortunately rendered their mother alien to the very black working-class tradition of resistance she affirms throughout the play. Rather than suggesting a utopian moment of racial integration, this reconstruction of Mama seems to recall the very problem of bourgeois assimilation raised by Harold Cruse, Amiri Baraka, Nelson Algren, and other vociferous critics of *Raisin*.

Yet Hansberry does not drop the scene at this point. The remaining portion of this small drama of naming demonstrates how Mama's new position as homeowner points not to bourgeois assimilation but rather to the politics of race and class. Hansberry transforms the implications of the Mrs. Miniver moment through the presence of a tacky, outrageously decorated, gardening hat that Walter Lee and Ruth's son, Travis, gives his grandmother. Travis is eager to have Mama wear a hat like the hats "ladies always have on in the magazines when they work in the garden," and his gesture seems at first little more than one more attempt to reconstruct Mama as Mrs. Miniver (111). With the exception of *Ebony* and *Jet,* most periodicals of the era offered their readers images of white bourgeois lady gardeners in their advertisements and photo spreads. Garson herself demonstrates an interest in hats in the opening scene of the movie. Yet, by giving his grandmother the kind of outrageous, immodest hat Mrs. Miniver would never wear, Travis troubles this entire scene of race and class transformation. Benethea and Walter Lee suggest as much as they watch Mama model the accessory. The former finds the hat evocative of Scarlet O'Hara, while the latter views the hat in considerably less extravagant terms. "I'm sorry, Mama," says Walter Lee, "but you look like you ready to go out and chop some cotton sure enough" (103–4).

Instead of appearing as a genteel white woman associated with roses, Mama now takes on the appearance of an antebellum southern belle or a southern black sharecropper—figures whose extravagant headgear suggests either decadent adornment or a desperate need for protection during long hours of backbreaking labor. The outlandish hat speaks historically through its violation of modern bourgeois taste, as does Mama's bedraggled plant in the earlier scene. And just as the forlorn bit of greenery returns us to the South of Mama's impoverished youth, so too does the outrageous gardening hat recall the long history of unjust southern race relations and their persistence in the North. Indeed, both commodities link the North and South to suggest that the black experience with white racism in Dixie is not so much a phenomenon that the family has left behind as an experience its members regularly encounter in the North as well.

In the end the notion of Mama as "Mrs. Miniver" does not confirm her newfound identity as an assimilated, middle-class property owner, as Harold Cruse argues, but rather suggests her historical connection to the South, black labor, and the oppressive plantation system. By opening up of issues of middle-class taste and middle-class identity to the history of black working-class exploitation and struggle, Hansberry troubles what might have been a typical celebration of embourgeoisement with suggestions of popular memory. And this moment of leftist education resonates within the world of the play as well. Behind Walter Lee and Benethea's laughter at the comic sight of their mother in a large hat, the audience should sense their inadvertent recognition of the way in which a black family's destiny and the destiny of labor have been intertwined. Walter Lee and Benethea's comments suggest that they are beginning to understand the way in which black labor has paid for the postwar dreams they entertain. Indeed, by imagining their mother chopping cotton or pretending to be the slave mistress, they reveal some sense of the class consciousness Hansberry links so closely with any sense of political identity, black or white.

What makes this scene particularly interesting for my purposes is that it represents the money-oriented and consumerist Walter Lee as part of the process by which black women share and thereby sustain a tradition of memory and resistance. Rather than isolating himself from a fundamentally working-class tradition that leads the Youngers to integrate a neighborhood and work out what it means to dub Mama a Mrs. Miniver, Walter Lee seems comfortable with his role in what had been up to now an all-female process. That Hansberry follows this scene with the family's two most excruciating tests—the discovery that Walter Lee has lost his family's money to thieves and the decision by Walter Lee to try to recoup the loss by accepting payment not to move into Clybourne Park—does not so much undercut the notion that Walter Lee can learn from the black female tradition of resistance as emphasize the many crises that must inevitably precede and inform his acceptance of the tradition.

Thus when Walter Lee, the would-be black capitalist, confronts Lindner—the white racist petit bourgeois—in the penultimate scene of the play,

Walter Lee recovers his dignity not only by asserting himself as a proud black man but also by identifying himself as a black working-class man—indeed, one in a family of black working-class people—and thus suggests that he has learned the lesson Mama has been offering Ruth, Benethea, and the entire family throughout the play. Walter Lee first emphasizes what Mama has always asserted—the Youngers' identification with the masses. "Well—we are very plain people," he tells Lindner (137). And Walter Lee goes on to recite the Youngers' recent labor history: "I mean—I have worked as a chauffeur most of my life—and my wife here, she does domestic work in people's kitchens. So does my mother. I mean—we are plain people." And: "And—uh—well, my father, well, he was a labourer most of his life" (138). In reciting his family's history of labor in the United States, Walter Lee memorializes its presence; his speech is not so much a testament of his faith in domesticity or middle-class values as an expression of his belief that "five generations" of black people laboring in America have a right to fair wages and to live where they choose.

Yet even as Hansberry gives this important speech to Walter Lee, she is careful in the play's last moment of dialogue to emphasize that her male lead's articulation of resistance, of race and class consciousness, has come about because of the collaborative work of two black women. When Mama tells Ruth that Walter Lee has "finally come into his manhood today," she is not so much affirming the superiority of black male identity or the need for every black family to be headed by a male as she is celebrating what two black women have accomplished together: the creation of a black male activist no less tolerant of capitalism than he is of racist oppression (130). In sharing their pride that Walter Lee has proved capable of resisting racism *and* capital, both women attest that, in this domestic melodrama, the reconstitution of the patriarchal nuclear family has in fact been something of a cover for the reproduction of the tradition of black female militancy. In demonstrating through melodramatic means how ordinary black women bond together to sustain the struggle, Hansberry has shown that the black female tradition of resistance can produce black male militancy as well.

In many ways the last moment of dialogue in *Raisin* suggests the power of the black female tradition to sustain itself and the black struggle, female and male, in the face of overwhelming adversity and temptation. The growth of the movement in the sixties would certainly testify to the truth of the melodrama's final moment. Yet the civil rights movement during the 1960s would, as well, reflect another irony implicit in the final exchange between Mama and Ruth. The very tradition of black female resistance that they represent would not only help produce a larger, stronger civil rights movement by the early 1960s, it would also, in encouraging greater male involvement, inadvertently create a situation in which black militants would push black women out of leadership positions in activist organizations. In their final moment of pride in both Walter Lee and themselves, Ruth and Mama at once suggest the power of the black female tradition in supporting the struggle and, at the same time, look ahead to a historical moment when both black women and black women's culture would be forced to play supporting roles in the black community's struggle for civil rights. Walter Lee learns his political responsibilities, only to take exclusive charge of politics.

By the early 1960s it had already become clear that black deployment of melodrama on behalf of the civil rights struggle could not continue much longer. The film version of *Raisin in the Sun* (1961) brought the melodrama of civil rights to millions more viewers but did not command the same critical acclaim or popularity. Made with a screenplay written by Hansberry but altered significantly for both budgetary and ideological reasons, the film version of *Raisin* served as the 1961 U.S. entry at the Cannes film festival but was only modestly successful at the box office.[25] As the black struggle grew steadily away from black women's culture and eventually away from black women, the future of civil rights melodrama on film would focus increasingly on the white response to desegregation. In 1968 the film version of *Raisin* was re-released with the timely ad "Guess Who's Moving in Next Door?" but this reference to the more expensive, higher-grossing film *Guess Who's Coming to Dinner?* did not simply refer to a more successful civil rights film; it also acknowledged that the melodrama of civil rights had become for the most part concerned with representing the white response to blacks "moving next door"—with representing the white family's response to desegregation—rather than an examination of black familial politics and their relationship to the struggle with poverty and hatred.

Yet *Raisin* still has much to teach us about postwar African Americans and their relationship to middle-class American dreams. *Raisin* urges us to rethink the assumption that discourses of domesticity—including melodramatic discourses—are white and middle class, an assumption that leaves little room for any consideration of how other Americans, people of color, the working class, might also respond to and transform stereotypical sentimental signs of home. And such considerations are, as *Raisin* suggests, of enormous importance to understanding the postwar era—an era when many Americans were transmuted by the seductive power of middle-class consumer culture. By insisting that the rhetoric of domesticity is open to appropriation by black working-class women as they struggle against racism, Hansberry asks us to understand the pervasiveness of middle-class tropes and images in the 1950s, not simply as a means of disciplining other classes and races but also as a phenomenon inadvertently productive of the counterhegemonic rhetoric of civil rights. As Martin Luther King Jr. recognized when he celebrated the character of Mama in a Mother's Day speech in 1961, the civil rights movement may have fought its most famous battles in the streets, but it had its origin in the home.[26]

## NOTES

1. See Harold Cruse, *The Crisis of the Negro Intellectual from Its Origins to the Present* (New York: William Morrow, 1967).

2. For a more complete description of *Raisin*'s popularity, see Stephen Carter, *Hansberry's Drama: Commitment amid Complexity* (Urbana: University of Illinois Press, 1991); James Baldwin, "Sweet Lorraine," in *The Price of the Ticket: Collected Nonfiction, 1948–1985* (New York: St. Martin's, 1985), 444. A recent example of the play's appeal is that the February 25, 2008, ABC broadcast of *Raisin* allowed the network to win the ratings battle for the first Monday in months.

3. Mark Reid, *Redefining Black Film* (Berkeley: University of California Press, 1993), 124. The Baraka quotation comes from a *Jet* article on the American Playhouse production of *A Raisin in the Sun* in 1989. See "PBS Broadcast of 'Raisin" Draws Record Nielsen Rating," *Jet Magazine*, May 22, 1989, 31–34.

4. By presenting the white middle class with the most serious economic downturn of

the postwar "boom" period, 1958 in particular forced a new awareness of how the nation's affluence was hardly assured. In that year the gross domestic product continued a post-1955 decline to reach a point of negative growth (-0.5 percent), while the unemployment rate reached 6.8 percent for all American workers and topped 13 percent for African American workers.

5. Arthur Schlesinger Jr., "The New Mood in American Politics," *Esquire*, January 1960, 58–60.

6. By using the term *Popular Front*, I refer to the loose coalition of Communist, Socialist, and liberal activists and cultural producers that worked together to defeat fascism during the late 1930s and early 1940s.

7. Peter Brooks, *The Melodramatic Imagination* (New Haven, Conn.: Yale University Press, 1995), 12.

8. George Lipsitz, "The Meaning of Memory: Family, Class, and Ethnicity in Early Network Television Programs," *Cultural Anthropology* 4 (1986): 355–87.

9. Kenneth Tynan, review of *A Raisin in the Sun*, New Yorker, April 1959, 95.

10. Tom Driver, review of "A Raisin in the Sun," *New Republic*, April 13, 1959, 21; Cruse, *Crisis of the Negro Intellectual*, 280.

11. Lillian Ross, "Talk of the Town," *New Yorker*, May 9, 1959, 101.

12. Christine Gledhill, *Home Is Where the Heart Is: Studies in Melodrama and the Woman's Film* (London: BFI, 1987), 31.

13. Lorraine Hansberry, *A Raisin in the Sun* (1959; repr., New York: Vintage, 2004), 22. All quotes are from this edition.

14. We are informed that Big Walter was so distraught that Mama lost a child because of their poverty that he allowed "the system" to work him to death.

15. Adrienne Rich, "The Problem of Lorraine Hansberry," in *Blood, Bread, and Poetry: Selected Prose 1979–1985* (New York: W. W. Norton, 1994), 251, emphasis in original.

16. Paula Giddings, *When and Where I Enter: The Impact of Black Women on Race and Sex in America* (New York: William Morrow, 1984), 259.

17. Rich, "Problem of Lorraine Hansberry," 251.

18. I am aware that in criticizing Rich for overlooking the possibility that for Hansberry black female resistance might emerge through her representation of black female connection and friendship, I take to task the woman who has articulated one of the most powerful conceptions of female friendship and interfemale erotics. See Adrienne Rich, "Compulsory Heterosexuality and Lesbian Existence," in *Blood, Bread, and Poetry: Selected Prose 1979–1985* (New York: W. W. Norton, 1994), 23–75.

19. In his 1979 essay "Lorraine Hansberry at the Summit," James Baldwin offers a powerful description of Hansberry's interaction with Kennedy. For another, less celebratory, commentary on Hansberry's role at this meeting, see Harold Cruse's *Crisis of the Negro Intellectual*. Baldwin's essay appeared in *Freedomways* 19, no. 49 (1979): 269–72.

20. Although Hansberry's papers are still sealed, we do know that Hansberry was an anonymous contributor to the *Ladder*, one of the first openly lesbian journals in the United States. Rich discusses Hansberry's letters to the journal in her essay about the playwright.

21. See Deborah McDowell, "The 'Nameless, Shameful Impulse': Sexuality in Nella Larsen's *Quicksand* and *Passing*," in Joe Weixlmann and Houston A. Baker Jr., eds., *Studies in Black American Literature*, vol. 3 (Greenwood, Fla.: Penkevill, 1988).

22. Terry Castle, *The Apparitional Lesbian* (New York: Columbia University Press, 1993).

23. We should note that while it was Lorraine Hansberry's father, William, who in the midforties moved his family into a home in an all-white area of Chicago, in *Raisin* it is Mama who makes this decision. The shift from the father's making this decision to the mother's well illustrates Hansberry's sense that by the fifties, at least, black women are leading the fight to confront and defeat segregation.

24. Needless to say, Hansberry's insistence on the centrality of working-class memory appears in the play in rather muted form. Unlike, for example, Philip Rahv or Michael Harrington, white male leftists beginning to criticize the status quo more vocally at the turn of the decade, Hansberry still had to contend with federal harassment. For a brief but useful discussion of the FBI report on Hansberry, see Ben Keppel, Ben, *The Work of Democracy: Ralph Bunche, Kenneth B. Clark, Lorraine Hansberry, and the Cultural Politics of Race* (Cambridge, Mass.: Harvard University Press, 1995).

25. In *Redefining Black Film*, Mark Reid cites a January 10, 1962, *Variety* story as reporting that Raisin's domestic rentals reached 1.1 million—a solid, though hardly remarkable, return on the filmmakers' investment.

26. I have not yet located the King speech. I take information about this speech from Izzy Rowe's *New York Amsterdam News* column, May 15, 1961, 37.

# Performing Sexuality

# 15

# The Black Church and the Blues Body

## Sexual Wrong

*Ooh, there's something going all wrong*

*Ooh, ooh there's something going all wrong*

*The way I'm thinking, I know I can't last long.*

■ Ma Rainey, "Mystery Record," 1924

"There's something going all wrong" in the black church. So that we may appreciate what that is, let me first clarify what I mean by the black church. The black church is not a single entity. It is a diverse grouping of churches that reflects the rich complexity of the black community itself. Though very different, black churches share a common history and maintain a pivotal role in black sociocultural life; these commonalities suggest their collective identity as the black church.

Historically, the black church emerged as a fundamental part of black people's resistance to white racial oppression, particularly slavery. This church continues to play a central role in the black struggle for life and freedom. Socioculturally, the black church has been one of the most significant influences upon black values. It shapes black people's notions of what is morally acceptable or unacceptable. The black church is also a critical resource for black well-being, whether physical, emotional, or spiritual. Black men and women tend to look to the black church to provide the social and cultural resources routinely denied them in a society defined by white privilege and shaped by white cultural standards. W. E. B. Du Bois rightly recognized the black church as both the "religious center" and "social center" for black people."[1] The black church's significance to black life is undeniable.[2] That there is something going wrong within it is therefore of vital concern. What is going wrong in the black church? Its attitudes toward issues of sexuality help answer this question.

Black churches consistently garner headlines for what many consider backward, if not unjust, views of sexuality, particularly homoerotic expressions of sexuality. Black clergy have been vocal in their reluctance to support lesbian, gay, bisexual, and transgender (LGBT) efforts to gain legal protections.[3] Various black church leaders have fundamentally refused to equate the "put-upon" LGBT body with the "put-upon" black body—even when the LGBT body is a black body. They have been just as die-hard in their refusal to recognize as civil rights matters issues concerning LGBT equality. Some in the black church community have gone so far as to accuse the LGBT community of hijacking the term *civil rights* as a ploy to gain black community support.[4] The persistence and passion with which too much of the black church opposes the LGBT struggle suggest that more is at stake than the rights of LGBT people. Black church responses to issues of sexuality point to a deeper concern at the center of the black church itself.[5]

It is no coincidence that sexuality would provide a window into what might be going wrong at the core of the black church. Sexuality is about more than sex. As the ethicist James Nelson said, while sexuality is certainly not the whole of who humans are, it is basic to being human. It is about body-selves. It involves how women and men relate to their own bodies and to the bodies of others. Sexuality is what propels human beings into relationships with themselves, one another, and even with God. According to Nelson, sexuality is a "sign, a symbol, and a means of our call to communication and communion." In short, sexuality involves embodied self-understanding, a way of relating to others and of relating to transcendent reality.[6]

Given the primacy of sexuality to the ways in which humans see themselves and interact with others—human and divine—it follows that passionate reactions to hot-button matters of sexuality might involve several layers of meaning. Such is the case with the black church when it comes to LGBT sexuality. Black church discomfort with the LGBT body points to its anxiety with the body in general. So to return to the question, what is going wrong in the black church? The answer is that the black church cannot accommodate what I call here a blues body.

The blackness of the black church, however, depends upon its morally active commitment to advance the life, freedom, and dignity of all black bodies. When this church, for whatever reason, rejects blues bodies, its very blackness is threatened. This has caused many to wonder whether the black church can last long, if it casts off or looks down on blues bodies. If the black church is to maintain its singular relevance in the lives of black women and men, it must mend the relationship between itself and blues bodies.

## The Blues and the Blues Body

No tradition is more suitable for understanding the relationship between the black church and blues bodies than blues itself. While it is important not to fetishize or romanticize the blues as if it is a pure reflection of black life and culture, it does capture a profound side of black living that other forms of black expressive culture do not. In so doing, it provides an informal yet precise perspective on the relationship between the black church and blues bodies and thereby provides some idea of the depth of the wrong in the black church. Let me therefore begin my exploration of this relationship by briefly examining what the blues tells us about the blues body.

## A Nonbourgeois Body

---

*One day every week, I prop myself at my front door*
*One day every week, I prop myself at my front door*
*And the police force couldn't move me 'fore that mail man blow*

*'Twas a little white paper Uncle Sam had done addressed to me*
*'Twas a little white paper Uncle Sam had done addressed to me*
*It meant one more week, one more week of sweet prosperity*

*After four long years, Uncle Sam done put me on the shelf*
*After four long years, Uncle Sam done put me on the shelf*
*Cause that little pink slip means you got to go for yourself*

■ Ida Cox, Pink Slip Blues, 1940

---

Blues is more than a musical form, that is, a twelve-bar, three-line structure. Blues is a story of black living. The blues emerged from black people who existed on the edges of life. These were sharecropping, migrating, hand-to-mouth-poor black people. Their bodies provided the hand-to-ground labor for the white plantation/farm economy. The blues tells personal yet shared stories of the common realities of poor black existence. Blues stories are of everyday hardships, disappointments, sorrows, loves, and desires of plain black women and men. These are the stories of black women and men propped at the front door waiting for government checks. They are the stories of black lives put at risk when the pink slip arrives to tell them that their government check will be no more. As Ida Cox sang, "Uncle Sam done put me on the shelf," and somehow she and others like her had to find a way forward for themselves. Essentially, blues tells "the story of humble, obscure, unassuming [black] men and women" trying to create a life worth living in a world that devalues their life and exploits their bodies.[7]

Blues bodies are nonbourgeois bodies. They are the bodies of the black underclass. They are the bodies that provide the hand-dirtying work that keeps the white economy going, yet they are bodies that have virtually no access to the benefits of that economy. The life conditions of blues bodies offer no middle-class, bourgeois illusions. These bodies suffer not simply because they are black but also because they are poor. They personify the notion of racialized poverty, that is, that blackness and poverty are intertwined realities. Yet, while the blues body seeks a better life, it is not impressed by black bourgeois compromises with white middle-class culture, nor is it captivated by white middle-class values.

Although the bodies of those on the underside of black life are readily identifiable as blues bodies, and hence blues people, it is crucial to understand that what it means to be a blues body is not essentially defined by class or social privilege. It is not a category fixed by social status. In other words, being educationally advantaged and socially middle class is not a disqualification for being a blues body. Blues bodies, and hence blues people, reflect a choice about their identity and accountability. Blues people are those whose black bodies are accountable to blues realities—they do not identify with white mainstream norms and values but with the experiences, values, and struggles that characterize the realities of blues people and thus blues existence. In short, a black middle-class body does not have to become a bourgeois body. A black middle-class body can be a blues body.[8]

## A Sensuous Body

*Seem like the whole world's wrong since my man's been gone*
*I need a little sugar in my bowl*
*I need a little hot dog in my roll.*

■ Bessie Smith, "Need a Little Sugar in My Bowl," 1927

Blues is often depicted as a highly sexualized, if not lewd, music. To be sure, sexual themes are prevalent within blues, especially those songs sung by women.[9] Blueswomen sing, seemingly without shame or restraint, about their sexual needs, desires, and preferences. No one could mistake what Bessie Smith is hankering for when she sings that her man is gone and she needs "a little sugar in my bowl" and "hotdog in my roll." Yet as titillating as blues can be, to become preoccupied with its suggestive lyrics is to miss the underlying meaning of this admittedly sexy music. The sexiness of the blues is about more than bawdiness. Rather, it points to the essential sensuous character of the blues. Blues is intrinsically a sensuous music.

To be sensuous is be in touch with one's feelings. Blues does not begin with ideas in the head. It begins with the experiences of the body. Blues does not intellectualize those experiences—it passionately expresses them. Blues listens to the call of the body and responds by conveying what the body is communicating. The blues is the voice of the blues body. Blues makes visible that which is invisible. Through lyrics, music, and performance the blues boldly utters what the body feels: pain, sorrow, loneliness, and desire as well as joy, happiness, solitude, pleasure, and satisfaction. The feelings of blues bodies resound through the rhythms and inflections of the music. If various blues songs are provocative, it is because they provoke their audiences to recognize and answer to the feelings of their own bodies. The blues affirms blues bodies by validating all that these bodies go through and providing a vehicle for them to vent all that they feel. Blues speaks to the listener, becoming virtually a mirror as the lyrics and music reflect previously unarticulated feelings.[10] They give back to listeners their very own experience. This is why I say that blues is sensuous music: it is animated by the feelings of blues bodies, including those feelings that are sexual.

Thus the blues body is not ashamed of itself. Black people who have blues bodies are not embarrassed by their bodies and what their bodies feel. They celebrate the individuality of their bodies in terms of size, color, shape, and other characteristics. They affirm the various sensations of their own bodies—the pain, disappointment, pleasure, and desire. And they respond to the call of their body by satisfying that call, whether that satisfaction is physical, emotional, or sexual. Essentially, blues bodies are those of sensuous black people, people who do not shun or deny their bodies but embrace their body's liveliness. Blues is a body-affirming musical expression for a body-affirming people. It follows, then, that blues bodies belong to those who do not bend to a nonsensuous culture—that is, a culture that is ashamed of or disapproves of the body and all its needs.

## A Rejected Body

> Everybody cryin' mercy, tell me what mercy means.
> Everybody cryin' mercy, tell me what mercy means.
> If it means feeling good, Lord, have mercy on me.
> ■ Ma Rainey, "Blues the World Forgot, Part 2"

The black church has typically regarded the blues as the devil's music. Some have suggested that it got that name because it often refers to the devil or because of the legendary crossroads meeting of bluesmen like Robert Johnson with the devil. Whichever apochryphal story you care to credit, there can be no doubt that the explicit sexuality of the blues earned it its association with the devil. And inasmuch as the sensuality of the blues speaks the language of the devil, the blues is not welcome in the black church. At the same time the black church regards those who sing the blues as singing the devil's music and doing the devil's work. Blues-singing men and women are therefore as unwelcome in the church as the blues they sing—at least so long as they continue to sing the blues. Essentially, the black church has not been a place of mercy for the blues or for those who sing it. Perhaps this is what led Ma Rainey, considered the mother of the blues, to ponder the meaning of *mercy*, which is what the church is supposed to offer. What does mercy mean, she wonders, if it is not the good feeling one gets in singing the blues?

Given the black church's disregard for blues, the message for blues bodies is clear: Don't come looking for mercy here. The black church judges and rejects both blues and blues bodies. The blues body is a cast-off, unwanted body. But in finding a way to appreciate the blues, the black church will be able to accept blues bodies and perhaps safeguard its own blackness.

## The Blues: A Signifyin' Lament

*Lord, one old sister by the name of Sister Green*
*Jumped up and done a shimmy you ain't never seen*
*Sing 'em, sing 'em, sing them blues, let me convert your soul.*
■ *Bessie Smith, "Preachin' the Blues," 1927*

One gift the blues has to offer the black church is its tradition of signifyin' lament. Lament is prominent within the biblical tradition to which the black church holds itself accountable. The ability to lament was essential to the Israelites' journey from an enslaved people to a free people. Lament allowed them to "rend their hearts," as Townes puts it, and to recognize the ways in which they had betrayed their own faith tradition. Lament was both a pastoral activity and a prophetic activity.[11] It served the Israelites most notably as a vehicle for voicing their suffering, engaging in self-critique, and as a call for accountability to their faith.

Ironically, the blues—deemed by the black church to be devil's music—echoes the biblical tradition of lament. Both a pastoral and prophetic activity, the blues, like the Israelites' laments, allows black women and men to rend their hearts and identifies particular crises that beset the community; in so doing it compels the black community to recognize its role in perpetuating some of these crises. As lament, blues becomes a means through which the black community can confront and transform its own situation. More to the point I want to make here, when functioning as lament, blues confronts the black church with its behavior, in a manner reflective of its biblically based faith, and then challenges this church to transform its behavior in a way consistent with its faith.

Blues lament also carries on a poignant black cultural tradition of resistance known as signifyin'.[12] While signifyin' has taken many forms, with each generation adding its own nuances, two characteristics stand out in this tradition: double-speak and intuitively astute commentary.

Double-speak itself may take a variety of forms. It may use wordplay, performative or verbal sarcasm, mocking repetition, or mimicking behavior. Discerning double-speak typically requires an awareness of the signifyin' tradition as well as knowledge of cultural codes, so that the signifyin' message itself can be decoded. In other words, someone who is not aware of the signifyin' tradition would not know to look for it. And even if one does recognize the art of signifyin' at play, it is still not easy to decode the message behind the words.

Because signifyin' double-speak is usually not about the literal meaning of words, discerning the meaning requires hearing beyond the words and reading between the lines. In order to do this one must be versed, to some degree, in certain cultural protocols, conventions, and habits. In fact, this is why signifyin' has become such a persistent part of black culture. It has functioned as a survival tool, allowing a powerless people to speak the truth of who they are as well as the truth of who their oppressors are without jeopardizing the speakers' very lives. Signifyin' allows one to send a message while hiding it from those for whom it is not intended. Reflecting again its place in a black culture of resistance, signifyin' allows a powerless people to speak truth that those who wield power over them cannot discern. It essentially turns the dynamics of power upside down. It is the signifyin' "weak" who have power over the oppressing "strong" because the oppressed speak a language to which their oppressors have no access. This leads to the second prominent feature of the signifyin' tradition—intuitively astute commentary.

While some signifyin' moments are simply meant to be playful, more often than not signifyin' reveals keen insight into some aspect of black existence. Such signifyin' is intuitive because it reflects knowledge that does not depend on abstract reasoning and analytical thinking. It is not knowledge that emerges from the head. It is born from the raw, everyday reality of black living. It is knowledge ushered forth from the bodies of black people. Hence it is a fitting aspect of a music that also springs from the experiences of black bodies.

Signifyin' is astute in that it provides smart and incisive perspective on a given situation or predicament. In its own clever way signifyin' can deliver wise judgment on certain areas of black culture and life because it emerges from the very life about which it speaks.[13] Such is certainly the case with the blues in regard to the black church.

As signifyin' lament, blues provides shrewd insight into black church culture and practices. This is evident in Bessie Smith's rendition of "Preachin' the Blues." The title itself provides a signifyin' play upon the relationship of the blues and the black church. That one could actually preach the blues places it in a context in which it is not wanted—the church. This signifyin' title foreshadows what is to come in the song.

Using lyrics ripe with sexual innuendo, Smith sings about Sister Green. To know black church culture is to know that the "sisters" of black churches are routinely considered the most holy, sanctified, saved ones. In many instances they are held in high esteem as models of virtue and salvation. They are also known to cast a scornful and harsh eye on the "unsaved." For Bessie Smith to suggest that Sister Green is shimmying to the blues is to signify upon this high-and-mighty black church culture. Smith does this specifically by mocking the point in many black church services when the choir's soul-stirring rendition of a particular hymn or spiritual leads a sister in the church to "get happy," jump up and shout, that is, engage in a holy dance. This dance supposedly demonstrates the sister's salvation and how touched she is with the Holy Spirit.

Playing upon this dramatic display of salvation, Smith portrays Sister Green as jumping up to the blues. In this instance, Smith employs a signifyin' tool of humor. For it is as if Sister Green herself has confused the devil's music with the church's music. Her shimmy is her shout. Resonating with the message of the blues, she cannot help but jump up and shout/shimmy. It is as if the blues touches her in a place that even being saved cannot erase. The blues speaks deeply to who she is in a way that perhaps the church does not. Through the blues she is put back in touch with her body.

While "Preachin' the Blues," certainly contains other signifyin' messages, one is especially clear: Smith is signifyin' upon a church culture that draws a judgmental line between the saved and the unsaved. In singing about Sister Green, Smith suggests that no matter how holy Sister Green may be, she still has a blues body that calls out to be satisfied. Thus, try as the black church might to keep the blues out of its holy space, blues resides in the bodies of those in the pews, even in the holiest of people. Smith therefore reveals the black church's naive view of the saved and the hypocrisy of its scorn for the blues and blues-singing people. Through a blues lament Bessie Smith draws attention to the black church's misguided rejection of blues bodies.[14]

The final signifyin' irony of Smith's blues is found in its intuitive astuteness. That Smith chooses to sing about Sister Green shows her profound wisdom concerning the ways of the black church. The implication of such a song is that Smith, who as a blues-singing woman is scorned by the black church, undoubtedly knows this church better than it knows itself—and, to be sure, she knows the Sister Greens of the church better than they know the Bessie Smiths of the blues.

"Preachin' the Blues" is just one example of the many signifyin' laments found in the blues that offer intuitively astute commentary on various aspects of black church culture and life. But through the blues-signifyin' laments on sexuality we are able to discern the magnitude of what is going wrong between the black church and blues bodies and how to fix this urgent problem.

# Blues Signifyin'

I'm a one-hour mama, so no one-minute papa

Ain't the kind of man for me

Set your alarm clock, papa, one hour that's proper.

I may want love for one hour.

Then decide to make it two.

Takes an hour fore I get started

Maybe three fore I'm through.

I'm a one-hour mama, so no one-minute papa

Ain't the kind of man for me.

■ Ida Cox, "One Hour Mama," 1939

They said I do it, ain't nobody caught me

Sure got to prove it on me

Went out last night with a crowd of my friends

They must've been women, 'cause I don't like no men.

■ Ma Rainey, "Prove It to Me Blues," 1928

As I pointed out earlier, blueswomen in particular sang unapologetically about their intimate sexuality. They sang about their sexual needs and preferences, as in Ida Cox's making clear that she is a "one-hour mama" who does not want a "one-minute papa." They also sang rather matter-of-factly about their homoerotic appetites, as in Ma Rainey's making clear that she "don't like no men." While these women sang about the most intimate aspects of their lives, they did not do so unreflectively or simply to provide lurid entertainment. Rather, they sang and performed with seemingly thoughtful signifyin' intent. Through sexualized lyrics and sexually charged performances, blueswomen signified upon a time-honored way of thinking within black culture—especially black church culture. This is a way of thinking that distorts black people's relationships to black bodies, even their own bodies, and fails to recognize the power in black men and women as sexual beings. Essentially, these very blues, so offensive to the black church, engage in a signifyin' lament that reveals a perceptive awareness of the menacing interplay of various narratives that render black people sexually impotent and threaten their power over their own bodies.

## Intersecting Sexual Narratives

The fundamental narrative is a white cultural narrative that reinforces white privilege and justifies violence against black bodies.[15] This narrative stereotypes black people as hypersexual animals. It portrays black men and women as driven by the unrelenting urges of their genitalia. Their libidos are presumably out of control and insatiable. This white cultural narrative essentially relegates black people to a constant state of lust.

Such a depiction clearly renders black people as little more than beasts, driven—like other beastly creatures—by their baser instincts and bodily desires. Because of this, this narrative also assumes that black people have no capacity for rational thinking. Their bodily desires simply overwhelm their rational faculties. Inasmuch as black men and women are governed by their hypersexual nature, they are at best inferior to whites (who are governed by reason) and at worst subhuman. For it was erroneously believed that it was the ability to reason that separated the beastly animal from the human animal. This white cultural narrative clearly has no regard for the sensuous body.

This same white cultural narrative deems black people dangerous because they are controlled by that which is uncontrollable, their insatiable sexual appetite. It brands black men as predatory bucks and black women as promiscuous seductresses. Throughout history just such portrayals have provided ideological justification for violent attacks upon black bodies, such as the lynching of black men and the rape of black women. Essentially, according to the stereotyping narrative of white racist culture, blackness is synonymous with abnormal hypersexualized behavior.

Such sexualized stereotyping is typical of cultural narratives designed to sustain oppressive power. The French philosopher Michel Foucault explains that discourses of power invariably attack the sexuality of those they subjugate, primarily because of the significance of sexuality to the human being. Not only is sexuality instrumental in relationships, but it is also the site for reproduction. To manipulate someone's sexuality is to therefore have power over that person's reproductive capacity as well as her or his capacity for positive relationships.[16] To reiterate a point I established earlier, sexuality is integral to one's ability to be in relationship with one's body-self, the bodies of others, and even with one's God. In this regard the sexualized stereotyping of black people serves not only to question their very humanity but also to disrupt their web of relationships.

The black community has produced its own narratives to counteract the notion that black people are hypersexual. The first is a sociocultural narrative driven by a determined effort to sever the link between blackness and hypersexuality. It urges black people to conform to a "hyperproper" standard of sexual conduct. What it means to be proper is based upon what is acceptable to mainstream white society. Thus that which is ostensibly unacceptable according to white sexual standards is absolutely intolerable for the black community.[17] This standard is as hyper in its attempt to desexualize black men and women as the white cultural narrative is in its attempts to sexualize them.

This hyperproper standard of sexual conduct has been influential within the black community. Most notably, it is reflected in black middle-class aspirations to be accepted within white mainstream society. In this regard this standard is also classist, manifested in efforts by the black middle class to promote this standard.

It ostensibly becomes the task of the black middle class to display a hyperproper sexuality (whether these people actually do is not the point) and to encourage the black working class to do the same. Those black people who do not conform to this standard are regarded as uncouth and fulfilling the hypersexualized stereotype. In addition, the black middle class considers the nonconformists to be a threat to the black middle class's acceptance into white society. For while the black middle class is part of the black minority, it enjoys certain white majority privileges that it is determined to protect. This black middle class is typically a more educated group, one that does enjoy certain social acceptance within white society: W. E. B. Du Bois's "talented tenth." Unfortunately, this more privileged class of black people too often harbors a patronizing mentality behind its efforts to civilize the uncouth black bodies. If their civilizing efforts fail, the black elites marginalize or reject those they deem uncouth.

This particular dynamic of the hyperproper sexual narrative and its elitist implications has played out in various black middle-class organizations, movements, social clubs, and even historically black colleges and universities. Generally speaking, various middle-class black organizations, while sincerely committed to black well-being, have modeled standards of white acceptability and have too often been infused with a determination to protect a privileged status in white society.[18]

Unfortunately, the black church has also been a part of this elitist dynamic. It too has produced a narrative to govern black sexuality with similar rejections of nonconforming black bodies. The black church narrative is perhaps more troubling because it claims sacred authenticity. It is, in other words, a holy narrative—one that has a long history.

During the eighteenth-century religious revivals, a significant population of black women and men were converted to an evangelical Protestant Puritan tradition. Black churches most influenced by this tradition tend to affirm the assertions of the apostle Paul that one should "make no provision for flesh," but if one must engage in sexual behavior, "it is better to marry than to burn."[19] This evangelical sexual ethic is based on an influential Western philosophical tradition, a Platonist tradition that places the body and soul in an antagonistic, oppositional relationship. The soul is seen as the seat of salvation, while the body is seen as the source of sin. The prevailing locus of bodily sin is sexual pleasure/lust. Desires of the body, especially sexual desires, are therefore to be overcome at all cost. Sexual desires are viewed as the ultimate temptations of the devil. Engagement in sexual intimacy must therefore be strictly regulated. This leaves only two ways for one to engage sexual activity, one tolerable and not inherently sinful and the other intolerable and unrelentingly sinful. Procreative engagement is tolerably good; nonprocreative engagement is intolerably sinful.[20]

Thus the black church inherited a body-negating sexual ethic and has used it as the religious counterpart of the black community's sociocultural sexual narrative. This sexual ethic provides a sacred cover for the black community's standard of hyperproper sexuality, making violation of this hyperproper sexual standard not simply a social breach but also a sin.

Ironically, the black narratives of hyperproper sexual standards validate the very white cultural narrative they attempt to contest. They do so in two ways. First, they affirm the nonsensuous norm of white culture. As I suggested earlier, white culture views the body as a source of danger to one's humanity, since it is the seat of sexuality. And so long as the body is seen as dangerous or incidental to human existence, one can attack it with self-righteous indignation.

Second, these black narratives also affirm the white cultural narrative by implicitly validating the white cultural stereotype of black people as hypersexualized beasts. In accepting this stereotype, the black narratives attempt to get black people to squelch their bodily desires and sexual proclivities, as if black people must pay attention to these aspects of themselves in a way that others do not. The hyperproper narratives attempt to mask the stereotypic behavior with proper behavior. They do not deny the authority of the original white stereotype. In that failure they may actually serve the purposes of white culture far better than they protect the well-being of black people.[21] From this we can see that the narratives of hyperproper sexuality and demonizing of the body are constraining and confining narratives. They alienate black people from their bodies and seize control of black sexuality by limiting the ways in which black people may express their sexuality. In this respect these black narratives have become as oppressive to certain bodies within the black community as white cultural narratives have been to all black bodies. This leads us to the heart of what is going wrong in the black church—which the blues addresses with signifyin' lament.

## A Blues Class of People

Thus the black church's sanctioning of a hyperproper standard of sexuality makes it virtually impossible for the church to accept, let alone be a sanctuary of support and empowerment for, blues bodies—which, as I discussed earlier, are invariably sensuous bodies. This is nothing new. Throughout history the black church has rejected various black people because of its presumption that they do not comply with its hyperproper standard. Black churches become more of a place of judgment than a place of refuge.

In recognizing this tendency within the black church, a disturbing aspect of black church tradition becomes crystal clear: almost as intrinsic to the black church as its black identity is a tendency toward the bourgeois.

That is, in its sincere efforts to advance the life of the people—thus making them more acceptable to white society—the black church has fostered a bourgeois culture. Bourgeois, in this regard, reflects an adherence to values and standards of acceptability according to the dominant cultural group—in this instance, white society.[22] The defining narrative to which all are supposed to conform is the hyperproper narrative of sexuality. I cannot emphasize enough that this narrative takes on such overwhelming significance because of the centrality of sexuality to human dynamics. As I have shown, sexuality is a key and irreplaceable aspect of what it means to be human, and to impugn the sexuality of a group of people is to diminish the very humanity of that people. In this way bourgeois culture inexorably creates a blues class of people who are rejected by the dominant sexual narratives, people who don't fit in. To reiterate, this is seen in the black church, which has spawned a tradition of rejecting those who do not comply in one way or another at any given time with the hyperproper narratives of the black church. Today LGBT people most clearly represent this class.

It is important to clarify that this tendency to foster a bourgeois culture and thus sustain a blues class persists in the black church because of its sanctified allegiance to the hyperproper sexual narrative, which accepts the nonsensuous standards of white culture. In this sense these sexual narratives, the social and religious, are themselves bourgeois narratives. Interestingly, in accepting this nonsensuous standard and valorizing standards of hyperproper sexuality, black church culture takes on the characteristics of the dominating oppressive culture. One striking way in which it does this is by sexualizing those people it finds unacceptable, just as white culture sexualizes black people. The black church basically seizes this effective tool of oppressive power. In short, the blues class is a hypersexualized class, a class of people ultimately defined in the black church by their intimate sexual behavior. To reiterate, those whom the black church finds unacceptable for reasons that usually reflect sexist, classist, or heterosexist values, the black church sexualizes, thereby creating a blues class. For instance, women are seen as sexual temptations to the men of the church, just as they are viewed by white culture as temptresses to white men. Therefore various black churches expect women to cover their sexuality by placing cloths over their legs. At the same time the black church often blames women for the sexual transgressions of "holy men" and even for the domestic violence these supposedly holy men may perpetrate against female bodies. The church similarly hypersexualizes gay and lesbian people. To be gay or lesbian is to be promiscuous, viewed by the church as people controlled by an abnormal, homoerotic libido. They are thus expected to remain celibate. While they may not be able to do anything about who they are as sinners (gay and lesbian), they are expected to renounce the sin of homoerotic engagement. In the end, because the black church's sexual narrative conforms to the nonsensuous norm of the white cultural narrative, the black church finds itself fostering a blues class and thus not only disrespecting but rejecting various black bodies.

The seriousness of what is going wrong in the black church is about more than LGBT sexuality, even as it is precisely about the LGBT body. The LGBT body is a vibrant reminder to the black church of what it has strived to overcome and all that it is trying to escape. It is as if the LGBT body itself is a demonic temptation. Thus for the black church to lend its support to LGBT issues would mean not simply making a compromise with bodily sin but perhaps a pact with the devil as well.[23] At the least, the black church often regards LGBT issues as a trap set by white society to once again link black people with abnormal, beastly sexuality. Black church leaders often therefore back off such issues by proclaiming them to be white issues, not matters of concern to the black community. One effect of this position is that it turns the tables on white people—linking them to abnormal sexuality while disassociating their black selves from it. This body-denying narrative of hyperproper sexuality has become so embedded within the black church that it all but defines contemporary black church culture. It assures the palpable reality of a bourgeois mentality. And, most seriously, it shapes black church responses to various social justice issues. Inasmuch as the issues at stake concern blues bodies' rejected sexualized bodies, they are issues about which the black church will at best provide an ambivalent response and at worst ignore or contest.

In this regard the hyperproper sexual narrative results in a church that is at times manifestly bourgeois, which means it is also sometimes classist, sexist, and heterosexist. And, perhaps most troubling, it is a church that sometimes ignores the pain and suffering of black bodies. Unquestionably, the hyperproper narrative of sexuality frequently overwhelms the black church's very identity. The end result is that the black church is unreliably black, and it is not trustworthy when it comes to protecting and advocating for the well-being of all black bodies. So long as the black church harbors narratives that fuel a bourgeois mentality, fosters and justifies a blues class of people, it is not black. In fact, it is effectively an advocate of the very white cultural norms that sexualize and reject black bodies. It is a church that acts against its unique existence and the well-being of its people.

It is time for the black church to adopt a new narrative, one that is true to its roots. This requires a narrative that benefits all black bodies and actually contests the white cultural sexualizing narrative of black people. This narrative should not forfeit a black identity for bourgeois aspirations. It is in the signifyin' lament of blues that the possibility of such a new narrative comes into focus.

## Saved by the Blues

**A Crossroads Worldview**

*I went down to the crossroads, fell down on my knees*

*I went down to the crossroads, fell down on my knees,*

*Asked the Lord above have mercy now, save poor Bob if you please.*

■ *Robert Johnson, "Crossroad Blues," 1936*

The notion of a crossroads has played an important part in blues lore. As I mentioned earlier, Robert Johnson presumably struck a deal with the devil at a crossroads in Mississippi in order to become a guitar legend. Lore has it that for the price of his soul the devil gave Johnson the gift of guitar playing. Within black folklore the crossroads is an ominous place, a site of ghosts and other spirits. Most significantly, it is the place where the devil hangs out. This crossroads mythology traces back to African mythology about the gods. The crossroads is where the prominent god Esu resides. Esu is a trickster god, acting sometimes for good, sometimes for bad; he is also the messenger god, interpreting the messages of the Great High God for other lesser gods and humans. In this way the crossroads suggests a worldview that is instructive for decoding the signifyin' lament of the blues.

The crossroads is a place where various realities intersect, interact, and influence each other. A crossroads worldview therefore is one that denies rigid, antagonistic realities, even when two dimensions of existence may seem to be intrinsically oppositional—such as sacred and secular dimensions of life. Instead a crossroads paradigm suggests that the truth of life is found in appreciating the inherent dialectic nature of human existence and thus forging a harmony of the ever-present dialectics of living. The meaning of this is clear in the signifyin' lament of blues in relation to sexuality. It is worth noting that understanding the significance of the crossroads enables us to decode blues signifyin'.

As I pointed out earlier, blueswomen sang without inhibition about their sexual appetites and preferences. Just as Bessie Smith clamored for a hot dog in her roll, she also confessed that she couldn't get enough of "papa['s] thing." Likewise, Ida Cox let it be known that she was a "one-hour mama" who did not want a "one-minute papa." The black church has interpreted such declarations of sensual sexuality as affirming the sexualized stereotype that the black church and community have so desperately tried to escape. But, again, to see the blueswomen as fulfilling and affirming the sexualized white cultural stereotypes of blackness misses the subtlety of what they were doing. For instead of reinforcing the stereotype, they were subverting it. That they sang so fervently and so often about sexual/sensual matters should be construed as a form of signifyin' protest against the sexualized stereotype of blackness. Indeed, unlike the black social and religious hyper-proper narratives, the blueswomen did not avoid the white cultural stereotypes of black people. They confronted them head-on by repeating them. In so doing, they provided a different approach to dealing with them, turning the stereotype on its head. They refused to be confounded by the sexualized stereotypes of black people or even restrained by the hyperproper response to those stereotypes by the black church and community. And so, while black sexual narratives contested the stereotype by projecting a hyperproper sexual norm, blueswomen dealt with this stereotype by not granting it any authority. They did not validate it. They transcended the white sexualized caricatures of blackness and crafted a new black identity, denying the white cultural narrative any claims over their sexual selves.

Furthermore, through their lyrics blueswomen did not adopt the non-sensuous norm upon which the white cultural narrative was based. By making love and desire the key for decoding the signifyin' message, they were contesting the notion that erotic sexuality is an impediment to life. Instead they advanced sexuality as the tool for grasping life's truths. As various blues singers boldly declared what blues bodies crave, they proclaimed the necessity of being in touch with the needs of one's body. They moved sensuality and sexuality out of the "private and into the public sphere."[24] As they did so, they moved sexuality from a place of shame to a place of ultimacy. They grasped the nature of sexuality itself. As blueswomen foregrounded sexuality, they affirmed its centrality to human existence.

Moreover, by flaunting their sexual tastes and preferences, blueswomen were protesting not only their hypersexualization by white culture but also the very systems and structures that such sexualization serves—the very ones that would seek to deny them freedom. A fundamental task of cultural narratives of power is to seize control of a people's sexuality; this has been the case for black men and women since slavery. The lack of freedom has meant the lack of sexual agency, or the inability to determine how to express one's sexuality and to chose one's sexual partners. By taking back their sexuality, blueswomen were stripping oppressive power of one of its most crucial weapons.[25]

As these women sang of their tastes and preferences, they also challenged a heteroerotic norm. They sang about their homoerotic desires as freely and openly as they sang of their relationships with men. In so doing, they recognized and valued the fluidity of human sexuality. They did not project a sharp distinction between different ways of expressing sexuality. They made clear that they sometimes preferred the love of women and sometimes the love of men. Each was a fulfilling and acceptable way to love. Neither was considered better or more holy than the other.

Just as the sexualized blues lyrics signified upon the sexualized stereotypes of white cultural narratives, so too did they provide a signifyin' lament on the black church's sanctified hyperproper sexual narrative. In the process they were doing more than disrespecting black church piety (if they were doing that at all). They were rescuing sexuality from its taboo space in the black church.

Here we can begin to understand the depth of blues signifyin' lament. An appreciation of the crossroads worldview helps us with this understanding. Blues signifyin' lament puts forth a crossroads approach to sexuality—and hence to navigating life. As blueswomen sing of sexuality, they refuse simple either/or choices. They instead navigate the dialectic of what it means to be a human, to have a body and a soul. They suggest not an oppositional relationship between the two but a harmonious one. For as I showed in Bessie Smith's "Preachin' the Blues," the sanctified soul resides in a sexual body. Moreover, the blues body can be a saved body. The sacred and the secular are part of the same reality. They are intersecting, interacting crossroads of human existence.

To hold the body and soul together in recognition of the intrinsic crossroads nature of being human actually maintains the integrity of the black religious tradition. This tradition is rooted in an African religious heritage that considers all life, including the body and sexuality, sacred. This tradition does not foster rigid splits between the divine and human. Simply put, African religions have no notion of secularity.[26] They have no taboo, inherently demonized, space of human living.[27]

The point I am making is this: as blueswomen signified upon the black church in singing their celebration of their sexuality, they implicitly lamented the black church's betrayal of its own African-informed, body-affirming religious tradition. At the same time they called the church back to this tradition. If blues lore has it that Robert Johnson and others made a pact with the devil at the crossroads, then perhaps the black church has made a similar pact by not stepping into the crossroads. It is as if the black church has made a pact with white Protestant Puritanism, thus trading its sensuous African religious heritage for a chance to be accepted within nonsensuous white mainstream society. It has betrayed its blackness for bourgeois standards.

The blues further reflected a crossroads in its refusal to reject the people the black church so frequently rejects. Blues does not make choices between the acceptable and unacceptable, the saved and unsaved. The blues recognizes the sacredness of all black people.[28] Most important, the blues recognizes two dimensions of what it means to be saved and how those two dimensions interact with one another. Essentially, for blues bodies both the body and the soul need to be saved. Additionally, a concern for one's soul's salvation cannot be addressed unless matters of the body are also addressed. So long as black men and women, notably blues bodies, do not have what it takes to cope with their earthly existence, they will be impeded in dealing with their heavenly existence. It is no wonder, then, that a blues class of people experiences mercy in the juke joints, where blues is performed. The juke joints do what the black church does not—they provide sanctuary for blues bodies. They make the body feel good. In this way the juke joint becomes the church. The blues itself functions as church. For the juke joint is place where the needs and desires of the body are tended to, and the blues is where the demands of the body are vindicated. The challenge to the black church is to be for blues bodies both church and juke joint, speaking to the soul and body.

Essentially, the blues challenges the church to acknowledge the crossroads reality of black existence. Inasmuch as the church does this, it remains true to its own crossroads-informed black religious heritage, not bourgeois narratives. This means not only rejecting either-or standards that make certain people unacceptable but also rejecting narratives that establish a blues class of people.

In "Preachin' the Blues" Smith sings:

*I will learn you something if you listen to this song*
*I ain't here to try to save your soul*
*Just want to teach you how to save your jelly roll*

She concludes the song by singing, "Sing 'em, sing 'em, sing them blues, let me convert your soul." True to what it means to be a signifyin' lament, "Preachin' the Blues" reveals to the black church a way to right what is going all wrong within it. The problem is not about the black church's ability to save souls but its effectiveness in saving "jelly rolls," that is, the sexual black body. The way to right this wrong is clear: the black church must lament. It must appreciate the blues. For until the black church is able to accept the blues as sacred discourse, it will not be able to accept blues bodies. In effect, the black church must come to recognize what the blues man Willie Thomas recognized: God gives black people the blues.[29] If the black church is to ever become more dependably black and less reliably bourgeois, it must become blue, for through the blues the black church can discover a way to be black.

## NOTES

1. W. E. B. Du Bois, *Souls of Black Folk* (1903; repr., New York: Alfred A. Knopf, 1993), 153.

2. In a 2002 study Anthony Pinn noted the black church's continued significance, even for those who had once abandoned the church. He noted that educated and middle-class blacks return to the church for support in their struggles against racism. Pinn suggests that despite an apparent decline in black church attendance it remains the strength of the black community. See Pinn, *The Black Church in the Post–Civil Rights Era* (Maryknoll, N.Y.: Orbis, 2002).

3. See, for instance, Michael Paulson, "Black Clergy Rejection Stirs Gay Marriage Backers," *Boston Globe,* February 10, 2004, www.boston.com/news/local/articles/2004/02/10/black_clergy_rejection_stirs_gay_marriage_backers.

4. See, for instance, Jay Tokasz, "Black Clergy Opposing Gay Marriage Resent Civil Rights Comparison," *Buffalo News,* May 18, 2009, http://preview.buffalonews.com/2009/05/18/674748/black-clergy-oppossing-gay-marriage.html.

5. Although I am addressing a prevailing homophobic tendency within the black church community, there are notable exceptions. Some black church leaders have been quite vocal in their criticism of homophobic attitudes within the black community. They have also been vocal in supporting LGBT rights and have been progressive in addressing HIV/AIDs. See Michelle Boorstein, "Black Churches Renew Focus on AIDS Fight," *Washington Post,* May 26, 2006, www.washingtonpost.com/wp-dyn/content/article/2006/05/26/AR2006052601070.html. This article provides a good picture of the passion and range of responses within the black church to the HIV/AIDS crises and hence to LGBT issues. It also addresses the effect of the HIV/AIDS epidemic on the black community in Washington, D.C. See also Sheryl Gay Stolberg, "Eyes Shut, Black America Is Being Ravaged by AIDS," *New York Times,* June 29, 1998.

6. James B. Nelson, *Embodiment: An Approach to Sexuality and Christian Theology* (Minneapolis: Augsburg, 1978), 117–18.

7. Paul Oliver, *The Story of the Blues* (Boston: Northeastern University Press, 1997), 3.

8. In this regard I do not accept what appears to be a pessimistic and fixed view of the black middle class offered by Leroi Jones (later known as Amiri Baraka). He seems to equate middle-class status with a "slave mentality" and an inexorable orientation toward white mainstream values and culture. For him, the black middle class cannot be blues people. See his argument in *Blues People: The Negro Experience in White American and the Music That Developed from It* (New York: Morrow Quill Paperbacks, 1963), esp. chap. 5.

9. I am focusing on blueswomen in this essay because the black female body is so often the target of the multiple interacting/interactive forms of oppression that are visited upon black bodies, that is, racism, sexism, classism, and heterosexism.

10. Charles Keil provides a similar analysis of the significance of the blues with his perceptive insights regarding the role of the "bluesman and the black preacher." See his *Urban Blues* (Chicago: University of Chicago Press, 1966), esp. chaps. 6 and 7.

11. This analysis of laments draws upon that of Emilie Townes, as found in her chapter "The Formfulness of Communal Lament," in *Breaking the Fine Rain of Death: African American Health Issues and a Womanist Ethics of Care* (New York: Continuum, 1998).

12. I first identify a culture of resistance in my book *Sexuality and the Black Church* (Maryknoll, N.Y.: Orbis, 1999). See esp. p. 67.

13. This discussion of the signifyin' tradition is informed by the analysis and discussion of the signifyin' tradition by Henry Louis Gates Jr. in *The Signifying Monkey: A Theory of African American Literary Criticism* (New York: Oxford University Press, 1989). Though my analysis is an independent analysis, a similar theory concerning the significance and meaning of the signifyin' tradition can be found Kermit E. Campbell, "The *Signifying Monkey* Revisited: Vernacular Discourse and African American Personal Narratives," *JAC* 14, no. 2 (1994), available at www.jacweb.org/Archived_volumes/Text_articles/V14_I2_Campbell.htm.

14. Angela Davis provides similar insight into Smith's rendition of "Preachin the Blues," in *Blues Legacies and Black Feminism* (New York: Pantheon, 1998).

15. The white culture I am specifically referencing here is a culture that nurtures white racism and is undergirded by a white supremacist ideology. It devalues anyone who is not white and thus serves as a haven for white patriarchal hegemony. See a

fuller discussion of this in Douglas, *Sexuality and the Black Church*, esp. 13–18.

16. Michel Foucault, *The History of Sexuality: An Introduction*, vol. 1, trans. Robert Hurley (New York: Vintage, 1990).

17. For a more complete discussion of this sociocultural narrative, see Douglas, *Sexuality and the Black Church*.

18. A more detailed discussion of this dynamic, particularly as it is manifested in the Negro Women's Club Movement, appears in Kelly Brown Douglas, "Testifying to the Blues: Sexuality and the Black Church," in Traci West, ed., *Defending Same-Sex Marriage* (Westport, Conn.: Praeger Perspectives, 2006), 2:53–65.

19. See Paul's First Letter to the Corinthians 7:9.

20. See an in-depth discussion of this tradition in Kelly Brown Douglas, *What's Faith Got to Do with It? Black Bodies/White Souls* (Maryknoll, N.Y.: Orbis, 2006).

21. Of course, black men and women need to be hyperaware of their conduct, sexual or otherwise, given the price that they have too often paid for displaying what white racist society considers offensive. In this regard such hyperproper narratives can be viewed as a Faustian pact that the black community has made with white society in order to survive. Inasmuch as these narratives have influenced black lives, they have no doubt prevented black people from engaging in behaviors that would not simply hamper their life chances but actually end their lives. Cornel West speaks of this Faustian pact in *Race Matters* (Boston: Beacon, 1993).

22. It is worth noting again that to be black and middle class does not automatically render one bourgeois. Adherence to a bourgeois culture in this regard reflects a choice one makes concerning how to relate to mainstream white society as well as to blues people. Again, those who are nominally black middle class by virtue of education, economic privilege, or status can indeed be blues people in the sense that they hold themselves accountable to and affirm the realities of blues bodies. In this regard they take the blues seriously.

23. In *Blues Legacies and Black Feminism* Angela Davis speaks of how the black church views blues-singing women as having made a pact with the devil.

24. Hazel Carby, *Cultures in Babylon: Black Britain and African America* (New York: Verso, 1999), 18. Carby argues as well that blueswomen "had no respect for sexual taboos." Daphne Duval Harrison similarly argues that through their songs blueswomen assert their power and "project a new image of themselves" (Harrison, *Black Pearls: Blues Queens of the 1920s* [Brunswick, N.J.: Rutgers University Press, 1988], 100).

25. Angela Davis provides a compelling analysis of the relationship between sexual agency and freedom in *Blues Legacies and Black Feminism.*

26. See Peter Paris, *The Spirituality of African Peoples: The Search for a Common Moral Discourse* (Minneapolis: Fortress, 1995).

27. The black church's roots in African religions have many theological implications that go beyond the scope of this essay and that I explore in other places. Suffice it to say that an appreciation for this African worldview undoubtedly made it possible for enslaved Christians to grasp the meaning of a god who entered into history as "fully human and fully divine." A lack of appreciation for the body is certainly inconsistent with a religion that has an incarnate God.

28. Bluesman Henry Townsend offers a sharp critique of the black church as he recognizes its rejection of blues people by proclaiming that "the Church should take in everyone" (Paul Oliver, *Conversations with the Blues* [Cambridge: Cambridge University Press, 1965], 181).

29. Oliver, *Conversations with the Blues,* 22.

# "A Kind of End to Blackness"
## Reginald McKnight's *He Sleeps*
## and the Body Politics of Race and Class

*One of the problems in the U.S. is that . . . down-home bedrock blackness is closely associated with being poor, and [being from] this slave background and [having] simple virtues and values. To step outside of that community of the poor means to step out of blackness.*

■ Reginald McKnight, "Under the Umbrella of Black Civilization"

The novelist Reginald McKnight confesses that he has often felt he was not "two-fistedly black" because he grew up in largely white environments and was not raised in the "community of the poor" that he describes in the epigraph.[1] McKnight's words provide a clue to why notions of black authenticity continue, in the twenty-first century, to be linked to black poverty, despite contemporary evidence of a visible, vocal, and sizable black middle class. The image of the black fist recalls the black power movement of the late 1960s and early to mid-1970s and an associated black cultural nationalism that grew to prominence during the period. Along with the movement's emphasis on a black community unified in its resistance to racist oppression, however, came its greatest misstep: the movement's nationalist rhetoric collapsed intraracial differences, particularly class differences, and represented all African Americans as essentially the same.

Thus, while the "black nationalist affair" of black power may have been "principally a 'new' black middle class phenomenon," as the scholar Cornel West has written, it was hardly acknowledged as such at the time; instead black power contributed to the public redefinition of blackness as militant urban rebellion. In the writer Randall Kenan's words, "to be black was to be poor, disenfranchised, to live in . . . what became the 'ghetto,' to distrust 'the man' and to be very, very angry." In certain arenas—like hip-hop music and its associated cultural products, the vast majority of which position life on impoverished urban streets as an arbiter of the racial "real"—such perceptions of so-called authentic blackness seem hardly to have changed since 1980 and the beginning of black power's decline. Indeed, black nationalist ideology has become commonplace in racial discourse.[2]

Yet black cultural nationalism is now juxtaposed to, if not plainly opposed by, black postmodernism, which frequently seeks to challenge the accepted wisdom on black racial authenticity.[3] While many rap and hip-hop artists evoke a 1970s brand of nationalism in their music, writers like McKnight appeal to postmodernist sensibilities in their literary work, interrogating the so-called inauthenticity of the black middle-class self. Efforts like McKnight's surrealist 2001 novel, *He Sleeps,* suggest that while it might once have been plausible, if not entirely accurate, to invoke race and class as corollary concepts ultimately synonymous with black disadvantage—assuming the black person's position to be fixed on the lower end of social and economic hierarchy—such a correlation is no longer universally applicable to that multifarious and diverse group we might, with optimism, call "the black community."

Black postmodernism does more than critique discourses of racial authenticity, however. In moving us beyond empty assertions about who is (or is not) black enough, it allows us to ask a few related but perhaps thornier questions: How does class privilege inform our understanding of blackness in the postmodern or post–civil rights era?[4] And how does that privilege shape the black individual's relationship to race, to gender and sexuality, and to the very body she or he inhabits?

Asking these questions in a volume inspired by the fiftieth anniversary of E. Franklin Frazier's polemic on the subject of black class privilege, *Black Bourgeoisie*, demands that we grapple with one of Frazier's most incendiary assertions about the black middle class: his suggestion that middle-class black men are unable "to play the 'masculine role,'" and thereby "resemble women."[5] Frazier's seemingly odd recourse to male sexual identity in his discussion of black class privilege relates to what I see, in McKnight's novel, as an inevitable relationship between black middle-class status and black masculinity, as lived through the corporeal or bodily self. Indeed, for Mc-Knight black bourgeois status, especially as that status is localized in a wayward and inadequate black body, has everything to do with black sexuality and the intimate connections that underwrite or even create racial character.

Not coincidentally, McKnight's *He Sleeps* takes place in Senegal, West Africa. This African setting—which highlights the protagonist's Americanness, not just his blackness—ironically allows the novel to comment on, specifically, African American middle-class identity and that identity's relationship to larger narratives of the black body. The various predicaments faced by McKnight's protagonist, entwined dilemmas of geography, sex, and class, imply that, in the twenty-first century, being black and bourgeois not only complicates but redefines African American racial performance; *He Sleeps,* finally, raises the provocative question of whether the black middle-class self is really a black self at all.

## Sexuality and the Failures of the Bourgeois Body

McKnight's novel *He Sleeps* follows Bertrand Milworth, an African American doctoral candidate in anthropology, as he completes fieldwork in Dakar, Senegal, in the mid-1980s. Bertrand's racial identity is shaped by a peculiar sexual conundrum—he is a black heterosexual man who has never been sexually or romantically involved with a black woman. This is far less than a simple coincidence, and the text outlines clearly the childhood incident that leads to Bertrand's fear of black women. As a boy of nine, Bertrand is wearing his robe and pajamas, playing host to two childhood friends, African American sisters who are close to his age and the daughters of an air force captain temporarily stationed in the area. The passage, which I quote at some length, indicates how Bertrand's racialized sense of sexual inadequacy is shaped by narratives of social class tied directly to the body:

> [Bertrand] stretched for a blue piece on their side of the puzzle and ripped the already sizable hole in the underarm of his robe. "Oops," said Sally without looking up. Bertrand removed the robe, tossed it on the orange couch behind him, and sat lotus style. . . . By increments, he noticed that the girls were giggling, softly, behind their hands. He knew it had to do with him but pretended he didn't hear them, tried to surreptitiously inspect himself to see what he was doing wrong. He gathered it must have been his slumped shoulders since all his life he had been exhorted to stand and sit straighter. He squared his shoulders, unbent his spine. Suddenly he found the missing piece, and in his excitement, he whooped and rolled onto his back, and this made the girls shriek with laughter.
>
> "You better put your robe back on, Birdie," said Bunny, and she was pointing at his crotch. When he saw the hole in his pajama bottoms, he lowered his head, shrank into himself. His whole body pounded with shame. . . . The hole, he knew, was the size of his hand. They must have been able to see his ass and his balls. Shoulda never took my robe off. When he finally lifted his head, he couldn't look either girl in the eye, but perceived that they'd stopped smiling.
>
> "Are you guys poor?" said Bunny. "It's OK if you're poor."
>
> "Yeah, we don't care."
>
> "No, we don't. Jesus loved the poor. Do you want to put your robe back on?"
>
> "Maybe you should."
>
> Bertrand didn't know whether his family was poor, but when he finally spoke, he said that they were because he believed that if they thought so they wouldn't dare laugh at him anymore.[6]

Although Bertrand first responds to the girls' clandestine laughter by squaring his shoulders, which we might read as a classed behavior, a marker of bourgeois aspirations to physical (and, by extension, moral) rectitude, class and corporeality play an even greater role once Bertrand realizes that his crotch has been exposed. Although he is frozen with an apparently sexual shame, in the first moment when Bertrand can again raise his eyes to glance at the girls, he faces not a reference to his body but to his socioeconomic status: "Are you guys poor? . . . It's OK if you're poor." Of course, despite his holey pajamas, it is unlikely that Bertrand's family is poor—his is one of a few black households in suburban Colorado Springs, his parents appear to be homeowners, they pay for him to attend private school. Thus we must ask why Bertrand tells the two girls that he is poor; why would the fact of his poverty mean that the girls "wouldn't dare laugh at him anymore"?

Perhaps, as Bunny's assertion that "Jesus loved the poor" suggests, the social compassion that poverty elicits could somehow mitigate the sexualized disgrace that Bertrand has experienced. Part of this relies on an idea that the girls seem to understand quite well, the sense that a poor person probably does not have control over the condition of material goods designed to protect his or her body from polite scrutiny. Yet even with this small protection from the girls' laughter, Bertrand "could hardly fathom the bigness of his shame" (89). He might eventually escape mockery, but he cannot escape humiliation, particularly since the lack of responsibility implied by his assumed poverty only heightens his sense of his own body as a failure, a violated object (it is no coincidence that the vulnerable "ass" and "balls," and not the more symbolically powerful penis/phallus, are exposed in this moment).

Bertrand could not protect himself from the girls' gaze in the first place, and claiming that he is poor implies an even larger measure of lost control, as he becomes merely another sort of object, the object of pity. Masculinity seems to play a central role in Bertrand's discomfort. Because a signal feature of masculine power is control of one's environment and one's physical place within it—in other words, "the power to suppress [the white, male] body, to cover its tracks and its traces" —Bertrand is literally emasculated by not only his physical exposure but also, paradoxically, by his assumed poverty.[7]

It is perhaps no wonder that this experience leads Bertrand into a lifetime of avoidance tactics—after hiding from Bunny and Sally for the next two weeks, until their family is finally transferred to another military base, he then hides from all other black girls at his school, eventually hides from all black women. When his white wife discovers condoms in the bag he has packed to take to Senegal, she is certain that he intends to end his lifelong flight from black women while he is abroad. Her suspicions may be founded, for Bertrand does seem to crave racial legitimacy. It seems hardly coincidental that Bertrand seeks this legitimacy in Senegal, West Africa; the West historically has invested African "blackness" with a mythological purity and power, particularly in comparison with the necessarily creolized and heterogeneous forms of black culture existing in the "New World." The black womanhood Bertrand finds in Senegal could provide a far more powerful route to racial legitimacy than any African American woman.

This connection is made explicitly early in the text, when, during a vivid dream about Senegal, Bertrand encounters a black American woman while on a plane: "A big beige woman in lime-green leisure, hair the color of ginger, blood fingertips . . . luggage-large hips and thighs" (65). The woman says to Bertrand, "Them niggers sure can do. . . . Got dicks as big as wrists. . . . And black? Real black like lava stones . . . tar pits, mine shafts, belts, and heels. Not that faded shit you see in Jersey. Make a woman out you, darlin' dear" (65). Ironically, given that Bertrand seeks to legitimize his masculinity in Senegal, the dream woman focuses on African manhood and its ability to "make a woman" out of the Western visitor. This aspect of Bertrand's dream, a reflection of his subconscious, likely reflects his fear that he too is "made a woman," emasculated, through his contact with this uberpowerful mythology of African manhood.

The social and sexual failure of the black middle-class body is clearly at issue here. After all, the dream woman's reference to "that faded shit . . . in Jersey" clearly suggests African American men, pallid in comparison with the deep "mine shaft" blackness supposedly found in Africa—a blackness she measures through the body, penis size and skin color. The significance of the corporeal in this passage reminds us of the subtle interconnectedness of sexual and racial identity—particularly for African American men, whose bodily manifestations in Western culture are always already invested with what another postsoul author and critic, Elizabeth Alexander, describes as "the forbidden spectre of black male mythological sexuality."[8] This mythologized sexual character, even as it literally pales in the face of fantasized African sexuality, may explain why Bertrand seeks to legitimate race through sex—in effect, this method is chosen for him by a social order that insists upon the unwritten truth of black male sexual excess.

Indeed, a peculiar irony is that Bertrand's dissertation project, the field-work he has traveled to Senegal to complete, is on urban legends: "Stories that are passed by word of mouth, but that can't always be found in news-papers and books" (7). The black male as sexual beast is, in its own way, a long-standing urban legend in American culture, indeed, in Western culture more broadly. Yet it is one story that Bertrand cannot seem to investigate, perhaps because as a middle-class black man he has a tenuous relation-ship to it. As Patricia Hill Collins notes, echoing E. Franklin Frazier, "In the post–civil rights era . . . assimilated, middle-class, Black men are somehow seen as being less manly," largely because of their perceived deference to and comfort within "the [mainstream] White world."[9] As a black man whose wife, closest friends, and colleagues are all Caucasian, Bertrand's character certainly evidences this sort of comfort with whites, and the added complex-ity of his (lack of) sexual experience with black women further excludes him from cross-racial narratives of black male sexual prowess.

This exclusion stems partially from the fundamental dependence upon the black female body for coherence of the Western mythology of black male sexuality—no matter how frequently it evokes the "forbidden" white female body as theoretical target. Historically, if white women have been presumed to be the unattainable objects of black male desire, black women have been the always available substitutes—indeed, the open terrain upon which an unbridled black male virility could play freely. Consider Eldridge Cleaver's famous admission, in *Soul on Ice,* that before raping white women—something he considered to be an "insurrectionary act" against the white world—he "started out by practicing" on black women. Echoing numerous other black feminist scholars, Angela Davis notes that "the fictional image of the Black man as rapist has always strengthened its inseparable companion: the image of the Black woman as chronically promiscuous."[10]

While Davis makes this point to emphasize the history of black wom-en's sexual exploitation by white men—"If Black men have their eyes on white women as sexual objects, then Black women must certainly welcome the sexual attentions of white men"—her statement also serves as unwitting reminder that black women are perceived to be always sexually available to black men.[11] The black woman is viewed as promiscuous by racist whites precisely because of her presumed accessibility to her black male counterpart. She becomes fair game for white male exploitation once her body is "sullied" by the black man (whether literally or only figuratively, through simple association). Yet this substitution is curiously reversed in McKnight's text, with white women repeatedly standing in for black in Bertrand's mapping of his own desire. This reversal points us, ultimately, to Bertrand's sexualized liminality as a black (male) subject, his positioning at the figurative end of blackness.

## "How Does It Feel to Be a Black Toubob?" Class and African/American Masculinity

Bertrand's tenuous black identity is highlighted in the very language of McKnight's novel—or, rather, in its depiction of African language. At several points throughout McKnight's narrative, Bertrand is called a *toubob*—a Wolof word that means both "stranger" and "white." While Senegalese characters occasionally correct others who define Bertrand in this way by noting that "he isn't a toubob; he's a black man" (70), in general the verdict is decidedly out on this point. Indeed, Bertrand's uncertain position in Senegalese society, his all-too-evident status as both cultural stranger and "white" man, surfaces repeatedly in the text and is frequently related to his class status.

Bertrand has rented a room in a large house in N'Gor Village, just outside the city, and on the first page of the novel readers learn that several other tenants, members of a middle-class Senegalese family by the name of Kourman, have unexpectedly become his housemates. The family's unexplained presence in the house unsettles Bertrand, yet it soon becomes clear to readers that he was never very settled to begin with, in part because of the unfamiliarity of his surroundings. Indeed, as I have already noted, the setting of McKnight's text is noteworthy early in the narrative, as particular aspects of Bertrand's Americanness, as opposed to his blackness, are foregrounded by his experiences in Senegal. Perhaps this opposition should not surprise us. Frazier makes little mention of Africa in his midcentury excoriation of the black bourgeoisie, except to note that "whatever memories [the enslaved African] might have retained of his native land and native customs became meaningless in the New World."[12] Still, the African American desire to seek one's black roots on the African continent emerges as a particularly bourgeois undertaking. Transatlantic air travel, the costly, fantasy-laden return "home," is a kind of classed performance—one in which McKnight's Bertrand participates willingly, despite his putative status as a researcher rather than a sightseer in the region.

Not surprisingly, class privilege is one way that Bertrand is immediately marked as an American in Senegal. Even without knowing his circumstances, strangers in Dakar make assumptions about his financial status; shortly after he arrives he is surrounded by a group of teenage boys who demand, "'Merican bruddah, you godt money?" (34). Bertrand recalls, "They weren't poor, even I could see that. Western clothed . . ., they dripped oil milk fat honey" (34). That these boys demand money from Bertrand although they "weren't poor" implies a global power differential in which Bertrand's status as (African) American traveler is automatically equated with economic excess—an excess so great that he is expected not to notice, or to acknowledge, the relative privilege of his interlocutors. Bertrand is asked to play the role of "wealthy American" to the boys' (literally) assumed poverty, in the process participating in a monetary exchange that plays on the supposed kin relationship—"'Merican bruddah"—between him and his Senegalese hosts.

There is uncanny overlap, here, between McKnight's fictional narrative of one black American's experience in Senegal and the recent nonfiction account of another black American's experience in Ghana. Saidiya Hartman's 2007 *Lose Your Mother,* a text that weaves memoir, travelogue, and history into critical analysis, tells a similar story of solicitation, also couched in the slippery language of kinship: "As I climbed the muddy incline leading to the entrance of Elmina Castle, a group of adolescent boys approached me yelling, 'Sister!' 'One Africa!' 'Slavery separated us.'" These boys hand Hartman well-worn letters proclaiming their brotherly feelings for her and asking her to help, presumably financially, with their "need of pencils and paper." Hartman goes on to note, "It was a hustle, and we were all aware of this; nonetheless, we assumed our respective roles." These roles, of patron and supplicant, beggar and benefactor, imply a pecuniary relationship that is inimical to the family affinity that the boys affect: "But how could these scruffy adolescents love me or anyone else like me? You could never love the foreigner whose wealth required you to inveigle a handful of coins."[13] For Hartman, as for Bertrand, lip service to diasporic brotherhood cannot adequately conceal the structures of economic exchange that shape the interaction.

This incongruity perhaps explains why Bertrand has similar problems even with those with whom he is more intimately involved. The fellowship money that he uses for his living expenses is considered a small fortune by many in Dakar, and as a result the Senegalese people to whom Bertrand becomes close also read him as affluent—a perception that both corresponds to and exceeds his actual material resources in the United States. After all, in many ways he is rich by Senegalese standards, as are most Americans, even if by U.S. measures his lifestyle as a graduate student is more than modest. Hartman is chastised by a fellow black American, a permanent expatriate living in Accra, "You're still sitting pretty compared to most. Do you know how many families could live on your Fulbright fellowship?" (28). Because he is unable to reconcile, or even acknowledge, this contradiction, Bertrand is unable to connect fully with any of the Senegalese men close to him, as money and status always create a barrier between them.

For instance, even though the man who will become Bertrand's assistant and confidant, Idrissa, refuses a tip from him when they first meet because he recognizes Bertrand as a scholar, not a tourist, their subsequent relationship is complicated by Idrissa's status as both Bertrand's employee and his guide to the Senegalese cultural marketplace. In one crucial exchange Bertrand believes that Idrissa has gotten him a good price on his rented room, but when Alaine Kourman, one of Bertrand's housemates, discovers how much Bertrand is paying, Alaine accuses Idrissa of cheating his American employer: "He's take advantage of you" (69). Confronted by Bertrand, Idrissa is unrepentant and resentful of Bertrand's dependence on him: "You told me that . . . the university was paying you, and this other foundation, too, who pay you. I didn't think it was your own money" (80). Idrissa's comment highlights the way that Bertrand's money is viewed by his Senegalese acquaintances as a kind of windfall, rather than his own earned money. Indeed, in many ways Bertrand's intellectual work—not labor in the conventional sense—situates him outside the economic system in which many of the Senegalese men who surround him operate, creating further distance between them.

Ironically, however, given his apparent anger on Bertrand's behalf, Alaine also takes advantage of Bertrand financially. Alaine, who appears to be solidly middle class by Senegalese standards—he was educated in France, he works in a civil service job—manipulates Bertrand into buying a new refrigerator for the house and into paying Alaine's wife, Kene, extra money for weekly supplies. Bertrand deeply resents these efforts but is paradoxically unable to refuse Alaine's requests. As Bertrand writes in his journal, "I remember every franc he's robbed me of, how frequently he's lied to me: There *was* coffee in the house last Monday. He *did* have the money for the water bill. He *did* forget my quinine tabs, and he does owe me the eleven thousand CFA. But do I stand up to him? I do not" (31). Bertrand sees his own behavior as weak, even imagines himself as "the new Mrs. Kourman" (68) because he is unable to stand up to his housemate.

Again, Bertrand is "made a woman" by his African counterpart; differing conceptions of masculinity are clearly at the center of this conflict. Ironically, Bertrand's sense of his own frailty is based on his sexist adherence to a Western model of manhood predicated upon rugged individualism and defensive displays of bravado. Bertrand imagines himself as what the scholar Paul Smith, referencing the film icon Clint Eastwood, has called the "rebellious, maverick, sometimes Promethean hero," or what the postsoul critic Mark Anthony Neal defines as the "Strong Black Man," whereas the Senegalese men whom Bertrand encounters privilege interdependence and mutual respect—hence Alaine's seemingly emasculating treatment of Bertrand as a younger brother, a member of his family.[14]

In addition to his conflict with Alaine, Bertrand's Westernized approach leads to numerous other misunderstandings in his interactions with Senegalese men. One central example is his encounter with a local man named Doudou, whose home Bertrand visits during an ultimately disappointing search for Senegalese palm wine. Indeed, Bertrand's expectations of this native African wine, which he had "craved . . . ever since [he] read Amos Tutuola's novel *The Palm-Wine Drinkard* in college" (97), reveal the extent to which his perceptions of Africa are informed by fantasy and even misinformation and foreshadow the subsequent interpersonal conflict. That Bertrand's interest in palm wine is piqued by a work of fiction indicates the manner in which his expectations of West African culture are grounded in invention, in what the historian E. Frances White calls the "collective political memories of African culture" that African Americans "construct and reconstruct" for their own purposes.[15] That Bertrand is in Senegal seeking a beverage more common to Nigeria is also significant here—to him as an (African) American, perhaps these two countries appear interchangeable, despite their divergent cultures and histories.

Although Bertrand describes Tutuola's fantastical novel, which is set in Nigeria, as "so strange, like a dream," and although Tutuola "never attempts to describe the taste, color, or smell of palm wine" (97) Bertrand nonetheless bases his beliefs about the wine's magical properties on the improbable adventures of the novel's central character. Bertrand muses to himself, "It would be cold as winter rain. It would be sweet like berries, and I would drink till my mind went swimming in deep waters" (99). Bertrand expects not only to encounter a sort of delicious and heavenly nectar but that drinking it will lead him to new levels of mental profundity. These expectations parallel his expectations for West African culture more broadly—as he imagines that his first taste of that culture will confer a physical or emotional sweetness, and an intellectual depth, to him as middle-class (African) American consumer.

Again, this connection is made explicitly earlier in the narrative, when, during the same vivid dream referenced earlier, an American journalist discusses Senegal with Bertrand: "Strike out on your own. Take it in; drink it up. You'll like it. Can't help but. It's home, homey. Drink deep, young man" (64). There is an odd opposition in these words, between Bertrand's American origins and his nationalist (or diasporic) claims on global black culture.[16] The linguistic parallel between "drink deep, young man" and the old American saw "go West, young man," particularly as coupled with the individualist instruction to "strike out on your own," evokes a spirit of exploration and the sense that West Africa is uncharted territory, conquerable by the solitary (white) American explorer—a position that Bertrand's work as scholar-ethnographer forces him to occupy. Yet the journalist's insistence that "it's home, homey"—use of the slang term *homey* here calling attention to Bertrand's black Americanness—also implies that Bertrand will quickly, even automatically, feel at ease within the culture of his presumed ancestors. This assumed belonging extends to palm wine, which Bertrand believes will taste delicious to him precisely because he is a black man, not a *toubob*. Bertrand does not recognize the dual message of his dream, however. When it comes to palm wine, and to African culture more broadly, he is as much (or more) an American outsider as he is a black insider.

Not surprisingly, then, the reality of palm wine falls short of Bertrand's sweet fantasies; indeed, it turns out to be awful, even "impossible to drink" (107). Notes Bertrand after his first taste, "If you could make wine from egg salad and vinegar, this palm wine is pretty much what you'd get" (107). Instead of an initiation into the "deep waters" of Senegalese or broader West African culture and experience, Bertrand is confronted with his own difference from them. He is shocked by the wine's sour, sulfuric bouquet (107), quite literally its foreignness. Of course, Bertrand's negative perception of the palm wine has been completely colored by what he as cultural outsider imagines it should be. The implicit imperialism of this perspective—Bertrand's privileged positioning on the American side of an African-American divide—puts Bertrand at odds with many of his Senegalese acquaintances, including Doudou.

Throughout the scene that follows—it spans fully seven pages in the novel—Bertrand seems unable to understand this Senegalese man's hostility toward him, although it is directly related to Bertrand's deliberate status as outsider to and scholar (but not student) of Senegalese culture. Almost immediately after meeting him, Doudou challenges Bertrand's academic work, highlighting the political meanings that historically have been embedded in the anthropological study of culture: "Omar tells me you're an anthropologist . . . the study of primitive cultures" (110). Doudou goes on to comment, with some sarcasm, "I knew an anthropologist once . . . who told me I should be proud to be part of such a noble, ancient, and primitive people" (111). Here Doudou critiques the exploitative and racist notion that black Africa is savage or primitive. He also, however, criticizes the paternalistic attitudes of figures like the unnamed anthropologist, who condescends to instruct the Senegalese on the relative value of their culture, even as he sets up a hierarchical relationship between "noble savage" and Western modernity, intellect, and technological advancement.[17]

Bertrand's response, however, in broken French, reveals his inability or refusal to grasp the meanings behind Doudou's statement and particularly ignores the condescension of teaching so-called savages that their culture has value: "Maybe . . . he trying to tell you that primitive. . . . I mean, that in this case primitive mean the same thing as 'pure'" (111). Here Bertrand takes the same paternalistic position vis-à-vis his African acquaintances, implicitly defending his fellow anthropologist's use of the loaded term *primitive* by euphemistically associating it with purity. "Who studies your people?" Doudou responds. "Do you have anthropologists milling about your neighborhood? Do they write down everything you say?"[18] Doudou points out the essential power imbalance that exists between American academics and the indigenous peoples of Africa. In this instance class supersedes race, and Bertrand's blackness ironically becomes irrelevant, because in his role as scholar he stands in for an entire history of Western exploitation of Third World cultures for the sake of knowledge.

Reiterating this point of view, another Senegalese man present during the exchange states hotly, "I get offended. I get very offended. You write us down. You don't respect us. You come here and steal from us" (112). In response Bertrand claims that he is "trying to help all black people by recovering our [lost] things" (112). Bertrand's "trying to help" argument here, and his use of the first-person plural possessive, *our,* suggest that he sees himself as a so-called native anthropologist, that is, an anthropologist who studies his own cultural group, often "for the explicit political benefit of those conatives under study."[19] Yet Bertrand, black American that he is, is not truly a native to West African culture. Worse, Bertrand cannot seem to recognize his outsider status, and the multiple arenas (geographical, national, ethnic, and material) in which his identity is not only marked as different from the Senegalese men's but is also privileged over theirs in historically informed ways.

Thus even when Bertrand tries to rearticulate his black identity in the face of the men's hostility, his efforts only highlight what the Senegalese men see as a fundamental difference between them. This is clear in Doudou's reply: "Things lost? . . . That must mean you're not pure. . . . You think you can come here and bathe in our primitive dye, legitimize your blackness to the folks back home" (113). Given Bertrand's fantasies of palm wine, the way that he imagines a taste of the liquid will send him to "deep waters," we might well take Doudou's words as an accurate description of Bertrand's motives. But rather than expressing contrition after being thus called out for his misstep, Bertrand attempts to turn his own status as American "other" against his adversary. In response to Doudou's hostile reference to Bertrand's cultural impurity, Bertrand himself highlights the narrative analogy of palm wine and African culture, this time through a rejection of that culture, in his own attempt to insult Doudou: "'Want some palm wine?' I said to Doudou. 'It really tastes like crap'" (113).

The exchange culminates with Doudou's asking Bertrand, "How does it feel . . . to be a black toubob?" (113). *Toubob,* a word that, as already noted, can mean both "stranger" and "white," is here rightly taken by Bertrand as a counterinsult, especially after he tries to clarify in which sense Doudou is using the word, and Doudou replies aggressively, "In Wolof, 'toubob' is 'toubob' is 'toubob'" (113). In other words, Bertrand's status as Western stranger here reduces him to whiteness; such an accusation is particularly painful for a middle-class African American man whose connection to black identity is already dubious.

## Dream Women in Black and White

Bertrand's perceived racial inadequacies vis-à-vis Senegalese men are mirrored in his sexual relationship to Senegalese women, or to one Senegalese woman in particular. Perhaps because of his "unconscious . . . , little-boy fears" (92), Bertrand cannot acknowledge his attraction to Kene Kourman, the black woman who is closest to him, literally inhabiting his home: "He won't let himself say that he wants Kene. He won't look at his own looking—her smooth throat, the silk-fine hair on her coppery skin . . . the lips that must be soft as breasts, the breasts made to fill his hands, the ass like a heart" (85). His attraction to the African woman instead is expressed most openly in that conventional bastion of the subconscious, his dreams.

Soon after Kene and her family arrive in the house, Bertrand begins to have vivid dreams, most often sexual dreams about Kene herself. Since he often falls asleep to the sounds of the Kourmans having sex (51), these

dreams should perhaps not be surprising, yet they are particularly significant in Bertrand's case because he has never before had such an experience:
"Never in all my thirty-four years have I ever dreamed. At least, I've never
remembered doing so. My sleep has always been black, empty, colorless,
silent—no impressions or thoughts of any kind" (30). After his first dream
about Kene, he writes in his journal, "I had always suspected that people
were talking about something they'd invented, imagined. I always believed
dreams took one's will. But this thing *happened* to me" (22). The emphasis on
*happened* here is a sort of foreshadowing. As the text progresses, readers are
given to understand that these dreams, which Bertrand faithfully records in
his journal, are not coincidental but rather the product of possibly malicious
external influences.

Another Senegalese male acquaintance, Allasambe, whom Bertrand
avoids for much of his stay because "Allasambe looks at him the way a man
would look at a friend who has come to a party with his zipper down and
wishes to get him in private to point it out to him" (36), eventually warns
Bertrand of the existence of these influences. Allasambe offers Bertrand
a *tere*, a Senegalese good luck charm—a small leather pouch containing
"herbs and other secret ingredients" (124) wrapped with Koranic prayers—
and warns him, "Someone close to you is trying to take all you have" (125).
Faced with Bertrand's skepticism, Allasambe adds, "There is someone in the
village whose entire association with you is false. You don't know it, but this
one robs you, little by little. The stealing is so small and grows so slowly
that you can't see it" (126). Bertrand's attempts to guess the culprit—"Idi?
Idrissa?"—are ignored by his protector, leaving both Bertrand and the text's
readers in the dark about who this sinister figure might be. Yet the combination of Bertrand's futile guesses and Allasambe's metaphorical references to
theft, a sort of forced economic exchange, suggest as culprits either Idrissa
or Alaine Kourman—both men who have been accused, in one form or another in the text, of stealing from or cheating Bertrand monetarily. These
accusations are ironic, given that Bertrand has himself been stealing from
his Senegalese hosts—recall the compatriot of Doudou's who compares Bertrand's intellectual work to cultural theft.

Interestingly, in an extension of the fiscal metaphor, accepting the *tere*
pouch from Allasambe requires that Bertrand make the gesture of offering

Allasambe money for it: "I offered him the coins, but instead of taking them he bent over and closed my hand with his long fingers. 'Keep the money. It's just a ritual, a way of showing respect. If you are not willing to pay for it, you are saying it isn't worth anything. But you put value in it when you pay" (126). This conversation again emphasizes Bertrand's interactions with Senegalese culture as a kind of material exchange, one that Bertrand participates in most fully when he abandons the scholar's distance and becomes willing to give something of himself in return for the cultural knowledge he has gained.[20]

The matter of Bertrand's dreams, however, seems somewhat less benign than this, particularly as they are linked to Allasambe's warnings that Bertrand is "in danger of belonging to someone" (125). Subsequent pages of the novel are filled with moments of suspicion, as Bertrand tries to determine whom he can trust. In one moment he suspects his guide: "I could feel [Idrissa's] eyes on me, and I wondered what effect the tere might be having on him, if any" (135); in the next he notices that "the Kourmans, particularly Alaine, have grown icy and distant" (156). Yet perhaps the most telling clue is that for the "twenty-three nights" (157) following his acquisition of the *tere*, Bertrand's vivid sexual dreams disappear: "Over his morning coffee, he'll screw as deeply into his mind as he can, but finds nothing but memories of the previous waking day. . . . He feels his dreamlessness deep in his stomach—a literal hunger—or he feels it run up and down his ribs in a nervous thrill" (157). Bertrand now experiences dreamless sleep, the sort of sleep to which he had been accustomed for the first thirty-four years of his life, as a bodily absence—and his lack of dreams has other corporeal effects as well. The text notes, "His penis is a dead thing these days, cold and flaccid by day, cold and tumescent most nights. He rarely thinks of sex at all and wonders, now and again, whether he is coming down with something" (156). Here Bertrand's lack of sexual desire—a lack that is more emotional than physical, as his continuing nightly erections reveal—is not only taken by him as a sign of illness but is linked to mortality ("a dead thing").

On the twenty-fourth day, after a sleepwalking incident during which Bertrand awakes to find himself in the shower, "his crotch, underarms, and hair . . . soaped white" (158), the truth about his dreams is finally revealed. He leaves the shower in a daze and encounters Kene in the living room of the house, crying because of Alaine's infidelity. She reveals, "I gave you those dreams. Almost every single one" (167–68). To his response of "You know everything about me," Kene replies, "Of course I know. . . . You belong to me" (168). Here the one person who had escaped Bertrand's suspicion reveals herself to be the figure who was stealing from Bertrand bit by bit, the one to whom he was in danger of belonging. Gender difference may explain why Bertrand had been unable to see Kene as his tormentor before this moment. On the one hand, the terms of economic exchange within which Allasambe framed his warning make Bertrand more likely to assume a man is at fault, given the ways that men are traditionally expected to control fiscal matters and the way that arenas of monetary exchange are assumed to be masculine domains.

In addition, however, Kene's femaleness operates as a diversion from the truth of her behavior. Allasambe intimated that the person who was working magic against Bertrand hoped to steal his life, just as Allasambe's life had been taken from him many years before: "Someone had intentionally taken my life from me. Someone I was close to. He got my job, my apartment, even my girl for a week or two" (123). Bertrand does not attribute this kind of theft, the desire to inhabit Bertrand's life, to Kene precisely because she is female. Yet perhaps her femaleness, and the consequences of it in Senegal, lead her to take action. Even as she admits to Bertrand that she has given him the dreams, she goes on at length about the limitations on her life as a woman in traditional Senegalese culture. Not only does her husband, Alaine, feel more than entitled to his own infidelity (ironically, with a white Belgian woman), Kene's tenuous privileged status as his wife is dependent upon her acceptance of it: "I'm in no position to leave him. I'd lose my child. Lapsed Muslim that he may be, he'll still claim his parental privileges and rights under Islamic law. [Their daughter] Mammi's the issue of his seed, and I'm his little vessel. You've lived here a while. You know how it works" (169–70).

Kene's desire to "take" Bertrand's life, then, may have more to do with her belief that "men are free" (163), free in a way that she cannot be. Indeed, Kene's desire for Bertrand recalls the theorist Lauren Berlant's reading of the desire between characters Irene and Clare in Nella Larsen's *Passing*: "There may be a difference between wanting someone sexually and wanting someone's body: and I wonder whether Irene's xenophilia isn't indeed a desire to occupy, to experience the privileges of Clare's body, not to love or make love to her, but rather to wear her way of wearing her body, like a prosthesis, or a fetish."[21] Similarly, although Kene's manipulation of Bertrand's dreams reads as her sexual desire for him, Kene may actually desire the corporeal and ideological freedom that Bertrand enjoys within Senegalese culture—the freedom of an outsider, a *toubob*, however problematic.

The brief kiss that Bertrand and Kene share after this exchange is the first waking moment in which Bertrand has expressed his own desire for Kene. Yet before that encounter Bertrand had another opportunity for sexual contact—a particularly ironic one. Weeks before, he pursued a woman whom he met in a hotel bar, an American with blue-green eyes. At the moment of their encounter, looking into those eyes, Bertrand "sees what he sees and is so disappointed in himself he feels his heart sink to his stomach" (94). In contrast to his unacknowledged desire for Kene, he not only is aware of his attraction to the American woman, Sue, but he is aware, and uncomfortably so, that that attraction is driven by her pale skin, her freckles, her "mint and hail" colored eyes.

Given that this encounter with Sue directly follows, in McKnight's narrative, the story of Bertrand's fateful exposure to Bunny and Sally, it is clear that Sue's pale body is here forced to stand in for the black women Bertrand has never touched, in the curious reversal of racial expectation mentioned earlier. Rather than black women standing in as always accessible substitutes for unattainable white womanhood, in Bertrand's case black women (like Kene) remain unattainable, while white women—from his wife to the colleague with whom he has an affair while in the States (46) to this potential new conquest—present an ever-available alternative sex object. In this moment Bertrand's character must confront the ultimate irony that on a continent full of African women, the woman with whom he comes closest to "breaking his sexual fast" is a white-skinned American.

This irony, however, itself proves to be a red herring; Sue shows Bertrand a picture of herself at twenty-two, standing next to "a light-skinned black man of about forty" (153)—her father. Bertrand is filled with a profound chagrin at her revelation, because he believes, rightly or wrongly, that he should have been able to tell she had black ancestry. This assumption on his part reveals his participation in the very structures of authenticity that have constrained his own life; what else are his insistent claims that "I can usually tell. I've *always* been able to tell" (154) but attempts to link racial recognition to inherent racial knowledge? Or perhaps class knowledge. As the philosopher and performance artist Adrian Piper notes in her essay "Passing for White, Passing for Black," it is middle class blacks in particular who assure her that despite her pale skin, they "always knew [she was] black."[22] As this scene in *He Sleeps* progresses, Bertrand sits mortified as Sue says, "Bert, if I weren't an ex-colored girl, I'd have loved to have been your first. But I don't count. There is a kind of end to blackness, and I'm it" (153). To his retort of "I don't buy it, black is black. . . . Are you saying that you're white?" Sue replies categorically, "Absolutely not, Bertrand. I'm invisible" (155).

In an unexpected transformation of Ellison's racial allegory, the quintessentially invisible black subject here is not a man but a woman—and she is invisible not merely to whites but to other blacks as well. As she explains to Bertrand in describing her decision to leave the United States (and her black identity) behind, "What's the point of being black if you have to flash an ID before anyone lets you in the door?" (154). Sue suggests that invisibility, not whiteness per se, is the social consequence for a black person who does not phenotypically signify as such. Yet Sue's invisibility ultimately does seem to be a capitulation to whiteness, given that whiteness is the only racial identity allowed to remain invisible, unmarked, in the United States—indeed, the one-drop rule of racial classification in the United States "represent[s] whiteness as the absence of the racial sign."[23] Without deliberately resisting this invisibility by showing her father's picture as ID, Sue continually arrives at the visual "end of blackness."

This dilemma perhaps explains her defection to Europe, where presumably her white body can at least signify a number of ethnicities—as evidenced in the African men's speculation about her while she sits mutely at the hotel bar where she and Bertrand meet. Guessing first German, then Dutch, "Definitely not French. Look at that ass" (93, 94), Bertrand's Senegalese companions Medoune and Saliu script Sue into a number of variations on whiteness, ironically reading the shape of her body against that of an African woman and finding it identical except for their erroneous racial classification: "If she were black, you couldn't tell the difference between her and a Senegalese woman" (94).

Sue's pale skin and blue eyes, if not her "ass," obviate her immediate inclusion within the African American community, but Bertrand too seems to inhabit a racial space dangerously close to the "end of blackness" that Sue describes and for reasons far more complex. In fact, perhaps the greatest irony of Bertrand and Sue's exchange is Bertrand's uncritical assertion that "black is black." Bertrand refers to skin color, acknowledging the wide variations in phenotype among those who are considered to be, or who consider themselves to be, African American. Yet what of other, less tangible, racial markers, especially those inflected by class, gender, sexuality? What is Bertrand's private sexual conundrum but classed and gendered evidence that in some instances black is clearly *not* black? As Bertrand himself acknowledges, in the eyes of many African Americans, his (conscious or unconscious) choice to be only with white women marks him, and other men like him, as "self-hating freaks, turncoats, . . . enemies of their own history" (144). Such thinking seems to indicate that just as there is an imagined phenotypical boundary to black identity, outside of which lies white-skinned, blue-eyed Sue, there is also an imagined sexual boundary, a line that just as easily excludes Bertrand. In both cases the body's failed performance of blackness emphasizes this line, and the material context for Bertrand's liminal status with regard to race indicates that social class plays a crucial role; perhaps one can be simultaneously colored and classed out of blackness.

McKnight's postmodernist novel, with its attention to the risks and contradictions of black material privilege, and to the vexed relationship between class and sexual identity, thus subverts nationalist discourses of blackness in crucial ways by emphasizing that blackness's contingent nature. While E. Franklin Frazier's assertion that black middle-class men "resemble women" takes these figures' racial identities as a given and questions only their sexual and gender performances, He Sleeps ultimately argues the reverse: that these corporeal performances also have the potential to fracture and mitigate blackness. As perhaps the quintessential black postmodern figure, Bertrand therefore denotes a radical shift in black cultural production—indicating that in our contemporary moment, blackness can no longer function as an all-powerful, meta-identity category because of the ways that it is modified, in some cases even erased, by other facets of experience.

This notion of blackness as conditional, fairly or not, has long been acknowledged in the work of black women and black gays and lesbians, marked as they are by the stigma of an embodied otherness; indeed, members of these groups have often been forced to defend their black identities or argue for their inclusion in the communal fold.[24] Conversely, black cultural nationalism has positioned the heterosexual black male as the naturalized representative of black identity, a figure whose racial belonging could rarely, if ever, be disputed. Male and heterosexual Bertrand's position at the "end of blackness," a direct result of his material privilege and his body's attendant failures, thus marks his contingent, postmodern blackness, always on the verge of disappearing, as something new. Perhaps it is fitting that in this postmodern, post–civil rights era, the central narrative metaphor for African American racial alienation is not an impoverished black man in a tortured relationship with a white woman but a highly educated, bourgeois black man literally unable to touch his black female counterpart—except perhaps, as is ultimately the case in this novel, in his dreams.

## NOTES

1. Bertram D. Ashe, " 'Under the Umbrella of Black Civilization': A Conversation with Reginald McKnight," *African American Review* 35, no. 3 (2001): 440. McKnight is certainly not alone in his feelings of alienation from this racial norm; other contemporary black critics and artists repeatedly explore such issues in their creative work and in memoir or personal essay. Randall Kenan is one example of the latter; he writes with similar poignancy of his feelings of inadequacy after reading James Baldwin's *Notes of a Native Son* as a young man: "I . . . had grown up on land that had been in my family for five generations; my grandfather was a successful businessman and my cousins were college professors and colonels. . . . I felt in some way not black enough, somehow—ridiculously—inauthentic; that, because of his struggles, James Baldwin was somehow closer than I to being a real Negro" (Randall Kenan, *Walking on Water: Black American Lives at the Turn of the Twenty-first Century* [New York: Vintage, 2000], 15). As for black fiction, while this essay focuses on McKnight's *He Sleeps,* other late twentieth- and early twenty-first-century texts

such as Paul Beatty's *White Boy Shuffle* (1996), Percival Everett's *Erasure* (2001), and Martha Southgate's *The Fall of Rome* (2002), among others, pay similar attention to black material privilege and its relationship to black racial subjectivity.

2. Cornel West, "The Paradox of the African American Rebellion," in Eddie S. Glaude Jr., ed., *Is It Nation Time? Contemporary Essays on Black Power and Black Nationalism* (Chicago: University of Chicago Press, 2002), 31, 32; Kenan, *Walking on Water,* 12. Indeed, Lubiano calls black nationalism "black common sense" (Wahneema Lubiano, "Black Nationalism and Black Common Sense: Policing Ourselves and Others," in Wahneema Lubiano, ed., *The House That Race Built* [New York: Pantheon, 1997], 232).

3. Although a full exploration of the concept of the postmodern is beyond the scope of this essay, here I should note that my understanding of "black postmodernism" draws, first, on Jean-François Lyotard's suggestion that the postmodern moment in general is marked by "incredulity toward metanarratives" of culture, as well as Phillip Brian Harper's crucial rejoinder that minority literatures have a long history of engagement with the notion of the decentered and fragmented subject, erroneously assumed by some observers to be new to the postmodern period (Jean-François Lyotard, *The Postmodern Condition: A Report on Knowledge* [Minneapolis: University of Minnesota Press, 1984], xxiv; Phillip Brian Harper, *Framing the Margins: The Social Logic of Postmodern Culture* [New York: Oxford University Press, 1994], 3). In a recent study even more germane to my project here, Madhu Dubey writes persuasively on the subject of black intellectuals' present-day relationship to the postmodern: "[In African-American studies,] the postmodern moment is characterized by a widely registered crisis in the category of racial community—a crisis rooted in the specificities of African-American history (notably the changed conditions of racial community after the political transformations of the Civil Rights movement) but also conditioned by the national and global developments . . . that are said to be formative of the postmodern era" (Madhu Dubey, *Signs and Cities: Black Literary Postmodernism* [Chicago: University of Chicago Press, 2003], 24). Dubey's comments remind us of the larger social and discursive context for my discussion of black class privilege in the postmodern era, even if I cannot, in this brief essay, undertake a full investigation of that context. It may also be important to note that my interest lies less in the broad contours of race and postmodernism per se and more in black class privilege as a specific circumstance of the postmodern moment—one of the distinct factors contributing to the "changed conditions of racial community

after . . . the Civil Rights movement" to which Dubey alludes but does not address in detail.

4. In invoking the "post–civil rights era," particularly coupled with my earlier discussion of black power, I am implicitly referencing the related concept of the "post-soul," which I use in a few places during this essay as a rough synonym for the "black postmodern." My temporal understanding of the term *postsoul* relies largely on Mark Anthony Neal's definition of the concept in his book *Soul Babies:* "I use the term *post-soul* to describe the political, social, and cultural experiences of the African-American community since the end of the civil rights and Black Power movements." Yet for Neal, the postsoul also has at its core "a radical reimagining of the contemporary African-American experience," including attempts "to liberate . . . that experience from sensibilities that were formalized and institutionalized during earlier social paradigms" (Mark Anthony Neal, *Soul Babies: Black Popular Culture and the Post-Soul Aesthetic* [New York: Routledge, 2002], 3). This second half of Neal's definition makes clear the deconstructive and oppositional efforts of many postsoul artists and intellectuals, which helps to explain my use of the term as loosely synonymous with black postmodernism.

5. E. Franklin Frazier, *Black Bourgeoisie: The Rise of a New Middle Class in the United States* (1957; repr., New York: Free Press, 1997), 221.

6. Reginald McKnight, *He Sleeps* (New York: Picador USA, 2001), 87–89.

7. Lauren Berlant, "National Brands, National Bodies: *Imitation of Life*," in Hortense Spillers, ed., *Comparative American Identities: Race, Sex, and Nationality in the Modern Text* (New York: Routledge, 1991).

8. Elizabeth Alexander, *The Black Interior* (St. Paul, Minn.: Graywolf, 2004), 133.

9. Patricia Hill Collins, *Black Sexual Politics: African Americans, Gender, and the New Racism* (New York: Routledge, 2004), 76.

10. Eldridge Cleaver, *Soul on Ice* (New York: Dell, 1968), 14; Angela Davis, *Women, Race and Class* (New York: Vintage, 1983), 182.

11. Davis, *Women, Race and Class*, 182.

12. Frazier, *Black Bourgeoisie*, 12.

13. Saidiya Hartman, *Lose Your Mother: A Journey along the Atlantic Slave Route* (New York: Farrar, Straus and Giroux, 2007), 84, 85, 88, 89.

14. Paul Smith, "Eastwood Bound," in Maurice Berger et al., eds., *Constructing Masculinity* (New York: Routledge, 1995), 77; Mark Anthony Neal, *New Black Man* (New York: Routledge, 2005), 21; McKnight, *He Sleeps*, 68.

15. E. Frances White, "Africa on My Mind: Gender, Counterdiscourse, and African American Nationalism," in Beverly Guy-Sheftall, ed., *Words of Fire: An Anthology of African American Feminist Thought* (New York: New Press, 1995), 504.

16. For a much more in-depth exploration of how the postmodern black subjects of McKnight's *He Sleeps* and his earlier novel, *I Get on the Bus,* see Rolland Murray's comments on discourses of African diaspora and nostalgic narratives of black American/Caribbean return to the African continent in "Diaspora by Bus: Reginald McKnight, Postmodernism, and Transatlantic Subjectivity," *Contemporary Literature* 46, no. 1 (2005): 46–77.

17. Arguably, this hierarchy is built into the very foundations of the discipline of anthropology; as Ruth Behar suggests, traditional anthropology was "born of the European colonial impulse to know others in order to lambast them, better manage them, or exalt them" (Ruth Behar, *The Vulnerable Observer: Anthropology That Breaks Your Heart* [Boston: Beacon, 1996], 4).

18. McKnight, *He Sleeps,* 112. Doudou's question recalls for McKnight's readers the ways that black Americans have indeed been the objects of anthropological inquiry—yet in another ironic reminder of the American man's class privilege, Bertrand's inability to respond to this rhetorical assault suggests his estrangement from the impoverished black communities that have most often been investigated in this way.

19. John L. Jackson, *Real Black: Adventures in Racial Sincerity* (Chicago: University of Chicago Press, 2005), 156.

20. Notes Behar, on the increasing acknowledgment of the ethnographer's vulnerability in anthropological study, "We now stand on the same plane with our subjects; indeed, they will only tolerate us if we are willing to confront them face to face" (Behar, *Vulnerable Observer,* 28).

21. Berlant, "National Brands, National Bodies," 111. Berlant's interpretation of Larsen's novel departs from established readings by McDowell, Butler, and others of *Passing* as a covertly lesbian or queer text and of Irene's attraction to Clare as an indication of her character's unarticulated homoerotic desires. See Deborah McDowell, *Introduction to* Quicksand *and* Passing (New Brunswick, N.J.: Rutgers University Press, 1989); and Judith Butler, "*Passing,* Queering: Nella Larsen's Psychoanalytic Challenge," in *Bodies That Matter: On the Discursive Limits of Sex* (New York: Routledge, 1993).

22. Adrian Piper, "Passing for White, Passing for Black," in Elaine K. Ginsberg, ed.,

*Passing and the Fictions of Identity* (Durham, N.C.: Duke University Press, 1996), 238.

23. Gayle Wald, *Crossing the Line: Racial Passing in Twentieth-century U.S. Literature and Culture* (Durham, N.C.: Duke University Press, 2000), 13.

24. For an insightful discussion of this phenomenon in black queer studies, see Dwight A. McBride, "Can the Queen Speak? Racial Essentialism, Sexuality and the Problem of Authority," *Callaloo* 21, no. 2 (1998): 363–79.

# Black Ladies and Black Magic Women

he films *Daughters of the Dust* (1991) and *Eve's Bayou* (1997) challenge the overdetermined narrative of middle-class black romance presented in numerous movies released since the 1990s.[1] The long list of popular films includes *Boomerang* (1992), *Hav Plenty* (1997), *Love Jones* (1997), *Soul Food* (1997), *The Best Man* (1999), *Two Can Play That Game* (2001), *The Brothers* (2001), *Deliver Us from Eva* (2003), *Breaking All the Rules* (2004), *Something New* (2006), *Daddy's Girls* (2006), *Why Did I Get Married?* (2007), and *Why Did I Get Married Too?* (2010). Considered "feel-good films targeted at the black community, . . . [that assume] a middle-class black audience," they often feature handsomely dressed, attractive professionals navigating the pitfalls of urban romance in luxurious settings.[2] Besides presenting an insular black middle-class universe, these comedies consistently feature the black woman as professionally exceptional but personally doomed. Often regarded as frigid and asexual, she is continually frustrated by her inability to find satisfying intimate relationships. The striver's career and possessions substitute for unfulfilled sexual desires.

In their period dramas Julie Dash and Kasi Lemmons subvert the stereotypes perpetuated by these contemporary romantic comedies. *Daughters of the Dust* (Dash) and *Eve's Bayou* (Lemmons) escape the clichéd depictions of sexually frustrated, but highly professional, black middle-class women. The directors endeavor to redefine contemporary notions of black womanhood from a historical perspective without becoming mired in the horrors of the past. Critics have rightly pointed out that Dash's groundbreaking feature film "created a new way of seeing, and reading" African American life.[3] Indeed, *Daughters of the Dust* is a black feminist film that places black women at the center of African American history. But it and *Eve's Bayou* are also landmark depictions of black women's beauty and sexuality. Both Dash and Lemmons force viewers to think about the middle-class and the sexual values attached to these women in ways that transcend conventional depictions of African American women.

Instead of merely evoking southern culture, Dash advocates for a "New World African aesthetic" that honors a nonlinear African storytelling style. She considers her work "based upon the way an African griot would recount a story's history, would recount a tale based upon West African deities, like Ogun, Osun, Yemoja," and asserts that "contemporary filmmaking by African American artists is very much a part of the continuum of the past and the writers from the '60s."[4] While the use of this New World African aesthetic collapses and simplifies various West African spiritual, regional, and tribal traditions, the strategy does allow *Daughters of the Dust* and *Eve's Bayou* to celebrate an alternate belief system that honors black people and black women in particular.[5] In an interview by Houston Baker Jr., Dash defends her narrative style: "I think we need to do more than try to document history. I think we need to probe. We need to have the freedom to romanticize history, to say 'what if,' to use history in a speculative way and creative speculative fiction."[6]

The tendency toward speculative fiction is evident in Lemmons's film as well. The work of the two extends beyond reimagining black history; the films specifically reimagine black womanhood within a spiritual tradition that harks back to indigenous modes of expression, power, worship, and respect. Their reliance on the religions of the African diaspora allows the films to move beyond retelling the sorrowful stories of black female suffering and sexual abuse so often linked to southern history. While they do provide filmic renderings of middle-class women who are unfulfilled and romantically frustrated, they also offer images of black women as sexual agents whose choices complicate conventional notions of middle-class sexuality.

## Eve's Bayou

*Eve's Bayou,* one of "the most financially successful independent film[s] of 1997," caused the critic Mia Mask to ask a despicable, but telling, question: "*Eve's Bayou:* Too Good to Be a 'Black' Film?"[7] The film did enjoy critical acclaim: Lemmons was awarded the Independent Spirit Award for Best First Time Feature, and the film was nominated for seven NAACP Image Awards. The distancing of the motion picture from the genre of African American cinema partially derives from Lemmons's break from typical renderings of black life, which led some critics to wonder if it was genuinely a "black film." *Eve's Bayou* revises the overbearing iconography of African American females through a subtle and diverse representation of southern black middle-class women.[8] Within the strict confines and historical conventions of the upper-middle-class black family, Lemmons renders four distinct female characters, each with a different temperament and motivations.

Set in the summer of 1962 in a fictional small southern town, *Eve's Bayou* relates the tale of a popular black physician, Louis Batiste (Samuel L. Jackson), who not only engages in various affairs but, as the film also suggests, at best he encourages an unhealthy flirtation with his older daughter, Cisely (Meagan Good). The discovery of his infidelities and transgressions eventually leads to his murder. The film's intricate plot, with its various subplots, depicts a black middle-class family in crisis.

Although the patriarch is at the center of the film, *Eve's Bayou* offers an unusually layered portrayal of black middle-class womanhood. While literature, film, and drama repeatedly depict middle-class African Americans as repressed, shallow, and self-loathing or as unblemished moral leaders, the Batiste women encompass a more complex range. None is an asexual Mammy, hypersexual vamp, outcast lesbian, or emasculating tyrant. Lemmons also disregards the impulse to treat middle-class blacks as perfect citizens who rigidly adhere to normative codes of conduct or as apolitical, self-interested, unenlightened sycophants. Instead she endows her characters with both admirable and disagreeable qualities that foreground their humanity.

The narrative reveals how Louis's philandering unsettles his wife, Roz (Lynn Whitfield), who desperately holds to a notion of an ideal middle-class family. Roz's reactions to Louis's misdeeds shape how their two daughters, fourteen-year-old Cisely and the titular Eve (Jurnee Smollett), a precocious ten-year-old, imagine their futures as black women. The film's spiritual center, Louis's sister Mozelle (Debbi Morgan), is also crucial to Lemmons's unconventional rendering of black sexuality. While Roz offers an example of how to be a conventional colored lady, Mozelle provides an alternative model of womanhood. Through Mozelle *Eve's Bayou* reveals how middle-class black women develop creative strategies to undercut conservative notions of female propriety and responsibility.

This visually stunning film uses vivid colors, a haunting soundtrack, and delicate lighting to evoke the danger, mystery, and romance of the southern United States. The "stylish, southern Gothic tale" makes use of a gumbo of spirituality, biblical allusion, and mysticism. The first scene establishes the class and social position of the Batiste family. The camera pans from the dark mysterious bayou to a wooded yard filled with expensive automobiles. Slowly, the audience enters a large and beautifully adorned residence filled with laughter and Zydeco music. The house teems with jovial, well-dressed black guests of various hues who are dancing, gossiping, and laughing. The dining room table and sideboard boast a lavish spread of Creole cuisine and champagne. The Batiste children laugh, play, and flippantly recite lines from Shakespeare.[9] As the host, Louis, surrounded by an adoring family, friends, and community, takes pleasure in being the focus of gossip in the parish.

The opening scene also introduces the primary challenges facing the Batiste clan: sibling rivalry, marital betrayal, misplaced intimacy, and emotional estrangement. In a moment of competition Eve and Cisely vie for their father's attention. When Louis dances with Cisely in front of the crowd, Eve retreats to the carriage house. Pouting, she falls asleep. Later in the evening, however, she is awakened by her father's sexual encounter with a party guest, Matty Mereaux (Lisa Nicole Carson).[10] This act of infidelity and Eve's witnessing of it signal the beginning of the family's destabilization and departure from proper middle-class decorum. When Eve confides in her older sister about seeing their father's tryst, Cisely becomes upset and immediately rejects the possibility of Louis's unfaithfulness. She consoles Eve by suggesting an alternative and sanitized version of the episode that maintains their father's image as a charismatic gentleman. Despite Cisely's attempts to comfort Eve, she remains traumatized by the incident. The moment serves as a catalyst for Eve's maturation, and she begins to question the advantages of becoming a colored lady if doing so requires her to privilege respectability and poise over acknowledging an unpleasant reality.

From the outset the film contrasts the flirtatious, voluptuous Matty with the glamorous yet respectable Batiste women and suggests the subtle ways in which the performance of black middle-class womanhood passes from generation to generation. When Matty dances a slow grind with her husband at the party, another guest whispers to Eve's grandmother, Gran Mére (Ethel Ayler), that Matty's husband "ain't the only one getting it." Clad in a tight black satin dress covered with hot pink flowers, Matty embodies the stereotype of the Jezebel. The spectacle of her full body and the close-up of her buttocks invite derision from Gran Mére, who conveys her irritation in sarcastic Creole. Matty's physical excess signifies sexual excess, and Gran Mére's commentary firmly establishes the behavioral boundaries for proper colored ladies.

The history of sexual objectification and abuse haunts all black women, but the figure of the colored lady in particular haunts middle-class black women and influences their behavior and sensibility. In the early twentieth century the "colored lady," a female member of W. E. B. Du Bois's "talented tenth," regarded her role of representing the race as paramount because "African American female reformers embedded bourgeois respectability in racial uplift ideology."[11] The colored lady was the sort of black woman who subscribed to Anna Julia Cooper's belief that "the intelligent wife, the Christian mother, the earnest, virtuous, helpful woman, [is] at once both the lever and the fulcrum for uplifting the race."[12] Cooper called on black women to battle the "all-leveling prejudice as that supercilious caste spirit in America which cynically assumes 'A Negro woman cannot be a lady.'"[13] The idea of being both black and a lady is a dichotomy that continues to haunt African American women.[14] It is this dichotomy that characterizes the possibilities for Eve and Cisely in their southern black middle-class community. Both sisters define themselves in relation to—and often in opposition to—the older women they most admire or to whom they are closest. Cisely competes with her mother, Roz, while Eve patterns herself after her aunt Mozelle.

The Batiste family history is crucial to understanding the sisters' choices and roles. The legend of Eve's Bayou frames Batiste womanhood in terms of African American history. Their ancestor, an African slave—the first Eve—worked as a conjurer and healer. According to legend, her "powerful medicine" saved the life of her owner, General Jean Paul Batiste, who was stricken with cholera. And "in turn for his life he freed her" and gave her a piece of land by the bayou; afterward, "perhaps in gratitude," she bore him sixteen children. The family originated in slavery yet endeavors to position the matriarch, Eve, as powerful.

*Eve's Bayou* uses biblical references as well as historic symbolism. Eve symbolizes the first human woman, often denounced in Christian cultures for original sin because she disobeyed God and ate from the tree of knowledge. The matriarch Eve used her knowledge to save her master's life, thus earning freedom and ensuring a better life for her descendants. But this first Eve Batiste's freedom is conflicted by her concubinage to her former master, underscoring the ways sexuality complicates the lives of her female descendants.

Eve gained freedom because of her knowledge as a healer, but that freedom is fraught because of her role as concubine and mother of her former master's children. Her special status within the nonwhite community is disconcerting; her relationship with the father of her children calls to mind the relationship between Sally Hemmings and Thomas Jefferson, as well as the arrangements between other white men of means and countless black women of the antebellum South that Lorraine O'Grady regards as a "still under-theorized, historic relationship."[15] It is more complicated than the obvious features of exploitation and abuse. Eve's descendents gain valuable land in the bayou because of a powerful white man. Instead of the usual arrangement—a female slave as property that produces property (more enslaved children)—the Batiste family inherits land and social prominence through the matriarch's body.

The land represents bondage as well as liberation for the Batiste clan. The original Eve's sacrifice of her body makes it possible for Louis to become a respected, even envied, physician. But sexuality proves to be a thorny issue in the lives of her female descendants. Ironically, her female progeny find their choices limited and their lives complicated by gender, sexuality, and class status. Nonetheless Eve and Mozelle, who inherit the gift of "sight," try to control their destiny, while Cisely and Roz fall victim to the dictates of middle-class decorum.

The spiritual gifts that give young Eve and Mozelle agency also derive from their family origins. It is not only their ancestor's role as a concubine that changes the family's destiny but also her skills as a healer and conjurer. Black female sexuality and black magic, both considered mysterious, powerful, wicked, and uncontrollable, are the foundation of the Batiste family's financial and social standing. The same space that their ancestors occupied as slaves is now the location of their grand home.

For Lemmons family history is but one tool to disrupt stereotypical depictions of black womanhood. The bayou symbolizes African American dynamism, boundlessness, hope, and power, a deep dark space offering both beauty and danger. An area of slow-moving water coming from a river or lake, often overgrown with reeds, the bayou is as languid as the colored ladies of the story. The film treats the landscape as an additional character that is female, even maternal. Given the Batiste family history, the gendering of the land as female is particularly intriguing. Spirituality, land, and sexuality all resonate as elements controlled by women, and in Eve's Bayou these elements destabilize middle-class propriety.

Roz best fits the cultural stereotype of the colored lady. Lemmons portrays her as untouchable, asexual, and respectable. Carla Peterson points out that, in order to become respectable, the black female body is normalized and made "culturally white" by performing in ways that are "regulated and disciplined." That is what Roz does. To maintain her status as a colored lady she uses strategies of decorporealization and normalization.[16] To uphold her middle-class identity Roz presents her black female body as attractive but desexualized. While other women in the film flaunt their sexuality in hopes of attracting Louis, Roz acts shrill, unhappy, desperate, frustrated, and vulnerable. She refuses to compete with others for her husband's affections through sex; the demands she makes on him are based on family, duty, responsibility, and morality. She performs what she perceives to be the role of the proper colored lady, who uplifts the community by adhering to the highest codes of sexual conduct.

Roz's performance of the normalized black middle-class identity allows for her to demonstrate passion only through motherhood, and here it is her young son, Poe (Jake Smolett), who receives a disproportionate share of her attention. His affections substitute for Louis's neglect. She embodies the ideal middle-class housewife (a doctor's wife, no less) and mother, with her power confined to the domestic sphere. Unlike the barren Mozelle, Roz's role as mother defines and normalizes her. When Mozelle warns of impending doom because of a vision, for instance, Roz forbids the children to go outdoors all summer. Only within the home, she believes, can she protect them.

Although Roz is quite beautiful, she appears in bed only when she comforts the children after Louis's death. The image of the newly widowed Roz is stunning; she sits surrounded by her children, who protect her from harm like a fortress. In this instance we are reminded how motherhood helps her to maintain the inaccessibility of the colored lady's body.

Throughout the film Roz either suffers her husband's behavior in strained silence or throws tantrums. Performing as a true colored lady, she never considers retaliating by taking a lover. Roz confesses that she married because she desired a carefree middle-class life. During a walk along the water with Mozelle, she explains her attraction to her husband: "When I first met Louis I watched him set this boy's leg who'd fallen out of a tree and I said to myself, 'Here's a man who can fix things. He's a healer. He'll take care of me.' So I leave my family and I moved to this swamp and to find out, he's just a man." Disappointed when she realizes Louis's humanity and embarrassed by his faults, Roz reluctantly becomes a frustrated colored lady with an unfaithful husband.

Roz expects Louis to live up to her ideal of marriage by being the man who takes care of her financially and emotionally. She unquestioningly embraces the myth of a classic American marriage. Uncritical of the marriage contract, Roz falls victim to naive beliefs; she becomes a beautiful, respected, honored woman trapped in a gilded cage. The fantasy of a normal middle-class family proves disastrous for her. She understands that to challenge Louis would risk her position within the community and threaten her perfect family. To maintain her status she finds herself in the same position as white middle-class housewives before the second wave of feminism. Normalization requires her to sacrifice her sense of self. Roz maintains a facade of normality because upholding the family's social position for her children, community, and race is more important than her personal happiness.

Throughout the film Lemmons questions the notion of the colored lady. Even Eve's conversation with her father evokes this impossible standard of womanhood:

**LOUIS:** Daddy loves you very much.

**EVE:** I know. You love Mama?

**LOUIS:** Your Mama is *the* most beautiful perfect woman I ever met. Your Mama is a lady and I'll always love her. Always. Understand?

In both Louis's and Eve's imagination the perfect Roz represents a colored lady with impeccable morals and flawless beauty. Louis delivers this message to Eve in a hushed, reverent tone that denotes the intensity of his love and respect for Roz despite his infidelities.

The exchange between father and daughter is especially poignant because the scene occurs directly after Eve has discovered her father with Matty. Louis's comments nearly suggest that he is unfaithful because Roz is a colored lady. A lover could never be the mother of his children or hold the position of wife. Just as Louis's presence ensures Roz's position, Roz's grace, beauty, domestic talents, and social standing ensure his role "as the most respected colored doctor in all Louisiana." She represents the type of woman Louis hopes their daughters will emulate—colored ladies, not imperfect women like his lovers. However, instead of behaving like a proper young colored lady who accepts the fictions of middle-class black society, Eve rebels. When she questions her father about the rumors she has heard, she aligns herself with Aunt Mozelle within the family discourse.

Mozelle is anything but a conventional colored lady. Her reddish hair, expressive eyes, and saucy speech distinguish her from the decidedly prim, reserved Roz. Mozelle exemplifies an atypical, uncommon style of womanhood that moves beyond the colored lady. She uses neither decorporealization nor normalization to maintain her class status; rather, she embraces her sexual life and romantic entanglements. Fortunately for Mozelle, her membership in a prominent family exempts her from the kind of scrutiny that Matty suffers. The eccentric Mozelle is the only woman who smokes (she even allows Eve an opportunity to puff on a cigarette), and her work as a psychic counselor places her outside normative boundaries for proper colored ladies. As a respected spiritual healer, Mozelle doctors the spirit like her brother heals the body. She does not work for financial reasons; psychic counseling, Louis remarks, is "something the family lets her do."

Indisputably, Mozelle's work marks her as a spiritual descendant of the matriarch Eve. Both are closely aligned with the supernatural. Although hoodoo and visions dominate her landscape, Mozelle's emphasis on the spiritual world does not place her outside the corporeal. She also defies other cinematic representations of middle-class black women in that she is comfortable with her sexuality; unlike the women in popular romantic comedies, she has no trouble finding love. Perhaps because of her multiple marriages and penchant for affairs Mozelle still radiates a sensuousness that the repressed Roz lacks.

Mozelle refuses to abide by her middle-class family's expectations. Louis dismisses his eccentric sister as one who is not "unfamiliar with the inside of a mental institution."[17] After Mozelle's third husband dies in an automobile accident early in the film, she temporarily capitulates to the community's label of black widow and concentrates solely on her work as a psychic counselor. Instead of remaining a long-suffering widow, however, she becomes engaged yet again. Mozelle's refusal to succumb to the misfortune of widowhood or become more conservative also marks her as different from her sister-in-law Roz and expands the representation of middle-class black womanhood. Although she is childless, Mozelle is gratified by her role as aunt and especially close to the precocious Eve with whom she shares the gift of second sight. Mozelle is a romantic character who carries her tragedies as a badge of honor. Her three dead husbands lend her an air of mystery.

The trust that exists between aunt and niece allows for mutual confidences. Mozelle is the only adult in whom Eve confides; when she tells Mozelle about Louis's infidelity with Matty, Mozelle reciprocates by revealing that she witnessed her lover murder her second husband. Mozelle's revelations about her sexual infidelities allow the precocious Eve to further imagine a life that troubles the boundaries of middle-class propriety. Instead of adopting the role of the long-suffering wife or celibate widow, Mozelle has forged a unique path. She insists on her own rules. Although her sexual choices and work as a psychic counselor place her outside the expectations of the black middle class, Mozelle still manages to earn the respect and trust of her community and family. Some consider her peculiar, but Mozelle skillfully negotiates her status as both an insider and outsider. At the end of the film she demonstrates bravery and independence by defying her "black widow" curse and agreeing to marry for the fourth time. She disregards most conventional notions of propriety while also managing to maintain her position within the black middle class.

Mozelle's connection to the spiritual world offers her solace in tragedies and a link to her past. Spirituality also helps her imagine a future. She resists expectations of a sexless widowhood and maintains sexual agency. After Matty's cuckolded husband murders Louis, Mozelle consoles Eve with another story: "Last night I had a dream that I was flying. It was such a fine feeling. But from the corner of my eye, I saw a woman drowning in the very same air that was keeping me afloat. And I knew without looking that it was me. Should I save her? Then I heard Louis's voice saying, 'Don't look back.' So I kept on flying . . . and I let her drown."

Unlike Roz, Mozelle accepts the inevitability of disappointment and loss. She survives because she refuses to embrace the victimization that comes with the prescribed role of a colored lady. The drowning figure in her dream represents not only her past but also her rejection of the role and codes that suffocate and stifle the spirit. Mozelle allows the colored lady to drown and models for Eve and Cisely a defiant middle-class black womanhood. Her life includes tragedy and misfortune, but Mozelle's refusal to stop flying suggests that a black woman can fashion her life in creative and liberating ways.

*Eve's Bayou* challenges assumptions about black middle-class respectability and southern gentility by illustrating that despite efforts to sublimate desire, the middle-class black female body retains its signification as a site of danger and contamination. Although Roz and Mozelle respond quite differently to social expectations, Lemmons initially presents both women as isolated and untouchable. Roz, although stunningly attractive, remains unimpeachable, modest, and pure. Mozelle, the doomed barren "black widow," conveys a sexual potency that threatens to devour every man who loves her. These narrative positions initially strip both women of agency, yet Mozelle's reluctance to tolerate the restrictions of her social position allows for her humanity. Of all the Batiste women, she is the most like the Louisiana bayou—powerful, enchanting, dangerous, and beautiful.

Lemmons grants her audience a nostalgic vision of black life in the southern United States. Like other artists, she redefines the South for African Americans and reclaims what is useful about the region. She casts it not only as a site of pain and horror but also as a place of culture, history, myth, and mysticism. The depiction in *Eve's Bayou* of a South without poverty, racial violence, and civil rights activism may be troubling, but Lemmons's strategy allows her to deliver a complex and rare portrayal of middle-class black sexuality.

## Daughters of the Dust

In Julie Dash's poetic *Daughters of the Dust* (1991), the tasteful decor of the Batiste home gives way to the rustic cabins of the Peazant family. As in *Eve's Bayou*, the southern landscape is a character in its own right. Expansive white sand beaches, the blue sea, lush fields, and dramatically crooked trees provide a serene but potent, almost sacred, backdrop. Like Lemmons, Dash not only features an enchanting landscape but populates her film with gorgeous black women. Dash has acknowledged that one of her objectives was to "show black families, particularly black women, as we have never seen them before."[18] The women in the cast are mostly dark skinned, wear natural hairstyles, and adorn their ample frames with lovely rich white fabrics. By casting black women as undeniably desirable, *Daughters of the Dust*, like *Eve's Bayou*, challenges dominant notions of beauty that privilege whiteness.

This first nationally distributed feature film directed by an African American woman addresses the issue of black middle-class sexuality indirectly. *Daughters of the Dust* does not portray a financially and socially secure black family. Instead, Dash situates her narrative within the tensions of Gullah culture, West African–inspired spirituality, and the Victorian notions of respectability and propriety espoused by the black middle class. The film is set on a day in 1902 when the Peazant family plans to migrate from its ancestral home in the Sea Islands to the mainland and life in the North. The family members spend the day celebrating their departure, negotiating their connection to each other, and mourning the inevitable losses their journey necessitates. The women are particularly cognizant of the dangers their new world may present to their bodies and notions of self.

*Daughters of the Dust* presents two ways for black women to assure their survival and understand black female sexuality. Women must either embrace Victorian values and pious Christianity in order to achieve colored-lady status or, in a more radical or subversive tactic, claim their worth as an essence, something derived from their ancestors that cannot be destroyed despite the experiences of slavery and postbellum racial violence. This juxtaposition is played out through two cousins who have come back home to chaperone the family's migration north: Viola Peazant (Cheryl Lynn Bruce), a Christian missionary, and her cousin, Yellow Mary Peazant (Barbara O. Jones), a prostitute. Yellow Mary and Viola, who have thrived away from the island, both cross from the mainland to celebrate the family's departure and offer advice influenced by their experiences. The ideological battle between what these two women symbolize plays out before the family and allows the other women to imagine how their lives may change after migrating.

The film uses an array of diverse personalities, in addition to Viola and Yellow Mary, to tell unfamiliar stories about black womanhood. Another principal character, Eula Peazant (Alva Rogers), is a rape victim. The knowledge of her rape haunts Eula and torments her husband, Eli (Adisa Anderson). That Eula's violation came at the hands of a white man evokes the family's recent slave past and reminds its members that while their home on Ibo Landing contains their roots, it does not offer complete safety. Eula's unborn child is a major presence. Unborn Child (Kai-Lynn Warren) unites the past and future with voice-overs and appearances at key moments that add to the film's mythical quality. She knows that her duty is to help her family make the transition to the mainland, and she also knows that because she is her father's child and not a product of the rape, her arrival will restore the bond between her parents. The Unborn Child also bridges the story's African-centered nonlinear narrative, its elements of magical realism, and the film's belief in family as a healing balm.

Eighty-eight-year-old Nana Peazant (Cora Lee Day), the family matriarch, represents spirituality, the family's connection to ancestors, culture, and the earth. Nana tries to instill in her offspring the lessons that
she learned growing up on Ibo Landing. She explains the importance of the
bottle tree as a way of remaining close to the "old souls" who protect the
family from "evil and bad luck." Nana asks her children to consider what
it means to abandon their ancestral roots, traditions, and home. When she
visits her husband's grave, she reminds Eli that "it's up to the living to keep
in touch with the dead." By stressing the importance of the family's history
on Ibo Landing, she underscores the family's African past as well as its ties
to the land the Peazants have occupied for generations. She embraces fragments of African spirituality that she has retained despite slavery, and her
non-Christian faith stands in stark contrast to Viola's religious beliefs. Some
dismiss Nana as living in the past and praise the migration for its promise
of class ascension, even though Viola's repressed manner and the film's al-
lusions to Yellow Mary's suffering sexual exploitation call that promise into
question.

Viola embraces a different set of values and represents the proper colored lady who looks forward to the future and new beliefs. She brags to Mr.
Snead, the photographer she has hired to document the family's historic
crossing, that she "sees this day as their first steps toward progress, an en-
graved invitation . . . to the culture, education, and wealth of the mainland."
The relationship between Viola and Mr. Snead best illustrates her transformation during that day, although nothing could be less apparent at the
start. Mr. Snead's first name is never revealed, making clear his standing as
a gentleman. Dash refers to Snead in the script as a "Philadelphia Negro," a
term based on the W. E. B. Du Bois study of urban African Americans in the
late nineteenth century; the term came to describe upstanding, respectable,
middle-class blacks. Although both parties are unmarried, no hint of impro-
priety exists in Snead and Viola's traveling together without a chaperone.

The proper photographer operates as a symbol of Viola's sophistication
and class position. Viola is the proper colored lady whose status is enriched
by her standing as a Christian missionary. She incorporates the strategy
of decorporealization even more than Roz Batiste does. As Angeletta K. M.
Gourdine suggests, Viola's clothing illustrates her repression. Viola's "A-

line skirt has a taut waistband, which along with the billow of the skirt both accentuates and conceals her body's natural curves . . . the constricting clothing displaces her rigid sexuality onto her religious convictions."[19] However, more than clothing contributes to her conservative performance. Viola wears her hair in a tight bun, carries herself with restraint, and keeps her hands folded in her lap. As the unimpeachable colored lady, she is adamant that the family should depart from the island that she considers backward. She pleads with her relatives to accept Christian values and relinquish their spiritual beliefs.[20] Ironically, Viola's ideological rival, Yellow Mary, dons a St. Christopher medal, which also links her to Christianity: the patron saint of travelers ushers Yellow Mary to Ibo Landing. Unbeknown to both women, their homecoming will grant them an opportunity to address their disparate sexual histories.

Both Nana Peazant and Viola worry about the threat of further ruination that awaits black women outside their island enclave, but the two advocate different survival strategies. The family's response to Yellow Mary and her mysterious companion, Trula (Trula Hoosier), indicate that the Peazants harbor fears about the mainland and the moral challenges life in the North may present. Yellow Mary initially left the island to work as a wet nurse for a white family. The husband's harassment forced Yellow Mary to "fix the tit" in order to be released from her job.[21]

Eula's rape, like Yellow Mary's subjugation, is another residue of slavery, a theme that arises once again. Being a wet nurse allowed Yellow Mary the freedom to travel, yet that occupation trapped her in domestic service where she was vulnerable to abuse. The finery in which she arrives on the island demonstrates that Yellow Mary, like Viola, has obtained a measure of success. Although it is never explicitly stated, it is implied that she eventually becomes a prostitute because prostitution, one of the few employment options for black women at the time, affords her a measure of autonomy. While Yellow Mary has material goods, she nevertheless seems spiritually and psychically bereft. Like the ancestral Eve in *Eve's Bayou* who bore her former master sixteen children, Yellow Mary's body pays a high price for freedom.

The narrative links Eula and Yellow Mary because both have been sexually victimized. The family considers Eula an innocent victim, but Yellow

Mary's life disturbs her relatives. The Peazant women must accept both women if its members are to envision themselves as whole and fully human. At Nana Peazant's farewell ceremony the matriarch calls on the family to embrace its past and culture. Sensing a rift caused by Yellow Mary's presence, Eula breaks into a frantic monologue: "As far as this place is concerned, we never enjoyed our womanhood. . . . Deep inside, we believed that they ruined our mothers, and their mothers before them. An' we live our lives always expecting the worst because we feel we don't deserve any better. . . . There's going to be all kinds of roads to take in life. . . . Let's not be afraid to take them. We deserve them, because we all good 'omen."

As the innocent one, Eula invites her relatives to consider how they experience the family's worth. Her passionate speech raises the uneasy issue that especially influences the lives of black women. Eula defends Yellow Mary, the woman in the family whose chosen road marked her as an outsider and as impure. Eula implores the Peazant family—especially its women—to believe that "we are all good women." A victim of rape by a white man, Eula makes a plea that suggests that despite violation, a black woman can embody goodness and deserve respect. Eula posits a transformative belief, especially considering that these descendants of slaves were taught to believe that African Americans are property and that black women are vulgar. Eula's appeal is raw. Because it comes at the end of the film, it emphasizes the lengths to which black women must go in order to convince the world, and even their own families, of their worth. She wants the family to understand that if the Peazant women want to "love yourselves then love Yellow Mary cause she a part of you just like we part of our mothers." To accept and embrace Yellow Mary is to accept the contradictions inherent in being a black woman in the new world.

Dash uses an excerpt from *The Gnostic Gospels,* "Thunder Perfect Mind," to underscore the contradictions that black women confront and the dichotomy, for women, of the black middle-class ideal and their real experiences. Yellow Mary's voice-over lays bare the irony of black womanhood in a haunting but defiant tone:

**YELLOW MARY:** I am the whore and the holy one.
I am the wife and the virgin.

I am the barren one, and many
are my daughters.

Black women have difficulty bridging the chasm between Mary, mother of Jesus, and Mary Magdalene, the alleged prostitute. Dash's film evokes other powerful images of black women with characters like Eula, the wife; Viola, the virginal woman; and Yellow Mary, the barren one.[22] Because they are black women, all the Peazants must consider the legacy of sexual abuse that marks them as "ruint." When Yellow Mary first returns to Ibo landing she does not receive the same warm welcome as Viola, and the tension mounts among the family members as they prepare to depart the island. Most of the Peazant women distinguish themselves from Yellow Mary in order to establish their own propriety and respectability. Dash, however, proves the weakness of this strategy; she suggests that scapegoating Yellow Mary reveals their anxiety about their own inherent value.

Unwilling to present a neat tale, Dash shows how migration fragments the black family: some daughters choose not to cross to the mainland. Yellow Mary's decision to stay on the island signals the need for black women to embrace their history and community so they can survive assaults on their psyches. Those who decide to migrate are changed by the afternoon's events. Even Viola, who repeatedly insists that the family relinquish its "old ways" as it departs for the mainland, finds herself transformed, and she begins to recognize the value of what she left behind on Ibo Landing.

Dash bolsters her romanticizing of black history in the epigraph that opens the film: "At the turn of the century, Sea Island Gullahs, descendants of African captives, remained isolated from the mainland of South Carolina and Georgia. As a result of their isolation, the Gullah created and sustained a distinct, imaginative, and original African American culture." This prologue signals viewers that they are about to be immersed in a culture they know little about. Some viewers complained that the characters spoke a Gullah dialect, but the film included that element because Dash expects her audience to want to know the culture and because she is invested in showing the connection between "African" culture and the lure of the future.[23] By the end of the film the person who most represents the future, with his camera and kaleidoscope, is Mr. Snead. He has become fascinated by the family's history, Gullah culture, and the island's mythical qualities. Mr. Snead's kiss shocks Viola, but his expression of desire and her slow acquiescence mark her departure from middle-class decorum and free her. She is thus able to reconnect with her family's culture and history and her own sexuality. Viola allows her hair, which throughout the film remained in a tight bun, to fall free. The loosened hair, a symbol of Viola's repressed sensuality and status as a colored lady, calls into question the overdetermined narrative in feature films whereby middle-class black women are unable to find love.

Although *Daughters of the Dust* romanticizes the African American southern past, it also reclaims the site of black women's victimization as one of regeneration and hope. This film joins Lemmon's middle-class black family narrative in exposing for African American women the limits of conventional middle-class morality. Placing issues of female sexuality at the center of these films is an important intervention in black film. In her conversation with Houston Baker, Dash rightly acknowledges the timidity of many independent black filmmakers in regard to presenting sex and applauds Spike Lee's controversial and groundbreaking *She's Gotta Have It* (1989):

> I think one of the most magnificent things that Spike reintroduced into black film was sex. Because the rest of us were making these righteous films, like: no sex, none of that. And he introduced all this sex and sensuality and eroticism and it's just like: "Oh yeah, we have a sex life, too. Why can't we show . . . ?" I think most of the filmmakers were so afraid to depict anything sexual because we were trying to stay away from the black exploitation films of the early 1970s. And so our films became very dry, and very didactic and so on. [24]

The gratuitous depictions of the black body in American iconography as well as blaxploitation-era films justify the reluctance of black directors to represent black sexuality. They appear to be even more hesitant about depicting middle-class blacks as sexual.

Dash's *Daughters of the Dust* and Lemmons's *Eve's Bayou* render black sexuality unapologetically. By bringing multiple representations of southern colored ladies to the screen, Dash and Lemmons reveal that the perception of the black body as harshly sexual is a lie; the directors' soft and gentle renderings allow the audience to envision middle-class black women be-yond the asexual stereotype. Their dramas are also instructive because they evoke the recent past when black women had limited access to middle-class status. Wealth and privilege, more often than not, were contingent upon a romantic partnership that subsequently defined and restricted women's sex-ual agency. Therefore the insistence of these films on upending conventional images not only calls into question a sepia African American southern past but also places their heroines in conversation with the financially indepen-dent lovelorn black ladies of contemporary romantic comedies. Although few opportunities exist for African American women to direct feature films, filmmakers such as Cheryl Dunye, Darnell Martin, Leslie Harris, and Sanaa Hamri have joined Lemmons and Dash with complex narratives that allow for a broader range of African American characters. They continue to pri-oritize compelling, realistic, and nuanced depictions of black women with sexual agency.

## NOTES

1. A version of this chapter appears in my book, *Beyond the Black Lady: Sexuality and the New African American Middle Class* (Champaign: University of Illinois Press, 2009). In it I provide a more in-depth discussion of black romantic comedies, as well as the films *Eve's Bayou* and *Daughters of the Dust.*
2. Sarah Warn, "The Right Time: Lesbianism in Middle-Class Black Movies," June 2002, www.afterellen.com/movies/blackmovies.html.
3. Joel R. Brouwer, "Repositioning: Center and Margin in Julie Dash's *Daughters of the Dust*," *African American Review* 29, no. 1 (1995): 5.
4. Houston A. Baker Jr., "Not without My Daughters: A Conversation with Julie Dash and Houston A. Baker, Jr.," *Transition* 57 (1992): 151.
5. Dash sets the film on Ibo landing, but the deities she names, Ogun, Osun, and Yemoja, are all Yoruba.
6. Baker, "Not without My Daughters," 163.
7. Mia L. Mask, "*Eve's Bayou*: Too Good to Be a 'Black' Film?" *Cineaste* 23, no. 4 (1998): 26. For a more nuanced reading of the reasons for the film's success, see Kara Keel-ing, *The Witch's Flight: The Cinematic, the Black Femme, and the Image of Common*

*Sense* (Durham, N.C.: Duke University Press, 2007), 149–51.

8. In the first few weeks of theatrical release the film made $13 million, after an initial investment of $4 million, making it a box-office success. The final domestic gross was nearly $15 million when it was pulled from theaters in March 1998. Lemmons's second film, *Cave Man's Valentine* (2001), also starring and coproduced by Samuel L. Jackson, suffered from a sophomore jinx, grossing a mere $687,081 domestically. *Talk to Me* (2007), a biopic about the Washington, D.C., radio personality Ralph "Petey" Green, was also a box office disappointment, grossing only $4.5 million domestically during its theatrical release.

9. When the Batiste children act out scenes from Shakespeare, it not only marks the family's class status but also foreshadows the film's disastrous ending: Cisely calls her brother and sister Tybalt and Mercutio, characters from *Romeo and Juliet,* a tragic tale of star-crossed lovers.

10. This would not be Carson's last turn as a siren. In the groundbreaking television comedy *Ally McBeal,* she played a sexually insatiable attorney and Ally's roommate. The character, whose sexual availability Carson played for laughs, is consistently frustrated by her lack of available lovers. Instead of being constructed as Ally's equal, she is consistently depicted as a freak whose sexual desires prohibit eligible partnership. Carson's character became an icon of the frustrated black middle-class woman.

11. Victoria W. Wolcott, *Remaking Respectability: African American Women in Interwar Detroit* (Chapel Hill: University of North Carolina Press, 2001), 6. For a more extensive discussion of terms such as the *colored lady,* see Thompson, *Beyond the Black Lady,* 6–7.

12. Anna Julia Cooper, "Womanhood: A Vital Element in the Regeneration and Progress of a Race," in Charles Lemert and Esme Bhan, eds., *The Voice of Anna Julia Cooper* (Lanham, Md.: Rowan & Littlefield, 1988), 70.

13. Ibid., 64.

14. Wahneema Lubiano called attention to the dichotomy of the term *black lady* in her analysis of the 1991 hearings held by the Senate Judiciary Committee on the nomination of Clarence Thomas to the Supreme Court. The phrase describes the recent incarnation of a figure that comes from a long line of icons of black female respectability. See Wahneema Lubiano, "Black Ladies, Welfare Queens, and State Minstrels: Ideological War by Narrative Means," in Toni Morrison, ed., *Race-ing Justice, En-Gendering Power: Essays on Anita Hill, Clarence Thomas, and the Construc-*

*tion of Social Reality* (New York: Pantheon, 1992), 323–63. Morrison also uses the term *black lady* in her introduction to the same volume.

15. Deborah Willis, *The Black Female Body: A Photographic History* (Philadelphia: Temple University Press, 2002), 89.

16. Carla Peterson, foreword to Michael Bennett and Vanessa D. Dickerson, eds., *Recovering the Black Female Body* (New Brunswick, N.J.: Rutgers University Press, 2001), xiii.

17. Although Aunt Mozelle represents another option of womanhood, Louis denounces his sister in front of the children and dismisses her mystical powers.

18. Julie Dash, *Daughters of the Dust: The Making of an African American Woman's Film* (New York: New Press, 1992), 32.

19. Angeletta K. M. Gourdine, "Fashioning the Body [as] Politic in Julie Dash's *Daughters of the Dust*," *African American Review* 38, no. 3 (2004): 505.

20. Viola is disturbed by her distant relative Bilal Muhammad's Muslim practices; she makes a point of criticizing him around the children and tells Mr. Snead that he's "an old heathen."

21. The colloquial expression "fixing the tit" suggests Yellow Mary somehow physically mutilated her breasts in order to stop producing milk.

22. It is noteworthy that both Mozelle and Yellow Mary, the women in each film who have the most lovers, are childless, which undermines the myth of the promiscuous, fertile black woman.

23. See Dash, *Daughter's of the Dust*, in which the director speaks about the film's critical reception.

24. Baker, "Not without My Daughters," 161.

# "Boojie!"
## A Question of Authenticity

This collection is an articulate intellectual space for exploring the interplay of class and blackness under the traveling, if not transformative, construction "from bourgeois to boojie." It is a space of both empowerment and entrapment. So, as a relatively articulate black/teacher/ performer/scholar working inside both the comforts and confines of the academy (the white ivory tower), I cannot address the issue of boojieness, in any manner or in my own defense without seemingly succumbing to the very critique to which the statement is directed.

The criteria that are used to evaluate and determine the charge of being boojie establish a trap for all black people in that they restrict the range of performing blackness to a limited space of what is socially, if not culturally, acceptable. For many black people such limitations actually threaten the possibility of their exploring the range of black performativity: What new and expansive ways could they perform themselves within their own skin? This is particularly challenging if the accusation of being boojie is reductively linked with educational attainment, where black people live, their social engagements, class distinctions, attitudes toward social issues and relational interactions with other black people, or the ways in which they speak and carry themselves in the world. In many ways the performance of culture, as described in the aforementioned categories, is conflated with a performance of race. This conflation threatens to limit the interpretive frame of what it means to be black both within and outside communities of social recognition, that is, groups of individuals who share cultural understanding, without the need for translation of behavior, words, speech, and the like— they can easily recognize and interact with one another.

Cultural and racial performances expand to uplift and inform both individuals and communities. The performance of race neither shifts nor fades with class elevation; it modulates, tuning itself to different environs but always with the undercurrents of historical truths that conduct the rhythms of bodily actions in time and space. It is, in fact, the wish that black parents often have for their children: the earned dexterity of performative accomplishment to transcend location and circumstance, to achieve, without forgetting the meaningfulness of home and the substance of black character.

The subtitle of this book refers to both "black middle-class performances" and the actuality of invited performances by middle-class blacks. The project then becomes a space for middle-class blacks to engage in both writing about being and expressing being in writing, using performance practice as a site of opposition. Such performance practice coalesces in ways evocative of black culture's use of performance as acts of resistance and protest, as well as modes of social and cultural maintenance. These are key strategies used by E. Franklin Frazier in his monograph but used as a standard to pathologize the rising black middle class, who in his construction seemingly resist the performative tropes of a delimited black authenticity. He writes that middle-class blacks are trying to become what they could never be, and, "living largely in a world of make-believe, the masks which they wear to play their sorry roles conceal the feelings of inferiority and of insecurity and the frustrations that haunt their inner lives."[1] Here he speaks of performance as faking, not making, a presence of what is actual versus the realization of possibility. In this passage Frazier writes of performance as a subterfuge without acknowledging the transformative nature of performance: performance as a transcendent rehearsal and a dexterous enactment of revealing one's own possibilities.[2] Such expansive performance possibilities are reflective not only of the individual but also of the racialized categories that they claim and those communities that claim them.

In this essay I offer three critical autoethnographic movements in which I loosely address Frazier's concerns of/for the rising black middle class as it relates to issues of gender and sexuality, performances of professionalism, and racial authenticity. In this project I find that I might be operating in a defensive mode against the accusation of being called boojie by actually engaging a boojie performativity. For me a boojie performativity references those perceived repetitive actions performed by black people, plotted within grids of power relationships and social norms that are presumably relegated exclusively to white people; hence, by virtue of their enactment and in the presumed absence of black folk, these performances are critiqued as rejecting or abandoning some organic construction of black character and black people. These are often concretized in critiques on social mobility, stylistics of language use and appearance, as well as middle-class distinction linked to occupation and social affiliation.

In the process of developing the construction of boojie performativity, I am not just thinking of performativity as the repetition of behaviors that are already expected in social and cultural contexts. I am also thinking of performativity as "non-essentialized constructions of identity; performativities as significantly and powerfully layered [behaviors] in the day-to-day, yet they are heightened and embossed in cultural performance. It is cultural performance where performativities are doubled with a difference: they are re-presented, re-located and re-materialized for the possibility of a substantial re-consideration and re-examination" of the delimited constructions of being and doing.[3] I am addressing performativities as a range of behaviors within racial and cultural communities that are engaged not just as an established script so that everyone knows what to expect but as an open set of skills and possibilities that are used improvisationally based on individual and cultural circumstances. I am thinking about performativities as others talk about the cultural expressiveness and creativity of black people—the inventiveness, ingenuity, and resiliency of black culture that has allowed black people to not only survive but to thrive.

As a black male academic, I find that critiques of my being boojie often call into question my dedication to race and even question my masculinity.[4]

*Tell me if you notice a defensive tone in my writing. And if you detect it, please know that it is a coy strategy that I am using to explore how discussions of racial authenticity often establish a space of entrapment for all involved.*[5]

# In Defense of Being with White People

I must admit that I have been with white people. The phrase "been with" suggests an intimate engagement, a sharing of flesh. I am a black man who identifies as gay. My partner for the last twelve years has been another man, a white man, but not "The Man." For some the history of gender, sexual, and racial politics collides within the idea of our partnership. Other black gay men have indicted me as a race traitor and assume that in my selection of a white man I have rejected all black people. This assumption of preference is most certainly enough to have my race card revoked.

And while the choice to be with this man was conscious, my choice was not centered in a preference for white over all others. And without feeling the need to chronicle my history of intimate engagements with people of varying hues, what I find in this man is more about care and compassion than it is about skin color. What I find in this man is what I have looked for in any man, more about a sense of warmth and welcome than the color of eyes and the texture of hair. What I find in this man is more about potential and possibility than histories of privilege or oppression. And these findings are less about what I have found in him than what I have not found in particular others whom I have encountered. And while this man is white, he does not perform whiteness. You know what I mean? And in my selection of him, neither am I performing whiteness or performing to whiteness or striving to become white by association.

I have a black gay friend who once told me: "A black person who chooses to be with a white person is not willing to work with black love. It is about being lazy, that the attraction has to be about exoticism or jungle fever or the desire for a 'snow queen.'" And I love this black man. So I want to apologize to him, not for being with a white man but for what my choice seems to engender in him, a kind of anger or sadness. I also want to apologize because I once saw, staring back at me from the mirror, the sad eyes of a black gay boy looking for another black gay boy—and every now and then, I still do.

And while I pondered what he said for a while, I have also thought about the amount of time and effort that all relationships take. I have thought about the amount of effort and energy it takes to negotiate and collaborate in any relationship. I have thought about the sometimes daily negotiations of otherness that accompany my relationship in circulating contexts of racial specificity. And I would be fooling no one if I didn't ask myself: Would negotiating the relationship be easier with a black man? (In past relationships with black men, it has and it has not.) I have thought about the struggles and strength it takes to be with someone in the face of public scrutiny or just to be yourself in the face of public scrutiny. I have thought about my process of thinking about this thought and the amount of work that I was engaging in (both then and now) and the effort to somehow justify my choice against criticism.

This criticism inevitably calls my race loyalty into question. It questions my performance of blackness merely on the basis of an intimate relation, on my chosen partner. And for some it also inevitably links my selection of a white partner to a performance of class, as if to suggest that if I were not Dr. Alexander, I would be with "an average black man," whatever that means. While addressing the dilemmas of black intellectuals Cornel West echoes the general distrust and suspicion of black intellectuals by the black community in general because, among other things, "the relatively high rates of exogamous marriage, the abandonment of Black institutions, and the preoccupations with Euro-American intellectual products are often perceived by the Black community as intentional efforts to escape the negative stigma of Blackness or viewed as symptoms of self-hatred."[6] And while I understand these elements of suspicion, the content of my character cannot be reduced to the suspicions of others but evaluated only on the actuality of my meaningful involvements in community.

So I find myself in that trap of performing to blackness against accusations of boojie performativity and the ways in which my choice of a partner questions my loyalty to race, which is now reduced to issues of class and cultural associations. I am of course aware that, for many black people, gayness is presumably asynchronous with blackness anyway. Hence, according to Franz Fanon in *Black Face/White Masks*, homosexuality is a white contagion that would negate my black social significance altogether.[7] I am aware of the problematic manner in which Frazier coyly characterizes black male homosexuality as "cultivated personalities." This is a criticism of a particular performance of masculinity that Frazier suggests is the result of a lack of power in white society and the dominance of women in black society (220–21). These arguments offer dispositive constructions of black gay men while also questioning the role of black women in the socialization of black boys and their social orientation to black men. Each critique serves as a foundation on which to build some ideal notion of black performativity— reductively stated as an expectation of heteronormativity, hatred of whites, and black male dominance.

My blackness, my queerness, and my choice of partners are separate aspects of who I am. Each operates in its own home place of comfort yet informs the choices that I make as a social agent who claims his commitment to black culture in the fullness of his self-presentation, public life, and social activism. These actions bleed the borders between race mobility and gender equality. But, of course, this is not the exclusive criticism of my black gay brother who suggested that having a white partner is an act of being lazy. For he too would be drawn into a critique of the complicity of his own same-sex black male desire that he criticizes and yearns for, using race once again to trump gender.

And I know that my partnering with this man who is white has nothing to do with being lazy. It has nothing to do with a desire for the other. It has nothing to do with his otherness, as much as it has to do with someone who values in me the things that I value in him, which is not about skin but substance. And I know that desire cannot be reduced to being a "crusader of the inner life" or an attempt to "grasp white civilization and dignity and make them mine" through intimate engagements. For no one can grant such authority, and the person seeking the self or redemption in the other is a fool. And, for that matter, the person who makes assumptions about racial identity based on intimate couplings struggles with her own sense of what constitutes the real. And for every heterosexual black man who has fucked a white woman as sport, I invite a critique of that complicated construal of race, sex, dominance, desire, and revenge in terms of racial authenticity and cultural commitment. Frazier might interpret this act as an excusable mechanism of black males' practicing or reclaiming power over white men (by conquering their women), but this is a problematic construction of black heteromasculine performance that I believe Fanon would also support.

In relationships the landscape of desire cannot be reduced to just skin but the personal histories of those encased within acting/performing bodies. So we negotiate, my partner and I, as all couples negotiate, those sometimes conflicting histories of race and class that are perceived as mediating variables in our relationship. And while "fragile relationships don't thrive best in overexposure," we find ourselves coming back to places of compassion, comfort, and care in the company of each other—sometimes shading our selves from the searing critiques of others and at other times offering our face to the sun of a new day.[8]

In her quintessential book on the black vernacular, *Black Talk: Words and Phrases from the Hood to the Amen Corner,* Geneva Smitherman offers a dictionary of words that serve as a "cultural map that charts word meaning along the highways and byways of African American life." Within the compendious volume Smitherman offers the following definition of the term *boojie* (or boojee, in her spelling): "An elitist, uppity-acting African American. Generally with a higher education and income level than the average Black, who identifies with European American culture and distances him/herself from other African Americans. Derives from 'bourgeois/bourgeoisie.' 2) Describes a person, event, style, or thing that is characteristic of elitist, uppity-acting Blacks. 'It was one of them ol boojee thangs.'"[9]

The specific construction of this definition invokes a critique and a commentary on the performative expectations of blackness as differentiated by class and social affiliation in relation to the ubiquitous yet somewhat specious notion of "the average black." I can only assume that the celebrated "average Black" in this definition is also the reified average Negro whom E. Franklin Frazier bolsters in order to stabilize the social construction of blackness in his comparative analysis of the rising black middle class.

In the definition of *boojie* provided by Smitherman, the shift in terminology from "an elitist, uppity-acting African American" to "the average Black" actually serves to reinforce a distinction in which the term *African American* might also be associated with an elite politicized construction of race grounded not in the materiality of bodies but in an assessment of performance, or, in Frazier's terms, "the elevation of class." Yet such an evolutionary cycle is suggestively catalyzed, not by the evolution of time and circumstance—from slave to freedman to citizen to self-determining mobile, social, and political being that Frazier also tracks in building a case of middle-class blacks—but as an assumed desire to escape blackness and the actuality of being black for some assumed safe space in the margins of white culture.

The hurling of the term *boojie*, which I believe is the accurate contemporary assessment of Frazier's usage (and or intention), is an accusation of passing for and striving to be what one can presumably never be. In Frazier's analysis this is about trying to be white and not the more attainable performance of whiteness—which might be a simulated discursive practice that in fact is the basis of his stinging critique.[10]

*Do you think it is boojie of me to break it down in this manner?*

# In Defense of Tamed African Locks

In their book *Dreads*, Francesco Mastalia and Alfonse Pagano write: "Dreadheads represent a cross-section of society, and the reasons for letting hair lock are as diverse as the wearers themselves."[11] About seven years ago I decided to lock my hair. The choice came for several reasons but, more important, at a time when I was ready to embrace a presentation and actualization of self that operated against the grain of my social reality as a black academic working in the white ivory tower. The decision came after I received early tenure, a reward for my performance of good academic citizen and before I was awarded early promotion to full professor.

The locks (African or dread—with the ensuing politics of origins and orientations) liberated me from a particular tyranny of hair while also exposing a presentation of blackness that signaled the politics of hair, propriety of performance, and polemics of place, space, and embodiedness. As if my dark brown skin were not enough, my hair signifies a particular racial performativity within the academy and an insider-outsider status. This insider-outsider status is a positionality that Frazier does not easily acknowledge as a desired location for many black middle-class people.

The insider-outsider status is a not position of being betwixt and be-tween in some transitional state of desirous becoming. As I am approaching it here, the chosen insider-outsider status is a political location, a chosen space that shows the duality of my being as a black man working in a white space, an elemental black man manipulating the institutional privileges of the white academy to my own purposes. In the insider-outsider status I am both a stable referent and a floating signifier to those who would see me as either one or the other. *I am both and . . .*

I began growing my hair—from the closely cropped bald fade that seemed a professionally appropriate performance of neatness for a black male college professor. And soon the growing hair resembled a short Afro, another performance of blackness that engendered comments from students and colleagues wondering what was coming over Dr. Alexander. ("Coming over"—as in a wave of resistance or rebellion. Maybe they saw me as sud-denly becoming black, as if my performances of good academic and good institutional citizen were performances of whiteness). All of which seemed to be associated with the politics of hair and not the everyday performances of my being.

The locking of my hair was particularly premeditated and strategic. The desire was accelerated by the convenience of the hair salon and the formulation of a series of equally and evenly graphed shiny twists. From some blacks my then-growing twists provoked critiques of fashion and style instead of their seeing in them some deeper organic commitment to culture and a way of living. They characterized my growing locks as a boojie perfor-mance of middle-class blackness, an assumed commercial performance of blackness to somehow override the otherness of the black intellectual work-ing in the white ivory tower.

During the workday I now often wear my locks, which are now sweep-ing my shoulders, rolled and tied back. They are slightly tamed against the daily suits and ties demanded by the workplace environment of a university administrator. To the uncritical eye it might appear that my tamed locks against the business suit suggest that I am trying to pass as the typical administrator in academia, trying to hide a distinction of race that might go otherwise unnoticed—never mind that growing dreads is counterintuitive to the desire to pass.[12]

The notion of passing is sine qua non in black cultural identity politics. It serves as a critique and observation of the performance practices of blacks who are unmarked by racial signifiers, such as dark skin pigmentation. Because they look white, those who are thus better able to engage a performative identity of whiteness assume the rights, benefits, and opportunities of whiteness. The notion of passing is also presumably kernel to Frazier's monograph—not only in his momentary coverage of the "passing of the gentleman and the peasant" (112–19) but his larger approach to critiquing the black middle class as performing whiteness.

Allow me to offer some basic descriptive tenets of passing: Passing is an active process of doing, yet not just doing but an assessment of what is being done. Someone makes the assessment of the desired effect by monitoring or accepting the seamlessness of the performance as a given of what it pretends to be. In the case of racial passing, not to be recognized, in the company of whites, as a person of Negro heritage is an issue not only of looking white but also of acting white. Hence, in the sense of performativity, the success of passing is dependent on the ritualized repetition of communicative acts known and interpreted within specified social or cultural systems linked with race. The act of passing is an existential accomplishment, one that exists in the historical presence of human social engagement. The person who is passing exists in a space of liminality, between the actuality of who they are and who they pretend to be, with the fear of being censured and alienated if caught by either side.

While performance as a transgressive practice has the potential to subvert and challenge prescribed rules, practices, and identities that oppress, passing (or the performance of passing) limits the possibilities of transgression. Instead it licenses the circumstances that prompt the passing in the first place. In the case of blacks passing for white, the first criterion is the actuality of skin color that is closer to white than black. For people of Negro heritage with darker skin tones, the visual signifiers of race automatically override any presumed ability to pass for white. The act of passing is an existential accomplishment that always resides in liminality—being betwixt and between what you are and what you assume or desire to be.[13]

So such a misperception of me as trying to pass by merely taming my locks during the day-to-dayness of business activity would feed into

Frazier's assumption that I want to suppress the obviousness of my being for purposes of my mobility and access to the same privileges as my white colleagues. What such a reading does not see is the intentional performative juxtaposition of competing presentations of social and cultural identity. The materiality of my dark brown (black) body and the African locks actively work against the staid institutionalization of the suit and the presumptions about my character and commitment to black culture as I work in the ivory tower.

My locks work against the assumed assimilation that Frazier speaks of in terms of field slaves versus house servants, whose "behavior and ideals approximated those of whites," which for him are seemingly the signifying characteristics of boojie performativity (13). My locks are an intentional act to further disrupt the assumption of what a college professor and administrator should both look and act like. I cannot further argue against those who would characterize my locks as an assumed performance of blackness to somehow override the otherness of my being a black intellectual working in the white ivory tower. However, I often sense that their critique is less about me and more a validation of their own performance of authenticity, marking them as real and marking me as the opposite of real. My efforts in such cases are lost.

The accusation of being boojie is a critique of cultural performance. "Cultural performance" refers to performances of normative behavior for the purposes of social agency within a particular cultural context. It also acknowledges the unidirectionality of cultural performative agency, whether as a fulfillment of cultural traditions that build community or the appropriation of presumed-to-be racially designated privilege (e.g., education, money, and options of living) to advance beyond social roadblocks or the perceived limitations of race.[14]

While the notion of passing, as I have discussed it, suggests a level of intentional subversion, the core logics of passing are grounded in expecting certain social and cultural behaviors. This is also the core of any impulse toward cultural performance as a means of maintaining cultural membership by assuming the necessary and performative strategies associated with that community. I presume this to be Frazier's desired expectation of black people—*to engage presumed natural and restrictive enactments of blackness* in ways that sustain the black community and black identity politics.

Hence, within the context of this project, to call someone boojie is an accusation of passing, as in the perceived lack of adherence to a set of social and performative executions of identity that are seen as less in association with black culture and more with white culture. The uttered descriptive of someone as being boojie is a kind of black performative act, one that declares a particular critique of the performative otherness of the person at whom the term is directed, while claiming the authenticity of the blackness of the person hurling the accusation.[15] *Because, of course, you cannot be boojie and call somebody else boojie. It would be like the pot calling the kettle black—or maybe not black enough.*

## Teaching Like a Black Man

When I completed my master's degree my father said to me, "Keith, Daddé is not an educated man, but let me tell you something. You have a lot of education, but don't ever forget that you're a black man with a black man's history. So when you're sitting in your college classes or teaching your college classes, remember what you learned in school and what you learned at home. Know the difference. It's all right to talk like a teacher, but remember that you're a black man. Don't forget who you are. Talk like a black man teacher." In my father's words I have often struggled to figure out which I want to foreground in the classroom—that I am a black man who is a teacher or the reality that I am a teacher who is a black man? How can the languages and voices of these two positions inform each other? In doing the research for my dissertation, I found myself asking these same questions as I interviewed black male teachers and the black male students in a predominantly white university.[16] As I listened to their experiences, I began to formulate my own answers.

To teach as a black man is to acknowledge the historical legacy of slavery and the cultural perceptions of black men with the social expectations and status of higher education. In the process of teaching, the black male teacher (like other "teachers of color") explores the academic arena while actively engaging in a process of denying the socially constructed image of himself. This is followed by the painstaking process of reconstructing in the minds of others an identity that is reflective and representative of who he really is and who he wishes to be. This self-defining program is an ongoing act that works against a historical backdrop and the prevailing social and class-based intentions that mark and minimize us—both by white America and sometimes by our own black communities.

This agenda is both personal and public. But it is not designed to un-weave the cultural tapestry that tells the story of our history. Rather, it is to reconfigure and offer alternate representations to those who view the display and those who blind themselves to cultural stereotypes. The agenda is to show the texture of our lives, to reveal the dimensions of our characters and the beauty in our souls. Within this vigorous program of self-identification and determination we also begin to see our possibilities. We are thus able to share our experience with others, particularly with students of all colors who are struggling to define themselves against all odds.

To teach as a black man is to push at the borders of these narrowly defined horizons. It is to use the classroom space for both cultural acknowledgment and cultural expansion. In teaching as a black man, I find that I draw upon a wide variety of my student experiences. From my black grade-school teachers, I have a developed sensitivity to the racial similarity that I share with black students. I try to allow our common racial designation to serve as a bridge to the curriculum by using particular cultural examples and invite their own. I draw upon my own sense of displacement in the predominantly white university classroom to close gaps of difference and indifference in curriculum and pedagogical practice.

Drawing from my experience with black professors, I acknowledge the tension that exists between being the "teacher" and the racially familiar to students of color. I realize that the "racially familiar" and the "culturally familiar" are at times different relational dynamics that can inform each other but are not intrinsically and experientially connected—given class and the socialized expectations of a performative blackness. To be the racially familiar is to acknowledge a broad history that joins people together by skin, blood, and points of origin. To be the culturally familiar is to acknowledge common traditions and orientations within a specified geosocial community.

Hence the assumption that all black people will have an initial affinity may be true in terms of racial issues that bind lived experiences. This may then be interpreted as a felt experience of blackness. Yet the dailiness of lived experiences, current location, class and circumstance, influences of family, community, and religion all may suggest difference. It is within these diverse lived experiences that cultural communities emerge within races. These cultural communities establish their own cultural performances that signify place and membership, displacement, and (re)membering, a concept that is not considered or respected in Frazier's analysis.

My inclination is to use the classroom as a space of intellectual and social negotiation. This approach confronts black students by saying, "We are different people in the world, yet we share some common historical, racial, and maybe cultural ties." This approach invites us to use those commonalties to come together and explore the differences as alternatives and ways of being. It moves toward expanding the repertoire of perceived performances of blackness—both in the perception of my nonblack students as well as with my black students.

I find that to teach as a black man is to address issues of race, culture, gender, and consequently difference in the classroom as an interstitial fact. To teach as a black man is to expand the pedagogical venture to include critical examinations of the human condition, to use the classroom as a site in which I am fully present. Not to address issues of blackness or the politics of race is to deny the existence of its visual presence (in my case) in the classroom (in the boardroom or society at large) and is always and already included on the social agenda, as well as in the presence of competing historicities.

In his essay "Face to Face with Alterity," Robert Simon speaks to the material facticity of the body. He writes: " 'Teaching as a Jew' does not necessarily imply teaching about Jews or exclusively for Jews. I am arguing that 'teaching as a Jew' denotes a pedagogical condition, initiated by my specificity as an embodied Jew, which enhances the achievement of knowledge through the interactive return of difference in the dynamics of teaching and learning."[17] Simon's notion of being an "embodied Jew" moves beyond any material fact of his body that might suggest a Jewish identity, if such a feature exists. It moves to an embodied political, social, and historical reality of his lived existence that filters his understanding of the world in which he lives and consequently informs his pedagogy. To teach as a black man is to teach in the face of such conditions. To teach as a black man (a person of color, as a gay or lesbian person, and so on) is to teach in the face of such conditions and to meet the challenge of presenting the specified course content, filtered through the implied influence of our particular beings in the world.

I have told this story to invoke the memory of and respect for my father, who passed away a number of years ago. I tell the story as a self-reflexive act, as an act of keeping myself in check. I offer the key component of his message again to make a point. "Remember who you are." I have long pondered my father's charge, for as a man from the South who was born in the 1930s, my father thought that to be a teacher meant to be white. Not just white, as we reductively use that word to depict the hue of someone's skin. For my father, to be a teacher signaled what he often referenced as the four P's of white-collar professionalism: privilege, positionality, power, and propriety.

For my father, to be a teacher meant to be engaged in a performance of whiteness. For him, to be a teacher meant to be somewhat distanced from working-class worries or having to encounter the tough cultural negotiations of otherness. But my father's message to me was as much a warning as it was a charge. He was warning me that despite my education, people would always see me first as a black man, even if I deserved the four P's of white-collar professionalism and even if I assumed the performance of whiteness that he associated with being a teacher and, more important, with being a college professor. His was a charge for me to be mindful of this complex of race, position, and class and how I would be positioned as a black male teacher.

And my father was right. As a tenured full professor and even as an associate dean, I have come to know the limited range of my socially constructed possibility. In times of conflict the criticism easily falls back on the "other" in this br(other), in relation to the population that is claiming me or disowning me. For other black folks the critique falls on what they perceive to be my privilege, positionality, power, and propriety as a professor and the perceived ability to practice power over them or in exclusion of them. Hence maybe whiteness can be studied through, as Shome puts it, "the interlocking axes of power, spatial location, and history"—who I am, what I do, and where I do it.[18]

These are also qualities of boojie performativity and, more important for this analysis, a germinal concept of what Frazier was critiquing as a doomed project of presumably trying to transcend blackness. So in this sense I do not completely reject the message in Frazier's now historic monograph or his critical analysis, only the totalizing reduction of possibility in striving for self-improvement that is read as a rejection of race and culture. Despite its critical implications, the reference to being boojie might also be, like my father's warning, a normal part of the cultural performance matrix of any community seeking to regulate the performances of its members as a form of cultural maintenance. But even in such cases, criticism does not always feel like love. So in remembrance of my dad and as my own commitment to blackness and black culture, I ritually perform resistance to assimilation, to living whiteness (even in living with a white man), and conflating the difference between what I do, where I do it, and who I am.

In particular, my father's warning was a form of both protection and an expression of his desire to keep me organically linked to the black community. His words of caution are with me every time I enter the classroom, the boardroom, the conference room, and the community. My evolving definition of what it means to teach as a black man is an attempt to negotiate the relational disparity of who I am and what I do with an acknowledgment that as a black male professor-administrator working in the white ivory tower, I am always operating in the margins of particular social expectations—of those who are claiming me and those who are rejecting me. Such a position allows me the opportunity to stand in resistance to the regimes of the so-called normal. It allows me a point of connection with my minority students and those who are struggling against the systematic erasure of difference. As bell hooks writes, it allows me to "continue to stand in political resistance with the oppressed, ready to offer [my] way of seeing and theorizing, of making culture, toward that revolutionary effort which seeks to create space where there is unlimited access to the pleasure and power of knowing, where transformation is possible."[19]

*My father's warning was really against becoming boojie, against becoming an Oreo.*

# An Ending without Foreclosure

E. Franklin Frazier ends his historic monograph by saying, "The black bourgeoisie suffers from 'nothingness' because when Negroes attain middle-class status their lives generally loose both content and significance" (238). As a black middle-class academic, I dedicate my scholarship to exploring and illuminating the intricate sophistication of what is presumed to be banal aspects of everyday black culture. In a series of essays on the black barbershop and salon as cultural space, and the relational dynamic of black male teachers and black students in the classroom, I seek to both illuminate and intervene in black cultural performance in these various locations.[20]

I acknowledge that I work within what Cornel West calls the "bourgeois model" of intellectual practices in higher education.[21] But within this model I work toward developing new paradigms of academic knowing and expressing the known. I work toward dismantling systems of oppression that deny the significance of emerging racial paradigms. And in my shifting roles as department chair, associate dean, and now an acting dean, I seek and accept positions of leadership that might work toward disrupting traditions of exclusion and white perspectives of what is real, what is worthy of study, and what is validated as scholarly production.

My research and scholarship have a sustained emphasis on the politics of black identity in terms of race, culture, and gender performance in the shifting contexts of home, campus, and community. Such projects have been engaged by using critical, poetic, and autoethnographic methods, in which I have positioned and embraced my indigenous membership in the black communities that I seek to research and illuminate. In my ethnographic work such as on black barbershops and salons, black/white family communication, and recently with black men living with HIV/AIDS, I often bring the voices of everyday black folk into the halls of the academy and place them between the boundaries of scholarly texts to give voice to experience and reason to theory.[22] But this is not by any means a tactical systemic problem of the bourgeois model in which as a black intellectual I am in the perpetual process of "defend[ing] the humanity of Black people, including their ability and capacity to reason logically, think coherently, and write lucidly," as

West describes it (137). In fact, I use their articulate voices not as evidence of defense but as ballast to theory. By situating heady thoughts of intellectual production in the everyday theorizing of the black community and then inverting the process to reveal new sources of knowing, I offer alternative conceptions of academic theorizing in the everyday practices of black cultural life.

My academic and professional work most often centers on the performance of culture in circulating contexts within the black community. Maybe such efforts evidence that while I work in the figurative white ivory tower and have attained middle-class status, I am (still) organically committed to black culture. But this is not an argument for authenticity or a defense against being called boojie. I am seeking neither authenticity nor the rather specious acceptance that comes from engaging the presumed-to-be-acceptable performances of blackness. I move through the world as the black man that I am with no apologies.

I am dedicated to illuminating the deep intellectual nature of indigenous and "endarkened epistemologies"—what black people know, how they know it, and how these knowledges contribute to larger social, cultural, and academic advancements.[23] I am ever reminded that the opportunity from which I have benefited as a particular black man is not distributed equally or evenly among all black folk.[24] I take this reality as a serious charge to represent, knowing that such representation will always be critiqued regardless of the intent or the effects of my efforts. And I take every opportunity, through service, mentoring, and active engagement in social and political issues, to translate, engage, and apply the nature of what I know and how I know it in the black communities that serve as foundation to my work and my being.

And unlike Frazier's description and near fatalistic prophecy for the black bourgeoisie, my life does not suffer from nothingness. My life, like my work, is replete with content and significance grounded in the everydayness of cultural activities that fulfill my sense of being a black man. So for me, the performance of race is relative, not to class but to embodied presence and the social relations that make manifest the meaningfulness of action. While class becomes the marker of situated being and the circulation or fixity within fields of opportunities, class negates neither the materiality of bodies nor the obligations to represent the possibilities of being within racial categories.

The relative nature of this position is of course contingent on positionality, that is, on which side you sit in the have–have not matrix of class distinction and whether you have built a bridge or a wall between the two.

## NOTES

1. E. Franklin Frazier, *Black Bourgeoisie: The Rise of a New Middle Class* (1957; repr., New York: Free Press, 1965), 213. bell hooks constructs her notion of "performance practice as a site of opposition" and further writes that "performance practice has, for African-Americans, been central to the process of decolonization. . . . Performance was important because it created cultural context where one could transgress the boundaries of accepted speech, both in relationship to the dominant white culture, and to the decorum of African-American cultural mores" (hooks, "Performance Practice as a Site of Opposition," in Catherine Ugwu, ed., *Let's Get It On: The Politics of Black Performance* [Seattle: Bay Press, 1995], 212).

2. Victor Turner writes: "If man is a sapient animal, a tool making animal, a self-making animal, a symbolizing animal, he is no less, a performing animal, *Homo performans*, not in the sense, perhaps that a circus animal may be a performing animal, but in the sense that man is a self-making animal—his performances are, in a way, reflexive, in performing he reveals himself to himself" (Turner and Turner, *On the Edge of the Bush: Anthropology as Experience* [Tucson: University of Arizona Press, 1985], 187).

3. D. Soyini Madison and Judith Hamera, eds., introduction to *The Sage Handbook of Performance Studies* (Thousand Oaks, Calif.: Sage, 2006), xix.

4. In my construction of "boojie performativity" I am signaling the specific constructions of performativity as offered by Judith Butler in which a performative is both an agent and product of social and political conditions in which it circulates. I also am referencing E. Patrick Johnson's notions of the performative as it includes not only gender but also race, class, sexuality, and other personal characteristics. See Butler, *Bodies That Matter: On the Discursive Limits of Sex* (New York: Routledge, 1993), and Johnson, *Appropriating Blackness: Performance and the Politics of Authenticity* (Durham, N.C.: Duke University Press, 2003).

5. Mae G. Henderson presented this concept at the Black Queer Studies in the Millennium Conference, University of North Carolina, Chapel Hill, April 7–9, 2000. Henderson defines a coy text as one that diverts or averts the reader's attention from one site or locus of meaning, one that is potentially risky or dangerous, to what appears to be a more comfortable and secure space but in fact becomes a place of entrapment. See Bryant K. Alexander, "Reflections, Riffs and Remembrances: The Black Queer Studies in the Millennium Conference," 23, no. 4 (2001): 1283–1305. 2001.

6. Cornel West, "The Dilemma of the Black Intellectual," in bell hooks and Cornel West, eds., *Breaking Bread: Insurgent Black Intellectual Life* (Boston: South End, 1991), 134–35.

7. Frantz Fanon, *Black Skin, White Masks* (New York: Grove, 1967), 78, 63.

8. Louie Crew, "Life in a Rural Two-Story Faggotry," in Michael J. Smith, ed., *Black Men White Men: A Gay Anthology* (San Francisco: Gay Sunshine Press, 1999), 206.

9. Geneva Smitherman, *Black Talk: Words and Phrases from the Hood to the Amen Corner* (Boston: Houghton Mifflin, 1994), 3, 66.

10. See how Raka Shome explicates the notion of whiteness and the politics of location in "Whiteness and the Politics of Location," in Thomas K. Nakayama and Judith N. Martin, eds., *Whiteness: The Communication of Social Identity* (Thousand Oaks, Calif.: Sage, 1999), 108.

11. Francesco Mastalia and Alfonse Pagano, *Dreads* (New York: Artisan, 1999), 14.

12. My use of the phrase "a distinction of race" is not to suggest that locks are specific to the particular of race. In fact, in *Dreads* Mastalia and Pagano chronicle a diverse history of people across boundaries of race who embrace wearing locks as a performative resistance against the restrictions of society.

13. I am drawing this discussion of passing and cultural performance from chapter 3, "Passing, Cultural Performance and Individual Agency," in my 2006 book, *Performing Black Masculinity: Race, Culture and Queer Identity* (Lanham, Md.: AltaMira).

14. See Deborah P. Britzman, Kelvin Santiago-Válles, Gladys Jiminez-Muñoz, and Laura M. Lamash, "Slips That Show and Tell: Fashioning Multicultural as a Problem of Representation," in Cameron McCarthy and Warren Crichlow, eds., *Race, Identity, and Representation in Education* (New York: Routledge, 1993); Turner, *On the Edge of the Bush*; and Erving Goffman, *The Presentation of Self in Everyday Life* (New York: Overlook, 1959), for further discussion of cultural performance.

15. My construction of a "black performative act" is drawing loosely on J. L. Austin's

construction of performativity as an utterance that does something—in that an effect coincides with its use, in this case an objective naming and a subjective claiming of identity. See Austin, *How to Do Things with Words* (Cambridge, Mass.: Harvard University Press, 1975).

16. See Bryant Keith Alexander, "Performing Culture in the Classroom: An Instructional (Auto)Ethnography of Black Male Teacher/Student Negotiations of Culture," PhD diss., Southern Illinois University, Carbondale, 1998.

17. Robert Simon, "Face to Face with Alterity: Postmodern Jewish Identity and the Eros of Pedagogy," in Jane Gallop, ed., *Pedagogy: The Question of Impersonation* (Bloomington: Indiana University Press, 1995), 94.

18. Shome, "Whiteness and the Politics of Location," 109. The narrative of my father's message is drawn from my essay "Black Skin/White Masks: The Performative Sustainability of Whiteness (with Apologies to Frantz Fanon)" and applied here to my discussion of boojie performativity. My essay appeared in *Qualitative Inquiry* 10, no. 5 (2004): 658–59.

19. bell hooks, "Choosing the Margins as a Space of Radical Openness," in Sandra Harding, ed., *The Feminist Standpoint Theory Reader: Intellectual and Political Controversies* (New York: Routledge, 2003), 153.

20. See the following essays: Bryant K. Alexander, "Gendered Labor: The Entanglements of Culture, Community and Commerce (an Experimental Ethnography)," *International Review of Qualitative Research* 1, no. 2 (2008): 145–72; "Fading, Twisting and Weaving: An Interpretive Ethnography of the Black Barbershop as Cultural Space," *Qualitative Inquiry* 9, no. 1 (2003): 101–28; "Telling Twisted Tales: Owning Place, Owning Culture in Ethnographic Research," in Judith Hamera, ed., *Opening Acts: Performance in/as Communication and Cultural Criticism* (Thousand Oaks, Calif.: Sage), 49–74; "Performing Culture in the Classroom: An Instructional (Auto) Ethnography," *Text and Performance Quarterly* 19 (1999): 271–306; "Br(other) in the Classroom: Testimony, Reflection, and Cultural Negotiation," in Rona T. Halualani and Thomas K. Nakayama, eds., *The Blackwell Handbook of Critical Intercultural Communication* (Hoboken, N.J.: Blackwell, forthcoming); "Negotiating Cultural Identity in the Classroom," in Mary Fong and Rueyling Chuang, eds., *Communicating Ethnic and Cultural identity* (New York: Rowman and Littlefield, 2003), 329–43; "Performing Culture in the Classroom: Excerpts from an Instructional Diary," in Sheron J. Dailey, ed., *The Future of Performance Studies: Visions and Revisions* (Annandale, Va.: National Communication Association, 1998), 170–80.

21. See West, "Dilemma of the Black Intellectual," 137–40.

22. See my work on black barbershops and salons, "Fading, Twisting and Weaving" and "Telling Twisted Tales." Also see Bryant K. Alexander with Paul Leblanc, "Cooking Gumbo—Examining Cultural Dialogue about Family: A Black/White Narrativization of Lived Experience in Southern Louisiana," in Thomas Socha and Rhuneter C. Diggs, eds., *Communication, Race, and Family: Exploring Communication in Black, White, and Biracial Families* (Hillsdale, N.J.: Lawrence Erlbaum, 1999), 181–208; Bryant K. Alexander, "Rhetorics of Loss and Living: Adding New Panels to the AIDS Quilt as an Act of Eulogy," in Charles E. Morris III, ed., *Remembering the AIDS Quilt* (East Lansing: Michigan State University Press, forthcoming).

23. On "endarkened epistemologies" see Cynthia Dillard, *On Spiritual Strivings: Transforming an African American Woman's Academic Life* (Albany: State University of New York Press, 2006).

24. In the epilogue to his important book *Black Intellectuals,* William M. Banks captures what might be the overarching dilemma of black intellectuals. He writes: "Intellectuals who advocate an organic relationship with the black community, and those who aspire to transcend ethnic consideration—are part of the unfolding saga of race and social thought in the United States. . . . The individualists affirm the essential openness of the social order. . . . In contrast, intellectuals such as Cornel West, Adolph Reed, Manning Marable, Derrick Bell, and Lani Guinier remind us that individual successes are not the measure of social justice, that the accomplishments of the newest Talented Tenth should not blind that Tenth to the group reality that still limits the choices of African Americans" (Banks, *Black Intellectuals: Race and Responsibility in American Life* [New York: W. W. Norton, 1996], 245–46).

# Afterword

*Mary Pattillo*

"We used to have to walk five miles to and from school in the hot sun with shoes that hardly had soles to get to a classroom that held all the kids from first to sixth grade." Who hasn't heard this line from their parents (or grandparents) as their testimony to how poor they were?

My mother's version was more about rationing beans for days on end in order to make the money and the meals stretch. One day I asked my mother, "But, Mom, wasn't Grandpa a postman, and didn't y'all own that house you lived in?" I was feeling pretty bold with my sociology PhD and as a budding scholar in African American studies. And I stumped her. As my mother and I have talked more about her childhood, she's had to recognize that her family was more lower-middle class than poor, although her father's poor money management did create some rough times.

What this story shows is that there is never an easy answer to the vexing question of how to define *class*. And it gets even stickier when we include stories of people with money who still get foreclosed on—the bourgeoisie who can't be boojie—and people with almost no money who regularly go on cruises—boojie but not of the bourgeoisie. My challenge in this afterword is to take a step toward clarifying these quandaries, using the excellent contributions in this volume as my examples.

The root of the confusion is that our intellectual guide in this project—E. Franklin Frazier—used a Marxian term (*bourgeoisie*) to describe a Weberian phenomenon (better captured by *boojie*). I warned you that I am a sociologist. While Marx surely did not invent the terms *bourgeois* and *bourgeoisie*, he formalized these words as analytical categories for describing the relations of production under capitalism. Marx wrote: "Society as a whole is more and more splitting up into two great hostile camps, into two great classes directly facing each other: Bourgeoisie and Proletariat." And who belongs in this category of the bourgeoisie? Marx answers: "The place of manufacture was taken by the giant, Modern Industry, the place of the industrial middle class, by industrial millionaires, [and] the leaders of whole industrial armies, the modern bourgeois."[1] In strict Marxian terms, then, the bourgeoisie are the owners of production: the industrialists, the capitalists, the bosses. Therefore, Oprah Winfrey is a member of the bourgeoisie, but my fourth-grade teacher, Mrs. Johnson, is not. The problem is that Frazier included Mrs. Johnson—and countless other white-collar workers, small business owners, professionals, and even well-paid manual laborers—in his definition and critique of the black bourgeoisie, in stark contradiction to the original use of the word by Marx, who would never consider Mrs. Johnson as part of the bourgeoisie.

It's no surprise, then, that the black bourgeoisie as Frazier constructed it was greatly disappointing to him since he saw this group as "subsist[ing] off the crumbs of philanthropy, the salaries of public servants, and what could be squeezed from the meager earnings of Negro workers."[2] That's a far cry from the owners and bosses of Marx's bourgeoisie. Frazier even has a whole chapter titled "Negro Business: A Social Myth." If Frazier is dismissive of the small capitalists in the black community—whom Marx would have called the petit bourgeoisie—it is no wonder that Frazier is positively scornful of blacks who owned little, if anything, but still postured as members of the capitalist class.

Whoever coined the term *boojie*, on the other hand, must have been a Weberian, someone who understood that stratification happens on many different planes, not just in the world of production. This is an instance when the analytics of everyday life, which are expressed in the slang and informal categories used by everyday people, are instructive for academics. Boojie is about consumption, not production. Max Weber argues that alongside and interconnected with the world of class—which is rooted in the economic order—exists the world of status—which is of the social order (and party, in the political/power order, to which I will return later). Weber elaborates that "status *may* rest on class position of a distinct or an ambiguous kind. However, it is not solely determined by it." Hence one's status is not defined by being a worker or an owner but by ones "style of life," a combination of education, heredity (were you born to a "good family"?), occupational prestige, and, most central for my argument here, consumption. Weber defines consumption as the "monopolistic appropriation of privileged modes of acquisition or the abhorrence of certain modes of acquisition."[3]

Despite Weber's nearly impenetrable definition, we all know well this world of style of life (or lifestyles) and its manifestation through consumption. For example, instead of crassly speculating about how much money someone makes (her economic position), we describe her overseas vacations or her fancy car (her "appropriation of privileged modes of acquisition"). Instead of looking at a person's résumé to see someone's work history, employers make assumptions based on appearance—he has cornrows or she wears long press-on nails ("the abhorrence of certain modes of acquisition").

Status, and the social honor or dishonor that it bestows, is directly related to consumption. Moreover, we do not only acquire goods and evaluate the goods that others acquire, we also wear them, display them, flaunt them, or are ashamed of them. In other words, we *perform* our consumption. Hence moving from bourgeois to boojie, as the book's title chronicles, is more than making the historical journey from 1957, when E. Franklin Frazier published his book, to 2007, when the commemorative conference was held at which some of these chapters were delivered as papers. It is also a necessary corrective to Frazier's original project because it foregrounds performance as different and apart from, albeit connected to, the materiality of economic class.

In other words, Frazier, among others, confuses us by using the Marxian term *bourgeoisie* when he would have been better served by the Weberian-inflected notion of *boojie*. We have gotten it more right in this book, as the examples of consumption-based distinctions are numerous: Lisa B. Thompson's play features an entire act in which the women describe their tastes and acquisitions. "Don't call me stuck up," SBF 2 says, "but, sorry, my panties get moist when I weave my basket through the aisles of Whole Foods, picking up organic cranberries and shiitake mushroom soup." We can also see the power of consumerism in Harilaos Stecopoulos's treatment of *A Raisin in the Sun,* in which Lena Younger's motivating dream of homeownership (especially of a house outside her current black neighborhood) is essentially about consumption. In another chapter Sara F. Mason shows how the entire booster apparatus of the city of Atlanta taps into the self-image of consuming black folks. Atlanta changed its brand from the "New South," which was associated with new industries and good jobs, to the "*Now* South," which casts Atlanta as a place of leisure, illustrated by references to its successful music scene and its touristic recasting of the King legacy.

These are all examples of status as it accrues to *positive* consumption, but Weber also directs our attention to the "abhorrence of certain modes of acquisition," or the negative status of certain lifestyles. The main character in Venise Berry's short story eats only the carrot sticks from the spread of soul food served at her cousin's repast. "All the traditional black foods of death," she says scornfully of what her working-class relatives have offered, before departing in a huff of boojie ridicule and in search of a salad. Damion Waymer begins his chapter by juxtaposing his Tommy Hilfigger past and his Walmart present. In the social order of the hip-hop world of which Waymer writes, this is a status demotion. Perhaps the most powerful illustration of the negative valences of consumption is the event that Candice Jenkins analyzes from the book *He Sleeps.* In the novel the main character, Bertrand, accidentally exposes himself to his two little girlfriends through his "holey pajamas." "Are you guys poor?" one of his playmates asks, with a combination of pity and compassion. Although Bertrand's family is probably not poor, Jenkins points out that even young children make associations and express "the sense that a poor person probably does not have control over the condition of material goods designed to protect his or her body from polite scrutiny." But these girls are also generous, and they try to console Bertrand by saying that it's okay. After all, "Jesus loved the poor." This last statement illustrates how consumption creates status groups. "The poor" is a status group, and it is "exposed" by its consumption of inferior goods.

Once we think of the social order as consisting of groups arrayed in hierarchical and relational fashion, it becomes clear that throughout *From Bourgeois to Boojie* the category of boojie cannot exist without some alterego, some comparison group. Frazier juxtaposed the black bourgeoisie with the Negro "folk." In our historical moment the terms "average black person" and *ghetto* pop up as the antitheses of *boojie,* or we rehearse the familiar Chris Rock typology of black people and niggahs. Status groups aim for social closure by defining what practices place you inside or outside the group's boundaries. Transgressions inevitably lead to name-calling. People who really desire membership bend themselves to get back in line lest they be ousted from the group. Kelly Brown Douglas shows us one such axis of status discrimination, sexuality. Black church members and leaders exclude "the blues body," which is a "nonbourgeois" body, one that is born of hard work and racialized poverty. But Douglas's illustrative example is not a body defined by the world of production but rather by the world of consumption and performance, in particular of sexual consumption. Black churches exclude same-sex-loving people because it is "the task of the black middle class to display a 'hyper-proper' sexuality." Douglas continues: "Unfortunately, this more privileged class of black people too often harbors a patronizing mentality behind its efforts to civilize the uncouth black bodies." Here we have an example in which the lines are not between boojie and ghetto (or average or folk) but between boojie and gay.

This is not to say that black gay men and lesbians cannot be boojie, a topic on which Bryant Keith Alexander reflects in his chapter. Instead, the insertion of sexuality into the discussion of race and class illustrates that multiple status hierarchies can be in operation at any given time.[4] Whatever the terminology, that there are lines of demarcation between boojie and some other category of people is clear, and those lines are drawn not just because of people's jobs or positions of ownership, as the Marxian term *bourgeoisie* might suggest, but instead between those who "privilege respectability and poise over acknowledging an unpleasant reality," as Lisa B. Thompson tells us Eve was called to do in the film *Eve's Bayou,* and those who do not.

So far I have proceeded as if the idea of boojie can be completely explained by consumption and the exhibition and performances of lifestyles. Of course, that is not true. Boojie is a racialized term. Boojie has no relevance outside the black community because it describes a status system that was fashioned only after a system of racial domination had created "the black community." Black churches, black friendships, black funerals, black movies, and other black spaces are the settings of the chapters in this volume, and the performances are directed at, and receive the approbation or condemnation of, other black people. While the idea of respectability is predicated on a white audience that might be convinced of the worthiness of the race for full inclusion, the term *boojie* exists completely within the world of black folks. Whereas a white person might describe a black person of a certain type as respectable, you'd almost never hear a white person calling a black person boojie. In other words, boojie describes a status group within an already defined status group, that is, African Americans. The boojie black people under Frazier's microscope and in this book (i.e., the subjects of analysis and sometimes we authors) are not trying to escape the black community but want instead to be at the *top* of it.

This is not to say that there aren't some black people who try to escape the black community and the boundaries of black identity altogether. Of course, they exist. There are a host of pejorative terms for them—*sellout, Oreo, Uncle Tom*. Such terms have little sting for black people who are committed to exiting the black community since their measuring sticks are not calibrated to the opinions of other black people but, instead, to the opinions of whites. So they are not boojie. To be defined as boojie requires enough interaction with the black world to occasion such an evaluation from other black people. Vershawn Young describes this scenario well in his introduction. Some blacks "attempt unsuccessfully to identify with only one [status], the white racial world, or the other, the black class world, since, to repeat the familiar expression, they're caught between the two." If being caught is a reality that seems unavoidable, then the more advantageous position is to be at the top of the black world rather than at the bottom of the white one. This is the location of boojie-ness.

Young's opening kernel about the middle position of (upper) middle-class blacks—between rich and poor and between white worlds and black ones—is echoed by Houston Baker's use of the term *black comprador,* or intermediary. I develop this idea of intermediaries, or middlemen and middlewomen, in my own work on the role of black professionals who have moved into a poor black neighborhood on Chicago's South Side and who sometimes take political positions that further marginalize or disadvantage their poor neighbors.[5] Marx believed that as the proletariat became more and more aware of their exploitation, and cognizant of the material wealth gained by the bourgeoisie at their expense, they would rise up and vanquish the bourgeoisie. But Marx did not anticipate the upward mobility of some members of the proletariat. He also did not consider the realities of racial oppression that would persist despite upward class mobility. So, here we are with black professionals who are just one step out of the proletariat themselves and who still experience racial discrimination despite having a little money. What do we find? In some instances, and this was one of the early contributions of Frazier, we find that rather than aiming to overthrow their tyrants, the oppressed become obsessed with *being* them. Hence the political perspective of black compradors, or intermediaries, or middlemen/women is sometimes clouded by their desire to have what the oppressor has, to protect it once they have it, and even to wield it against those less fortunate than they, even of their own race.

Thinking about the bourgeoisie and boojie as political categories further illustrates the usefulness of separating the materialism of Marxian analysis from the multilayered explanation that Weber offers for inequality. Struggles for rights and economic justice happen in the realm of the power order, or by "parties," as Weber discusses them. Whereas Marx saw the proletariat as the protagonists of a class revolution, Weber sees neither economic classes nor social status groups as capable of affecting or changing power relations or the distribution of resources. Moreover, status groups are particularly weak agents of change because they draw their boundaries for the purposes of social closure—not economic or political power—and because the basis of their existence is so rooted in the ephemera of consumer goods, representations, and claims to status prestige. It is the world of parties, politics, and power that must be engaged in order to shift the balance of power away from the wealthy and privileged and toward the masses.

This analysis does not cut off the possibility for transformational leadership within the black community. It simply says that such leadership is not going to come from the ranks of those who are fully invested in a boojie status position. And, of course, no black person really is so uniformly committed to boojie-ness. Greg Tate reminds us of the "Ellisonian fluidity of black identity," which means that many of us professional black folks have made claims to boojie-ness at one time or another. I hope we also have the capacity to snap out of it.

To conclude, this book has elucidated the importance of separating the world of consumption and performance from that of material economic position and political power, even if Frazier too often muddled the three. It also makes clear that boojie-ness has its sensual pleasures, its psychological tolls, and limits transformational politics because it represents an attempt to divide a group by status that is already set apart and subjugated by race. The result is something to be avoided, the target of Amiri Baraka's criticism, black folks "who kick they own ass." This is the trap that requires our constant vigilance.

## NOTES

1. Karl Marx and Friedrich Engels, *The Communist Manifesto* (New York: Oxford University Press, 2008), 3, 4.

2. E. Franklin Frazier, *Black Bourgeoisie* (New York: Free Press, 1957), 194.

3. Max Weber, *Economy and Society*, ed. Gunther Roth and Claus Wittich (Berkeley: University of California Press, 1978), 306.

4. See also Cathy Cohen, *The Boundaries of Blackness: AIDS and the Breakdown of Black Politics* (Chicago: University of Chicago Press, 1999).

5. Mary Pattillo, *Black on the Block: The Politics of Race and Class in the City* (Chicago: University of Chicago Press, 2007).

# Contributors

**BRYANT KEITH ALEXANDER** is acting dean of the College of Arts and Letters and professor of performance, culture, and pedagogy in the Department of Communication Studies at California State University, Los Angeles. His published essays have appeared in a range of scholarly journals and collected works, including *Men and Masculinities* (2006); *Handbook of Performance Studies* (2006), *Handbook of Qualitative Research* (2005), *Handbook of Critical and Indigenous Methodologies* (2008), *Handbook of Communication and Instruction* (2010), and the forthcoming *Handbook of Critical Intercultural Communication*. He is coeditor of *Performance Theories in Education: Power, Pedagogy, and the Politics of Identity* (2005, with Gary L. Anderson and Bernardo Gallegos) and author of *Performing Black Masculinity: Race, Culture and Queer Identity* (2006).

**HOUSTON A. BAKER JR.** is Distinguished University Professor and professor of English at Vanderbilt University. His most recent book is a critique of black public intellectuals, *Betrayal: How Black Intellectuals Have Abandoned the Ideals of the Civil Rights Era* (2008). He is also a published poet whose most recent volume is *Passing Over*.

**AMIRI BARAKA** was born Everett LeRoi Jones in 1934 in Newark, N.J. His reputation as a playwright was established with the production of *Dutchman* (1964). The controversial play subsequently won an Obie Award and was made into a film. He and his wife, Amina Baraka, edited *The Music: Meditations of Jazz & Blues* (1987) and *Confirmation: An Anthology of African-American Women* (1983). The *Autobiography of LeRoi Jones/Amiri Baraka* was published in 1984. Other publications include *Y's/Why's/Wise* (1992), *Funk Lore* (1993), *Eulogies* (1994), *Transbluesency* (1996), *Somebody Blew Up America & Other Poems* (2002). His recent book of short stories, *Tales of the Out & the Gone* was published in late 2007. *Home,* his book of social essays, was re-released in early 2009. *Digging: The Afro American Soul of Music* was also published in 2009.

**JEAN BERRY** (cover art and part pages) is an internationally known artist whose provocative series *Blood on the Fields: African Roots Emerging* was acquired by the Gencor-Gallery at Rand Afrikaans University in South Africa. Berry holds a degree in art from Drake University in Des Moines, Iowa. She is best known for her unique work in cardboard collage with charcoal, her favorite medium. Her work includes several other series, among them, *Black Women: The Souljah Series* and *The 14 Contemporary Stations of the Cross,* both of which focus on important African American issues.

**VENISE BERRY** is an associate professor of journalism and mass communication at the University of Iowa. She is the author of three national best-selling novels: *So Good, An African American Love Story* (1996), *All of Me, A Voluptuous Tale* (2000) and *Colored Sugar Water* (2002). She is at work on her fourth novel, *Pockets of Sanity.* In 2003 she received the Creative Contribution to Literature award from the Zora Neale Hurston Society. Berry is also part of the Solstice Low-Residency Master of Fine Arts in Creative Writing Program in Pine Manor College in Massachusetts and teaches novel writing at the University of Iowa Summer Writing Festival. Her website is www.veniseberry.com.

**KELLY BROWN DOUGLAS** is Elizabeth Connolly Todd Distinguished Professor of Religion at Goucher College. She is author of *What's Faith Got to Do with*

*It? Black Bodies/Christian Souls, The Black Christ,* and *Sexuality and the Black Church.* She is completing her manuscript for *Black and Blues: Body Talk/ God Talk for the Black Church.* Douglas is an ordained Episcopal minister and previously taught theology at the School of Divinity of Howard University.

**EILEEN CHERRY-CHANDLER** is assistant professor of theatre and film at Bowling Green State University. She has held academic appointments at Columbia College Chicago, Northwestern University, and DePaul University. Her work includes numerous appointments as artist-in-residence, the development of community-based arts organizations, publications of poetry, fiction, essays, and playwriting, as well as solo performance. Her current research in performance studies explores cultural diversity through performance.

**CLAIRE OBERON GARCIA** is a professor of English at Colorado College, where she teaches in the race and ethnic studies and the feminist and gender studies programs. Her publications include "'For a Few Days We Were Dwellers in Africa': Jessie Redmon Fauset's 'Dark Algiers the White'" in *Ethnic Studies Review* (2007) and "'Have YOU Ever Lived on Brewster Place?' Teaching African American Literature at a Predominantly White Institution" in Sandra Jackson and Jose Solis Jordan, eds., *I've Got a Story to Tell: Identity and Place in the Academy* (1998). Her research interests lie in African American women's literature, gender and modernism, and Henry James.

**CANDICE M. JENKINS** is associate professor of English at Hunter College, City University of New York. Her first book, *Private Lives, Proper Relations: Regulating Black Intimacy* (2007), examines how African American writers articulate the political consequences of intimacy for the already-vulnerable black subject. In 2008 *Private Lives, Proper Relations* was awarded the William Sanders Scarborough Prize by the Modern Language Association. Jenkins is now at work on two new manuscripts: an exploration of black middle-class embodiment in post–civil rights era African American fiction, and a feminist defense of commercial hip-hop, which theorizes the music as a visionary and peculiarly American discursive form.

**E. PATRICK JOHNSON** is chair of the Department of Performance Studies and a professor in the Department of African American Studies at Northwestern University. A scholar-artist, Johnson has performed and published widely in the area of race, gender, sexuality, and performance. He is the author of *Appropriating Blackness: Performance and the Politics of Authenticity* (2003). He is also coeditor (with Mae G. Henderson) of *Black Queer Studies: A Critical Anthology* (2005). His most recent book is *Sweet Tea: Black Gay Men of the South—An Oral History* (2008).

**SARA F. MASON** is a lecturer in the School of Social Sciences at Gainesville State College. Her research interests lie at the intersections of culture, knowledge production, and power, with a particular emphasis on cultural practices, history, memory, and racial identities. Her essay in this collection is based on her dissertation research on the heritage tourism industry in Atlanta.

**DWIGHT A. MCBRIDE** is dean of the College of Liberal Arts and Sciences and professor of African American studies, English, and gender and women's studies at the University of Illinois at Chicago. His published essays are in the areas of race theory and black queer studies. He is author of *Impossible Witnesses: Truth, Abolitionism, and Slave Testimony* (2001) and *Why I Hate Abercrombie and Fitch: Essays on Race and Sexuality* (2005), both of which were nominated for the Hurston-Wright Legacy Award. He received his BA from Princeton University and both his MA and PhD from the University of California, Los Angeles. He previously taught at the University of Pittsburgh and at Northwestern University.

**ANGELA M. NELSON** is an associate professor in the Department of Popular Culture at Bowling Green State University. She has edited *"This Is How We Flow": Rhythm in Black Cultures* (1999), coedited *Popular Culture Theory and Methodology* (2006) with Harold E. Hinds Jr. and Marilyn F. Motz, and published several essays on different aspects of African American popular culture. Nelson's current teaching and research focus on black popular culture, including African American popular and religious musics and representations of African Americans in comic art and television.

**MARY PATTILLO** is the Harold Washington Professor of Sociology and African American studies at Northwestern University. Her areas of interest include race and ethnicity, urban sociology, and qualitative methods. She is the author of two award-winning books, *Black Picket Fences: Privilege and Peril among the Black Middle Class* (1999), and *Black on the Block: The Politics of Race and Class in the City* (2007). She coedited *Imprisoning America: The Social Effects of Mass Incarceration* and has published numerous journal articles. She is a founding board member of Urban Prep Charter Academies, Inc., a network of all-boys public high schools in Chicago.

**HARILAOS STECOPOULOS** is the author of *Reconstructing the World: Southern Fictions and U.S. Imperialisms, 1898–1976* (2008) and the coeditor of *Race and the Subject of Masculinities* (1997). He teaches U.S. literature and culture at the University of Iowa.

**GREG TATE** is a writer and musician who lives in Harlem. He is currently working on *James Brown's Body,* a book about the Godfather of Soul, for Riverhead Press. He and the poet Latasha Nevada Diggs edit the journal *Coon Bidness.* In 2010 Tate's fourteen-piece band, Burnt Sugar The Arkestra Chamber, provided music for the Paris stage revival of Melvin Van Peebles's "hood opera" *Sweet Sweetback's Badass Song.* The band's website is www.burntsugarindex.com.

**LISA B. THOMPSON** is a playwright and associate professor of English at the State University of New York at Albany. The centerpiece of her scholarship is her book *Beyond the Black Lady: Sexuality and the New African American Middle Class* (2009). Thompson's critically acclaimed off-Broadway play, *Single Black Female,* which was nominated for a 2004 *LA Weekly* Theatre Award for best comedy, has been produced throughout the United States; in 2010 the play received its international debut in Toronto. Her current projects are a play about black motherhood in the age of Michelle Obama and a monograph examining cultural trauma in contemporary African American theater and performance.

**BRIDGET HARRIS TSEMO** is an assistant professor of African American studies and rhetoric at the University of Iowa. She studies the African American literary and rhetorical tradition, and race as a class performance. Her other academic interests include contemporary African American film and music, cultural studies, and issues surrounding writing studies. She also writes for public audiences. She is at work on her monograph, tentatively titled *Confronting an "Unwashed Democracy": African American Literature at the Turn of the Twentieth Century.*

**DAMION WAYMER** is an assistant professor of communication at Virginia Tech. His research sheds light on issues of culture and diversity in general and issues of race, class, and gender specifically. Additionally, his research uses communication theories to explore some issues that marginalized or underrepresented publics can and do encounter and the strategies that are available to them to challenge these issues. Journals that have published his work include *Qualitative Inquiry, Journal of Applied Communication Research, Public Relations Review, Communication Quarterly,* and the *Journal of Communication Inquiry.* He received his PhD from Purdue University.

**DEBORAH ELIZABETH WHALEY** is an assistant professor of American and African American studies at the University of Iowa, where she teaches courses on the theory and methods of American studies, comparative ethnic studies, black cultural studies, and popular culture. Her first book, *Disciplining Women: Alpha Kappa Alpha, Black Counter-publics, and the Cultural Politics of Black Sororities* (2010), is an interdisciplinary examination of a historically black sorority. She is working on her second book project, tentatively titled *Sequential Subjects: Black Women in Graphic Novels, Comics, and Anime.*

**NAZERA SADIQ WRIGHT** is an assistant professor of English at the University of Kentucky. She is the recipient of national fellowships through the Ford Foundation, a Thurgood Marshall Fellowship at Dartmouth College, and an Erskine Peters Fellowship from Notre Dame. Her research and teaching areas include nineteenth- and twentieth-century African American literature, African American studies, childhood studies, girlhood studies, gender and women's studies, and archival studies. She is completing her book manuscript tentatively titled *Girlhood in African American Literature.*

**VERSHAWN ASHANTI YOUNG** is a performance artist and associate professor in the Department of English at the University of Kentucky. He teaches African American studies, performance studies, and rhetorical studies. He is the author of *Your Average Nigga: Performing Race, Literacy, and Masculinity* (2007) and is lead editor of the forthcoming *Code Meshing as World English: Policy, Pedagogy, Performance.* He is also completing a monograph tentatively titled *The New Equality: Stories of Race and Triumph.* He was previously on the faculty of the University of Iowa.

# Index

black female body, target of multiple forms of oppression, 258n9

black girls, post-Reconstruction era: behavior of as important topic in conduct rhetoric, 92; rules of "duty" and "beauty," 92; urged to return to domestic sphere, 92

black heritage tourism: Emmett Till Memorial Commission, 76–77; growth in, 75–76; response to surge in black tourism, 75; tourists' view of King Center as affirmation of their middle-class identity, 79. *See also* Atlanta; Martin Luther King Jr. National Park Historic Site (King Center)

black intellectuals, 330n24; distrust of by black community, 313; insider-outsider status, 316–17; public, 46; relation to postmodern, 283n3; role of in struggle of black masses, 23

black leaders: encouraged proper conduct in post-reconstruction era, 92; marked by race, 65; and politics of racial representation, 65–66

black male, masculinity and class, 268–75

black male mythological sexuality, 266–67; dependence upon black female body, 267–68

black male teacher, 320–24; classroom as space of intellectual and social negotiation, 322; self-defining program, 321

black Marxist ideology, 9

black media, 26

black middle class: charge of "make belief" against, 4–5; class status linked to white racial identity, 16; and gentrification of black neighborhoods, xix; hyperproper standard of sexual conduct, 247–49; identity related to narratives of black body, 263; ideologies shaped images of black Americans post-WWII, 175; increasingly associated with whiteness and disavowal of blackness, xiv; lessons extolling middle-class virtues against negative images of lower-class blacks, 2; mid-twentieth century advice of parents to children, 2; performed by those in range of economic positions, xx, 11; poor and working-class roots, xix; racial conservatism, 5; racial identity linked to lower-class status, 16; required to "act white" in post-Jim Crow era, 16–17

black middle-class female: haunted by figure of colored lady, 291–92; and limits of middle-class morality, 304; marriage rate, 145–46; sexually truncated image of, 28; single, in post-civil rights era, 143–52

black middle-class girls, lower-class performance, 131–42

black middle-class male, effeminized, 28, 263, 266–67, 271, 281, 311

black middle-class performance: in American culture and literature after Reconstruction, 35n15; as desire for first-class citizenship, 13; everyday self-presentations, 12; "Pockets of Sanity" (Berry), 49–60;

Hurst, Fannie, 17
Hurston, Zora Neale, 17; *Dust Tracks
  on a Road*, 106
"Hustler Musik," 172
hyperproper sexual narrative, 249–52,
  335; and centrality of sexuality to
  human dynamics, 250; survival
  pact of black community with
  white society, 259n21

Ice Cube, 155
identity markers, bound to ideological
  and cultural discourses, xx
*I Hear a Symphony* (Woods and
  Hiddell), 202
Imani Uzuri, 157
insider-outsider status, 316–17
institutionalized racism, xvii, xviii
intermediaries, 337
intersectionality, 36n23

Jack and Jill of America, 42
Jackson, Maynard, 73
Jackson, Samuel L., 289, 306n8
Jackson, Tim, 189n16
Jay Z, 157, 161, 165, 170–71
Jefferson, Thomas, 292
*The Jeffersons*, xv
Jenkins, Candice M., xxi, 334; "A Kind
  of End to Blackness: Reginald
  McKnight's *He Sleeps* and the
  Body Politics of Race and Class,"
  28; *Private Lives, Proper Relations:
  Regulating Black Intimacy*, 35n15
*Jet*, 26, 157
Jim Crow, 14–16, 41, 71
Johnson, E. Patrick, 327n4
Johnson, James Weldon: *Along This

*Way*, 18; *The Autobiography of an
  Ex-Colored Man*, 2, 18, 35n15
Johnson, John H., 176
Johnson, Lyndon, 43
Johnson, Robert, 241, 252, 255
Jones, Barbara O., 299
Jones, Grace, 157
Jo's Collector Club, 203
Joyce, Donald Franklin, 178, 179
"Juicy," 167
juke joints, as sanctuary for blues
  bodies, 256
Just Original Images, Ltd., 192

Keil, Charles, 258n10
Kelis, 172
Kenan, Randall, 262, 282n1
Kennedy, John F., 72
Kennedy, Robert, 219
Khruschev, Nikita, 211
King, Coretta Scott, 78; events
  surrounding death of, 79–81; final
  memorial at New Birth Baptist
  Church, 80–81
King, Lonnie, 73
King, Martin Luther, Jr., 63, 72, 82,
  229; "I Have a Dream" speech, 77;
  understanding of poverty as civil
  rights issue, 81
King Center. *See* Martin Luther King
  Jr. National Park Historic Site
  (King Center)
Kington, Raynard, 66–67
kitchen-sink plays, 212
Kristof, Nicholas, 13

lament, 241–42. *See also* signifyin'
  lament